LIBRARY SERVICE AND LEARNING:

Empowering Students, Inspiring Social Responsibility, and Building Community Connections

edited by *Theresa McDevitt and Caleb P. Finegan*

Association of College and Research Libraries
A division of the American Library Association
Chicago, Illinois 2018

The paper used in this publication meets the minimum requirements of American National Standard for Information Sciences–Permanence of Paper for Printed Library Materials, ANSI Z39.48-1992. ∞

Cataloging-in-Publication data is on file with the Library of Congress.

Table of Contents

INTRODUCTION

Everybody Wins:
Empowering Students and Enhancing Community Connections through Library Related Applied Learning Experiences

Who hasn't been transformed by reading a book? For centuries libraries held their place at the center of college and university intellectual life by storing and lending accessible and portable receptacles of knowledge that enabled readers to learn on their own. Enhancing the value of the informational resources themselves were spaces that promoted serious and silent study and services that assisted in the research process. With doors that were open to all, academic libraries were popular gathering spaces where generations of college students and faculty came to be transformed.[1]

Currently, information exchange, teaching, and learning practices are rapidly changing academic life. Classroom work is shifting to include more activities that are relevant, include action, develop agency in students, and are truly transformational. In response to these changes in the main community for which we serve, today's libraries are changing to provide our students with the environment most likely to help them succeed.[2]

In these new libraries, well-organized and comprehensive collections of information resources, individual learning spaces, and research support services are still essential, but they have taken on a new appearance and quality. The learning that is occurring there is no longer exclusively silent or solitary. Spaces are colorful, comfortable, often noisy, and clearly collaborative and interactive. Newly renovated libraries include social learning spaces that encourage group work and the exchange of information. These lively and welcoming spaces are intentionally designed to encourage visitors to join the scholarly conversation, regardless of an individual's discipline or level of study. Visitors select what they need from a vast array of available information, share what they know with others, and refine ideas as they are shared to create new knowledge. Users are taking an even more active role in creating their own learning.

New teaching practices, such as experiential learning and service-learning, are becoming more and more important on college campuses. McDonnell has called them "a powerful force" that is "transforming how teaching and learning is conducted in the twenty-first century."[3] They are considered to be among the "high-impact practices" that lead to higher levels of student engagement, retention, and success.[4] Colleges and universities are actively promoting them by including them in strategic plans, creating high-impact-practice-themed faculty development programs and initiatives, and offering grant funding to support their development.

Experiential learning can be defined as "education that emphasizes personal experience rather than learning from books or other secondary sources" that "broadens the classroom experience by providing concrete opportunities to observe, conceptualize, and apply knowledge and experiment.[5] In its most effective form, it "engages the learner in a transformational journey, moving her through a cycle of *concrete experience, reflective observation, abstract conceptualization,* and *active experimentation,* in order to integrate learning for overall personal development."[6] While traditional teaching methods left students to passively absorb knowledge provided, these methods require action and application on the part of students and deep involvement in their own learning and acquisition of new skills.[7]

Service-learning is defined by Barbara Jacoby as "a form of experiential education in which students engage in activities that address human and community needs, together with structured opportunities for reflection designed to achieve desired learning outcomes."[8] Today's students—who want to work in groups, apply what they learn to real-life problems, and work in environments that are "relevant and participatory"—respond well to active teaching techniques that build community, that are relevant to their current lives and future career goals, and that allow them to work together to solve real problems and shape their own learning.[9]

Proponents of the use of these teaching techniques note positive outcomes for students, instructors, and collaborating community partners. They argue that student learning is significantly enhanced by experiences that call upon them to work with new people in new circumstances and apply course content to often messy real-world problems. This process leads to improved understanding and ability to apply theory, and to growth in areas like acceptance of diversity, increased compassion and caring for others, self-confidence, and growth in social responsibility and civic engagement. Instructors, too, learn more in the process and may develop closer and long-lasting connections to students. Community partners gain service work that can benefit them but also form connections to students who are empowered to make a difference in their world. In the end, everyone serves, and everyone wins.[10]

Providing services that solve problems has always been something that libraries have done. Service-based and experiential assignments have long been an integral part of professional training for careers in these service-based organizations.[11] With experience in learning with these active methods, librarians are well-equipped to share their knowledge of these practices and work with others to develop new applications. Librarians recognize that these approaches to teaching are also highly effective in library and information literacy instruction and are using them more in their instruction. When they work with faculty colleagues to develop information literacy elements in courses in the disciplines, librarians are sharing these positive teaching practices.

Welcoming to all, libraries are popular academic gathering spaces, now more than ever the center of campus academic life. They are expanding their role as informal learning spaces through creating or hosting passive and active educational programming and by space redesign that is conducive to new types of information sharing. Programs and space redesign is done in collaboration with individuals on-campus and members of the community beyond their campus boundaries. These partnerships and spaces allow libraries to connect faculty with partners for application-based learning on and off-campus or offer an ideal setting to host them. Always living a "vocation based upon service to the community," librarians are helping the community as they facilitate the development of meaningful learning experiences for their students. The possibilities for the creation and sharing of new knowledge, the development of authentic skills, and doing good are expanding as a result.[12]

The chapters in this book are case studies, win-win stories, written by librarians, university faculty, and students who have successfully employed service-based or experiential learning experiences for students in higher education. Included are classes or programs that have been taught by librarians or developed in collaboration with librarians. All include information literacy-related outcomes, and/or utilize library resources or take place in library facilities. In each case, the course or educational event developers have intentionally included service to a partner, real work applications of theory, mutual benefit for all involved, and opportunities for thoughtful reflection.

Each chapter describes activities, motivations, curriculum materials, and outcomes in enough detail to assist others in building upon their experience to bring this positive practice to their institutions. Appendices include assignments, rubrics, and other materials that will enable readers to replicate and adapt the activity to their own needs. A chapter with a review of the literature concludes the volume to provide readers with more to consider. Chapters are divided into case studies where the librarians are taking the lead, those where the librarians are the partners in development of the learning experiences, and those where the library is hosting a public educational event, activity, or program.

Chapters where libraries take the lead include assignments for between one- and three-credit stand-alone classes offered by librarians. This includes a class for upper-level undergraduates where students learn about preparing grants through developing a funder research portfolio for a local non-profit. In three other classes, students investigate the work of local service organizations and prepare research products for the partner's use. Student projects include research portfolios, video introductions to the work of partnering organizations, and informative infographics that address community issues. Another chapter in this section describes how students in a graduate LIS program support the development of information literacy skills in undergraduate students and gain teaching experience by lending a hand in teaching bibliographic instruction sessions for Research in the Disciplines classes. In the final chapter in this section, a large research university library system offers mini-grants and librarian mentorship to students who wish to pursue service-based undergraduate research projects. In all cases, the research performed by the students increases their awareness of a problem that affects the community and the work of organizations whose mission it is to address those needs, and provides a service and/or product for partner's use.

The next set of chapters are case studies where librarians are partnering with faculty to offer service-based activities that develop information literacy skills or use library materials to address a campus or community need. Classes in this section show how information literacy skills and libraries can enhance, and be enhanced by, service opportunities in archeology, art, communications, education, English, history, and international business classes.

In this section, first-year students in an arts course work with a community program for young authors to bring the young authors' writings to life through the creation of "moving words," or short films. Graduate and undergraduate public history students learn the practice of public history as they build community history digital exhibits and finding aids to benefit future researchers. An English class asks students to investigate social problems and community organizations who are working to address them and develop remedies and responses. In this course, one assignment builds students' information literacy skills as well as their level of civic engagement with the task of writing letters to editors on societal issues. A pre-service teaching class in elementary education prepares students for the technologically rich teaching world they will be soon entering by challenging them with an assignment to create digital products to help tell the story of those who might otherwise be voiceless. Archeological students used special collections and archives materials to enhance investigations of a burial site. Students at a small private university in a writing for public relations course investigated the topic of fair trade and created buzz about the practice by developing campus-wide events to increase awareness of fair trade and promote the purchase of fair trade items on their campus. Completing this section is a chapter where business students build workplace research skills as they apply information literacy skills to help local companies to design international business plans with the assistance of a librarian research consultant.

In the library as educational service center section, active and passive educational outreach events are offered by students in the library and are designed to educate library clientele and build an educated community. The section begins and ends with events developed to address the needs of children and families. It begins with the description of a children's literacy fair that was created in collaboration with a number of community literacy service groups and staffed by students in elementary education and held in a university library. It ends with the account of students in a community nutrition class who promoted health awareness and gained experience in providing community nutrition programs at a public library with an ABCs of Nutrition interactive expo. In between, there are other classes where programming was developed by students for their peers. In an English course, students offer an interactive Banned Books Week Read-Out in the library coffee bar area. Students in a senior-level communications research course promote scholarly communication through coordinating all aspects of an undergraduate research forum held in the library. Interior design majors developed library displays to educate university visitors, spread awareness of their vocational choice, highlight related library materials, and in the process gain hands-on experience with the creation of appealing educational library displays. Students in history practicum courses work in a library Oral History Center and provide virtual programs with the production of oral history podcasts that feature the stories of community members and are shared online beyond the campus as a culminating project. Students in political science offer library poster sessions on online privacy and the Constitution and promote safe and secure online sharing activities to their peers during National Cyber Security Awareness month. In a Wikipedia edit-a-thon for gender balance, students in English and women and gender studies address the gender gap as they staff an open edit-a-thon designed to increase Wikipedia coverage of women and women's authorship in the evolving online encyclopedia.

The book ends with a chapter that briefly surveys professional literature on experiential and service-learning in libraries and information literacy instruction. Resources included in the chapter were intentionally chosen to provide readers with more information on why these authentic practices are beneficial for libraries, instructors, students, and community partners, and how librarians are joining with those who promote these practices to create successful and empowering learning for all involved.

Notes

1. Leonard Jolley, "The Function of the University Library," *Journal of Documentation* 18, no. 3 (1962): 133–142; Patricia A. Frade and Allyson Washburn, "The University Library: The Center of a University Education?" *portal: Libraries and the Academy* 6, no. 3 (2006): 327–346.

2.   Loanne Snavely, *Student Engagement and the Academic Library* (Santa Barbara: ABC-CLIO, 2012).

3.   Pete McDonnell, *The Experiential Library: Transforming Academic and Research Libraries through the Power of Experiential Learning* (Amsterdam: Chandos Publishing, 2016): xxvii.

4.   Catherine Fraser Riehle and Sharon A. Weiner, "High-Impact Educational Practices: An Exploration of the Role of Information Literacy, *College & Undergraduate Libraries* 20, no. 2 (2013): 127–143.

5.   Amy York, Christy Groves, and William Black, "Enriching the Academic Experience: The Library and Experiential Learning," *Collaborative Librarianship*, 2, no.4 (Oct, 2010): 193.

6.   Pete McDonnell, *The Experiential Library: Transforming Academic and Research Libraries through the Power of Experiential Learning* (Amsterdam: Chandos Publishing, 2016), xxviii.

7.   Ibid, xxviii.

8.   Barbara Jacoby, *Service-Learning Essentials: Questions, Answers, and Lessons Learned.* (Hoboken, NJ: John Wiley & Sons, 2014), 1–2.

9.   Christy Price, "Why Don't My Students Think I'm Groovy?: The new "R"s for Engaging Millennial Learners," *Essays from E-xcellence in Teaching* IX (2010) https://teachpsych.org/Resources/Documents/ebooks/eit2009.pdf#page=29.

10.   Nancy K. Herther, "Service Learning and Engagement in the Academic Library: Operating Out of the Box," *College & Research Libraries News* 69, no. 7 (2008): 387; Marcia Hernandez and Lorrie A. Knight, "Reinventing the Box: Faculty-Librarian Collaborative Efforts to Foster Service Learning for Political Engagement," *Journal for Civic Commitment* 16, no. 1 (2010): 1–2.

11.   Lorna Peterson, "A Brief History of Service Learning in LIS," in *Service-learning: Linking Library Education and Practice,* eds. Loriene Roy, Kelly Jensen, and Alex Hershey Meyers (Chicago: American Library Association), 1–4; Melville Dewey, "School of Library Economy at Columbia College," *Library Journal* 9 (1894): 118; Robert E. Wolverton, Jr. and April K. Heiselt, "US Academic Librarians and Community Service: A Case Study," *New Library World* 111, no. 9/10 (2010): 381–390.

12.   Katherine Kott, "Service Learning in Academic Libraries in the United States," in *Service Learning, Information Literacy, and Libraries,* ed. Jennifer E. Nutefall (Santa Barbara: ABC-CLIO, 2016): 1–20; Frances Yates, "Beyond Library Space and Place: Creating a Culture of Community Engagement through Library Partnerships," *Indiana Libraries* 33, no. 2 (2014): 53–57.

PART I.

Library and Information Literacy Credit-Bearing Courses or Sponsors of Undergraduate Community Based Research

CHAPTER ONE

Research for Non-Profits, a Service Learning Class in Grantseeking Research

Alyssa Wright
Research Librarian for the Social Sciences
West Virginia University Libraries
Alyssa.Wright@mail.wvu.edu

THE ACTIVITY

Description: Research for Non-Profits is a 300-level course that gives students an introduction to non-profits and grantseeking while teaching them research and information literacy skills. Students complete a funder research portfolio for a non-profit "client" with a funding need. The portfolio contains detailed profiles of funding agencies that are most likely to give to the non-profit, as well as statistics and research studies useful for writing a grant proposal. While creating the portfolios, students hone their research skills and grapple with larger information literacy concepts—particularly that information has value, information creation as a process, and authority is constructed and contextual.

Students are encouraged to work closely with their non-profit clients to better understand the organization and its needs. Each student is required to complete a minimum number of volunteer hours working for the non-profit in addition to the work they complete for the portfolio. They also learn to use good communication practices in interviewing and contacting their non-profit clients. Course readings and class discussions cover tax rules that govern US non-profits, broad issues surrounding non-profit funding, as well as best practices for grantseeking research and proposal writing.

The course was a success in the first semester with strong student reviews and positive interest from other units on campus. It was offered as a cross-listed course from the Libraries and the Communication Studies. I plan to teach it once a year in the future, cross-listed with multiple departments.

Getting Started: Three personal experiences occurring at roughly the same time led me to develop the Research for Non-Profits course. First, I had been teaching West Virginia University Libraries' Introduction to Library Research course for six years and had grown increasingly dissatisfied in students' engagement with the class. It was difficult to effectively demonstrate the usefulness and importance of information literacy skills to students. I felt that if I could somehow better apply the lessons to a real-world information need that students would be more inspired to learn. That same year, our library became a Funding Information Network Partner of the Foundation Center. The Foundation Center maintains databases of funding opportunities and offers research and planning support to non-profits. As a network partner, we offer funder database access to local non-profits and the university community. We also provide regular grantseeking workshops for the public. I serve as one of the supervising librarians for the program and receive regular training from the Foundation Center. It was energizing to be a part of the Foundation Center program. I helped groups with immediate research needs that required teaching both practical research tools as well as information literacy skills. That spring I was also fortunate to attend two service-learning events: one was a day-long workshop hosted by WVU's Center for Service and Learning, the other was a panel presentation on service-learning at a library conference. Both events gave me encouragement and practical tips for developing a service-learning course. Panelist Maureen Barry from Wright State University was particularly generous in giving me advice and sharing course materials from her service-learning course. Her articles in *College & Research Library News* and *LOEX Quarterly* were also useful.[1]

Motivations: I developed a service-learning course because it filled a need in our community and offered a better learning experience for WVU students. Students are able to directly apply the skills they learn in class to a project that makes a direct and immediate impact on the community. The students are also accountable to more than just me and themselves; their work is going to be used by an organization trying to better the community.

THE PEOPLE

Libraries: West Virginia University is a public land-grant institution that enrolls more than 28,000 students on our Morgantown Campus. We are the state's flagship institution with a Research I Carnegie Classification offering undergraduate, graduate, and professional degrees. WVU has a strong presence in the state with two regional campuses and a state-wide extension service. The university promotes service among students, faculty, and staff through The Center for Service and Learning and has earned the Carnegie Foundation's Community Engagement Classification. The WVU Libraries encompass five libraries on the Morgantown Campus with thirty-eight library faculty. We have an active instruction program that includes a one-credit-hour basic information literacy class taught by all instruction librarians as well as a small number of advanced subject-specific information literacy courses. Library faculty are allowed to develop advanced courses as fits the needs of the campus. Some examples of topics for advanced courses that the libraries have offered are film and media literacy and advanced research in Women's Studies.

Instructors: I am the social sciences librarian at WVU and liaison to WVU's departments of Communication Studies, Psychology, and Sociology & Anthropology. I manage library collections in those areas and collaborate with faculty to incorporate information literacy into their courses. I also teach the introduction to information literacy class and one-shot instruction sessions to 100- and 200-level courses across the campus and serve as one of our libraries' Foundation Center librarians. I developed and teach the three-credit course ULIB 302: Research for Non-Profits.

Courses: ULIB 302: Research for Non-Profits is included in WVU's general education course listing and is cross-listed as Communication Studies 393D. In spring 2018, the course will also be cross-listed as a 400-level political science course and will be promoted to a group of honors students in our pre-Peace Corps program. It will also be offered to communication studies masters students at the 500 level with higher grading expectations.

Students: Students taking the course in its first semester were predominately juniors and seniors. Their majors varied widely including business, political science, history, and parks and recreation. About half of the class had a communication major or a communication minor. All of the students had some interest in either working for a non-profit after graduation or were currently involved with a non-profit. Several were dog and cat enthusiasts drawn to the course because our non-profit partner worked with animals.

Community Partners: The first community partner to work with the course was Mountaineer Spay and Neuter Assistance Program, MSNAP. They are a local non-profit that provides vouchers to individuals to cover the cost of spaying and neutering their pets. Many other organizations have expressed interest in working with the course, including a local free medical clinic, children's dance company, and an international exchange program. Faculty in communication studies and political science have not been involved in developing or teaching the class but they have been important partners in recruiting students to take the course.

Finding and Working with Partners: Finding community partners to work with the course was not difficult. WVU's Center for Service and Learning connected me with potential partners and promoted the class to local non-profits. After holding the class for one semester, several organizations interested in partnering with the class have contacted me. The need for grant research help in our community is great and many organizations are interested in working with the class.

In the coming semesters, we plan to work with multiple organizations, one for each student team. An interest questionnaire is being sent out to all organizations who work with WVU Center for Service and Learning. The questionnaire is short, with four questions designed to gauge if the organization's needs fit with the class. Applications were sent out in the summer and are due by September for the class held in the spring semester. We plan to hold an information session for interested non-profits in early October and to choose the organizations who will work with the class by November. By choosing the partner organizations early, we hope to be able to better plan volunteer activities for the students and class meetings with the organizations. We also hope to steer interested students to volunteer at the partner organizations before the course begins so that they have as much knowledge of the organization as possible.

The course is designed to require our partners to do minimal work. In talking with potential partners early on in the planning process, I found that some non-profits that had worked with students on similar projects in the past were at first hesitant to work with the class because they found working with students created more work for them than it saved. Partners found that they had to spend time teaching students basic business communication skills as well as proposal writing skills. I spend time early in the class discussing best practices for business communication. I have also structured the class like a client/business relationship and encourage students to treat their non-profit partners like clients.

Benefits

Instructor Benefits: When asked what they learned most from the research for non-profits course by a class guest, my students all mentioned research skills as the first or second most important thing they learned. They also all felt that they would use the skills they learned in the class as they entered the workforce. As a teaching librarian, this outcome is the best benefit I got from the course. I also felt that my work teaching the course had a greater impact than just the student's education. I know that the non-profit partner is using the information prepared by my students to forward their mission and better the community. These factors are a great motivation for me to continue working on the course.

Student Benefits: Students benefited by gaining skills and confidence in grant writing that they can use in the job market and in their future careers. Students also gain a sense of satisfaction for contributing directly to a non-profit to help solve a community problem. They also develop a better understanding of information literacy concepts and have better overall research skills that can be used in their lives and the classroom as well as on the job.

Community Partners Benefits: Our non-profit partner was grateful for the funder portfolios. They learned about at least two promising funding opportunities that they were not aware of before. They also were able to use some of the academic research supplied by the students not just in grant proposals but also in promoting their services to the public. Finally, our partner was thrilled for the opportunity to have young adults in our community learn about and get involved with their mission. They see our students as additional promoters of their services and potentially future board members.

Institutional Benefits: The Research for Non-Profits course benefits the WVU Libraries as well as the university as a whole. The course helps round out instructional offerings from the libraries and raises our profile on campus. It also fills a need on campus for a grant writing-related course and adds to the array of service-learning courses offered on campus.

THE PROCESS
Expected Learning Outcomes

The expected learning outcomes for the course are primarily centered on research and information literacy skills with the addition of knowledge of the non-profit organization.

After completing the course, students will be able to

- demonstrate a basic understanding of how non-profit foundations are organized and their role in the United States society;
- determine the type and amount of information required for grant proposals;
- employ reflective research strategies, including effective use of specialized databases such as the Foundation Center Grant databases, relevant academic research databases, and statistics sources;
- evaluate sources to identify the most authoritative and useful references for a grant proposal;
- identify and analyze potential grant funding opportunities for a non-profit organization;
- articulate the best communication strategies for approaching potential funders; and
- present their research effectively and professionally.

Curriculum Materials

The course is designed to be a guided work/internship experience and therefore does not have extensive reading or lecture components. The primary assignment for the course is the team research portfolio and presentation to the non-profit client. Students also complete individual research reports that contribute content to the final team portfolio, reading quizzes, personal reflections, and team progress reports. There is no assigned textbook for the course. Readings are available through the libraries' eReserves and are drawn primarily from *Foundation Fundamentals* from the Foundation Center, grant writing manuals, as well as one chapter from Badke's *Research Strategies: Finding Your Way Through the Information Fog*. The readings are designed to give students necessary background information and practical examples for their own work.

Steps Involved

The entire course is designed as a service-learning experience. A member of WVU's Center for Service and Learning visits the class the first week to talk about service-learning and how it benefits both students and the community. They also cover the practical procedures for students logging service hours in our iServe tracking system. The system creates a central place for students, community partners, and faculty to track service hours. Students log both the service hours they spend on-site working for their organizations as well as the hours they spend working on grant research. Students complete four short reflection papers evenly spaced through the semester that ask them to reflect on the course, their progress, and how their service hours connect with what they are learning in the class.

Students are assigned a non-profit client the first week of class. They then spend some time doing background research on the client and preparing for an informational interview with their clients in the second or third week of class. In the first semester the course was run, we worked with only one non-profit client. I divided the class into three teams of four and each team competed for the best client portfolio. At the end of the semester, the client chose the winning portfolio. This method worked well for the first semester, but because of growing interest in the class, we have decided to work with multiple non-profit clients in future semesters: one client per student team.

The course content is divided into three modules designed to help students build the required sections of their portfolios. The modules are: 1) Finding funders, 2) Finding statistics and secondary research, and 3) Communication strategies. The first two modules of the course focus on tools and background knowledge needed to complete research for the portfolios. Individual students are required to submit source reports to me and their teammates for each type of source covered. Assigned readings cover the nature of non-profits and the rules that govern them, as well as research strategies.

In the final third of the semester, teams concentrate on creating their portfolios. At the beginning of module three, student teams review the source reports submitted by individual members and select the best sources to include in their portfolio. Teams can also decide at this time that more research needs to be done to complete their portfolio. Assigned readings and some class time are devoted to reading and analyzing successful grant proposals. The remaining class time is given to teams to meet and prepare their portfolios. Each team meets with the instructor twice during this time period to report on their progress and create a plan to complete the remaining tasks. The teams are required to submit written action plans to the instructor prior to the meetings.

At the end of the course, each team gives a short (no more than ten minutes) formal presentation on their research to their clients, the rest of the class, and class visitors from the Center for Service and Learning. The clients are given copies of the portfolios in a format best suited to their needs. Most teams choose to give their client paper portfolios in binders with an electronic copy available online or on a USB drive. The teams are encouraged to keep in contact with their clients throughout the process to ask for clarification and give updates. (See entire course syllabus and reflection prompts in the Appendix Materials for this chapter.)

POST-PROJECT ASSESSMENT
Methods of Reflection

- Students are asked to complete three short reflection papers. The assignments are evenly spaced throughout the semester. The first two reflection papers ask students to think about how their volunteer hours and their grantseeking work contribute to their learning for the class. These assignments follow the DEAL Model for Written Critical Reflection developed by Ash and Clayton. The model gives students a structure to follow for their papers. It also gives them a process of reflection that helps them make connections between their service experience and the course learning objectives.[2] The third reflection paper is assigned at the end of the course. It asks students to describe skills they learned in the course as they would to a potential employer during a job interview. I developed the assignment prompt from one posted on a Duke University service learning website.[3] The reflection paper prompts are included at the end of this chapter.

Post-Project Feedback

- Selected student reflections:
  - Students were generally surprised by the amount of work and time involved in searching for grants: "I spent nine hours searching for

four potential funders…. This exercise required learning patience and perseverance." "I learned how extensive the process is for creating a final grant proposal recommendation. From creating a need statement to doing the statistical research to back up your claims, the time it takes to create a quality grant proposal is unbelievable."

o Students felt that their overall research skills were much stronger by the end of the course: "I don't think I started out as a good researcher, but now I know what I'm doing."

o Students felt a sense of accomplishment by the end of the course for having both learned new skills and helped a local cause: "Spending hours finding data for an argument fuels a passion to help others. This coursework has enabled me to make a difference in my community. After this course is over, I plan to apply this knowledge to help other non-profits."

- Community partner feedback:

o Mountaineer Spay and Neuter Assistance was our community partner for Spring 2017. They were impressed with the quality of the student portfolios, so much so that they found it hard to choose a winning portfolio because they felt all three groups did professional work. They have been pursuing a couple of the grant opportunities outlined in the portfolios and have used some of the academic research from the portfolios in their promotion work.

Project Assessment and Reporting Methods

- WVU's Center for Service and Learning tracked service hours completed for the course. In the Spring 2017 semester, students logged ninety-six service hours for the course with an estimated impact value to the community of $2,014.
- Formal student evaluations for the course were generally positive, although only half of the students completed the optional online evaluation form. In future semesters, we may include an additional end-of-the-semester evaluation or an added incentive for completing the course evaluation.
- The quality of work completed for the final portfolios was high and the overall course average was a high B.

Difficulties Encountered

Student issues: Most students underestimated the difficulty of grantseeking research and the time required. Despite detailed class instruction and class workshop time, most of the students' initial grant maker profiles were less than adequate. The quality of their research and profiles improved only after graded feedback and guided revision.

Contacting their clients with questions and contacting potential funders for more information caused anxiety for some students. They were reluctant to ask all the questions they needed to of their clients. They also needed quite a bit of coaching in how to best approach potential funders.

Instructor issues: The single largest roadblock for this course was getting enough students to enroll. The course began as an elective outside of WVU's general education requirements. It was advertised widely on campus and promoted to advisors in key departments, including social work, sociology, English, business, and others. After failing to get more than three students enrolled in each of the first two semesters it was offered, I re-tooled the class as an upper-division course and submitted it to the campus curriculum committee to be included as a general education course. Most importantly, I successfully negotiated with the communication studies department to have the course cross-listed as a communication studies elective. Slightly more than half of the thirteen students enrolled in the course's first successful semester were communication studies majors or minors. This process took several years from the time I first envisioned the course to the first semester it was taught. I have had to continue to build campus relationships to ensure an ongoing student audience for the course. It will be cross-listed in both communication studies and political science for its next semester.

This course required me to move beyond teaching information literacy. It necessitated that I have lessons and readings on non-profit operations and on the rhetoric of successful grant writing. My training from the Foundation Center as well as my previous experience teaching rhetoric and composition were helpful, but I also needed to do a lot of reading to prepare.

Community partner issues: Our initial community partner had very little difficultly working with the course because it required minimal effort on their part. The Center for Service and Learning and I did all of the coordinating and scheduling. The community partner needed to be willing and able to provide the class with detailed accounting records and other data they had collected on their operations. They also had to be able to meet with the student teams at least once and answer email inquiries.

Our first community partner was not able to give students tasks to do to fill their required volunteer hours. Students completed volunteer hours with a related organization that handled pet adoptions. This situation was less than ideal for the students and the community partner because they did not have as much time together to develop a relationship.

Conclusion

Teaching Research for Non-Profits has been the positive and engaging experience that I hoped it would be. Designing the course, building campus partnerships, and growing a student audience took a significant amount of effort over several years. These tasks continue to take time and effort in addition to teaching the course, but the product has been worth the effort. Giving students a real-world information need helps them learn information literacy skills and appreciate the value of those skills more than they would in a pure classroom setting. The course has built positive and productive relationships between academic departments and the libraries that help build our profile as a partner in education on campus. Since I started work on the course, the libraries have engaged in other projects with the Center for Service and Learning and the course continues to gain attention on campus and in the community.

APPENDIX MATERIALS
- Course Syllabus
- Reflection Prompt

Course Syllabus

ULIB 302 / COMM 393D Research for Non-Profits

Spring 2017

Tuesday/ Thursday 1:00pm–2:15pm 2036 Downtown Campus Library

Contact hours: 3hrs/wk.

Instructor: Alyssa Wright

alyssa.wright@mail.wvu.edu

(304) 293-0337

1004D Downtown Campus Library

Office hours by appointment

COURSE DESCRIPTION

This course covers advanced research skills, including precise, effective use of discipline-specific databases and grantseeking research. Students will apply these skills working in teams to produce a research portfolio for a local non-profit organization.

COURSE LEARNING OUTCOMES & GOALS

WVU GEF LEARNING GOAL	LEARNING OUTCOME	ASSESSMENT
Personal or Social Responsibilities (specifically civic knowledge and engagement)	Students will be able to demonstrate a basic understanding of how non-profit foundations are organized and their role in the United States society.	Reading Quizzes, Funder Source Reports, and Personal Reflections
Intellectual and Practical Skills (specifically information literacy)	Students will be able to determine the type and amount of information required for grant proposals.	Research Portfolio with annotated bibliography
Intellectual and Practical Skills (specifically information literacy)	Students will be able to employ reflective research strategies, including effective use of specialized databases such as the Foundation Center Grant databases, relevant academic research databases, and statistics sources.	Personal Reflections & Team Action plans
Intellectual and Practical Skills (specifically information literacy)	Students will be able to evaluate sources to identify the most authoritative and useful references for a grant proposal.	Source Reports & annotated bibliography
Intellectual and Practical Skills (specifically information literacy)	Students will be able to identify and analyze potential grant funding opportunities for a non-profit organization.	Funder Source Reports & Research Portfolio
Intellectual and Practical Skills (specifically written and oral communication)	Students will be able to articulate the best communication strategies for approaching potential funders.	Research Portfolio
Intellectual and Practical Skills (specifically written and oral communication)	Students will be able to present their research effectively and professionally.	Client Presentations

GENERAL EDUCATION FOUNDATION AREA 4, SOCIETY & CONNECTIONS

(Students will demonstrate understanding and analysis of human behavior, societal and political organization, or communication.)

This course will give students a general understanding of how the United States non-profit sector is organized and its role in US society. Students will also learn how to analyze and create rhetorical strategies used in grant proposals for non-profit organizations.

MAJOR ASSIGNMENTS

The following are basic overviews of the major assignments for this course. More detailed assignment guidelines and grading rubrics will be distributed in class.

Team Research Portfolios and Client Presentations: The final project of the course will be a research portfolio and presentation for a non-profit organization. The portfolio will be created in teams and will include an executive summary, profiles of potential funders, useful statistics, a need statement, and an annotated bibliography.

Source Reports: Students will individually write at least twelve detailed reports on potential sources for the final team research portfolio. Source reports will be due at the end of each unit, and each student will be graded individually. Source reports will be posted to a team Google Drive or other web tool. Report formats will be determined by the teams.

Personal Reflections: Each student will write three personal reflections that give an account of his/her research process and his/her work with the non-profit.

Team Action Plans: Team action plans will be due at mid-term and near the end of the semester. Action plans will be brief outlines of work that needs to be done to complete the portfolio, including further research, and will assign specific tasks to team members.

Service Hours: Students will be required to complete 2.5 to four volunteer hours for a related non-profit organization. Volunteer hours should be scheduled by the end of the second week of class and should be completed by the end of the thirteenth week of class. Your service hours will be logged using iServe, the online service management system provided by WVU's Center for Service and Learning. You can learn more about iServe here: http://iserve.wvu.edu.

GRADING

- 35% of the final grade for this course will be based on group work, 65% of the final grade will be based on individual work.
- Team research portfolios & presentation (group work), **30%**
- 3 written personal reflections on the course and research process (individual work), **25%**

- 12 or more source reports (individual work), **28%**
- Reading quizzes (individual work), **10%**
- 2 team action plans (group work), **5%**
- Volunteer hours with related non-profit (individual work), **2%**

GRADING SCALE

A+=100–98, A=97–92, A-=91–90, B+=89–88, B=87–82, B-=81–80, C+=79-78, C=77–72, C-=71–70, D+=69–68, D=67–62, D-=61–60, F=59 and below

COURSE READING

Readings will be posted on WVU Libraries' eReserve. There is no required text-book for this course. Assigned readings are designed to give you background knowledge of the US non-profit sector, grant-seeking, research tools, and academic articles. The research project you will complete for this course will also require a significant amount of independent reading.

Due by week 2:
Collins, S. (2008). *Foundation Fundamentals*. New York: The Foundation Center. (Chapter 1 whole chapter, & Chapter 4 pages 35–38).

Due by week 3:
Collins, S. (2008). *Foundation Fundamentals*. New York: The Foundation Center. (Chapter 4 pages 39–49, & Chapter 5 pages 51–70).

Salamon, L. (2012) What is the nonprofit sector and why do we have it? In *America's Nonprofit Sector: A Primer* (pp. 9–25) New York: The Foundation Center.

Due by week 4:
Collins, S. (2008). *Foundation Fundamentals*. New York: The Foundation Center. (Chapter 7 pages 103–127)

Due by week 5:
Kester, C. L. (2015) Chapter one: How federal grants work. *Writing to Win Federal Grants: A Must-Have for Your Fundraising Toolbox.* (pp. 1–8) Nashville, TN: CharityChannel Press.

Kester, C. L. (2015) Chapter four: Finding the best match: Prospect research. *Writing to Win Federal Grants: A Must-Have for Your Fundraising Toolbox.* (pp. 28–38) Nashville, TN: CharityChannel Press.

Due by week 6:
Mallory, M., & Forte, E. (2001) Government Documents and statistics sources: Important statistical sources. In Bopp, R & Smith, L (ed). *Reference and information services: An introduction.* (pp. 564–568) Englewood, CO: Libraries Unlimited.

Samuelson, R. J. (2011, Aug. 21). Please, save the Statistical Abstract of the United States. *Akron Beacon Journal Online.* Retrieved from http://www.ohio.com/editorial/robert-j-samuelson-please-save-the-statistical-abstract-of-the-united-states-1.230800

Samuelson, R. J. (2012, Dec. 12). The stat abstract lives! *The Washington Post.* Retrieved from http://www.washingtonpost.com/blogs/post-partisan/wp/2012/12/12/the-stat-abstract-lives/

Due by week 7:
Laubepin, F. (2013) How to read (and understand) a social science journal article. Ann Arbor, MI: Inter-university Consortium for Political and Social Research.

Badke, W. B. (2011). Journal databases in *Research Strategies: Finding your way through the information fog* (pp. 76–95) Lincoln, NE: iUniverse.

Due by week 10:
Tremore, J., & Burke Smith, N (2009) Chapter 10, writing a statement of need in *Grant Writing: A complete resource for proposal writing* (pp. 91–101) Avon, MA: Adams Media.

ATTENDANCE POLICY

Attendance will not be graded; however, you will not be able to make up in-class work and quizzes without prior arrangement with the instructor.

SERVICE-LEARNING STATEMENT

Service-learning courses include four essential elements. They
1. enable students to enhance learning while engaging in hands-on service;
2. provide service that benefits the community partner and the student;
3. engage students in reflection and critical inquiry that link learning from service to academic learning; and
4. have the potential to promote community and civic engagement by relating service experiences to issues of public concern. (Adapted from the CSU Center for Community Engagement, cecenter@csus.edu)

We'll be using our service project, conducting research for Mountaineer Spay Neuter Assistance Program as field experience, informing our study of information literacy and at the same time using our academic and intellectual skills to fill a real need in the community.

INCLUSIVITY STATEMENT

The West Virginia University community is committed to creating and fostering a positive learning and working environment based on open communication, mutual respect, and inclusion.

If you are a person with a disability and anticipate needing any type of accommodation in order to participate in this class, please advise me and make appropriate arrangements with the Office of Disability Services (293-6700). For more information on West Virginia University's Diversity, Equity, and Inclusion initiatives, please see http://diversity.wvu.edu.

ACADEMIC INTEGRITY STATEMENT

The integrity of the classes offered by any academic institution solidifies the foundation of its mission and cannot be sacrificed to expediency, ignorance, or blatant fraud. Therefore, I will enforce rigorous standards of academic integrity in all aspects and assignments of this course. For the detailed policy of West Virginia University regarding the definitions of acts considered to fall under academic dishonesty and possible ensuing sanctions, please see the Student Conduct Code (http://studentlife.wvu.edu/office_of_student_conduct/student_conduct_code). Should you have any questions about possibly improper research citations or references, or any other activity that may be interpreted as an attempt at academic dishonesty, please see me before the assignment is due to discuss the matter.

COURSE CALENDAR
Week 1:
- 1/10/17: Class overview and service learning presentation
- 1/12/17: Form teams, prep for client interviews by formulating research questions about the organizations

Week 2:
- 1/17/17: Reading quiz on Foundation Center Foundation Fundamentals: Chapter 1, What is a foundation, pp. 1–8, and first half of Chapter 4, Planning your Funding Research Strategy pp. 35–38
- Overview of the different types of foundations and charitable giving. Introduction to the Foundation Center and FC Databases

- 1/19/17: Team members share what they found out about the client and their environment and formulate questions to ask the client in the interview
- **Volunteer hours sign-up deadline**

Week 3: Begin Module 1: Finding potential funders
- 1/24/17: Client interviews with non-profit partner
- 1/26/17: Reading quiz on Foundation Center Foundation Fundamentals: second half of Chapter 4, pp 38–49; Chapter 5, online resources for funding research, pp. 51–70; and Salamon, L. (2012) What is the nonprofit sector and why do we have it? In America's Nonprofit Sector: A Primer (pp. 9–25)
- Teams create funder profile forms to use in their research and select online file sharing platform

Week 4:
- 1/31/17: Reading Quiz on Foundation Center Foundation Fundamentals (Chapter 7, Corporate giving, pp. 103–127)
- Lab day, search Foundation Center databases
- 2/2/17: Guest lecture on the non-profit sector and fundraising; Paula Martinelli, Director of Development, WVU Libraries
- 4 funder profiles due by end of the week

Week 5:
- 2/7/17: Reading quiz on Kester, C L. (2015) Chapter one: How federal grants work. *Writing to Win Federal Grants: A Must Have for Your Fundraising Toolbox.* (Chapter 1, pp. 1–8 and Chapter 4, pp. 28–38)
- Government funding sources
- 2/9/17: Lab day, search grants.gov and CFDA
- **2 government funder profiles due by the end of the week**

Week 6: Begin Module 2, Statistics
- 2/14/17: Reading quiz on Mallory and Forte, Important Statistical Sources, pp. 564–568; Samuelson, "Please, Save the Statistical Abstract of the United States; & Samuelson, "The Stat Abstract Lives!"
- Discussion about Census data and demo of American FactFinder, Census.gov, & Statistical abstracts
- 2/16/17: Funder profile workshop

Week 7:
- 2/20/17: **Revised Funder Reports due (private and federal)**

- 2/21/17: **Reflection 1 due,** non-governmental statistics sources demo and search in teams
- 2/23/17: Audience analysis for grant applications and teams meet to assess statistics needed for grant applications.

Week 8:
- 2/27/17: **3 Statistics source reports due**
- 2/28/17: Reading quiz on: Badke, "Journal Databases," pp. 76–95; EBSCO & Web of Science databases demo and search in teams
- 3/2/17: Discussion about White papers and reports; copyright and open access; and Google Scholar and Issue Lab demo and search in teams

Spring Break

Week 9:
- 3/14/17: Reading: Laubepin, "How to Read (and Understand) a Social Science Journal Article"
- Lesson/workshop on writing source annotations and citations; **bring the full text of at least one source to class**
- 3/16/17: **Reflection 2 Due** Portfolio discussion

Week 10:
- 3/21/17 & 3/23/17: **2 Academic source annotations due by the beginning of the week**
- Team mid-term conferences with instructor and optional meetings with client
- **Team action plans for further research and portfolio prep due by the end of the week**

Week 11: Begin module 3: communication strategies
- 3/28/17: Reading quiz on Tremore, J & Burke Smith, N (2009) Chapter 10, writing a statement of need in *Grant Writing: A complete resource for proposal writing*, pp. 91–101
- Analysis of winning proposals
- 3/30/17: Analysis of winning proposals and group work day

Week 12:
- 4/4/17: **Annotated bibliography drafts due,** peer review
- 4/6/17: **Needs statement/literature review drafts due,** peer review

Week 13:
- 4/11/17 & 4/13/17: Team conferences with instructor and work on further research, optional client meetings
- **Team action plan for further research and portfolio creation due by the end of the week**

Week 14:
- 4/18/17: Presentation workshop
- 4/20/17: **Final reflections due.** Teams work on final portfolios and client presentations

Week 15:
- 4/25/17 & 4/27/17 Presentations
- Final portfolios due to clients

PORTFOLIO ASSIGNMENT

ULIB 302/COMM 393D Research for Non-Profits

Funder research portfolio and client presentation

30% of final grade

Due dates:
- 4/4/17: Annotated bibliography drafts due
- 4/6/17: Needs statement drafts due
- 4/25/17 & 4/27/17 **Presentations & Final portfolios due to clients**

Required portfolio components:

Each team's portfolio should contain the following sections. If your group believes additional information is needed for your client—i.e., charts, sample budgets, or sample letters of introduction—please feel free to include them.
- Executive summary
- Profiles of potential funders
- Annotated bibliography
- Sample need statement

SECTION DESCRIPTIONS:
Executive summary:

The executive summary should be a clear and concise overview written for the people in your client's organization who will not have time to read the entire portfolio. It should give a short overview of the current climate for funding in your client's area, explain the value of the portfolio, highlight the most important information, and make recommendations (for example, which grant opportunity should be perused first). Please see http://www.umuc.edu/current-students/learning-resources/writing-center/writing-resources/executive-summaries/index.cfm?noprint=true for more information on writing an executive summary.

Profiles of potential funders:

This section will arguably be the most useful part of the portfolio for your client. The funder profiles should include all the information your client will need to write and send a grant proposal to a funder. They should be in a consistent, easy-to-read format. You should include profiles for funders that are good matches for your clients. There is no required number of profiles for your portfolio. The funder profiles included in your portfolio can, but do not have to be, the same profiles individual team members submitted earlier in the semester. Your team may want to adapt or consolidate individual team members' profiles or you may want to create new profiles based on further research you completed in the second half of the semester.

Annotated bibliography:

The annotated bibliography should provide your client with full citations, short summaries, and use statements for statistics sources, academic articles, white papers, and reports. The citations should generally follow APA formatting. The goal of the annotated bibliography is to make information easy to use for your clients. If a source is available online, include a usable link. If the source you are citing has restricted access, you might want to include a copy in the portfolio. There is no required number of sources for the annotated bibliography. It should provide enough information for your client to support their claims in a grant proposal.

Sample need statement:

A need statement is the part of a grant proposal that argues why a particular organization or project should be funded. It is not an accounting of the funds needed by an organization to operate or complete a project. The need statement should convince readers that an organization or project is needed by the community.

Your statement should use clear and convincing rhetoric and make liberal use of the research you found for this class. We will discuss more about how to write a convincing need statement in weeks 10 and 11 of the course.

You should provide in-text citations that follow a consistent format and make it easy for readers to find and read your sources. Strict adherence to APA formation rules is not necessary and may not be preferable for your audience. Any source cited in your statement should also be included in your annotated bibliography.

Your need statement can be a generic statement your client can adapt to fit any grant proposal, or you may want to write a need statement to be used to apply for a particular grant that you recommend to your client.

Portfolio format:

The portfolio should be in a format best suited to your client. You may want to create a digital portfolio using the web tool of your choice, or a paper portfolio, or both. The portfolio should be easy for your client to access and use. If you choose to create a digital portfolio, it will be up to your group to figure out which technology will be best suited to your needs and how to use that technology. A digital portfolio must be freely and permanently accessible to your client.

Whichever format you choose, the portfolio should look professional and be clearly organized and easy to read. Its formatting should be consistent; it should be written in formal language and be free of grammatical errors.

Presentation:

Your presentation should give an overview of your research and make recommendations to your client. The format of your presentations is up to your group. They should be informative and engaging. We will discuss the element of successful presentation in week 13 of the course.

Presentations should be no longer than **ten minutes** and will take place in our classroom 2036, Downtown Campus Library. You should budget time for questions and be prepared to answer any questions your client might have.

All team members do not need to speak in the presentation, but all team members need to be present and participate in some way.

Presentations will be given during the last week of class. Your audience will be your client, your instructor, and potentially class guests.

Reflection Prompt

ULIB 302/ COMM 393D
Personal Reflection 1
Due Tuesday, February 21, 2017
Length: 1.5 to 3 pages double-spaced

Points: 8 points (8% of final grade)

FORMAT:

Following the DEAL Model (see below), reflect on your class experience so far. What have you learned? What has surprised you? What have you found difficult and why? If you have completed your pet adoption service hours, please reflect on that experience as well as your research experience.

The DEAL Model for Written Critical Reflection:

- First paragraph: **D**escribe in fair detail and as objectively as possible the experience, the activity, the reading, etc.
- Second paragraph: **E**xamine, in accordance with the learning objectives.
  - o What specific academic material is relevant to this experience?
  - o What academic (e.g., disciplinary, intellectual, professional) skills did I use/should I have used? In what ways did I/others think from the perspective of a particular discipline and with what results?
  - o In what specific ways are my understanding of the material or skill and the experience the same and in what specific ways are they different? What are the possible reasons for the difference(s) (e.g., bias, assumptions, lack of information on my part or on the part of the author/instructor/community)?
- Third paragraph: **A**rticulate Learning
  - o What did I learn?
  - o How did I learn it?
  - o Why does it matter?
  - o What will I do in the future in light of it?

Notes

1. Maureen Barry, "Librarians as Partners in Service-Learning Courses (Part I)," *LOEX Quarterly* 38, no. 6 (2011): 345–348; Maureen Barry, "Research for the Greater Good: Incorporating Service Learning in an Information Literacy Course at Write State University," *College & Research Libraries News* 72, no. 1 (2011): 8–10.
2. Patti Clayton, "The DEAL Model for Critical Reflection," *Curricular Engagement*. Accessed July 24, 2017. https://curricularengagement.com/.
3. Katie Halcrow, "Reflection Activities: Service-Learning's Not-so-Secret Weapon," *Resources for Responsible and Ethical Engagement Duke University*, accessed July 24, 2017, https://sites.duke.edu/responsibleengagement/files/2015/04/Reflection-Activities-for-All-Classrooms.pdf.

CHAPTER TWO

A Picture is Worth a Thousand Words:
Using Infographics to Visually Present Student Research

Dr. Terri Summey

Professor
Emporia State University Libraries and Archives
tsummey@emporia.edu

Bethanie O'Dell

Assistant Professor
Emporia State University and Archives
bodell1@emporia.edu

THE ACTIVITY

Description: For several years, Emporia State University has incorporated principles from the Kansas Leadership Center (KLC) in selected courses with the purpose of teaching students to develop leadership skills by identifying and solving problems in their communities.[1] In line with the focus on leadership competencies, the University Libraries and Archives has adopted a service-learning emphasis to guide students enrolled in a two-credit information literacy course in topic selection. In this course, UL100: Research Skills, Information and Technology, students are asked to identify a community organization and a social issue linked to that organization to guide their research for the semester-long course. Students are required to present their findings to their selected organization in a variety of ways, utilizing various technological tools. One method is using visual storytelling through infographics, where students are required to use a combination of visuals, data, and text to present focused information on their topic.

Students use an online tool (such as Canva or Piktochart) for creating infographics and present a minimum of five information sections on their topic. They will utilize a combination of visuals and text to present the information and cite any sources used in creating their infographic. To introduce students to the concept of infographics, one lesson in the course uses infographics as an information resource. Students evaluate infographics using standard evaluation criteria such as currency, relevancy, authority, accuracy, and purpose. Course instructors have discovered that students enjoy the creativity essential to the effective completion of this assignment and the unique nature of the product that they are creating. This helps illustrate the success of incorporating the infographic evaluation assignment along with presenting the infographic project as an alternative to traditional research assignments.

Getting Started: For many years, students in the UL100 course, Research Skills, Information, and Technology, used their own topics for the projects in the course. Topics ranged from personal interest topics to more professional topics based on assignments for courses in which students were enrolled. After several library faculty members participated in a program under the auspices of the KLC regarding adding leadership competencies to their general education courses, a couple of library faculty members decided to change the parameters for the topics students selected for their research in the UL100 course. Many of the KLC competencies could be applied to research such as Diagnose the Situation and Seek Multiple Interpretations. Library faculty members teaching the UL100 course wanted students to begin to consider future leadership roles in their communities and to think beyond themselves. One way to do this is to be involved in service organizations. Inspired by the principles and teachings of the KLC, the UL100 instructors had students select service organizations in which they had an interest and where they might want to volunteer in the future. For their research topics, students researched these organizations. In addition to researching the organizations, students also selected a social problem that these organizations wanted to solve or help alleviate. For example, students selecting a food bank would research that organization. They might also seek information on poverty or hunger.

Additionally, for one of the final projects in the course, students conducted research and gathered information about their topics. This information about their topics and a discussion of the sources they used was presented in a bibliographic essay. After experiencing some difficulty in explaining the purpose of a bibliographic essay, instructors teaching the UL100 course decided to make a change from a bibliographic essay to an infographic. Inspired by infographics used in marketing and to present data, the library faculty believed that this would be a new and fresh way for students to present their findings on a selected topic. The resources that students used to locate information on their topic was still presented in an annotated bibliography. In the annotated bibliography, students discuss the process they used to find relevant sources in an introduction and include citations and annotations for each source used. Each annotation consists of two paragraphs, one which summarizes the resource and a second paragraph evaluating the resource.

The inspiration for using infographics to teach students about infographics came from a lesson by McClure and Toth on using infographics to teach the value of information and the authority of infographics as sources of information in *Teaching Information Literacy: Threshold Concepts Lessons Plans for Librarians.*[2] This lesson was used as a starting point and its accompanying worksheet was adapted for this class activity. Students are provided a variety of infographics to analyze and evaluate in pairs or small groups. Students use the CRAAP criteria created by librarians at California State University, Chico to evaluate the infographics.[3] Additionally, students analyze the infographics using tips for creating good infographics, paying attention to content and design. After groups finish evaluating and analyzing the infographics, the instructor leads the students in a discussion to debrief the class activity and present what they found in their evaluation and analysis of the infographics. The infographics selected for this activity are on similar topics and of varying quality.

Motivations: The two primary motivations for utilizing infographics is to encourage students to present information in formats outside of the traditional presentation style and to avoid overloading students with too many research papers. Because individuals typically spend only a few seconds looking at the information presented in an infographic, students need to learn how to present the information on their topic in a concise manner. In addition to the infographic assignment, students also submit an annotated bibliography listing eight sources related to their research topic and an online portfolio which presents key assignments and students' reflections throughout the course. This variety of assignments helps keep students engaged and motivated throughout the course because they are able to express their creativity and take ownership of their research.

Because UL100 is a lower-level general education course, many of the students enrolling in this course are freshmen and sophomores. As mentioned earlier, a primary motivation for changing the way students selected topics was to help students think beyond themselves. In line with the KLC principles, learning about community organizations provides these students with opportunities to volunteer and give back to their communities in the future. Another secondary motivation was to help students connect the content taught in this course to real-world experiences in order to engage them in the learning experience and bring meaning to the course for the students.

THE PEOPLE

Library: The University Libraries and Archives (ULA) is the primary library at Emporia State University. Emporia State University (ESU) is a public university located in the Midwest that serves approximately 6,000 undergraduate and graduate students. The mission and vision of the ULA are to inspire lifelong learning and engaging adaptive learners (University Libraries and Archives, 2017).[4] The ULA provides "enrich[ed] academic experiences and achievements by providing resources, space for creation, cooperation and fraternization, and teaching information literacy skills across the curriculum" (University Libraries and Archives, 2017).

Instructors: UL100: Research Skills, Information and Technology is taught by the ULA reference and instruction librarians. Currently, there are five librarians teaching UL100:

- The director of assessment and instruction oversees the information literacy sessions by coordinating the assessment as well as collaborating with the English composition courses to schedule and oversee library instruction.
- The reference and research services librarian serves as the point person for ESU's Reference and Information Services, along with the Children's Literature Collection and Children's programming. This librarian also teaches the two largest face-to-face sections of UL100.
- The head of technical services provides tech support for the library and introduces new technology features to the library atmosphere.
- The lifelong learning librarian oversees the lifelong learning activities for ESU students and expands the library's relationship with community programs.
- The virtual learning librarian oversees virtual learning for ESU students by developing online workshops and teaching the online section of UL100.

All of these librarians have participated in workshops and strategic initiatives focused on the KLC principles. Therefore, the librarians have taken an interest in adapting leadership themes in each information literacy course.

Course: UL100: Research Skills, Information and Technology is a two-credit (soon to be three-credit), one-hour general education course that introduces the skills and concepts of locating, evaluating, and using information from a variety of resources. This course meets the information technology requirement for undergraduates by teaching students how to identify credible information while using it ethically and responsibly. This course is offered face-to-face, online, and in eight-week blocks in order to meet the scheduling needs of ESU students.

Students: Because this is a lower-level general education course, a majority of the students enrolled in the course are freshmen and sophomores. The Department of Psychology, Department of Nursing, and several other departments in the College of Liberal Arts and Sciences require their students to take this course as a part of their degree requirements. It was believed that the community service aspect of the assignment would appeal to psychology and nursing students, who will eventually seek employment in service-oriented positions.

Community Partners: Initially, students have been allowed to seek out their own community partners or service organizations. Because the students are only learning about the organizations and the social problems that the organizations seek to address, instructors do not contact the organizations to form partnerships at this time. Students are encouraged to contact the organizations and interview leaders in the organization to learn more about the mission and operations of the service organization. Course instructors have discussed selecting local community service organizations to partner with in the future, especially those affiliated with mental health and medicine to provide real-world experiences for our nursing and psychology students enrolled in the course.

Finding and Working with Partners: Currently, students are allowed to select their own community service organizations in either the local community or their hometown. Students are encouraged to select an organization with which they are familiar, that interests them, or aligns with their future professional goals. Students utilize a variety of information sources to learn about the organization, including interviewing an individual affiliated with the community service organization. Emporia State University is proud of its town-gown relationship with the community of Emporia. All of the Recognized Student Organizations (RSO) have to perform a required number of community service hours. Therefore, connections have already been formed with community service organizations. Furthermore, in a town of 25,000, community leaders are well-known and supportive of the university's initiatives. Initial contacts have been made with community service organizations such as the local hospital, the mental health center, the addiction recovery facility, and skilled nursing facilities. Other organizations will be contacted to match with students' interests, majors, and future professions. For example, the community theatre organization may be contacted to work with theatre majors. Community service organizations will be asked to identify information needs to guide students' research for the course. Students will be required to interview an individual affiliated with the community service organization and present their infographic to the organization at the end of the course.

Benefits

Instructor Benefits: One of the primary benefits for the instructors is the experience of seeing the creativity of the students as it is expressed in this infographic assignment. Very rarely are the infographics of the students similar in style and format because students either focus on presenting information with images, charts, thought bubbles, and more. Students also arrange their information in ways they feel is important to the presentation. While two students may create an infographic over the same research topic, they bring their own perspective to the design process which results in a wide range of information. This is a creative outlet that allows many students to express their ideas in ways that go beyond words. Additionally, it aligns with the ACRL Framework, especially with Information Creation as a Process.[5] Using the infographic as one of the major assignments allows course instructors to assess the information gathered by the student on their selected topic and the sources used. Additionally, instructors of UL100 learn more about the students in their courses and their interests through the organizations that they select for this assignment and the social problems on which they focus. It is amazing to see the commitment to community service that many of these students express in their assignments for this course.

Student Benefits: The biggest revelation students have when completing this assignment is the ease of creating an infographic with the information they located throughout the course of the semester. Many students will utilize the pre-made themes provided by graphic design tool websites like Canva and Piktochart so that they can focus on the information they find valuable to present instead of stressing over how to create the template and use proper design. The ability to be creative in designing their infographics appeals to a majority of the students in UL100. When asked about their favorite assignment in the course, a majority of students select the infographic as that assignment. Students also express that they enjoy the opportunity of learning a new presentation tool that they can use to present information for other classes and projects. After taking the course and learning about infographics, students have indicated that they used infographics to present information in other courses. Because of the brevity of an infographic, students must select the most important information to present concisely in their infographic. Students are presented tips for the creation of quality infographics and told to introduce their topic well through images, graphs, and words. One of the greatest benefits for students might be learning about social and service needs in their communities. As one student indicated, she did not know that food insecurity was a problem in our local community and that children often went hungry at nights and on weekends. Through her interest in a "food for students" program, she learned that for many students, the only meals they eat are the ones they receive at school.

Partner Benefits: Through this assignment, students learn about community service organizations and the problems that they seek to alleviate. Because of their new knowledge about these organizations, many students will seek out these organizations as volunteers when they need to fulfill community service hours as part of an RSO or desire to give back to their community in the future. When the infographics are posted on the University Libraries and Archives Facebook page or displayed in the library, the information regarding the community service organizations is shared bringing more awareness to the organizations and their missions.

Institutional Benefits: This assignment has several benefits for Emporia State University. It aligns with the Strategic Plan of Emporia State University, the Adaptive University.[6] According to the ESU Strategic Plan, the core values of ESU are excellence, respect, responsibility, and service. As stated in the strategic plan, "With service, the university values engagement in leadership and community that positively impacts our global society." The vision for ESU is "Changing Lives for the Common Good." Students are learning about the needs of a community and that volunteering in that community helps change the lives of the people that those organizations serve. One of the goals of the ESU Strategic Plan is to provide students with opportunities to develop leadership skills. Incorporating leadership competencies from the KLC into this general education course facilitates the achievement of this goal. Finally, students working with local community service organizations enhances the town-gown relationship and the reputation of the university within the community of Emporia. Since students are allowed to select community service organizations in their hometowns, it also enhances the reputation of ESU throughout the State of Kansas. Recently, the infographics from one of the UL100 course sections were shared on the Facebook page of the ESU Libraries and Archives. The local paper, the Emporia Gazette, noticed the infographics and wrote a story featuring the students' work in the course providing positive publicity for the university.

THE PROCESS
Expected Learning Outcomes

The instructors of UL100 focus on keeping the learning outcomes up to date by aligning the outcomes with the Framework for Information Literacy for Higher Education provided by the Association of College and Research Libraries (ACRL). These learning outcomes are:

- Define, narrow, and focus on a topic for any research need.
- Develop the skills necessary to access information effectively and efficiently.
- Apply critical thinking skills, such as interpreting scholarly materials, considering multiple perspectives, and using reason and evidence in the evaluation of information.
- Analyze and synthesize information for the purpose of creating new knowledge.
- Cite sources in a format recognized by professional colleagues in scholarly communication.
- Identify ethical, legal, and social issues reflecting the changing nature of information in a technological society.

This course also focuses on aligning with the following General Education Requirements:

- Acquire proficiency in core skills necessary for academic success, including written and spoken communication, quantitative and mathematical reasoning, and information technology and literacy.
- Be able to think critically and analytically about an issue, an idea, or a problem.

The infographic assignment aligns with all of the course outcomes for the UL100 course. Students must find information and sources on their topic throughout the semester, which in this case is a community service organization and its accompanying social issue. Initially, students write a short paper introducing their community service organization and the social problem that it is trying to alleviate. Then throughout the semester, they engage in classroom activities designed to assist them in defining their topic. Because the amount of information that can be presented in an infographic format is limited, students must be able to narrow down and focus their topic on introducing the important facts about the community service organization and its social problem to make it more manageable. Students must then search for resources that will help provide them with the information they need to create the infographic. When they create the infographic, students must analyze and synthesize the information they found. We discuss how they are creating new knowledge that can be shared with interested parties. Students are required to cite any sources used in creating the infographic using both in-text citations and a bibliography. Because students in this course come from a variety of disciplines, students are required to use the citation style for their discipline. The majority of the students in the class use APA style from the American Psychological Association. Finally, we discuss ethical issues like plagiarism and crediting people for the information that the students use in creating their infographics.

Curriculum Materials

The students in this course complete a variety of assignments, including an introductory essay, topic development assignment, annotated bibliography, infographic, and final online research portfolio. However, for this chapter, we will present information only on the infographic assignment.

- To help students begin to think about how their actions might make a difference in someone's life, we watch a TedTalk, *Everyday Leadership* featuring Drew Dudley (https://www.ted.com/talks/drew_dudley_everyday_leadership). Throughout the course, we utilize TedTalks as discussion starters in class on various topics.
- The core competencies of the Kansas Leadership Center (KLC) are presented to students to help them learn about leadership principles

and how they can use them in their own lives and communities to make a difference for the common good (https://www.emporia.edu/dotAsset/631d8f1f-ff9c-47e1-9d05-4179779c1414.pdf).

- The introductory activity for the infographic assignment is an analysis and evaluation of infographics. It is based on the assignment in *Teaching Information Literacy: Threshold Concepts Lesson Plans for Librarians* developed by McClure and Toth. The activity sheet for this assignment is included at the end of this chapter. To identify infographics for this in-class activity, we select a topic that is of interest to the students and locate infographics of varying quality from a variety of sources.
- The infographic assignment information sheet and rubric are included at the end of this chapter.

Steps Involved

Introduction to leadership and volunteerism: During the first few weeks of the semester, students are introduced to the core competencies of the KLC and the concept of adaptive challenges. In addition, the class watches the Drew Dudley TedTalk, *Everyday Leadership* during the same class session. Following this presentation and video, the class engages in a discussion about lollipop moments or how individuals can make a difference in the lives of others with even small gestures. This leads to a discussion about giving back to communities by volunteering for community service organizations. A discussion of the core competencies of the KLC leads to identifying adaptive challenges that these community service organizations are trying to overcome.

Topic identification: Following this lecture, students are asked to identify a community service organization that they are interested in learning more about or that aligns with their professional aspirations. Students write a one-page essay introducing their selected community service organization and the social issue that the organization is working to alleviate. Students are told that they can use any sources for this essay. To learn more about their organization, students are asked to interview an individual who is affiliated with their selected community service organization.

Topic development: Students spend several weeks defining their topic and narrowing it down to make it manageable. Students use reference sources, such as encyclopedia articles, to build on the information presented in their introductory essay and develop a working knowledge of their topic. They use concept maps to help identify the key concepts in their topic.

Introducing the infographic: Students are introduced to infographics at the beginning of the semester through the syllabus for the course in an infographic format. During a class session later in the semester, students are introduced to the concept of infographics. Infographics are defined as presenting information using mainly graphics with some text as needed to add contextual information to the graphics. Students are then divided into pairs or small groups of three for an activity where students analyze and evaluate infographics on a specific topic selected by the instructor. This activity is based on the work of McClure and Toth in their "Louder than Words" lesson plan presented in the *Teaching Information Literacy: Threshold Concepts Lesson Plans for Librarians*. The sheet that students use in the activity is included at the end of this chapter. After the activity, class members debrief with the instructor by discussing their analysis and evaluation of their assigned infographic.

Creating a wireframe: Using what they have learned about their community service organization and social issue, students create an outline for their infographic or a wireframe. This is a skeletal outline for the infographic. Students can use it to lay out their infographic. Students are instructed to include the title for their infographic and an introduction to their topic at the top of the wireframe. Because they need to cite their sources, students are encouraged to include a bibliography of sources toward the bottom of their wireframe. The wireframe allows the students to outline their information sections, graphics, and data visualizations to make sure that the elements flow from one to another in a logical fashion. A sample wireframe is included at the end of this chapter.

Gathering and evaluating information: Students use several weeks to gather and evaluate information on their community service organization and its affiliated social issue. They are required to locate a minimum of eight sources. These sources are summarized and evaluated in an annotated bibliography.

Creating the infographic: Three weeks before the infographic assignment is due, students are introduced to infographic creation tools, "10 Free Tools for Creating Infographics" by Creative Bloq.[7] Many students use Canva or Piktochart to create their infographics.

Peer review: Prior to turning in the infographics, students are divided into groups of three. During a class session, each group of three takes turns evaluating their infographics. At the end of the evaluation exercise, the members of the group debrief in their small groups and share suggestions with group members. Students are given a week to make changes to their infographics using the information gained during the peer review session. The peer review evaluation guide and the rubric used to grade the infographics is included in the information at the end of this chapter.

Presentation of the infographics: At the end of the semester, students present their infographics to the class. Students rank each infographic on a scale from 1 to 5. These numbers are averaged to select the top five infographics in the class. Students are encouraged to share their infographics with their selected community service organization.

POST-PROJECT ASSESSMENT
Methods of Reflection

- Peer review: During the peer review process, students critique their classmates' infographics. This information is shared with each other. During a debriefing session, classmates reflect on the comments received from their classmates. After peer review, the students use the comments to modify their infographics.
- Final reflection: As part of the students' final projects, they write a final reflective essay. In this essay, they reflect on what they learned in the course, the course itself, and the assignments in the course, including the infographic.

Post-Project Feedback

- On the end of the semester surveys, a majority of students indicate that the infographic is one of their favorite assignments because it is novel and allows them to use their creativity.
- Students have come up to instructors in semesters after they have taken the UL100 course and indicated that they used infographics in courses they took later in their college career.
- Community service organizations indicate they enjoy talking to interested students about their organization because it brings awareness to what they do in the community.

Project Assessment and Reporting Methods

- End of the semester surveys: At the end of the semester, students are asked to fill out a survey beyond the IDEA Course Evaluations. In this survey, students are asked several questions, including what they liked about the course, which assignments were their favorite, which assignments were their least favorite, and what changes could be made in the course to make it better. Additional questions were asked about using community service organizations as the topics.
- Because this is a general education course, assessment data that is gathered regarding this UL100 course is reported as part of our general education assessment program. This data is reported on a semester basis.

Difficulties Encountered

Student Issues: One of the biggest challenges for this assignment is the learning curve required for creating an infographic using a graphic design tool program.

The instructors typically present a specific graphic design tool program (such as Canva or Piktochart) so that they can help troubleshoot any issues a student may encounter. These issues usually include downloading the file as a .jpeg, .pdf, or .png file and uploading it to the institution's learning management system, Canvas. This is a challenge when students want to add their infographic to the final project for the UL100 course, which is an online portfolio in which students gather all of their assignments.

Other issues included printing certain infographics as some students have a tendency to add multiple layers, which expands the infographic beyond what would fit on a standard 8.5 × 11 page. The instructors are familiar with these troubleshooting issues and can quickly assist students through step-by-step guides or short video tutorials. At times, students struggle to identify a topic or community service organization for their research. Since they select a topic early in the semester, some students decide during the semester that they are not as interested as they thought in their topic and want to change topics.

Instructor Issues: Because students are not generally familiar with creating an infographic instead of writing a paper, there is some hesitation when the assignment is introduced. Another challenge is getting students to narrow down their topic, making it focused enough to be adequately presented in an infographic format. From the online instructor perspective, it can be a challenge in assisting students that are experiencing computer issues when developing an infographic. One method that has helped ease this anxiety is becoming a semi-expert in the graphic design tool programs recommended for students to use so that video tutorials can be quickly created utilizing the comment feature built into Canvas. This feature allows an instructor to quickly provide specific feedback or customized recordings for a student to access directly in Canvas.

Community Partner Issues: Working with students requires time in already overloaded schedules, even if it is just an individual affiliated with the organization taking time for a student to interview them.

Conclusion

Throughout their collegiate career, undergraduate students undertake a variety of research projects utilizing multiple modalities to share that research. In response to the changing nature of how information is disseminated and presented, the instructors of the UL100 course at Emporia State University wanted to provide students with a way to present the information gathered in their semester-long research project beyond writing the traditional research paper. Our solution was to have the students present their findings in the form of infographics. Because the nature of infographics, students must narrow down their topic to make it manageable for an infographic format. Utilizing a combination of graphics, charts, figures, and minimal text, students are able to visually tell the story of their topic in a concise and brief manner. Additionally, utilizing infographics as information sources helps to meet some of the dispositions contained in the ACRL Framework for Information Literacy for Higher Education (2016), especially under the frame of Information Creation as a Process.

Since we have implemented this assignment in our UL100 courses, the infographic assignment has been the most popular assignment with the students taking the course. This may be because today's students are inclined to receive their information in visual formats. They also enjoy the creativity associated with developing their infographic. Students who have taken the course early in their collegiate career will come back to course instructors in subsequent semesters to indicate how they have utilized infographics to present information in other courses. We discovered that using the infographic as a final assignment allows students to express themselves in a format other than the traditional research paper.

In addition, the focus on service learning for the topics selected by the students achieves a couple of important outcomes. One, it incorporates elements from the Kansas Leadership Center (KLC) principles into the UL100 course. Second, it allows undergraduate students the opportunity to think beyond themselves and their present world to consider how they can make a difference in the lives of others. Hopefully, the inclusion of service learning in this course will help students to recognize that they can play an important role in making our world a better place and help to develop future community leaders. Our next step would be to explore adding interactivity in the form of video, sound, web links, graphics, and other interactive elements to the infographics using augmented reality (AR) applications. A few of our UL100 instructors have already started the beta assignment for incorporating a more interactive infographic using the AR tool, Blippar. Using AR tools allows the students to transform the "flat" infographic into an interactive experience providing a deeper level of information through web links, video, and other external resources. Overall, the student response to this next step has been mostly positive but students still favor the simplicity of the infographic instructions and the ability to be creative.

Acknowledgments

The authors thank ESU students, Christianne Parks and Jamie Gathright, for granting us permission to use the infographics they created as students.

APPENDIX MATERIALS
- Infographic Analysis and Evaluation Activity Sheet
- Infographic Assignment Description
- Infographic Wireframe
- Peer Review Guide Sheet

- Infographic Grading Rubric
- Sample Student Infographics

Infographic Analysis and Evaluation Activity Sheet
INFOGRAPHICS AS INFORMATION SOURCES

From the infographic and the website where it appears, try to answer the following questions:

Title of Infographic Evaluated:
1. Accuracy: Where did they get the information for this infographic? What sources are cited?
2. Authority: Who is the creator/author of the infographic?
3. Purpose: What is the purpose of the infographic?
4. Who is the intended audience?
5. Currency: How current is the infographic? The information presented in the infographic?
6. Relevancy: Would this be a good information source on your topic?

Using the Internet, try to find:
1. Where did this infographic appear originally?
2. Check out one of the sources cited. Does it appear to be legitimate? How can you tell?
3. Choose one claim that is included in the infographic. List a different source that confirms this claim.
4. Is this infographic trustworthy? Why or why not?
5. If you were the creator of this infographic, what would you change to make it more credible?

Infographic Assignment Description
UL100: Information Literacy and Technology
INFOGRAPHIC ASSIGNMENT

For this infographic assignment, you will need to use the information that you have discovered on your topic from your sources and visually represent it using an Infographic.

What is an infographic?: An infographic is presenting information in a graphical or visual format. "A visual image such as a chart or diagram used to represent information or data. A good infographic is worth a thousand words."

To successfully complete this assignment, you will create an infographic that fully introduces your topic using the information that you gathered throughout the semester. Make sure that you include enough information on your infographic so that someone can learn about your community service organization, its mission, and the social problem that it works to alleviate. You will want to use a combination of pictures and text to describe your topic. Additionally, you will want to make sure that your infographic is arranged logically and attractively designed.

ASSIGNMENT REQUIREMENTS:
- A title at the top: include the name of your community service organization
- Your name somewhere on the infographic, either at the top or the bottom
- A short introductory paragraph introducing your organization and social issue
- Provide a minimum of five factual or informational sections on your topic (statistics, a description, graphics, etc…)
- Make sure that you cite your sources on the various parts of your chart so that I know where you obtained your information, using full citations or in-text citations
- If you use in-text citations, then include a bibliography of sources cited at the end of the infographic

To turn in your assignment, submit the URL. Make sure that you publish your chart before submitting the URL.

TIPS FOR A GOOD INFOGRAPHIC:
- Be accurate: Make sure that the information you present is accurate and that your charts are accurate. Data visualizations must match the numbers.
- Pick a good topic: Make your infographic interesting.
- Search for prior infographics: Look for infographics on similar topics to get an idea of what to include. Don't plagiarize; make sure that you are not duplicating an infographic that exists.
- Focus on the key message: Before creating your infographic, define the message that you want to provide concerning your community service organization and social issue. Focus in on conveying that message in your infographic. Don't try to tell too much in your infographic. "Ideally, an infographic needs one clear message" and what you provide in data and pictures will support that central message. Be able to communicate the message in 5–10 seconds to the reader. Tell one story really well. Use the wireframe to logically layout your infographic.
- Visualize when possible: Use data visualization whenever possible—charts, graphs, icons, illustrations, and diagrams. Big fonts are not visualizations.

- Minimize text: Use text to introduce the topic and provide some detail to support the images.
- Eliminate chart legends: Make charts easy to understand. Create them in PowerPoint, save them as an image and import them into your infographic.
- Be data transparent: Tell your readers where you found the information contained in the infographic. This adds to credibility. Cite original sources of data and list the source references with the text or at the bottom of the infographic. Be exact on sources not vague.

Infographic Wireframe

Title and Introduction

Bibliography

Peer Review Guide Sheet

Infographic Peer Group Review Worksheets

Infographic Title: Infographic creator:

REVIEWER 1:

1. Introduction: How well does the introductory paragraph introduce the infographic and the topic? Can it be improved?
2. Information presented: Through the introduction and facts presented, are you able to learn about the topic?
3. Does the content cover the topic in-depth with details, meeting or exceeding the presentation of a minimum of five facts or information pieces on the topic?
4. Does the author make excellent use of font, color, text, and graphics to present the information on the topic? Is the infographic readable and are you able to understand everything that is presented?
5. Clarity/style: Did you find distracting punctuation, spelling, grammar, or word usage problems? Identify them.
6. Resources: Does the author clearly identify his/her sources? Is proper in-text and reference format used?
7. What did you like best about the infographic?
8. What can be improved in the infographic?

REVIEWER 2:

1. Introduction: How well does the introductory paragraph introduce the infographic and the topic? Can it be improved?
2. Information presented: Through the introduction and facts presented, are you able to learn about the topic?
3. Does the content cover the topic in-depth with details, meeting or exceeding the presentation of a minimum of five facts or information pieces on the topic?
4. Does the author make excellent use of font, color, text, and graphics to present the information on the topic? Is the infographic readable and are you able to understand everything that is presented?
5. Clarity/style: Did you find distracting punctuation, spelling, grammar, or word usage problems? Identify them.
6. Resources: Does the author clearly identify his/her sources? Is proper in-text and reference format used?
7. What did you like best about the infographic?
8. What can be improved in the infographic?

CRITERIA	RATINGS					PTS.
Requirements	All requirements are met and exceeded. 10.0 pts	One requirement was not completely met. 8.0 pts	Several requirements were not completely met. 5.0 pts	Few requirements were met. 3.0 pts	None of the requirements are met. 0.0 pts 10.0 pts	10
Introduction	Introductory paragraph introduces the topic well and in a concise manner. 15.0 pts	Introductory paragraph introduces the topic fairly well. 12.0 pts	Introductory paragraph may or may not introduce the topic fairly well. 8.0 pts	Introductory paragraph introduces the topic, but not very well. 5.0 pts	Introductory paragraph is missing. 0.0 pts 15.0 pts	15
Attractiveness/ Creativity	Makes excellent use of font, color, text, and graphics to present the information on the topic. Ideas presented are creative and inventive. 20.0 pts	Makes good use of font, color, text, and graphics to present the information on the topic. Ideas presented are mostly creative and inventive. 15.0 pts	Makes use of font, color, text, and graphics to present the information on the topic, but often these distract from the content. Ideas presented are lacking in creativity and inventiveness. 10.0 pts	Use of font, color, text, and graphics distract from the presentation of information on the topic. Very little creativity shown. 5.0 pts	Little use of color, text, and graphics. 0.0 pts	20

CRITERIA	RATINGS					PTS.
Content	Content covers the topic in-depth with details, meeting or exceeding the presentation of a minimum of five facts or information pieces on the topic. Subject knowledge demonstrated is excellent. 25.0 pts	Includes essential knowledge about the topic with at least four facts or informational items on the topic. Subject knowledge appears to be good. 19.0 pts	Includes essential information about the topic with three or fewer facts or informational items. 13.0 pts	Includes minimal information about the topic with two or fewer facts or informational items. May have factual errors. 6.0 pts	No information is provided on the topic. Many factual errors. 0.0 pts	25.0
Citations	Source information is provided for all of the information, facts, graphics, and quotes presented. All citations are documented in proper format with no errors. 10.0 pts	Source information is provided for all of the information, facts, graphics, and quotes presented. Citations are not documented in proper format or contain some errors. 8.0 pts	Source information may or may not be presented for all of the information, facts, graphics, and quotes presented. Citations are not documented in a proper format and contain many errors. 5.0 pts	Very little source information is provided for the information, facts, graphics, and quotes presented. Citations are missing or not documented in a proper format and contain many errors. 3.0 pts	Very little or no source information is provided Citations are missing. 0.0 pts	10.0

CRITERIA	RATINGS					PTS.
Organization	Content is well organized. 10.0 pts	Overall organization of the content appears flawed. 8.0 pts	Content is logically organized for most of the infographic. 5.0 pts	No clear or logical organizational structure. 3.0 pts	No organizational structure. 0.0 pts	10.0
Mechanics	No misspellings or grammatical errors. 10.0 pts	Three or fewer misspellings and/or mechanical errors. 8.0 pts	Four or more misspellings and/or grammatical errors. 5.0 pts	Project is full of misspellings and grammatical errors. 3.0 pts	Project is unacceptable as presented. 0.0 pts	10.0

Student Infographics

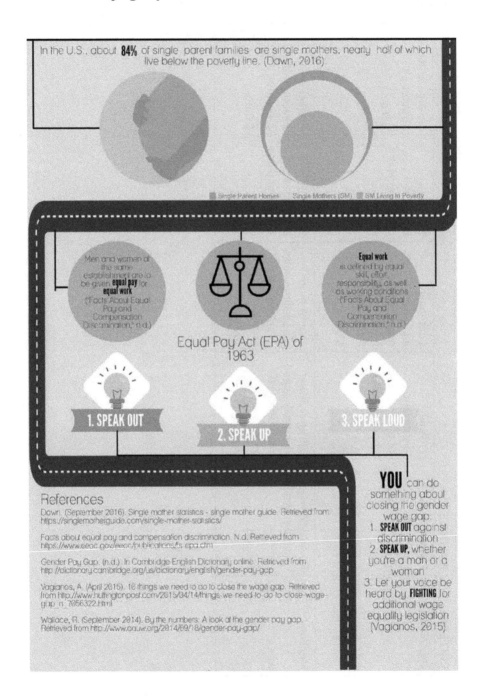

In the U.S., about **84%** of single parent families are single mothers, nearly half of which live below the poverty line. (Dawn, 2016)

Single Parent Homes   Single Mothers (SM)   SM Living In Poverty

Men and women at the same establishment are to be given **equal pay** for **equal work** ("Facts About Equal Pay and Compensation Discrimination," n.d.)

Equal work is defined by equal skill, effort, responsibility, as well as working conditions ("Facts About Equal Pay and Compensation Discrimination," n.d.)

Equal Pay Act (EPA) of 1963

1. SPEAK OUT

2. SPEAK UP

3. SPEAK LOUD

YOU can do something about closing the gender wage gap.
1. **SPEAK OUT** against discrimination
2. **SPEAK UP**, whether you're a man or a woman
3. Let your voice be heard by **FIGHTING** for additional wage equality legislation (Vagianos, 2015)

References

Dawn. (September 2016). Single mother statistics - single mother guide. Retrieved from https://singlemotherguide.com/single-mother-statistics/

Facts about equal pay and compensation discrimination. N.d. Retrieved from https://www.eeoc.gov/eeoc/publications/fs-epa.cfm

Gender Pay Gap. (n.d.) In Cambridge English Dictionary online. Retrieved from http://dictionary.cambridge.org/us/dictionary/english/gender-pay-gap.

Vagianos, A. (April 2015). 18 things we need to do to close the wage gap. Retrieved from http://www.huffingtonpost.com/2015/04/14/things-we-need-to-do-to-close-wage-gap_n_7056322.html

Wallace, R. (September 2014). By the numbers: A look at the gender pay gap. Retrieved from http://www.aauw.org/2014/09/18/gender-pay-gap/

Student Infographics

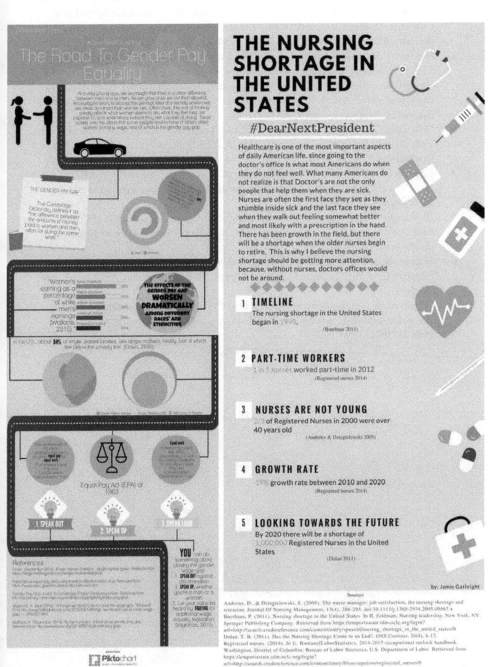

Notes

1.   Ed O'Malley, "The Competencies for Civic Leadership: An Introduction to the Core Curricular Underpinning of the KLC," last modified 2012, https://www.emporia.edu/dotAsset/631d8f1f-ff9c-47e1-9d05-4179779c1414.pdf.

2.   Hazel McClure and Christopher Toth, "Louder than Words: Using Infographics to Teach the Value of Information and Authority," in *Teaching Information Literacy: Threshold Concepts Lesson Plans for Librarians,* eds. Patricia Bravender, Hazel McClure, and Gayle Schaub, 166–172. (Chicago: Association of College and Research Libraries, American Library Association, 2015).

3.   "Evaluating Information: Applying the CRAAP Test," Meriam Library, California State University, Chico, last modified September 17, 2010, https://www.csuchico.edu/lins/handouts/eval_websites.pdf.

4.   Emporia State University Libraries & Archives, "University Libraries & Archives Mission and Vision," last modified November 16, 2015, http://www.emporia.edu/libsv/about-the-library/mission.html.

5.   "Framework for Information Literacy for Higher Education," Association of College and Research Libraries, last modified January 11, 2016, http://www.ala.org/acrl/standards/ilframework.

6.   Emporia State University, Office of the President, "Strategic Plan 2015–2025: The Adaptive University," accessed July 1, 2017, https://www.emporia.edu/president/strategicplan/.

7.   "13 incredible tools for creating infographics," Creative Bloq: Art and Design Inspiration, last modified September 1, 2016, http://www.creativebloq.com/infographic/tools-2131971.

CHAPTER THREE

Using Service-Learning Experiences to Engage Students in Information Literacy Classes

Breanne Kirsch

University Librarian
Briar Cliff University
Breanne.Kirsch@briarcliff.edu

Lola Bradley

Public Services Librarian
University of South Carolina Upstate
lbradley@uscupstate.edu

THE ACTIVITY

Description: Colleges and universities are showing increasing interest in incorporating service-learning and civic engagement in courses across the curriculum. The University of South Carolina Upstate is no exception. LIBR 201: Strategies for Information Discovery is a three-credit course taught on that campus by librarians and designed to help students develop information literacy skills for academic and workplace research. In the course, the research process, effective search strategies, evaluating sources, using information ethically, and emerging technologies are emphasized. In May 2015, the instructors of some sections of this course decided to incorporate a service-learning component.

Students in the course complete assignments that encourage in-depth research on topics related to the work of a local community service organization. Student research is intended to help the organization by offering suggestions of ways to improve services to the community. Students are required to volunteer at a service organization of their choosing for five hours or more before completing background research to decide on a research question to use for their projects. Then students are expected to spend at least five hours throughout the semester researching a topic that will benefit the organization. Their research work is incorporated into their final project both visually through an infographic and orally through a presentation or video recording discussing the research. Community service organization representatives are invited to attend the final presentations if the class is held face-to-face. If it is an online class, students are asked to share their videos with community service organization representatives along with the infographics. The community service organizations can then review the research results and use them in any way that they can. The service-learning component for LIBR 201 is unique on the campus since it is taught by librarians and its main purpose is to have students practice information literacy skills by working through the entire research process with a real-world topic.

Getting Started: At the University of South Carolina, the administration sought to expand service-learning opportunities for students beginning in fall 2014. Faculty believed that service-learning could offer a deeper learning experience, improve relationships with community organizations, and support the metropolitan mission of the University of South Carolina Upstate. There had previously been a few professors who incorporated service-learning into their courses but this was not widespread, and most faculty did not know how to begin using service-learning in their courses. A summer faculty innovation grant was offered for faculty who wished to develop a service-learning component in their courses or to use another innovative pedagogy, such as the flipped classroom model or active learning. The librarians had been teaching LIBR 201 for a couple of years and decided it would benefit students to incorporate service-learning into the course.

In 2015, the Office of Service-Learning and Community Engagement was established at the behest of the administration. Dr. Abraham Goldberg, a faculty member who had incorporated service-learning into his courses for a number of years, and Kara Davis, the Associate Director of Metropolitan Engagement offered support to faculty who were interested in developing service-learning courses. We sought advice from Dr. Goldberg a few years before the grant opportunity began in 2015. He was very supportive in helping us come up with an idea of what to do for the service-learning component in our course. In the spring semester of 2016, we offered our course online, and Dr. Goldberg and Kara Davis were again willing to provide assistance in reworking the service-learning-related assignment for online delivery.

Motivations: There are a growing number of libraries supporting the development of service-learning opportunities on their campuses. *Service-Learning, Information Literacy and Libraries* includes eight chapters that offer insights from a variety of librarians using service-learning in the library.[1] They demonstrate how service-learning can help build bridges between academic and community partners, how to use authentic service-learning experiences in the classroom, and how to incorporate service-learning into the pedagogy.[2]

Heiselt and Wolverton discuss a service-learning activity where students helped public library patrons with genealogical and historical research as part of their coursework.[3] In their article, they share a number of benefits and considerations when implementing service-learning that are important to think about when starting a service-learning initiative. They mention that service-learning helps students reflect and discover links between their personal lives and the surrounding community, particularly with the partnering organization.[4] This was one of our aspirations when we decided to include a service-learning component in our class. We wanted our students to gain an understanding of how their research could positively affect the local community. Some of the challenges to consider are how time-consuming service-learning can be and that uninformed students can actually do more harm than good in some service-learning situations.[5] Other studies involve the academic library serving as the community partner for service-learning classes and assisting students and faculty members by providing a convenient location for student service work and meaningful projects.[6] After considering the benefits and challenges, we decided to include service-learning as part of our LIBR 201 course for the fall of 2015.

The Summer Faculty Innovation Grant was offered during the summer of 2015. The timing of the grant opportunity, introduced right when we had begun considering the addition of a service-learning component to the course, served as a motivational factor for us to improve the course for our students and make the course more meaningful by showing how research has real-world applications.

We felt that our students were not engaged when they were expected to complete in-depth research on one topic throughout the semester since they did not select topics that were based on authentic experiences or had real-world ramifications. To encourage more engagement and passion from our students, we felt that showing how their research could directly benefit and affect the service organization would help them better appreciate the research process and realize the importance of information literacy skills. We believed a service-learning component could bridge the gap between research for classes and workplace research for our students.

THE PEOPLE

Library: The University of South Carolina Upstate Library has eleven full-time librarians and fifteen staff members in the access services and technical services areas. The current library building was built in 1976 and contains nearly 250,000 volumes and provides access to well over 200 databases. The library serves more than 5,000 FTE students, campus faculty and staff, as well as local community members.

Instructors: Several instruction librarians at the University of South Carolina Upstate Library teach LIBR 201. Other librarians assisted through their willingness to be interviewed by students during the research process to suggest additional databases or places to research based on their research question and topic. Any librarian that is interested in teaching LIBR 201 is required to take a teaching online course offered at USC Upstate. Two librarians team-teach the course on a rotating basis. So far, four librarians have taught LIBR 201. Lola Bradley, Public Services Librarian and Breanne Kirsch, Coordinator of Emerging Technologies have incorporated the service-learning component to demonstrate to students that research is important in the real world and future workplaces.

Course: LIBR 201: Strategies for Information Discovery, a three-credit course, provides a broad-based approach to developing information-seeking strategies and skills for academic and work-related research. Students are required to complete the composition sequence (English 101 and English 102) before taking LIBR 201. Emphasis in the course is on the research process, including effective search strategies, critical evaluation of information, emerging technologies and applications, and their use in research.

Students: The students of LIBR 201 vary from semester to semester since this is an interdisciplinary course and is used by a number of departments on-campus as a possible elective or prerequisite to other courses in the major. Students are usually sophomores and juniors, although some seniors have also taken the course. We have had nursing majors, interdisciplinary studies majors, journalism majors, and students with a variety of other majors take the course. The numbers have ranged from seven students to thirty students depending on the semester, how many sections are taught, and the format (online, face-to-face, or hybrid).

Community Partners: The community partners vary depending on the format that the course is offered. Students are expected to approach an organization to see if they are willing to have the student volunteer with them for five hours and complete a research project involving the organization or what services they offer to customers. Students and organization representatives fill out an agreement form that lists expectations for all people involved. We suggest the two organizations that we worked with during the first semester we offered the service-learning component as two possibilities for students. The organizations we most frequently work with are Miracle Hill Ministries and Forrester Center.

Miracle Hill offers housing for homeless individuals and children, addiction recovery services, and a number of other initiatives at locations throughout the Upstate region of South Carolina. They provide a variety of volunteer opportunities, making this an excellent organization for our students to work with. Forrester Center is a government organization that helps treat substance use disorders, behavioral health therapy, prevention, and education to the Spartanburg community. There is one location and privacy is an important consideration, so this organization is particularly valuable for our nursing majors to work with. We do not encourage a large number of students to work with them, though, because of the privacy concerns. The responsibility is on students to select and work with a service organization. This gives students a choice over who they work with and helps inspire them to work hard on a research topic that will directly benefit the organization of their choice.

Finding and Working with Partners: When we began to consider incorporating service-learning into LIBR 201, we discussed finding partners with Dr. Goldberg. He recommended that we attend the Spartanburg Spring Fling in May since a number of local organizations have tents set up and pass out promotional materials to market their services. This is where we found out about Miracle Hill, Forrester Center, and a number of other organizations that we could possibly work with in future semesters. Miracle Hill Ministries and Forrester Center are the two organizations discovered at the Spring Fling that we decided to work with, but it was definitely worth attending the Spring Fling to have the opportunity to learn more about all types of local organizations.

To begin our first service-learning community relationships, we sent out an email introducing ourselves to local organization representatives and included information about our service-learning component, assignments, and expectations to see if the organization was interested in participating. It is important to be upfront and clear about the service-learning project for the organizations so they are prepared and aware of what is expected of them in terms of students and volunteer hours. Setting clear expectations on what is required from everyone in the beginning helps avoid problems or complications that may happen during the semester.

It is also helpful to be professional and teach students to be more formal with the partnering organization since they are representing the course and university. At the beginning of the semester, we invited the service agency representatives to attend our course and give brief presentations on their organizations to introduce students to their purpose and services, as well as inviting them to attend the students' final project presentations. For the online course, we tell students that we expect them to share their final projects with their organization representative, although it is up to the student and representative to communicate with each other and share information.

Benefits

Instructor Benefits: The librarians have the benefit of seeing student research make a difference for a local organization. We also have the pleasure of grading assignments that students are more passionate about and engaged in than traditional assignments.

Student Benefits: Students are able to see the direct application of the research they complete in class in a real-world setting. Knowing that their research will be shared with the service organization causes students to become more engaged in the research and motivates them to work hard on their assignments. Service experiences help the students become more passionate about research since they choose both the organization to work with and the research question they will investigate. Of course, the assignments themselves help students advance their information literacy skills and develop as researchers. We believe that the benefits of service-learning greatly exceed the time and effort it takes to create and utilize a service-learning component.

Community Partner Benefits: The service organization reaps the rewards of student research. Student research may show an organization how to improve functionality or provide ideas for a new service that could be offered. Community partners also gain a student's perspective on issues at their organization and possible solutions. The student research can provide more information for the community partners to continue improving their services for the local population.

Institutional Benefits: The University benefits through increased student participation in local issues that demonstrate the importance of civic responsibility. This helps cultivate strong reciprocal relationships among the university, community organizations, and students.

THE PROCESS

Expected Learning Outcomes: Below are the learning outcomes that were used with the service-learning segment.

- After completing the Background Research Topic, Tutorial, and Reflection, the learner can find pertinent sources of information for academic and workplace purposes with 80 percent competency.
- After completing the Research Log, the learner uses appropriate resources for a research need in a service-learning organization with 80 percent competency.
- After completing the Infographic & Video Presentation, the learner uses appropriate resources for a research need in a service-learning organization with 80 percent competency.

Curriculum Materials

Course Themes. Three broad themes are woven throughout this course in instructional content and assignments:

- Differences and similarities between academic and workplace research
- Role of technology in research and awareness of how it is changing research
- Critical evaluation of information and its sources.

Students are expected to read *Research Strategies: Finding your Way through the Information Fog.* 5th ed. by William Badke. Library 201 is designed to develop information literacy and research skills and to help students engage in the research process. The instructional materials, readings, quizzes, and assignments are all designed to emphasize the processes involved. There are some terminology and facts to remember, but often students develop skills by practicing and reflecting on them.

Daily course work includes the following as explained to the students:

- **Readings from the textbook and other sources.** Keep up with the schedule since these readings form the "backbone" of content in the course.
- **Online instructional materials.** You will be assigned a number of videos, online modules, "library guides," and other online resources. These will expand on and supplement the text and often lead you directly into the assignments.
- **Quizzes.** These will be completed on Blackboard on a weekly basis. They will cover required readings from the textbook and other assigned material.
- **Assignments.** All assignments are process-oriented and three are designed to include all steps of the research process, from background research to completed presentation. Detailed instructions for each assignment are provided in Blackboard. All assignments are due on the day indicated unless otherwise specified by the instructors.

The following text introduces the service-learning nature of the course and requirements:

> "This is a course with a service-learning component. Service-learning is a combination of traditional instruction with service in the community to give students a practical, real-world learning experience. Students will be required to find and volunteer at an organization, for a minimum of five hours during two to three visits at the beginning of the semester. In addition, students will be expected to spend at least five hours researching a topic or issue about the organization and presenting conclusions in the final assignment."

Included in the Appendix Materials are:
- Service-learning Site Expectations and Responsibilities for LIBR 201: Strategies for Information Discovery
- Service-learning Organization Video Assignment with Grading Rubric

Steps Involved
- Service organization video is completed by students with general information about the organization. This helps students learn more before beginning their research.
- Background Research Topic, Tutorial, and Reflection is completed next. Students think of a possible research topic and complete background research focused on reference sources in order to fully develop their final research question.
- Research Log is completed by searching a variety of databases and sources for more in-depth research in order to answer their research question.
- Infographic and Video Presentation is the final for the course. Students complete an infographic and an oral presentation sharing their research process and results.

As part of the course, students are required to do the following:
- Select a service organization and share the organizational representative letter with them and have them fill it out and sign it.
- Read the service-learning expectations document and share it with your representative when they agree to be your partner.
- Volunteer for your organization a minimum of five hours during the beginning of the semester and fill out the volunteer hours form and have your representative sign it. After completing your five hours, you will need to scan and email this document to the instructors.
- Complete related assignments.

POST PROJECT FEEDBACK
Methods of Reflection

The LIBR 201 goals are designed with the six core principals of the Framework of the Association of College and Research Libraries, in mind. These principals are as follows:
- Authority Is Constructed and Contextual
- Information Creation as a Process
- Information Has Value
- Research as Inquiry

- Scholarship as Conversation
- Searching as Strategic Exploration.

Library faculty promote these six principles to students either during library instruction sessions or one-on-one at the reference desk. While working on their degrees, students learn how to research more effectively to achieve successful results and gain knowledge about the research process. Students come to the understanding that in order to succeed in the classroom, they need to know how to avoid plagiarism, discern accurate sources, and how to properly give the author credit. They are taught to recognize that information has to be credible and current, and that research is a continuing process that may not initially answer the question but could potentially lead to further exploration.

Very often, students fail to comprehend that these theoretical principles can be brought into play in the working environment. Library faculty have observed that, even though students might have a grasp of information literacy in theory, it gets completely abandoned when it comes to applying it toward practical uses. By converting LIBR 201 into a service-learning course, the library faculty has been able to convey the importance of the process of reflection on students' academic and real-world experiences.

Critical reflection leads learners to analyze their experience and draw meaning from it, which can lead to a different perspective. The process of critical thinking allows students to be challenged while contemplating their ideas and practices and seeking the possibility of applying the old skills to new issues.[7]

In LIBR 201, students not only get the opportunity to gain the experience of working with community partners but also reflect on their service experience while working on their assignments. Several assignments including Background Research, Research Log, Infographics and Presentation, and Organization Video motivate them to learn about the structure and mission of an organization, to investigate how the organization improves the lives of city/county residents, and to research the underlying issues of the organization and how they can be solved. Working on these assignments helps students see the importance of mastering research skills when trying to solve problems in the community. In addition, the library faculty interviews students and asks a set of questions based on student work and research experience.

Most of the time, students are happy to share their experience as a positive moment that shaped their understanding of analyzing and solving problems using their research skills. While working on the problem, students realize the value of research in making a difference in the functionality of an organization. Through these reflections, students are inspired to search for better solutions to the problems they have encountered.

Post-Project Feedback

It was essential for faculty to obtain post-project feedback from LIBR 201 students, community partners, and co-directors of the Office of Service-Learning and Community Engagement. All students agreed that applying research skills while volunteering at one of the local organizations let them build a stronger connection between education and work as well as becoming active participants. Serving people and the community has helped shape students' civic identity. At the same time, the volunteer work motivated them to work harder in the classroom and become better researchers. Hence, service-learning considerably enhanced the learning process and increased the engagement level for students. After completing their volunteer hours, many students expressed their desire to continue serving at the organization. Thus, the library faculty observed positive changes in the students and their sense of civic connection.

The librarians were also interested in learning the opinion of the community partners on their collaboration with the students and the research that students presented on the last day of class. The library faculty sent invitations to the local community partners to view students' presentations and fill out an assessment on collaboration with students, student volunteer work, and student research. It was helpful to have the community partners attend the class and hear recommendations to continue the collaboration with USC Upstate and the students.

The co-directors of the USC Upstate Office Service-learning and Community Engagement also attended the last class to view the students' final projects. They expressed the hope that the librarians would continue offering the service-learning course to students of various majors on a regular basis. The co-directors provided suggestions on incorporating a service-learning component into an online course for students outside the Spartanburg area.

Project Assessment and Reporting Methods

The librarians used both formative and summative assessment in order to assess the successfulness of the student performance and the content of the course.[8] Formative assessments are used to support the learning process and are divided into formal and informal or structured and unstructured subcategories. For formative formal assessments, we used structured class presentations, structured peer evaluations, class assignments, and structured student interviews. For formative informal assessments, we used class discussions, instructor observations, class activities, and community partner observations. To evaluate the learning outcomes and the program in general, we used summative assessments such as quizzes, surveys, community partner evaluations, and the final assignment and presentation.

All these methods allowed us to observe how well students gained cognitive skills, such as critical thinking and problem-solving. They also helped us observe the continuous personal growth of civic identity in our students with a strong responsibility to collaborate with local organizations. The data obtained from the assessments gave us a distinctive picture of how the course should be revised and taught in future semesters.

Difficulties Encountered

Librarians were excited about launching LIBR 201 as a service-learning course for a variety of majors, but we encountered unanticipated challenges too.

Student Issues: We were not able to anticipate the difficulties some students had with the more complicated nature of service-learning. Some students were unprepared for the extra efforts needed to both schedule enough volunteering time and to research relevant topics to help the organization's goals. We did see some students withdraw due to their lack of ability to commit to the course work. Fortunately, we have made some positive changes on campus to better promote service-learning to students. During the last two years, USC Upstate has established an Office of Service-Learning and Community Engagement and more departments have added service-learning opportunities to their courses. This newer collaboration, with the Service-Learning and Community Engagement Office working along with community partners and students, will help improve students' perceptions of service-learning. The use of local organizations as university satellites will also provide students with increasing awareness of the benefit of combining their learning process with hands-on experience.

We also experienced some difficulties with the online course due to its duration. While the face-to-face course stretches for fifteen weeks from the beginning until the end of the semester, the online course is condensed into ten weeks and may be challenging for some students who take it as an additional fifth course. The ten-week course creates timing challenges for students to find a service organization and volunteer for five hours before coming up with a research topic. The best way to overcome this problem is to schedule the online course for a full fifteen-week semester.

Instructor Issues: The librarian instructors also experienced a few unexpected issues. One challenge was a lack of control relating to student experience outside of the academic setting. We had to rely on community partners to encourage our students to learn while working at their organization. We realized the importance of staying connected with both the community partners and the students during the first two weeks of the class. In other words, communication was sometimes an issue when trying to gain feedback from both community partners and students about the volunteer process. We also allowed students to change the community partner if they found that their first choice of an organization was not suitable for them based on scheduling issues or the mission of the organization. Another potential issue is that multiple students ended up working with the same organization. While students could focus on different aspects of the organization for their research, it could lead to an overlap in research areas depending on the topics.

Community Partner Issues: Some community partner groups require a background check before a person can volunteer. This led to time constraints due to the length of the course, and some students had to change their organization due to this requirement. We found that it was important to work with organizations that did not require a background check.

We have been lucky in that we have not run into many issues with our community partners. Part of this may be due to the fact that we allow students to approach the organization about volunteering with them rather than assigning a specific organization to students. We do offer suggestions to students of possible community partners but students can also select a different organization. The agreement form that students and organization representatives sign also helps prevent possible issues.

Conclusion

Overall, adding a service-learning component to LIBR 201 has been a good experience for the librarians, students, and community partners. The benefits far outweigh any challenges that have arisen. The service-learning component has enhanced students' engagement with course assignments and research. The course design helps demonstrate to students how research skills are important in a workplace environment and can improve community partner services. Student research also strengthened the relationship between community partners and students. After course completion, learners often expressed a desire to continue volunteering with their organization.

The service-learning component has undergone multiple iterations based on feedback from students and community organizations. Related assignments have also been updated in response to this feedback. By introducing service-learning in LIBR 201, students complete more authentic research and master research skills and information literacy. Other academic libraries that teach a course on information literacy skills may also benefit by incorporating a service-learning component in a similar way.

APPENDIX MATERIALS

- Service-Learning Site Expectations and Responsibilities for LIBR 201: Strategies for Information Discovery
- Service Learning Site Video Assignment with Grading Rubric

Service-Learning Site Expectations and Responsibilities for LIBR 201: Strategies for Information Discovery

The service site expects students to

- behave professionally while carrying out assigned tasks, including observance of their established dress code;
- complete a service-learning agreement that indicates goals and schedule of hours, with reasonable assurance that this agreement will be honored;
- fulfill all hours and complete projects;
- notify the professors if the student or site supervisor terminates the volunteer position;
- provide a minimum twenty-four-hour advance notice of absence;
- respect the policies and expectations of the site, especially in regard to confidentiality and participation in required training sessions; and
- serve in a manner which preserves the reputation and integrity of University of South Carolina Upstate.

You can expect the site supervisor to

- afford sound guidance, direction, and input;
- provide an opportunity for the student to make suggestions and receive feedback;
- provide an orientation to the site and training for the position as necessary;
- provide meaningful and satisfactory work related to skills, interests, and available time;
- recognize your efforts as a volunteer; and
- share as much information as possible about agency organization, policy, clients, programs, and activities.

The Center for Service-learning and class professors expect students to

- accurately and dependably fulfill their committed hours;
- adhere to USC Upstate's honor code;
- approach safety on-site with common sense;
- complete a new service-learning agreement if placement site is changed;
- complete a service-learning agreement that indicates the goals and schedule of hours, with reasonable assurance that this agreement will be honored;
- complete course work in a timely fashion;
- follow USC Upstate's policy on alcohol and drug use; and
- respect client confidentiality in papers and class discussions.

A student can expect the professor, with support from the Center for Service-learning, to

- assist in developing service-learning objectives and agreement;
- furnish opportunities to receive feedback and evaluate your experience at the end of the semester;
- provide access to a resource center on service and leadership;
- provide information on service-learning, expectations, and responsibilities, and support in locating a service-learning site; and
- provide support through challenges or difficulties encountered at service sites.

Adapted from the "Expectations and Responsibilities in Service-Learning" from the Tennessee State University Center for Service-learning and Civic Engagement

Service-Learning Site Video Assignment

Purpose: This video will help your fellow students learn more about the organization you are working with for the semester. This assignment will be worth 5 percent of your final grade. Maximum 25 points. Use a webcam or smart phone to create a five-minute video on your organization. The video can be one long video or multiple shorter videos, as long as it is a total of five minutes in length.

- The video should include the name of your organization, the mission or purpose of the organization, and any other pertinent information about the organization that you want to share with the class.
- This video should NOT discuss your research project at all, but it can talk a little about some of the issues or problems that the organization faces.
- You are to upload the video to the following Padlet (provide the link). If you encounter difficulties in creating your video, try to work out the problems on your own first, then talk to the IT staff and/or peers. Only after you have tried these other methods, email the instructor.
- If you are a local student, you may borrow AV equipment from the Digital Media Lab located in the Admin 117.
- For more ideas on how to create a video, refer to the wikiHow recommendations: http://www.wikihow.com/Make-a-YouTube-Video.
- Post your video to Padlet (provide the link). As a part of the participation grade, view three videos of your peers and tell us in two or three sentences what you learned about their organizations, not the students' videos. The grading rubric is created to show you what criteria will be used to grade the assignment. Make sure you follow all steps in the Excellent column if you are striving for a higher grade.

Video Grading Rubric

CRITERIA	EXCELLENT 5	ACCEPTABLE 3	WEAK 1
Organization Name and Mission	The name and mission of the organization are clearly stated in the video.	The name of the organization is present but the mission is unclear.	Only the name of the organization is mentioned.
Length	Video is 5 minutes long.	Video is 3–4 minutes long.	Video is 2 minutes long or less.
Additional Information	Issues, problems, or other pertinent information is clearly stated.	Issues, problems, or other pertinent information is stated, but unclear.	Issues, problems, or other pertinent information is missing.
Creativity	Exceptional creativity is shown in the creation of the video.	Some creativity is shown in the creation of the video.	Video is not very creative.
Post	Video is posted to Padlet with a 2–3 sentence description of what tool/tools were used to create the video.	Video is posted to Padlet with a one-sentence description of what tool/tools were used to create the video.	Video is posted to Padlet without a description of what tool/tools were used to create a video.

See a sample video project at:

The Miracle Hill Organization Video https://view.knowledgevision.com/presentation/56e5eccbd527475b88c332877d5b54f5

Notes

1. Jennifer E. Nutefall, *Service-Learning, Information Literacy, and Libraries* (Santa Barbara: Libraries Unlimited, 2016).
2. Ibid., 51.
3. April K. Heiselt and Robert E. Wolverton, "Libraries: Partners in Linking College Students and Their Communities through Service-learning," *Reference & User Services Quarterly* 49, no. 1 (Fall 2009): 83–90.
4. Heiselt and Wolverton, "Libraries," 84.
5. Ibid.
6. John S. Riddle, "Where's the Library in Service-learning?: Models for Engaged Library Instruction," *Journal of Academic Librarianship* 29, no. 2 (2003): 71; Nedean J. Meyer and Ielleen R. Miller, "The Library as Service-Learning Partner: A Win-Win Collaboration with Students and Faculty," *College & Undergraduate Libraries* 15, no. 4 (2008): 399–413.
7. Janer Eyler, Dwight E. Giles, Jr., and Angela Schmiede, *A Practitioner's Guide to Reflection in Service-Learning: Student Voices and Reflections* (Nashville: Vanderbilt University, 1996).
8. Susan Waters and Karen Anderson-Lain, "Assessing the Student, Faculty and Community Partner in Academic Service-Learning: A Categorization of Surveys Posted Online at Campus Compact Member Institutions," *Journal of Higher Education Outreach and Engagement* 18, no. 1 (2014): 89–122.

CHAPTER FOUR

In Service to Rutgers University Libraries' Instruction Program:

LIS Students Gain Instruction Experience through a Mutually Beneficial Collaboration

Leslin H. Charles

Instructional Design Librarian
Rutgers, The State University of New Jersey
leslin.charles@rutgers.edu

THE ACTIVITY

Description: Rutgers University Libraries (RUL) have developed a strong partnership with the Rutgers Writing Program in the School of Arts and Sciences on its New Brunswick (NB) campus. Each semester, there are more than 50 sections of an undergraduate writing course, Research in the Disciplines, with over 90 percent of them requiring information literacy (IL) instruction. A large pool of skilled IL instructors is needed. To address that need, trained LIS students have traditionally been paid to teach in the program. One mutually beneficial option was to give LIS students enrolled in the School of Communication and Information's graduate course, LIS 519: Information Literacy: Learning and Teaching, 10 percent credit to teach a one-shot (IL) session in the NB Rutgers Writing Program. Thus, these students were provided with a service learning experience within their graduate course.

Learning styles, lesson planning, and classroom management skills were integrated into the course. ACRL Standards for Proficiencies for Instruction Librarians and Coordinators provided guidance as students performed self-assessments of their teaching.[1] They shadowed librarians and were observed by peers or library mentors using an official feedback form that was distributed before their teaching sessions.

Using feedback from these students, an online course using the Sakai learning management system (LMS) has been created and is being used to train future LIS students who teach for RUL as instruction assistants (IAs). All segments of this course can be accessed asynchronously. Topics range from common concerns about teaching one-shot information literacy sessions to active learning strategies. Interactive tutorials supplement the segments and relevant scholarly materials are available as optional reading material. Students can also share concerns, experiences and/or triumphs in a discussion forum as they form a community of learners. They can also reflect on their progress using the blog feature of the LMS. Thus, LIS students have structured opportunities to practice, reflect upon their experience and learning, and help their fellow students before they enter the profession.

Getting Started: As the new instructional design librarian I was seeking to collaborate with librarians, teaching faculty, and relevant campus partners to identify opportunities in existing curricula to integrate IL competencies and to define and execute appropriate methods of assessment of student learning. I had recently (summer 2014) implemented a new professional development approach to facilitate sharing of teaching strategies among library faculty. This TeachMeet series was created to leverage the culture of sharing of expertise in the New Brunswick libraries. In our organization, a TeachMeet is a vehicle to provide input in steering the instruction and assessment techniques in our IL program and fosters teamwork among library faculty. It had been well-received by faculty and, by the fall of 2014, some faculty members were already trying out new strategies that they had discovered over the summer. I decided to seek out collaboration with faculty and administrators in the Library and Information Science Department in the School of Communication and Information (SC&I) at Rutgers University to adapt a TeachMeet for the LIS 519 course. The topics would include active learning and classroom management techniques.

Motivations: There were two main motivating factors that influenced this decision. First, as a longstanding member of the Virtual Academic Library Environment (VALE) Shared Information Literacy (SIL) Committee, I had been participating in frequent conversations revolving around how we, as a professional organization, could work with LIS students in New Jersey (NJ) to sensitize them on the trends in the library profession—chiefly, the increasing focus on instruction. We subsequently established periodical visits to SC&I's graduate student organization, the Student College, Academic, and Research Libraries Association

(SCARLA), to convey this message. To further spread the message statewide, I presented a poster with three colleagues from the VALE SIL committee.[2]

Second, there was a need for more trained instructors in the Rutgers University Libraries (RUL) instruction program in NB. Through this proposed collaboration, the libraries would have more trained instructors and the students enrolled in this course would have the opportunity to provide a service to the institution and its students, deepen their learning by putting theory into practice, and make them competitive candidates as they sought employment. Thus, in fall 2014, I sought an audience with the administrators of SC&I and the instructor of the LIS 519: Information Literacy, Learning and Teaching course in preparation to launch the service-learning experience in spring 2015.

THE PEOPLE

Library: Rutgers University Libraries (RUL) in New Brunswick, NJ has a long-standing instruction program that is supported by faculty, adjuncts, and LIS students in SC&I. The majority of the instruction is for IL in the Rutgers Writing Program for undergraduate students. The RUL (NB) instruction program has a tradition of employing LIS students as instruction assistants (IA). These students are given opportunities to observe instruction and to work with a mentor in preparation to teach in the instruction program.

More recently, led by the instructional design librarian (me), the libraries established a structured program for communicating about IL instruction. These TeachMeets revolve around instruction strategies and assessment. They have become the main channel for sharing of expertise through demonstrations and conversations.

Instructor and Librarian: The instructor of the LIS 519 course had been teaching it for several semesters before our collaboration. I had recently come to RUL (NB) in summer 2013 and had a goal of increasing awareness of IL instruction within the libraries and to ensure that the library instruction for the Research in the Disciplines undergraduate course was explicitly aligned with the 2 IL learning outcomes in the syllabus.

Course: The LIS 519: Information Literacy, Learning and Teaching graduate course description from the SC&I website is as follows:

> Development of effective instruction in the use of information resources and technologies in all types of library settings. Special attention is paid to adult learning theory and to the integration of information seeking behavior with instructional design. Students practice instruction in cooperation with librarians and library users in various settings.[3]

Students: The students enrolled in this course were LIS graduate students in the Library and Information Science Department in the School of Communication and Information (SC&I) at Rutgers University in New Brunswick. Although the course focused on IL, not all the students were on the academic librarian track.

Community Partners: The NB Rutgers Writing Program collaborates closely with the RUL (NB) to provide IL instruction for the undergraduate students enrolled in the Research in the Disciplines course. IL learning outcomes in the course syllabus are: (1) evaluate and critically assess sources and use the conventions of attribution and citation correctly, and (2) analyze and synthesize information and ideas from multiple sources to generate new insights.[4]

The Library and Information Science Department in the School of Communication and Information (SC&I) located in NB runs the newly named Master of Information (formerly MLIS) program that is currently "...ranked 7th nationally by U.S. News and World Report; #1 School Library Media (tied with Florida State University)."[5]

Finding and Working with Partners: I first met with my immediate supervisor, the associate university librarian,Research and Instructional Services to share my idea and, since I was so new to the institution, to get direction on the best ways to approach administrators who would be best positioned to work with me. I also reached out to the library liaison for SC&I, who was very enthusiastic about the possibility of strengthening the libraries' relationship with her department. It was decided that I would reach out to the chair, Department of Library and Information Science.

In my email communication to the chair, I highlighted the ready-made opportunity for LIS students to gain classroom experience. I also explained the use of the TeachMeet model, where pedagogy, IL learning outcomes, and assessment strategies were demonstrated and shared in an experiential way. In addition, I pointed to the contents of the LIS 519 syllabus, where major topics included user instruction, instructional design, assessment, and evaluation. I made the linkages to the contents of the TeachMeet sessions. My email further stated:

> Would SC&I be interested in a partnership where our Teach-Meet is expanded to include LIS students and provide a rich experience in IL instruction so as to prepare them for a career in academic librarianship? We would use the ACRL Standards and Proficiencies for Instruction Librarians and Coordinators as standards to which our learning outcomes and assessment strategies are aligned.[6] We could further, provide feedback through classroom observation and include mentoring opportunities using a pool of library faculty and SC&I faculty if feasible.... This would be an opportunity to strengthen the relationship between SC&I and Rutgers University Libraries.[7]

Of note, the chair of the department took the lead with identifying and inviting administrators and instructors who should come to the table to discuss. The following positions in the Department of Library and Information Science were invited to a meeting: director, MLIS Program; associate professor; emeritus faculty; assistant teaching professor; and instructor. I realized that I had met with one of those invited before in my capacity as the chair of the VALE SIL committee. We had spoken about ways to sensitize LIS students on the need for more instruction experience. This was how we had been able to approach the student group, SCARLA, to establish periodical visits to have a dialogue on the profession and its ever-changing nature.

Although before the meeting the attendees had expressed great interest and excitement (via email) at the prospect of giving students enrolled in this course instruction experience, I presented the idea as a potential pilot activity. In this way, I would neutralize any possible misgivings that might have been lingering. In my experience, the term "pilot" puts potential partners at ease because if the project succeeds, they could be viewed as pioneers. If it is not very successful, then the stakes would not have been considered very high. During the meeting, it was noted that not all students enrolled in LIS 519 were considering academic librarianship. However, it was acknowledged that instruction is increasingly being done at non-academic libraries, so this experience would be relevant and beneficial to all students enrolled. The need for mentoring and shadowing opportunities was discussed as well as the inherent time commitment on the part of library faculty.

The meeting ended with these action items:

- The librarian would bring this pilot project to the Instruction Group in RUL New Brunswick to seek out mentoring and shadowing volunteers.
- The instructor and librarian would collaborate on the library instruction portion of the syllabus.
  - o The students would attend a TeachMeet tailored for them and instruction in the NB Rutgers Writing Program would be an avenue of instruction experience. The slides of the summer TeachMeet would be modified to blend with the LIS 519 course content: the teaching portion would be more focused on preparation to teach in the Research in the Disciplines courses.
  - o The instructor would insert this new activity in the assignment portion of the syllabus.
  - o Supporting instructional tools would be developed.
  - o The librarian would attend the first class session in the spring 2015 semester to provide an orientation to the procedures in the pilot project.

Next, I brought this project to the Instruction Group and my fellow library faculty members readily volunteered to serve as mentors and to observe students in their instruction sessions as well as to give feedback. Fortunately, there were fewer than ten LIS students, so there were enough volunteers. Further, in the RUL instruction program, the practice of observing before teaching was already well established. I would need to create an Instruction Feedback Form (See Appendix Materials) and to serve as the coordinator of the LIS 519 students, the library faculty, and IAs (LIS students who were already being paid to teach in our program) who could function as peer mentors. The instructor of the LIS 519 course and I communicated regularly via email as we planned for the spring 2015 semester. We also met in person at intervals during the running of the course to provide formative feedback to each other.

Benefits

Instructor Benefits: The instructor for this course would have a ready-made instruction program in which his students could gain practical teaching experience in fulfillment of his course objectives. He would also have a subject specialist (instructional design librarian) who would be able to provide specific guidance and instruction on active learning and classroom management techniques in the real-life environment of the NB libraries. His students would be able to teach actual undergraduate students.

Student Benefits: The students enrolled in this course would gain practical teaching experience that would support their class goals and their professional goals. They would gain invaluable experience in working closely with library faculty as they prepared their lesson plans and worked on their teaching and presentation skills per the ACRL Standards for Proficiencies for Instruction Librarians and Coordinators.[8]

Partner Benefits: The course syllabus stated, "Students practice instruction in cooperation with librarians and library users in various settings."[9] However, there was no established collaboration with the RUL (NB) as a means to accommodate this, neither for the entire class nor on a regular basis. Few students enrolled in this course that focused on instruction were IAs in the libraries. A more established partnership between the RUL NB and the administrators of this course would provide ready and convenient opportunities for all enrolled to gain practical instruction experience.

Institutional Benefits: The NB Writing Program and, by extension, the undergraduate students enrolled in the Research in the Disciplines course, would benefit from IAs who gained more training than traditionally. The LIS students (IAs) would be applying theory and practice in a concentrated manner over the course of an entire semester through the LIS 519 course and the TeachMeet components that would be integrated and catered specifically for their needs.

THE PROCESS
Expected Learning Outcomes

The learning outcomes for the LIS 519 course were:

- Identify their personal learning and teaching styles and be able to articulate their instructional philosophy.
- Demonstrate their ability to apply instructional design to meet the learning needs of specific audiences.
- Produce some basic learning aids.[10]

Revising the syllabus for this specific course entailed the creation of an introductory statement about the pilot project. I crafted the following statement: "In cooperation with librarians, students will be provided the opportunity to practice in-classroom instruction by participating in NB Rutgers Writing Program, an arm of the English Department." I also used the online course description to align the TeachMeet activities to the learning outcomes. The instructor assigned 10 percent of the course grade for "Library instruction with Alexander Library."[11] The learning outcomes in the syllabus that were aligned with this assignment were:

- Plan and design effective library instructional sessions based on the identification of users' needs.[12]
- Receive practice and feedback by applying theoretical ideas into a real-world setting.[13]

Curriculum Materials

It became clear that it would be best to divide the LIS student preparation into three segments delivered on three occasions and that the sessions should be done in the classroom rather than the library. My first visit would take the form of an orientation to the pilot project and to give an overview of the NB Rutgers Writing Program. The three visits would address:

1. Information Literacy in Context
   a. Learning Outcomes
   b. Expectations in an academic library presented by the library liaison to SC&I
   c. Student Learning Preferences & Styles
2. Active Learning Strategies/Characteristics
   a. Based on Sweeney, 2006[14]
   b. Based on ACRL Standards for Proficiencies for Instruction Librarians and Coordinators[15]
3. Classroom Management Techniques
   a. Based on ACRL Standards for Proficiencies for Instruction Librarians and Coordinators using the following classroom scenarios

    i.   the sleeping student
    ii.   the disengaged student
    iii.   students who speak incessantly with the potential of disturbing the class
    iv.   the student who wants to answer every question
    v.   the disengaged teacher or the absent teacher

Steps Involved
INFORMATION LITERACY IN CONTEXT

During the first classroom session, I provided an overview of the library partnership with the NB Rutgers Writing Program. The Research in the Disciplines course description is as follows:

> Students in Research in the Disciplines select their own research topic, and work to advance the conversation about it from a critical and analytical point of view. They learn the process of searching for books, journal articles, and Internet sources; develop strategies for managing notes and citations; extend their synthetic and analytical skills; respond to instructor and peer feedback; and become able to differentiate between and assess scholarly, credible, and non-credible sources.[16]

The IL learning outcomes of the Research in the Disciplines writing course were shared so that students could see the alignment to their instruction strategies and how this was integrated into their LIS 519 course syllabus.

The list of courses was provided so LIS students could have an idea of the breadth of potential research topics of the undergraduate students enrolled in Research in the Disciplines. Some of these were: natural disasters; science, medicine, and society; animal ecology; ethics of food; epidemics; the environment; nutrition and exercise science; and culture of healthcare. They were very engaged, and a few of them selected a course section of interest during this orientation session. Others selected their classes later but, in most instances, they chose one that related to their own undergraduate majors.

I made constant reference to the LIS 519 syllabus so students could see how this activity aligned with their course requirements. There was open discussion about the instructional spaces in RUL New Brunswick and scheduling their instruction sessions in the NB Rutgers Writing Program.

I covered learner-centered instruction, its characteristics, and student learning preferences. I also addressed instruction strategies and assessments that would be effective with millennial students, which represents the majority of undergraduates enrolled in Research in the Disciplines courses on our New Brunswick campus. For example, they prefer games and like to do things rather than being passive participants in a classroom. According to Sweeney, "colleges and universities have to find more ways to create and or use academic games in student learning environments."[17] Therefore, interactive activities are useful. This set the stage for the second session that would focus on Active Learning Strategies and Characteristics.

The mentoring aspect and its related shadowing opportunities that would be provided as well as the logistics were discussed. They would shadow their mentors and other librarians or experienced LIS students who were hired as IAs in our instruction program, as their schedule would allow. The ACRL Standards for Proficiencies for Instruction Librarians and Coordinators were examined and students agreed to focus on two proficiencies and specific performance indicators that would be relevant for their assignment. They would work toward achieving these competencies that also aligned with their entire course. These were Proficiency 9: Presentation Skills and Proficiency 12: Teaching Skills.[18] See Appendix Materials: Instruction Feedback Form.

ACTIVE LEARNING STRATEGIES/CHARACTERISTICS

Using learning preferences of millennials that Sweeney (2006) outlined, I presented potential approaches to engage undergraduates in Research in the Disciplines during my second visit to the classroom.

MILLENNIAL LEARNING PREFERENCES	SUGGESTED APPROACHES
Less Reading (Sweeney, 2006, 6)[19]	Use images and graphics in place of text to convey concepts as much as possible
Collaboration (Sweeney, 2006, 5)[20]	Peer assessment activities, group work
Impatience/Need Quick Feedback (Sweeney, 2006, 3)[21]	Utilize audience response systems like Kahoot, I-Clickers, Poll Everywhere
Experiential and Exploratory Learners (Sweeney, 2006, 3)[22]	Jigsaw Classroom, Hands on/lab work

I modeled an instruction session for a mock Research in the Disciplines class. The LIS students took on the role of the undergraduate students. This included a lecture that included searching demonstrations and hands-on learning. The main points that had to be covered in each Research in the Disciplines course were stressed. Parameters of flexibility were discussed. I also demonstrated a jigsaw classroom scenario (See Appendix Materials) active learning technique that allows

- students to work together in teams;
- students to come up with solutions to a problem;
- class interaction on a macro (collective) and micro (group) level;
- gives all students a voice but also allows ones with social challenges to feel safe in a team rather than singled out and allows the more boisterous ones to be tempered by the framework of a team atmosphere under instructor supervision;
- instructor to act as facilitator to the learning process;
- integration of constructivism as students start to build knowledge;
- ready assessment strategies; and
- ice breaking.

Thus, students had options on how to plan and execute their instruction sessions.

CLASSROOM MANAGEMENT TECHNIQUES

I began the third visit with an overview of the range of students in our classrooms. These ranged from millennials to returning adult students to young parents to veterans to international students to those with special needs. We then discussed various classroom scenarios. These conversations were very engaging and enlightening. It was evident that they were learning about scenarios that most of them had not yet considered. It was important for students to understand the possible implications of an academic librarian taking on a class without the presence of the instructor. They gained a clear understanding of the value of undergraduates seeing a team effort between librarian and instructor. Also, they realized that they are ultimately responsible for a classroom of students when they teach without the actual instructor present.

POST-PROJECT ASSESSMENT
METHODS OF REFLECTION

Reflection was integrated into the overall course structure and students were able to plan their instruction while working with a faculty librarian mentor or an experienced LIS student who was already working in the NB Rutgers Writing Program. I had two students shadow me and they were able to ask questions after the sessions.

To allow constructive feedback and to help students to reflect on their own progress, the Instruction Feedback Form was created and distributed (See Appendix Materials). The aforementioned ACRL Standards for Proficiencies for Instruction Librarians and Coordinators, namely, presentation and teaching skills that students had agreed upon were represented on this form. Observers of instruction (mentors) completed this form during the LIS student instruction session. They returned the form to the student and were encouraged to talk about the feedback when possible. This form was submitted to the LIS 519 instructor and these students had it as a reflection tool.

POST-PROJECT FEEDBACK

It became apparent that, in addition to the LIS 519 instructional segments that were devoted to the class, a supplemental set of resources that covered the three areas that I taught would have been helpful. All the information could be incorporated into an online module that would provide asynchronous access. Students would therefore have the ability to go back and review materials (lesson plans, active learning tutorials, etc.) as needed and at their convenience. The ability to reflect using electronic tools and to share these reflections with peers was also needed. This set of resources should be accessible for the duration of the semester.

PROJECT ASSESSMENT AND REPORTING METHODS

The repository of instructional tools and materials would also be useful in training future cohorts of instruction assistants in our program. It was subsequently created using the Sakai learning management system. It is called "Classroom and Instruction." It is available to all who are teaching in the RUL instruction program that supports the Rutgers Writing Program in New Brunswick, NJ. It is divided into the following categories:

- Before You Teach: Librarians and Instruction
- Before You Teach: Common Concerns
- Before You Teach: Nuts and Bolts of Teaching at RUL
- Planning to Teach: Active Learning Strategies
- Planning to Teach: Creating Lesson Plans
- After You Teach: Reflection

LIS students who are teaching in our program are able to form a learning community for collaborative learning and self-assessment. The blog feature of the LMS has been enabled so students can post reflections. Peers can comment and provide suggestions and encouragement.

They can post before they teach:

1. Select one performance indicator from the Instruction Feedback Form and reflect on:
   a. Where are you with this skill currently?
   b. What experience have you had to enhance or practice this skill?
   c. How will you work on it?
   d. What will doing well look like to you?
2. Focus on an active learning strategy that you are developing or are interested in or have observed and want to implement:

    a.   How will you work on it?

    b.   What will doing well look like to you?

After they teach, they can post about general observations, classroom management techniques, surprises, challenges, and success. The three segments that I presented on my three visits to the LIS 519 class were turned into interactive tutorials and are available as resource materials. There are also relevant scholarly materials that can be read as needed.

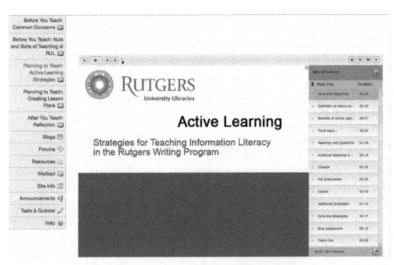

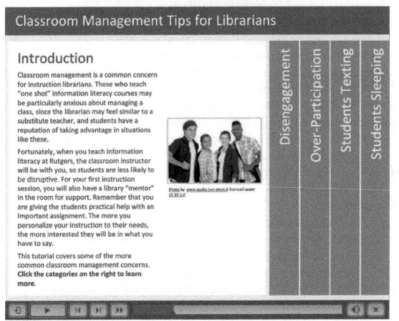

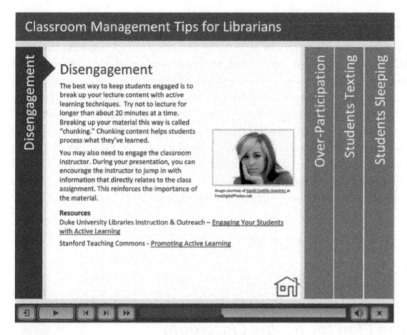

Difficulties Encountered

Scheduling shadowing sessions with their mentors before they taught a session was difficult because of student schedules. In a few instances, students had to shadow a different person because of this scheduling issue. However, each of them got constructive feedback using the Instruction Feedback Form. And each of them was also able to work with their mentor while planning the instruction session.

Student Issues: Observing more than one instruction session is ideal and it would have been beneficial if students could shadow more than one librarian/peer. The feedback form was very useful as a barometer for setting expectations so the students could work on specific proficiencies. Although students had lesson planning materials as a part of the LIS 519 course, provision of lesson planning templates from the libraries would have been beneficial.

Instructor Issues: The instructor and I met several times during the semester to ensure that we were both meeting the expectations initially outlined and to inform each other on any issues with students. He provided appropriate segues for my portion of the instruction when I was in the LIS 519 classroom. It was a good model of team teaching for the students.

Community Partner Issues: Communication is critical. This was a first for the LIS 519 students, library faculty, the LIS 519 instructor, and SC&I administrators, so it was important to check in at intervals and to clearly articulate expectations and plans. It took a great deal of effort to keep everyone informed as needed.

Conclusion

The pilot met the objectives of enhancing the relationship between the RUL and SC&I. All students enrolled in LIS 519: Information Literacy, Learning and Teaching were able to teach a class in the NB Rutgers Writing Program. All of them were mentored and they all received constructive feedback. Moreover, they gained a clear understanding on how to prepare to teach, potential classroom behaviors that they can manage, active learning strategies, and how to align specific teaching strategies to learner characteristics. Most importantly, they gained an understanding of skills needed for their chosen profession and they experienced the collegiality that exists among librarians. This service-learning model can be replicated by seeking out willing partners at iSchools.

APPENDIX MATERIALS

- Lesson Plan for Jigsaw Classroom
- Instruction Feedback Form

Lesson Plan for Jigsaw Classroom
LEARNING OUTCOMES

- Students will explore search tools and resources to determine capabilities of the library webpage.
- Students will demonstrate capabilities of search tools and resources to the class using the library interface.
- Students will find scholarly resources for their assignment.

METHOD/TOOL OF ASSESSMENT
- Student presentations/responses
- Scholarly resources found

OPPORTUNITIES FOR LEARNING
- Group work
- Guided worksheets
- Reporting/Demonstrating to the class
- Role Play (students become teachers)

CLASSROOM ACTIVITIES
Activity 1

Instructor explains the activity, the reasons for the activity, and expectations on class participation. There are three sets of worksheets, each addressing a particular library tool. For example, library catalog, Google Scholar, the library discovery tool called Articles+. Each worksheet has a step-by-step exercise for students to accomplish which aids in the exploration of the search tools in a guided way. Instructor distributes worksheets randomly to students by counting off 1, 2, 3, 1, 2, 3... so that students next to each other have different worksheets.

Activity 2

Students work individually on their worksheets. They can only consult the librarian for help because their colleagues to their left and right are working on a different worksheet than theirs.

After an allotted time, students with the same worksheet will form a team. They will confer to be sure that they all have a clear understanding of the search tool and that they have all come to the same answer. Students are asked to select a team leader and be prepared to demonstrate to the class how to use the tool.

Activity 3

Each team demonstrates how to use their particular search tool. They also field questions from the audience and the librarian ensures that all in the room have grasped the concepts.

Activity 4

Students use the three tools that were discovered to find appropriate resources for their assignment. The librarian and instructor work with students individually as needed to ensure each student gets an appropriate resource.

Instruction Feedback Form

RUTGERS
University Libraries

Instruction Feedback Form

Instructor:
Observer:
Class:
Class Date:

Overview

This form is based on performance indicators from ACRL Standards for Proficiencies for Instruction Librarians and Coordinators. Use this form to provide feedback for MLIS students teaching in the Writing Program. Please indicate with a check mark if a performance is observed/achieved.

Presentation Skills

1. Uses voice , eye contact , and gestures to keep the class lively and students engaged
2. Clarifies confusing terminology , avoids excessive jargon , and uses vocabulary appropriate to the level of students
3. Makes smooth transitions between classroom technology and class communication/interaction
4. Uses time effectively

Teaching Skills

1. Creates a learner-centered environment by employing active and collaborative learning strategies
2. Encourages students to ask/answer questions allowing adequate time . Rephrases questions . Asks probing and/or engaging questions
3. Encourages teaching faculty to participate in discussions to link library instruction to course content and to answer student questions

Evaluation

Please indicate the strengths of this instruction session:

_____

_____

_____

_____

If possible, please review the form with the student. Leave form with student.

Materials Used

List any supporting teaching tools used:

_____

_____

_____

Record general observations here:

_____

_____

_____

_____

Suggest possible resources (articles, workshops, etc.) that might be useful to this student:

_____

_____

_____

_____

Turn over if more space is needed.

Instruction Feedback Form   1

Notes

1. "Standards for Proficiencies for Instruction Librarians and Coordinators," *Association of College and Research Libraries*, accessed June 29, 2017, http://www.ala.org/acrl/standards/profstandards.

2.   Leslin H. Charles, Lynee R. Dokus, Jaime Donnelly, and Amanda Piekart, "LIS Students: Step into the Ring of Academic Librarianship—Becoming the Best Candidate," Poster presentation at the VALE Users' Conference, Piscataway, NJ, January 2014, doi: http://dx.doi.org/doi:10.7282/T3JD4ZR5.

3.   "Information Literacy, Learning and Teaching," School of Communication and Information, Rutgers University, accessed June 30, 2017, https://comminfo.rutgers.edu/academics/courses/32.

4.   Ann Alter, "Research in the Disciplines: Fashion," *Course Syllabus* (New Jersey: Rutgers University, 2015).

5.   "Master of Information," School of Communication and Information, Rutgers University, accessed October 1, 2017, https://comminfo.rutgers.edu/academics/graduate/master-information.

6.   "Standards for Proficiencies for Instruction Librarians and Coordinators," *Association of College and Research Libraries*, June 29, 2017, http://www.ala.org/acrl/standards/profstandards.

7.   Leslin H. Charles, email message to SC&I administrator, November 2014.

8.   "Standards for Proficiencies for Instruction Librarians and Coordinators," *Association of College and Research Libraries*, accessed June 29, 2017, http://www.ala.org/acrl/standards/profstandards.

9.   Ibid.

10. "Information Literacy," School of Communication and Information, Rutgers University.

11. Mark Alpert, "Information Literacy, Learning and Teaching," *Course Syllabus,* (New Jersey: Rutgers University, 2015).

12. Ibid, 6.

13. Ibid, 6.

14. Richard Sweeney, "Millennial Behaviors and Demographics," *Newark: New Jersey Institute of Technology*, accessed on June 30, 2017, 12, no. 3 (2006): 10.

15. "Standards for Proficiencies," *Association of College and Research Libraries*.

16. "Research in the Disciplines," Writing Program, School of Arts and Sciences, Rutgers University, June 29, 2017, http://wp.rutgers.edu/informationforstudents/134-355201-researchinthedisciplines.

17. Sweeney, "Millennial Behaviors."

18. "Standards for Proficiencies," *Association of College and Research Libraries*.

19. Sweeney. "Millennial Behaviors."

20. Ibid, 5.

21. Ibid, 3.

22. Ibid, 3.

CHAPTER FIVE

Community Research Assignments for an Information Literacy Class

Theresa McDevitt

Government Information/Outreach Librarian
Indiana University of Pennsylvania Libraries
mcdevitt@iup.edu

THE ACTIVITY

Description: Information literacy classes and other courses which have a research element often use research portfolios or annotated bibliographies as culminating assignments. Instructors see such assignments as challenging ways to provide students with practice with each of the steps in the research process and formative assessment tools to measure growth and mastery of information literacy skills. Students frequently see such assignments as having little practical application in their lives outside of and after college and do not find them engaging. These standard projects can easily be adapted to provide an indirect service-learning element for any class that involves doing research by asking students to investigate a topic provided by a non-profit organization.

For this activity, students in a one-credit information literacy class are given a list of community partners and the topics that these organizations would like to have researched. The assignment asks students to investigate the partner and the topic they have provided, prepare a research portfolio for the organization, and present their results at the end of the semester. The research portfolio preparation process asks students to apply information literacy skills, including formulating specific research questions, utilizing efficient research strategies, locating sources in a variety of formats using a variety of search tools, and evaluating what they find to choose the most relevant, current, and authoritative sources.

Reflection also takes place. Some class time is spent on defining and discussing the nature of service-learning and why it is beneficial. Students respond privately to reflective prompts at three points in the semester and more publicly in an end-of-semester presentation that includes a summary of their work, recommendations, and reflections.

I have used this assignment in classes for over five years in both face-to-face and online classes. It is easy to implement and so adaptable that I would recommend it for inclusion in a class in any discipline that contains information literacy elements.

Getting Started: Librarians at Indiana University of Pennsylvania (IUP) Libraries are lucky to have the opportunity to teach a one-credit library and information literacy class each semester if they so choose. I have taught this class for over thirty years. I enjoy working with students and hope to share my love of the research process with them, and to help them build strong information literacy skills that will enhance their lives. When I noticed that students recognized that the ability to do academic research was beneficial in college but seemed not to be seeing such skills as having much relevance when it came to their personal or professional lives, it bothered me. So I considered ways that I could make the class more relevant and engaging. Providing some connection between what was done in class and the real world seemed like one way that I could make it more relevant.

When I attended an on-campus faculty development workshop on service-learning, I got an idea. The presenter, a professor from Loyola's Center for Experiential Learning, told the group about a community researcher class that was offered there. Though the Loyola class was for upper-level students and included more extensive research than was appropriate for my one-credit introductory classes, I thought I might be able to adapt the idea. Over the summer, I spoke with the service-learning officer on my campus and she gave me the names of professors on campus who were teaching classes with service-learning elements. I contacted some of them and they were willing to share their course structure and actual assignments to help me plan for the fall. The week before classes began, the service-learning officer contacted local non-profit organizations who were seeking student volunteers and invited them to a meeting to discuss my idea about asking students to do research for them. A number of community partners showed interest and agreed to provide topics for my students to investigate.

Another experience that led me to use the service-learning assignment was teaching an Introduction to Women's Studies course a few years ago. The class used assignments that were consistent with feminist pedagogy, which were reflective and collaborative. The result was one of the most positive and memorable teaching experiences that I have ever had. I hoped that using a service-based and more reflective teaching method would provide a similarly positive experience, and I have been satisfied with the result.

From the beginning, this authentic assignment has been popular with the students. Though the community partners and topics students have chosen to work on have changed through the years, the central assignment where students consider real-world problems and the organizations that have been created to address them, choose one of particular interest to them, practice research skills in researching the problem, and create a research portfolio designed to assist an organization help the community has remained the same.

Motivations: The library profession is one that is rooted in service to others. There are many who have argued that professional training in library and information science is best when practical, application-based, and includes a service element. It stands to reason that just as LIS students learn better by doing something for someone else, students in information literacy classes, who are learning similar skills, should too. Interest in increasing the use of experiential and service-learning practices is growing in higher education, as is interest in building positive relationships with the community and giving back to them. Administrators and professors in many disciplines are promoting authentic learning experiences as ways to better prepare students for future careers, so there is a lot of support for using service and experientially based assignments to teach information literacy skills. I included service-based assignments in my classes because I felt that asking students to consider societal problems, to investigate the workings of organizations that are developed to address them, and to build their research skills by looking for information that could help find solutions to real problems provided an engaging and deeper learning experience. In addition, I believe the assignment allows instructors and students to become more closely connected with the community and possibly help others. In summary, it is a teaching technique that students like, is currently popular in higher education, supports university/community connections, helps students develop as citizens and future employees, offers an applied learning experience, and as a by-product might help those in need, allowing us to help others are while we are learning ourselves.

THE PEOPLE

Libraries: Indiana University of Pennsylvania (IUP) is a public university in southwestern Pennsylvania that serves approximately 13,000 graduate and undergraduate students in undergraduate, masters, and doctoral degree programs. IUP librarians support the development of information literacy skills through a comprehensive instruction program which includes hundreds of on-demand, one-shot sessions and one-, two-, and three-credit information literacy classes that are offered both face-to-face and online. Librarians who teach information literacy classes work with some common learning outcomes that are based on the original Information Literacy Standards. Instructors still have the flexibility to design classes to achieve maximum benefit to students. IUP actively promotes faculty and student engagement in community-based service opportunities through its Office of Service Learning. High impact practices, such as experiential and service-learning, are also encouraged through specific mention in the university's strategic plan. IUP's Center for Teaching Excellence also offers a teaching award to faculty who include experiential and service-learning elements in their classes. There is a lot of interest in experiential and service-learning on our campus.

Instructor: I am the government documents/outreach librarian at IUP. I have taught the LIBR 151 class for over thirty years. More rarely, I have taught two- and three-credit information literacy classes and an Introduction to Women's Studies class. I am also bibliographer for History, Women's Studies, and Religious Studies, as well as the embedded librarian for the College of Humanities and Social Sciences. As such, I provide one-shot instruction sessions when requested from faculty in these subject areas and work with students individually when they have discipline-related research questions.

Courses: The one-credit LIBR 151: Introduction to Information Literacy is the class for which I have most often used this assignment. It is intended to introduce the concept of information literacy to students and provide opportunities for the development of these skills.

Students: Though the class is an entry-level class, those enrolled are most often upper-level students who are taking it because they only need one credit to graduate. The majority of them are from criminology and nursing, though students with any major at any class level can and do sign up for the class.

Community Partners. Students can choose any partner/topic from a list provided. Partners that my students have most often chosen to work with have been the YMCA, Four Footed Friends Animal Rescue organization, the local hospital, and the campus Health Awareness office. Other partners have been our community gardens, a homeless shelter, our campus domestic violence support group, the campus LGBTQ support group, the public library, a local nursing home, and our campus Information Technology Support Office. Students are also permitted to use any non-profit group that will work with them to provide a topic with my approval, so a variety of other organizations have served as partners.

Finding and Working with Partners: I found community partners initially through my university's service-learning office. They contacted representatives of organizations that sought student volunteer workers and set up a time for us all to meet. My first semester, I included partners that I met at the meeting. Since then, I have found additional community partners by talking with those who attend a student engagement fair designed to connect students with community organizations seeking volunteers. Also, because I give students the choice of suggesting unique topics and partners, I have found other partners that were suggested by students. An instructor could also do a brainstorming session early in the semester and ask students for their ideas. They might then contact partners suggested by students to see if these organizations would be interested.

Course planners should keep the needs of the community partner service organization that is working with them foremost in their planning and be sure to balance student learning outcomes with benefits to the organization. When the service-learning experience is direct (students actually visit the organization and provide service there) training and supervision of students can further burden already overworked employees. Unless the volunteer student workers perform a significant task or serve for an extended period of time, non-profit employees may not see it as is in the best interest of the organization to have such students at their facility. Intentionally planning for mutual benefit to the organization, instructor, and student is necessary to maintain a good relationship with the partner.

Benefits

Instructor Benefits: I have derived greater satisfaction from including service learning elements in my classes than from any other instruction method I have ever used. Students like it, and I believe it is effective and benefits students in ways that I mention below, as well as resulting in a richer teaching and learning experience for me. Students choose topics they are interested in and sometimes even passionate about. Reading their reflections and research projects help me learn more about them, but also about community partners and the issues those organizations address. It feels good to make an effort to empower students and help them recognize that they can have a part in fixing a problem, even as they learn basic information literacy skills. Also, because service-learning is considered a High-Impact Practice (HIP), inclusion of service-learning assignments may increase student engagement, retention, and deep learning, and HIPs are specifically mentioned in the university's strategic plan, using service-learning assignments can be included on my annual report of impact relating to the strategic plan.

Students Benefits: Students are challenged by the assignment and generally indicate they enjoy the class because they feel their work is not just another paper that will go into the recycling bin but research that can address a community problem. They also state that they enjoy being able to pick topics whether they are related to their major or just something they are interested in learning more about.

Community Partners Benefits: Some partners have indicated that the research reports the students provide are helpful to them because their employees are too busy providing service and don't have time to search the literature for new ideas. Community partner employees reported that reading the projects have inspired them to try something new, and one partner told us they handed out some of the student portfolios at their Board of Director meetings. At least one organization was able to use the material included in the portfolios to support the writing of a grant.

Organizations may also get new volunteers or donations through the student's class experience. Finally, the assignments deepen student awareness of community problems and may lead them to support the work of the organization in the future.

Institutional Benefits: Colleges and universities struggle to maintain good relationships with the communities that surround them. Positive service-learning experiences can improve town/gown relationships. Service-learning is also a high-impact practice and could impact student success and retention, and this benefits the institution as well.

THE PROCESS
Expected Learning Outcomes

The expected learning outcomes are similar to those found in most information literacy classes.

When you complete the course, you should be able to
- define and articulate the community partner's need for information;
- choose appropriate sources from a variety of different types and formats of information available;
- retrieve information online or in-person using a variety of methods;
- evaluate information and its sources critically; and
- use information ethically and effectively to prepare a research report for the community partner, including an annotated bibliography with recommendations based upon research findings.

Curriculum Materials
- The main assignment in this class is the Research Portfolio assignment. It was adapted from the Paper Trail Project from Burkhardt, McDonald and Rathemacher's *Teaching Information Literacy* book.[1]
- When service-learning is discussed in class, we have watched Tom Shadyac's *I Am* film trailer (https://www.youtube.com/watch?v=iYtfnONaz-TU) to begin a discussion of why we should try to help others.
- The textbook I have used in the class most often has been *The Information Literacy User's Guide: An Open Online Textbook.*[2]
- Assignments used in the class can be found at the end of this chapter and include:
  - o   Research Portfolio Description
  - o   Reflective Exercises
  - o   Sample Community Partners Organizations and Topics
  - o   Exploring Your Topic and Community Partner Worksheet

Steps Involved

- During the first class, students participate in a discussion of why they took the class, what they expect to learn, and what will be expected of them. The syllabus is reviewed and service-learning is defined. The final project description and a sample final project are provided online for them to review. Students reflect on their pre-course perceptions of information literacy and service-learning and how they feel about taking a class with a service-learning element.
- During the first few weeks, topics such as exploring how libraries are designed to support student success, what ethical use of information is, and what standard bibliography style is are discussed.
- In the fourth week, students are provided with a list of community partners and topics the partners are interested in to use as a focus of their research that semester. Students may also suggest a partner and topic if they like but it has to be an organization that is non-profit, provides a service to the community, and is approved by the instructor. Students are asked to complete the "Exploring Your Topic and Community Partner Worksheet" by the next week. This assignment will be the basis for the research statement section of their final portfolio.
- Once students have chosen a topic and partner, they begin their research. Formulating research questions, creating efficient search strategies, the information cycle and the various formats that information may take, search tools, and choosing appropriate information for the particular information need are discussed.
- At mid-semester, students do a Start-Stop-Continue reflection that asks for feedback on the class and their thoughts about the service-based project at that point.
- Students use information literacy skills introduced to gather lists of appropriate information resources, choose the best, and create an annotated bibliography.
- Finally, students build upon assignments they have completed throughout the semester to assemble their final project.
- On the last day of classes, refreshments are served and each student briefly presents their findings. Each shares what their topic and partner was, what they believed about the topic prior to beginning their research, whether their beliefs were challenged or became stronger, what they felt the most useful sources of information on their topic were, and any recommendations they might have for their community partners. Representatives from the community partner organizations are invited to attend if they are available.
- Projects are turned in and they are given to the community partners.

POST-PROJECT ASSESSMENT

Methods of Reflection

- Students reflect as part of discussions, other assignments, and anonymous surveys at the beginning, middle, and end of the class. See reflective assignment and prompts used at the end of the chapter.

Post Project Feedback

- Student reflections:
    o Students report greater interest in doing the assignment because they feel that it will be used by someone to actually do something that will make a change in the world and benefit others. The following reflection shows typical sentiments expressed: "It feels good to know that others might benefit from the information I have collected. It is totally different than having to complete meaningless research for classes as busy work. At least this way we could develop our research skills while contributing to a greater cause."
- Community partner remarks:
    o Community partners have also reflected positively on the assignment. They have told us that they get some great ideas from the research portfolios and that they don't have time to sit down and do research, so the information is really helpful to them. Some have reported including some information and sources from literature reviews in successful grant applications.

Project Assessment and Reporting Methods

- This teaching practice has been popular with students, and I have gotten good teaching evaluations every semester that I have used it. While some students are not enthusiastic about the assignment at first, complaints are few, and it is inspiring the way some of them embrace causes and work hard to prepare something useful for their partners and clearly demonstrate a social consciousness at the end of class.
- Our service-learning office sends out a survey on student community service each year in preparation for a report that they do. I am able to mention the assignment in that survey and I am also able to include it in my annual report as an effort to employ a HIP in my teaching.
- I have presented on my assignment at a number of conferences in poster presentations and presentations.
- The closer relationships that I have developed with community organizations have also been useful to me as an outreach librarian. For exam-

ple, after students investigated the YMCA's topic of a summer reading program as a part of the YMCA's annual day camp, I was talking with our partner at the YMCA about the progress of the project. He informed me that he was having trouble obtaining books for the children attending camp to read. Our library was able to lend them books and a literacy element was added to their summer camp program. This probably would not have happened if I hadn't gotten to know them through the service-learning assignment.

Difficulties Encountered

Student issues: Students most often indicate in reflections at the end of the semester that they enjoyed the assignment and found it very useful and even rewarding, but in initial and mid-term reflections, they may report anxiety about the assignments. They are unsure because the application-based assignment is different from traditional academic assignments. Scaffolding assignments so that everything that will be asked of them will be introduced and practiced in the class, providing frequent feedback, and other structure such as detailed assignment descriptions, evaluation rubrics, and sample assignments seem to ease their anxiety. Depending upon the question, they also may have difficulty locating any scholarly sources that they can include. For example, the animal adoption agency asked for research on using social media to help in pet adopted. Issues like that may require some flexibility in sources accepted and is something that can be worked through and considered in revisions of the assignment.

Instructor issues: Applied assignments that involve outside partners offer lots of unknowns to instructors and can cause anxiety for them as well. Starting early, preparing by attending workshops and doing readings on service and applied learning can help to get started. Also useful is to take advantage of any campus support that is available, and reach out to a campus office of Service Learning and Student Engagement and Teaching Excellence faculty support groups. Faculty who have already used this technique are generally enthusiastic about the use of service-based experiences and are often willing to provide support as well. They all can provide encouragement and advice that can assist you in finding community partners, creating assignments, developing curriculum, and preparing you for challenges that may come your way.

Community Partner Issues: Remember that community partners have important work to do and are often operating with a skeletal staff and limited funding. They are likely to be receptive to offers of significant student assistance with their work, the potential for recruiting future long-term volunteers, and activities that create awareness of the work and the problems they address, They may not have time to work individually with students, though, and may react negatively if they feel that students are taking their time and they are seeing little or no returns on their investments in them. When working with them, be sure to balance what they will get from the student work for them with that they will have to invest.

Conclusion

Students may feel that traditional information literacy assignments are less than engaging and have little relevancy to their lives after college and instructors are likely to sense this. A community research assignment where students choose topics, use information literacy skills to investigate social problems, and seek solutions and motivate students is likely to increase student interest and satisfaction with the course, boost effectiveness of instruction and satisfaction of the instructor, and benefit the community as everyone learns.

APPENDIX MATERIALS

- Research Portfolio Description
- Reflective Exercises
- Sample Community Partner Organizations and Topics
- Exploring Your Topic and Community Partner Worksheet

Research Portfolio Description

Successful college students graduate and are hired by companies who expect them to come with the skills necessary to carry out research projects in their area of expertise. The ability of employees to formulate appropriate research questions and locate and effectively and ethically use the best information helps organizations make the best decisions and thrive. Underfunded and short-staffed non-profit organizations often do not have access to the best information resources or sufficiently trained staff who have time to carry out needed research.

For this assignment, you are asked to investigate a research topic that would benefit a non-profit organization and to prepare a research portfolio for them that will help them to do what they do better. The completed portfolio should include a title page, research statement, research outline, annotated bibliography in APA Style of five items, and answers to final reflection questions.

The following is a description of what should be included in each of the parts of your portfolio:

PROJECT SHOULD INCLUDE:

1. **Title page.** This section should include the title of your project, your name, and the name of your community partner.

2. **Research statement.** This section should be a few paragraphs and contain the
    following information: your research question, a little bit of information about
    your community partner, and why you chose that topic and that community
    partner. Explain what you thought was true about your topic before you began
    and then any new and interesting things you ended up finding out in the in-
    formation resources you located, including information that contradicts your
    original assumptions. Explain if the information you found confirmed your
    initial expectations or not, and list some conclusions you reached through
    your readings. Indicate what your best sources of information were. Finally,
    provide one or two recommendations for actions that your community part-
    ner might take to help address the problem at the base of your research topic.
3. **Research outline.** This section should include a few paragraphs that address
    the following questions about how you did your research: How did you get
    started? What were your first steps? What followed (listing steps from be-
    ginning to end)? What kind of resources (books, journal articles, interviews,
    internet blog entries, etc.) did you use for your portfolio and to back up your
    presentation? Why did you choose these sources? How did you search for
    information? What search tools did you use to find information? Did you
    use any particular method of searching (for example, did you use Boolean,
    phrase, or advanced searches)? How did you record the descriptive informa-
    tion about the sources you used (author, title, publisher, pages, etc.)? Did you
    copy and keep the sources you used until you were done with the project or
    just take notes? How did you organize your notes and sources? What did you
    consider when choosing sources to be sure that you had the best information
    available? Research outlines, which are not detailed, and do not address all
    questions, will receive few points.
4. **Annotated bibliography.** This section should include an annotated bibliog-
    raphy of five current, relevant, and appropriate resources. Citations should
    be in standard bibliographic style. Annotations should be descriptive and
    touch upon the points highlighted in the "How to Write an Annotation"
    handout provided in the Learning Management System.
5. **Final reflection.** This section should include a paragraph or two addressing
    the following questions: How did you feel about the doing a research that
    might have a real impact on the work of a non-profit organization? How does
    this compare to research projects that are simply academic exercises? Did you
    discover anything interesting about your topic that you think may have an
    impact on either your life or the work of the community partner that you did
    the research for? During this course, did you learn something (or some things)
    about doing research that you think will impact your life in the future in some
    way? As a result of this course, have you changed anything about the way that
    you search, evaluate, and use information? Finally, pass on one piece of advice
    about information research to a student who has not taken this course.

Reflective Exercises

Early in the semester:

- Private reflection prompts
  - o How would you define service-learning?
  - o Have you ever participated in service-learning activities before?
  - o What do you think of doing service-based research in this class? If so, please describe your experiences.
  - o What do you expect from this assignment?
  - o How do you define information literacy?

Around the mid-point of the semester:

- Private reflection prompts
  - o Why did you choose your partner and topic? What appealed to you about them?
  - o How do you feel about doing research for the partner?
  - o What is working well in this class that we should continue?
  - o What is not working and should be stopped?
  - o What aren't we doing and that we should begin doing?

At the end-of-semester:

- Private reflective prompts:
  - o Now that you have the final project, how do you feel about doing research for a non-profit organization as a final project?
  - o Do you think having worked with this partner and done this research will change anything about the way that you think about, or interact with, the partner and topic in the future?

Final Presentation. Students are asked to prepare a presentation for the final class period with answers to the following questions:

- What were your topic and your community partner? Why did you choose each?
- What were the most important things you discovered in the course of your research? Did you find what you expected or were you surprised by some of your findings?
- Please share any recommendations you have for your community partners or for your fellow classmates that you can make based on what you found in the course of your research.
- What is your opinion of using a service-based assignment in this class?

Sample Community Partner Organizations and Topics

Four Footed Friends. Topics:

- Types of service dogs and prison inmates training service dogs for people with disabilities
- Helping families to make a good decision when selecting a cat or dog— particularly when there are children involved; best practices in promoting pet adoption
- Programs that motivate children to read by having them practice reading aloud with registered and insured therapy dogs
- Programs for children to prevent cat and dog bites, interact more safely with cats and dogs, and be responsible pet owners
- Controlling the spread of disease and isolation procedures in dog shelters (we are seeking a grant to add an isolation wing to the existing shelter structure)
- Highly effective strategies for promoting the adoption of homeless dogs and cats
- Visiting nursing homes, rehabilitation facilities, residential facilities for adults with special needs, and healthcare facilities with registered and insured therapy dogs

Indiana Community Garden. Topics:

- Growing food year around in Western Pennsylvania
- Community gardens and food insecurity or local food banks
- Urban community gardens in abandoned lots
- Community gardens and school children

YMCA. Topics:

- Building community in summer camps for children
- Leadership programs
- After-school programs for K-12 students
- Innovative exercise programs
- Special Olympics
- Trends and fads for teen activities: What programs are popular leisure activities for teenagers?

IUP Center for Health Awareness. Topics:

- How to provide effective support for College Students with depression
- College students and stress reduction: rates and remedies

- How to avoid sleep disorders while in college
- Love Your Body campaigns for college campuses
- How to address disordered eating on college campuses
- College students and sexually transmitted diseases: rates and remedies
- Connection between tanning beds and skin cancer
- Keeping off the Freshman Fifteen: good nutrition for college campuses

Exploring Your Topic and Community Partner Worksheet

Student Name _____

After you have completed this week's background reading, considered the choices provided for partners and topics (see Community Organizations and Topics document in this module) and chosen a community partner and topic from the listing, please complete this worksheet.

- **Part One.** Who is your community partner, what do they do, and who do they help? Do some preliminary investigations of your community partner by going to their website, doing a Google search on them, or consulting the local newspaper database. Read through the information you find there and answer the following questions about them:
    - o What community partner have you chosen from the list?
    - o What is their website? List the URL (website address).
    - o What is their mission or main objectives? Hopefully, there is at least one listed. If not, what do you think their purpose is given what you find on the site?
    - o Who do they serve?
    - o What kind of services do they offer?
- **Part Two—Your topic**
    - o What is the topic that you have chosen from the list?
    - o Why did you choose this topic and partner? Does it relate to your major or are you just interested? Do you have any particular skills or interests that lead you to choose this topic?
    - o Do you feel like you already know something about the topic? If so, what do you expect to discover in your research?
    - o To get some background information on your topic, do a Google search on your topic and see if you can easily find some. Write a bit about the topic you are going to explore below.
- **Part Three—This assignment and service-learning**
    - o As you begin this research project, do you feel confident you will be able to do well in it or are you concerned? If you are concerned, explain why.

o How do you feel about doing a service-learning assignment as opposed to doing a traditional research project? Better, worse, the same? Please explain.

Notes

1. Joanna M. Burkhardt, Mary C. MacDonald, and Andrée J. Rathemacher, *Teaching Information Literacy: 50 Standards-Based Exercises for College Students* (Chicago: American Library Association, 2010).
2. Greg Bobish, Trudi E. Jacobson, Deborah Bernnard, Jenna Hecker, Irina I. Holden, Allison Hosier, Tor Loney, and Daryl R. Bullis, *The Information Literacy User's Guide: An Open Online Textbook*, accessed May 25, 2017, https://dspace.sunyconnect.suny.edu/bitstream/handle/1951/68218/The-Information-Literacy-Users-Guide-pdf.pdf?sequence=1.

CHAPTER SIX

Support for Student-Driven Projects:
Library Mini-Grants and Service Learning

Amanda Peters

Student Engagement Librarian
University of Michigan
arforres@umich.edu

THE ACTIVITY

Description: As an academic hub for all disciplines, the library is committed to actively engaging with the campus community to extend learning beyond the classroom. At the University of Michigan Library, we developed a Student Engagement Program to provide and support collaborative student experiences that focus on information, design, and research, enabling practical opportunities for students to explore, experiment, create, lead, and reflect—capacities and skills that are critical to addressing twenty-first century problems in any field.

One of the largest components of the program is a Student Mini-Grants initiative; grants of up to $1,000 are awarded to both graduate and undergraduate students who present proposals for projects that demonstrate innovation, collaboration, and that strive to make a real-life impact. Projects must also strengthen community partnerships, enhance global scholarship, and/or advocate for diversity and inclusion. Throughout the past two years, we have funded forty-seven projects and have plans to continue this level of funding.

Getting Started: In 2015, in an effort to respond to an increased trend of high-impact learning practices through experiential learning, in our annual budget request we asked for money to pilot a variety of programs to support this work, including the mini-grants initiative. We were highly aware that service-learning and social justice-oriented projects are often a catalyst for authentic learning experiences, and we structured our call to students with an expectation that we would receive proposals with a service-learning focus. Our students met and, in fact, exceeded our expectations with their proposals.

Motivations: The library has always worked with students in a variety of capacities, including working with students on service-learning projects and preparing them for learning abroad and other high-impact work, but we wanted to find a way to be more intentional about providing these services in an effort to make sure students understood they could come to the library for more than help with a research paper. We also wanted faculty to understand that we were natural partners in engaged learning and felt we could make more connections by making our work in this area more visible.

THE PEOPLE

Library: The University of Michigan (UM) Library is consistently ranked as one of the top ten academic research libraries in North America. We have more than 13 million volumes in our collection. We recognize that for undergraduate students, the size and scope of our libraries can be overwhelming, and we provide collections and programs to support their work as beginning researchers.

Instructors: Academic contacts for this activity were library mentors rather than course instructors. Amanda Peters is the Student Engagement Librarian, and in this role she manages and coordinates the Student Engagement Program, including an Engagement Fellows Program, Student Ambassadors, and the Student Mini-Grants initiative. As coordinator of this program, she invites her librarian colleagues from across the system to work as mentors and project managers for student projects. Students are awarded a grant and at that same time are paired with librarian mentors, many of whom have a subject specialization, who meet with the students regularly throughout their project. Through both interviews and surveys with both librarians and students, we were able to demonstrate the impact that librarians can have in this type of learning experience.

Course: In this case, the learning experience is connected to working on a project related to an award, rather than a specific course. The award is for mini-grants of up to $1,000 for projects that meet the criteria outlined in the description. Students must submit a proposal, budget outline, and faculty letter of support in order to be considered. A committee of librarians read proposals and choose grantees. We have been accepting about twenty to thirty projects per year.

Students: Both undergraduate and graduate students are eligible for this award. When we decided to make the grant available to both, we were concerned undergraduates might be at a disadvantage to more experienced graduate students, but this has not turned out to be the case. We have had a diverse mix of both undergraduate and graduate projects each year. We ask that the students are in "good standing" but otherwise depend on the application to speak for itself.

Community Partners: Students work with community partners across our region, including many partners based out of Detroit, which is only about thirty minutes from the University of UM Ann Arbor campus. Through a variety of faculty and student organization connections, students also work with international organizations. Examples of partnerships include:

- Washtenaw County Youth Detention Center
- The Detroit YWCA
- The Quipu Project
- Universidad de San Carlos de Guatemala
- KUYI Hopi Radio in Arizona and KYUK in Alaska
- And many more.

Finding and Working with Partners: Students at UM are able to identify community partners in a variety of ways—through faculty contacts, student organizations, and two very important campus offices: The Ginsberg Center and the Center for Engaged Academic Learning. Both of these offices work to connect faculty, students, and community members for mutually beneficial partnerships. These two centers also do a good deal of work with students to prepare them for community-based work, such as sessions on cultural humility, asking students to think about sustainability and how projects can continue even beyond their project, and much more.

The opportunity to work with community organizations both locally and abroad gives students a greater perspective on how their academic work can make a real-life impact. Students gain skills that cannot be taught in the classroom: how to work in teams, better communication skills, increased creative thinking, and an entrepreneurial mindset are just some of the challenges students find themselves presented with during this work. Community partners benefit from some very tangible things; they have access to students who are enthusiastic and full of energy for a project and benefit from a connection to the university community that can provide expertise and resources.

THE PROCESS
Expected Learning Outcomes

These learning experiences provide students from a variety of disciplines with practical, hands-on opportunities to lead and shape collaborative and innovative projects with direct support and mentorship from library faculty and staff. The projects present students with real-world challenges and the library offered a safe space for exploration. The program enhances engagement with library resources and services while empowering students to further develop skills critical for success as global citizens.

Description of the Award: Students receive up to $1,000, based on their budget outline.

Steps Involved

At the beginning of fall semester, a call for proposals is announced. Submissions are generally due mid-October, and a committee of six librarians chooses around thirty grantees. It generally takes a couple of weeks to make decisions. Students then receive their funds and they are matched with library mentors. Mentors are chosen based on their subject expertise and what students have outlined as a need in their proposals. Mentors and students are asked to meet at least three times during fall and winter semesters. Mentors have described helping students with navigation of campus resources, including introductions to other individuals in the library and across campus who would be useful to student projects. Mentors also help students find information, both scholarly and non-scholarly, that could be of help to a project. Finally, many mentors play a role in helping students design a way to present their work, both to an internal library audience and to other stakeholders, both in academia and beyond.

Benefits

Librarian/Instructor Benefits: The benefits of this initiative are both tangible and intangible; librarians describe building relationships with students which gives them insight into the student experience, both academically and interpersonally. This informs their work in other service experiences with students. We have become much more aware of the work of student organizations and students who are working on projects outside of a traditional course assignment.

Student Benefits: Students have communicated through surveys, interviews, and their end-of-year presentations that they have benefited from being involved in this program. Many of them were not aware of the resources or services recommended by librarians, and many described the impact that this mentorship brought to their project in unforeseen ways.

Community Partner Benefits: We have not closely assessed partner benefits but we are aware that students are working with community partners in many of their projects and that those partners have informally shared with both their students and with us that the experience was positive and fruitful. Some of the benefits are specifically monetary; in one case, a youth detention center received new books for their collection, and in another, a school in a developing country received needed supplies. However, as in many partnerships, all parties benefited from the relationships that developed and perspectives that were gained.

Institution Benefits: We have also not closely assessed how UM has benefited, but anecdotally, we know that we have developed closer relationships with campus partners who have a service-learning focus, and these relationships have the potential to create new possibilities in programming and services. We also believe that by offering services and resources that indirectly benefit community partners, those community members see our University as a reciprocal partner, not simply an institution looking to use the community as a research subject.

POST-PROJECT ASSESSMENT
Methods of Reflection

A requirement of the grant is that student grant recipients must present their projects at an end-of-the-year symposium. We give them suggestions on what to share about their project and to reflect on the ways the library and the university were able to support their work. This presentation serves to give the students a public speaking experience and helps communicate the outcomes of the program to librarians and the larger university community.

Post-Project Feedback

We also sent students surveys and did a number of one-on-one interviews with students to gain a greater understanding of the benefits of the program and places where the program could improve. This required several emails and personal follow-ups but we received a fair response. In the first year, we also asked students to participate in interviews, which were given by student staff who were not associated with the program. This helped the students to feel candid and we were able to gain a good amount of feedback. We received positive feedback from students and library experts, who valued the diverse opportunities and partnerships we provided.

Here are a few stories from grant recipients:

Global Health Case Competition: "Students at the School of Public Health, in collaboration with the Office of Global Public Health, have established the first annual global-health-focused case competition at the School of Public Health. The experience will call on students to work in multidisciplinary groups and create innovative, equitable, and real-world solutions to public health policy challenges around the world.

Our relationship with the library was pivotal to the success of this event, especially research support for developing the case itself. Gurpreet Rana was an incredible resource for our case writing team and helped us find reputable data and templates from other case studies. Not only did she offer invaluable feedback as we wrote, but also provided support for logistical snags and multidisciplinary advertising.

"The library partnership significantly enhanced the educational experience of the case writing team, as well as the competitors, because we were able to produce a much more solid final product than we would have otherwise."
—**Michael Budros**, MPH/MPP '17 Health Management and Policy

Your Voice is Not Forgotten: "Oral histories are sourced from women who have experienced intimate partner violence and [who] are utilizing services offered by the YWCA, the only domestic abuse shelter in Metropolitan Detroit. Audio narratives shatter typical stereotypes of women who are victims of intimate partner violence.

"The staff at the YWCA feels strongly that being present, listening, and using conversation as a form of therapy aids in the healing process. Copies of the interviews are given to participants and the YWCA retains an archive of stories. The library was immensely helpful in providing information that both challenged and supported my project sources that dealt with intimate partner violence in ways sensitive to both qualitative and quantitative manners. Library funding also provided the means to travel back and forth to Detroit."
—**Ruth Burke**, MFA '17 Art

Transnational Solidarity for Peru: The Quipu Project: "To help raise awareness and demonstrate solidarity for victims of coerced sterilization during the Fujimori regime in Peru, we held a screening of the interactive testimonial documentary by the Quipu Project, a multimedia exhibition, and a translation weekend where volunteers worked collaboratively to transcribe and translate testimonies of the victims.

"All the events were open to the community, and we feel that with their help, global networks of solidarity were created. English, Spanish, and Quechua speakers engaged in discussion about the ongoing consequences and future implications of sexual violence. Not only were interdisciplinary networks strengthened within the U of M community, but we created partnerships with the Quipu Project team in Peru, Chile, and England."
—**Lauren Darnell**, PhD '20 Romance Languages & Literatures

Violence and Voicelessness: Experiences of Survivors of Intimate Partner Violence on College Campuses: "The purpose of this project was to provide an evaluation of university and college services for survivors of intimate partner violence from the student survivors themselves. Through research on anti-violence movements and their impact on school administrations to qualitative interviews with twenty-four undergraduate students who self-identify as survivors of intimate partner violence, this project approaches service provision from an intersectional lens based on the lived experiences of these twenty-four students.

"The money I received from the UM library was essential to my research. It was used for compensation of participants, and without the additional funding I would not have been able to recruit as many participants and gain as wide of a spectrum of perspectives as I did. Through this funding, the library has participated in the compensation of survivors, which I believe to be incredibly important when sharing their stories of abuse and trauma, as well as to the creation of feedback that will be used by providers in the future to make services more inclusive to all survivors."

—**Katherine Irani**, BA '16 Women's Studies

ADAPT (Applying Design to Advance Patient Treatment): "ADAPT is an interdisciplinary team of students building products that promote independence for those utilizing assistive devices. Every design decision begins with real people and real problems. We work at the intersection of art, design, and engineering to create beautiful and productive designs.

"With the library resources, we were able to 3D print several of our prototypes in addition to receiving valuable information regarding patent law/resources. Moving forward, we will continue to use the 3D Lab while continuing to search the patent databases for possibly [sic] conflicts. These resources will be essential to implementing social change. Having enough room for our designer and engineer to work at the same time helps us remain efficient in our work."

—**Miranda Veeser**, BS '16 International Studies

Respiratory Health in Guatemala through Human—Centered Design: "M-HEAL's Guatemala Team conducted a needs assessment in Antigua, Guatemala in 2015. Through interviews and observations at clinics, schools, and hospitals, the team gained of the community's needs. The team has narrowed its focus to respiratory health through literature review and selection rubrics and is engaging with community partners to continue the project.

"The team has gained a better understanding of front-end design processes, namely in-country needs assessment, literature review, and down-selection. By tackling challenges during the project, the team has developed an understanding of the challenges with and importance of rigorous front-end design. The team has also experimented with and refined its organizational structures. Most importantly, the team has learned the importance and benefit of working with strong community partners and has begun to foster a growing partnership with the cohort at Universidad de San Carlos de Guatemala. The partnership with the UM Library has supported the literature review, benchmarking, and community partner search processes. Library experts have helped lead the team to relevant databases, introduce the team to the patent search process, and connect the team to potential community partners."

—**Kevin Jiang**, BSE '18 Biomedical Engineering

"Words Flying Through the Air": Tribal Radio as a Health Information Resource for Rural American Indian Reservation Residents: "My community-based participatory research project aims to explore the role of U.S. tribal radio stations in providing access to accurate, culturally relevant health information for residents of rural American Indian reservations. My two project partners and research sites are KUYI Hopi Radio in Arizona and KYUK in Alaska.

"A challenge the project faces is the very limited prior work that exists on U.S. tribal radio in general and the lack of scholarly work addressing tribal radio as a health information resource. This is also a unique opportunity for the project to make a contribution to the field of Media Studies but also to Native American Studies and Public Health. The library staff, particularly Judy Smith, has been instrumental in identifying sources for both the academic and the applied aspects of the project. I will work with library staff to create the National Tribal Radio website. I also learned a great deal about community-based participatory research, as the project is conducted in close partnership with the radio stations and their tribal communities. The project will not only be approved by the UM IRB but also by the respective tribal review boards in AZ and AK."

—**Jana Wilbricht**, PhD '19 Communication Studies

The strongest indicator of the success of the program has been through the students' own words. Here are a few quotes from students about the benefits they received by being a part of this program:

"Now, more students can volunteer at the center, helping to promote literacy because there are more materials there.... I greatly benefitted from working more closely with the Washtenaw Youth Center to get this project going.... Before, I was just a book club volunteer, but after this project, I've gotten a deeper understanding of how to make a more long-lasting difference.... Our Children's Librarian was amazing at recommending books that are great at interesting kids in reading. She pointed us in the direction of books that celebrate diversity and helped us invest in different types of books that would be good for the population there...."

"My mentors are wonderful. They helped me talk through my ideas for the present and future stages of the project, offered great feedback, pointed me to new resources (library and otherwise), and provided guidance on methods for lit review. I really enjoyed having the chance to talk through my ideas with such smart, supportive ladies and am all the more proud after this experience to have such a great library system at UM! Thank you!"

"I mainly learned about the librarians through the grant. I didn't realize what a wealth of knowledge we had at the University in terms of people. I'm often told what amazing resources we have in the library but it isn't often discussed what amazing people we have in the library. Getting this grant opened my eyes to the power of having a dialogue over a topic, instead of having a dialogue with a computer or catalogue."

Project Assessment and Reporting

Assessment of student performance during the projects was provided by librarian mentors who met periodically with students and at the end of the year through a survey and analysis of student presentations. Students were asked to address the following questions: Did students attend multiple meetings with their mentors? Did students appear to be on track with their projects or were they encountering problems? Were students open and receptive to presenting their work at the end-of-year symposium?

The student presentations were very positive and provided the audience with an informative snapshot of the outcomes of the program. We created a short video that encompasses the entire Student Engagement Program, but the last part of the video focuses on the mini-grants recipients: https://youtu.be/hCe0ZlqBTfQ.

Difficulties Encountered

We encountered a few different difficulties but they were mostly logistical issues. Since this is such a new program, we have a range of possibilities to strengthen the program that have not been fully explored.

Student Issues: When students received their grants, the money was distributed to students through the financial aid office. In a few cases, this impacted students' other awards. We found that by writing a letter to financial aid explaining the nature of the grant, any impact on the students' financial aid was reversed.

Instructor/Library Mentor Issues: We are still working through how to define the mentorship; right now, this ranges from more of a standard research consultation to a more in-depth relationship. Part of this may just be the nature of some of the projects as needing more or less intervention, but we are considering offering workshops or materials to the mentors that might help them to think more deeply about what they can do to increase student engagement with the library.

Community Partner Issues: Since the community partner relationships are brokered by the students, we don't currently have much of a way to measure this. It would be great to add an assessment piece here but we will need to think through our options.

Conclusion

Looking back on the goals for this new program, we have made great strides in creating and supporting engaged learning opportunities across a broad range of disciplines. Supporting service learning projects has been gratifying for all involved, and we have seen evidence of the development of richer relationships with both our students and the greater communities that they serve.

APPENDIX MATERIALS
- Call for Mini-Grant Applications
- End of the Year Presentation Email Reminder and Instructions
- End of the Year Survey Sent to Students

Email Call for Mini-Grant Applications
U-M LIBRARY STUDENT MINI-GRANTS NOW AVAILABLE

It's time to take your student project to the next level! Partner with the U-M Library!

The U-M Library is committed to actively engaging with the campus community to extend learning beyond the classroom. Apply today **for our student mini-grants (up to $1,000)**, which support innovative and collaborative projects that make a re-al-life impact. Selected projects must strengthen community partnerships, enhance global scholarship, and/or advocate for inclusion and diversity.

The U-M Library is your perfect partner every step of the way—with personalized training and support from library experts as well as direct access to world-renowned research collections and state-of-the-art design and technology labs, studios, exhibit galleries, and collaboration spaces.

Applications due Friday, October 30.

This initiative is sponsored by the U-M Library's Student Engagement Program.

For more information, please visit engage.lib.umich.edu/mini-grants/.

End of the Year Presentation Email Reminder and Instructions
FINAL REPORT DETAILS

Content: As part of your mini-grant, you are required to participate in the Spring Symposium. We realize the timeline for each project is a little different, so the report is really more of a presentation about your project work to date (even if you have not yet completed your project). We will add your final abstract and slides to our library website and will deposit it into *Deep Blue* (http://deepblue.lib.umich.edu/), the library's online repository of faculty and student work. In addition to your presentation, there may be other materials you'd like to submit (e.g., poster, video, website, slideshow, publication), but must include:
- **Abstract** (150 words or less)—a short summary of your overall project.
- **Presentation (PPT or Google Slides)**—PowerPoint presentation should be uploaded to this Box-Folder by noon on April 3rd.

We'd like you to address the following:

Objectives: What was your purpose? What did you hope to accomplish?

- **Challenges**
- **Real-Life Impact**—Address briefly how your project
  - o strengthened community partnerships;
  - o enhanced global scholarship; and/or
  - o advocated for inclusion and diversity.
- **What I Learned:** Address the impact of the project on you
- **Library Partnership:** How did the library contribute to the success of your project (person you worked with, resources used, etc.)?
- **Further Work:** What's next for this project?

Acknowledgments: Highlight all those (people, school/college, academic departments, teams, organizations, co-sponsors) who helped you along the way. For posters, this can be a smaller section at the bottom.

Audience: In addition to student presenters, the audience will include a mix of U-M students, faculty, staff, and invited guests. Think about the audience when designing your presentation. Keep text minimal and graphics simple and easy to read. Use your presentation time to enhance campus awareness of your work and possibly make great connections. You never know who might show up at the event or who could be a great resource for you down the line.

Licensing Your Work: Visit our U-M Library Licensing Your Own Material Under a CC License webpage (http://www.lib.umich.edu/copyright/licensing-your-own-material-under-cc-license) for more information about how to license your materials. Most students select "CC BY" or "CC BY-NC," but we suggest you consult with your primary library expert if you need a little guidance about the best choice for you.

Presentation Submission: Think about what you would like to include in your presentation. Talk through options as well as your anticipated timeline with your primary library expert. Remember to build in extra time for your primary library expert to review your materials and provide feedback. Please submit your presentations to us by **noon, Monday, April 3 to this Box-Folder**.

End of Year Survey Sent to Students

As part of your library mini-grant, we are asking you to complete a final feedback survey about your experience. Your feedback is important to us, as the data will be used to help us enhance the mini-grant experience for future recipients. This survey is brief and should only take you about ten minutes to complete. Please submit your responses by midnight Monday, April 24th.

What MLibrary resources were you familiar with before you applied for a mini-grant? (Select all that apply.)

o   Study Areas
o   Reference Desk
o   Ask A Librarian
o   Computers and/or other technology
o   Special Collections
o   Library workshops and/or instruction sessions
o   Online resources (electronic periodicals, data sets, etc.)
o   Physical resources (books, periodicals, maps, etc.)
o   None
o   Other

Please indicate your level of agreement with the following statements:

	STRONGLY AGREE	SOMEWHAT AGREE	NEUTRAL	SOMEWHAT DISAGREE	STRONGLY DISAGREE
It was easy for me to find time to meet with the assigned librarian					
The assigned librarian was available when I was available					
It was helpful for my project to have an assigned librarian					

The assigned librarian helped my project with (check all that apply):

o   Finding information about my project topic
o   Connecting with people and/or resources ON campus
o   Connecting with people and/or resources OFF campus
o   Honing the project's goals or its scope
o   Making important decisions
o   Planning next steps as the project progressed
o   Learning to use software or technology needed for the project
o   Other?

What factors influenced your decision to apply for a library mini-grant (check all that apply):
- o Funding up to $1,000
- o Opportunity to be paired with a librarian
- o Access to world-renowned research collections
- o Access to state-of-the-art design and technology labs
- o Access to library studios, exhibit galleries, and collaboration spaces
- o Ability to archive project work in Deep Blue

Briefly describe how the project experience was important to you. Consider including what you enjoyed or learned, or how your experience might inform your future projects.

What did you learn about MLibrary that you did not know before?

I would recommend this program to others
- o Yes
- o No

Please explain why or why not.

Other comments?

May we have your permission to include your responses in a library research project?

See a description of the award and links to past student projects on our library website: https://engage.lib.umich.edu/mini-grants/.

PART II.

Library Support for Courses with Applied Service-Based Projects in the Disciplines

CHAPTER SEVEN

Moving Words:
Building Community through Service-Learning in the Arts

Anne Marie Gruber
Instruction & Liaison Librarian
University of Northern Iowa
anne.gruber@uni.edu

Angela Pratesi
Fine & Performing Arts Librarian
University of Northern Iowa
angela.pratesi@uni.edu

Angela Waseskuk
Art Instructor & Foundations Coordinator
University of Northern Iowa
angela.waseskuk@uni.edu

THE ACTIVITY

Description: In this unique project, college students in a first-year Three-Dimensional Concepts art course are partnered with a local youth writing project to create short films based on participants' writings. This experience was born out of a campus Service-Learning Institute (SLI) to train faculty on best practices. The mutual goals included giving voice to area youth and connecting college students to the community. All participants explored and reflected on the importance of community engagement and citizenship by acknowledging their similarities and differences through creative lenses.

Participants from both groups generated ideas through shared journal exercises that the youth writers then used as inspiration for their written works. Art students at the University of Northern Iowa created short, stop-motion films based on the writers' works using Rod Library's Digital Media Hub. A faculty-coordinated hip-hop literacy group made up of area youth created the soundtrack for one film, providing another level of campus-community collaboration.

The goal of the information literacy portion of the service-learning project was to ground the university students in facts and data about the community, public arts, citizenship, and the community partner. By confronting stereotypes or lack of information with evidence and empathy, the authors hoped students would have a clearer sense of who their community partners were and the value of collaborating to create works of art.

This chapter will describe the project, its inception, and its exploration of social engagement as fine arts practice, learning objectives, lessons learned, and supplemental sources, including final projects. Student, youth participant, instructor, and librarian reflections will be highlighted, with emphasis on the areas of motivation, engagement, and learning outcomes, both formal and informal.

Getting Started: Inspired by university-wide conversations about diversity and inclusion, this project is a small part of a significant culture shift at the university from an already strong focus on community engagement to more formalized, systematic efforts and expanded capacity for campus work in this area.[1]

The formal development of this project began through the inaugural UNI Service-Learning Institute (SLI) in 2016, consisting of a three-day workshop held annually to help selected faculty use best practices to incorporate service-learning into a course. A hallmark of SLI is that all projects are co-created with community partners at the table. Waseskuk responded to a university-wide call for participation that had been sent to faculty during the spring 2016 semester. The program was supported by Iowa Campus Compact[2] and held great potential for addressing many of the issues around diversity, inclusion, and engaged citizenship that were currently affecting her students. Waseskuk also hoped to learn best practices in service-learning through SLI, as she was already doing some engagement work but had yet to deliberately write it into her coursework.

Gruber had been asked to present at SLI because of her research interests related to intersections between information literacy and service-learning. She had previous experience teaching information literacy sessions for service-learning courses using a model developed at the University of Dubuque; in this approach, students work in small groups to respond to questions about societal needs related to their service agency, using advanced Google search techniques and suggested resources such as government data.

In order to present a hands-on experience for participating faculty members at SLI, many of whom had never seen information literacy instruction before, Gruber conducted a session simulation. This consisted of faculty being asked to role-play as students engaging in research activities that are typically part of the service-learning information literacy model. Because part of the institute took place at the local food bank, Gruber used poverty and hunger issues as the simulation research topic. Faculty "students" worked in small groups to respond to questions about local, state, and national hunger and food insecurity issues. They made use of suggested resources provided on a research guide Gruber created with the LibGuide (Springshare) platform.

Following the simulation, Gruber presented the basics of the instructional model and rationale for the approach and offered to modify the information literacy session for various courses faculty were teaching in future semesters. She asked the faculty to verbally reflect about their research experience, focusing on information that surprised them and potential action steps. The hands-on experience for faculty was effective in helping them envision how library instruction could support their courses. As a result of the session, Waseskuk initiated conversations with Gruber about how to incorporate a research component in the 3D Concepts art course the following semester. Waseskuk had not previously realized the range of support librarians could provide for her studio art students, and Gruber's presentation proved eye-opening in this regard. Waseskuk had long struggled with facilitating motivation among her students for deeper research and the desire to draw from many resources but always seemed to fall short trying to instill this in them herself. After hearing Gruber's presentation, she realized that involving librarians was an ideal fit for her service-learning project and as a way to begin to address these other issues.

Motivations: As an instructor who works largely with first-year students, Waseskuk came to realize the limited perspectives of many students who were entering college. Many UNI students come from small rural towns from across Iowa and have not had exposure to people from diverse cultures and backgrounds. Waseskuk's classroom, most often made up of primarily first-year students, reflects the university undergraduate student demographic of 85.2 percent Caucasian students as of fall 2016.[3] While many UNI students work off campus and have pre-college service experiences, only about half reported participating in community service during college, according to a 2015 National Assessment of Service and Community Engagement survey of more than 1,800 students.[4] Waseskuk was inspired to address this lack of community connection among UNI students and developed an interest in creating holistic learning experiences to help students confront their assumptions and develop skills for responsible citizenship. Although she was teaching a formal studio art course where service-learning was rarely built into her department's curriculum outside of art education, Waseskuk wanted her students to acknowledge the importance of working with diverse populations while gaining insight into experiences that differed from their own as part of their art education. By doing so, she hoped her students would realize art is richer when rooted in the complexities of lived experiences, and that artists can and should be engaged in their communities and be encouraged to continue civic participation beyond graduation.

Concerns relevant to community engagement as well as diversity were made very clear in 2015–16 when racial tensions came to a head at the university, paralleling what was happening on campuses across the nation. Some students of color expressed concern about feeling unwelcome on campus.[5] Administrators responded immediately in a variety of ways, such as by holding meetings with student leaders, hiring a chief diversity officer, issuing a statement authored by the provost and distributed within a campus newspaper, and hosting a forum on campus sponsored by the Office of the President to begin elevating and addressing related experiences.[6] Waseskuk felt that if the university's goal was to provide a complete education and prepare students to be productive citizens who are motivated to contribute to society, then race, social justice, and inclusion must be addressed in all areas of study, art included. At the same time, students want to connect to what their assignments are asking them to do but feel that it can become difficult to find purpose in their work. Some begin to feel that their passion for art gets lost in the structure of academia. It became clear there was a need to create a space for students to gain knowledge through meaningful experiences, so Waseskuk began to incorporate these concepts more intentionally into her classroom.

THE PEOPLE

Libraries: Rod Library serves the University of Northern Iowa, a comprehensive regional university with approximately 12,000 full-time-equivalent (FTE) students located in Cedar Falls, Iowa. Within the library, there are several specialized collections and service centers designed to meet the needs of the various intellectual and creative pursuits of campus and community patrons. Included are the Fine & Performing Arts Collection, a Youth Collection, an Active Learning Classroom, ScholarWorks (the institutional repository), and a Makerspace. In addition to these resources, the library houses a Tech Desk and Digital Media Hub with specialized equipment and services, supported by the University's Information Technology Services (ITS). A focused education collection, HN Corporation Instructional Resources and Technology Services (IRTS), is part of the library system and is housed in Schindler Education Center, offering K-12 textbooks, equipment, and other resources specific to teacher education programs.

Two of the strategic goals of the library are to spark student success and to provide an excellent user experience via flexible spaces, technology, and high-quality services. Collaborating with art students and community partners on this service-learning project is one example of how the library is able to leverage our collections and services to achieve our goals, advance students' learning and scholarly outcomes, and further the library's mission of empowering and inspiring discovery, imagination, creation, and innovation. Supporting community engagement efforts has been an area of increasing emphasis at Rod Library in an effort to further connect with this priority within the university strategic plan.

Instructors: Angela Waseskuk is an art instructor and foundations coordinator who incorporates service-learning pedagogy to enrich first-year art student experiences. Anne Marie Gruber is an instruction and liaison librarian who elevates the library's role in campus-community engagement. Angela Pratesi is a fine and performing arts librarian who works at the intersection of information, learning, and the arts, with an emphasis on process.

Courses: ART1333, Three-Dimensional Concepts. This is one of the foundational studio art courses for first-year art students and includes beginning experiences in conceiving and making in three dimensions, emphasis on interaction between work and idea, skills in art making, and common vocabulary of art.

Students: Participating university students were enrolled in the foundational studio art class, 3D Concepts, primarily for first-year students and sophomores, with some transfer students included. All art majors and minors are required to complete this course, so the majority were art students going into different areas of study, such as art education, graphic design, and studio art. As mentioned in the Motivations section above, many of the students were Caucasian and long-term Iowa residents.

Community Partners: Waterloo Writing Project (WWP),[7] begun in 2015, is a local non-profit agency modeled on a nationwide initiative called 826. Its mission focuses on providing a third space for area youth, ranging from kindergarten through high school, to explore individual voice through creative writing and public performance. The volunteer-run program includes a weekly writers' workshop for students to learn about various writing techniques and receive feedback. Participants also perform their pieces at various community events throughout the area.[8]

Arts to End Violence (ATEV) is a program for area youth that provides space, opportunities, and mentors to help participants channel energy and talent into the arts, mainly hip-hop and dance, and to use creative means toward empowerment. It is an outlet to help youth avoid pathways to crime and violence. Both ATEV and WWP use the arts as a way to engage youth in creative expression, empowering them to articulate their voice and create an avenue for communication.

Finding and Working with Partners: Making community connections that grow into fruitful partnerships can happen in unexpected places. Waseskuk first learned of the Waterloo Writing Project when project co-creator Kevin Roberts, along with Alyssa Bruecken, attended a story circle event in February 2016. Roberts' story about their motivation and passion for creating a space for young authors to hone and share their voice stayed with Waseskuk throughout the semester. During this same semester, Waseskuk learned of the hip-hop literacy program, ATEV, run by Michele Feltes and Dr. Shuaib Meacham, a colleague in the UNI College of Education.

Inspired by the work of these two groups, Waseskuk began thinking about mutually beneficial collaborations. Connecting the skills she learned in the UNI Service-Learning Institute seemed like the best opportunity to partner and collaborate. Waseskuk, Roberts, and Bruecken planned the project through the summer. Waseskuk brought in librarians Gruber and Pratesi to lay the information literacy groundwork in the classroom.

The importance of a deliberate dialogue between community partners and the instructor throughout the planning process had been emphasized in SLI. Waseskuk and Roberts kicked off the project planning during the time allotted on the final day of the institute by discussing the goals and benefits to each stakeholder for a project that was truly collaborative. It was imperative that the creative voices of the young authors, musicians, and college art students were equally present and that no single vision overpowered others in the finished product. All leaders involved wanted to create spaces for the UNI students and youth authors to interact positively while ensuring that all participants would feel valued as stakeholders. This conversation continued into the summer with the addition of Bruecken and Meacham. It was through this time spent with each other that stakeholders built trust and began creating a lasting partnership.

Apart from the intentional nature of programs such as the Service-Learning Institute, meeting community partners can often be unexpected and serendipitous. Instructors and librarians who are active in their own communities will be better positioned to support campus-community engagement work. Those at other institutions may consider partnering with the community engagement office on campus to find out what projects are happening with various partners and to brainstorm how the library can support that work. While many academic libraries are creating their own engagement projects (i.e., partnering with public libraries, providing instruction for high school groups, and offering public lectures/events), supporting projects other campus entities are doing can help position the library as a vital partner for engaged learning.

Benefits

Instructor Benefits: This project had multiple benefits for all stakeholders. Rod Library saw benefits from these partnerships, helping further tie the library to the university's community engagement strategic planning goal. It enabled library faculty to support campus service-learning initiatives and encouraged faculty who incorporate community engagement to consider including library resources and services in their courses as well. Since this project began, there has been a marked increase in library instruction requests related to community engagement, particularly in the art department but in other departments as well. Waseskuk has requested library instruction in subsequent courses along with other teaching faculty who learned of the library's involvement in the project.

This experience enabled librarians to evaluate how the instructional model works in a different discipline and with first-year students. There was ample time within the 3D Concepts course for Gruber and Pratesi to teach advanced Google search techniques, as these were new to most of the students. This was an important reminder for librarians to modify instruction for various needs, including student levels and ranges of research experience.

The project allowed library faculty and staff to demonstrate ways that they serve campus in celebrating intellectual outputs of faculty and students alike. Librarians suggested and hosted a culminating learning event in the library's new ScholarSpace, designed to be a venue for sharing scholarship and creative work for the campus community. This project has provided an opportunity to add new content in digital formats, including the first-ever video materials, to the institutional repository.

Librarians benefitted from the co-teaching experience, enabling Pratesi in particular to learn new pedagogies and explore creative teaching ideas. Gruber engaged in a train-the-trainer model with Pratesi, as they worked together to prepare the information literacy session and materials, such as the small group questions and the LibGuide. Throughout this process, Gruber explained her strategies and motivations for the instructional model so Pratesi could see "behind the curtain."

This collaboration supported library faculty scholarship and service as well. Gruber is conducting research related to faculty perceptions of the library's role in curricular service-learning and this project was an important exemplar. Additionally, Waseskuk participated as an interview subject in Gruber's research. Waseskuk shared that her view of librarians' roles and scopes of practice broadened as a result of the service-learning collaborations. The librarians' experience with the project has led to increased requests for Gruber to serve on university committees related to community engagement, elevating the library's role in this area of campus priority.

Beyond the library, this and other library/faculty collaborations for community engagement have lent additional visibility to library resources and expertise on campus, including leading to both Gruber and Waseskuk being named to the campus-wide Civic Action Planning Team, which will work to elevate and formalize community engagement on campus. Institutionally, this project has been held up as an example of effective community engagement, particularly because it was co-created with the community partners from its inception.

Other librarians may consider initiating co-teaching or even simply observing others' teaching styles. Modifying or using select elements of the instructional model, such as the collaborative research activity or the Head-Heart-Hands reflection prompt, would offer some potential resources without requiring implementation of the entire model.

Student Benefits: Increasing the UNI students' experiences with community beyond campus and with diversity are major areas of focus on campus, and students articulated that this project enabled them to learn about and appreciate diversity in a community-based context. This project enabled them to confront assumptions they had about the community and it encouraged collaboration across age groups, racial divides, varied backgrounds, and creative method as artists collaborated with musicians and writers. Students appreciated becoming part of the community both at the university and beyond campus. (See the Post-Project Feedback section for additional details.)

Students had the opportunity to think about and use varied sources of information without the pressure of scholarly output/citation. As undergraduate students, they engaged in exploring what "counts" as research, realizing it might be broader than many students first consider. Exposure to campus resources was a very intentional part of the project, and the students experienced technology available to them through the Digital Media Hub at Rod Library. They connected with resources such as their liaison librarian, Pratesi, who not only helped with this project but is a resource for them throughout their college career.

Students benefitted from the opportunity to further develop soft skills, such as teamwork, communication, problem-solving, conflict resolution, and flexibility. They actively participated in the life and culture of the community and considered issues of citizenship, creativity, voice, and empathy. The art students also benefitted from added motivation to use a new art medium effectively since the service-learning component included a larger audience, primarily external to the university; students expressed a desire to honor the youth authors' work. Additionally, they realized their work can have a broader impact beyond the arts classroom and began developing a sense of the value of the arts in amplifying community voices. One student exemplified this sentiment in a reflection, stating the project "made what we did in class seem worth it. I think being able to display are [sic] artwork that has a community involvement brings me, the artist more pleasure. I feel like I did the work not just for myself but hopefully to share a personal moment with someone outside UNI." Future art teachers within the group expressed a growing understanding of how to incorporate community engagement in their own classrooms. Further descriptions of student learning and reflection are included below.

Community Partner Benefits: For the primary community partner, Waterloo Writing Project (WWP), this project served as a catalyst to engage more college students and other community members with the nascent organization. It enabled Roberts and Bruecken to engage potential student volunteers. It offered additional publicity and opportunities for youth performance to a broader audience.

It was a secondary benefit to the community that WWP participants were exposed to the university and to campus resources, such as spaces and technology. For example, youth writers had a chance to visit campus and explore using the green screen production studio in Rod Library. Performing at the Waterloo

Center for the Arts benefitted the youth participants by providing them an outlet and a supportive audience for their creative work.

Institutional Benefits: Community engagement is a strategic goal for the University. Positioning the library as a central player in supporting these efforts provides a richer experience, with the potential for improved academic outcomes, such as critical thinking, within service-learning courses. Capturing and preserving those experiences and artifacts demonstrates student learning; over time, this will serve as evidence for not only student learning but also for the university's impact in the community.

Additionally, the collaborative nature of this project serves as a model for library support of service-learning campus-wide. The project also provides an example of service-learning within a discipline that does not typically include it. In fact, it inspired other art professors to include library services into their new community engagement projects.

THE PROCESS
Expected Learning Outcomes

Learning outcomes expected were both formal and informal and were related to art, community engagement, and information literacy

Formal Learning Outcomes
ART OUTCOMES

Students will
- create imagery that effectively communicates a narrative;
- utilize compositional elements such as color, shape, movement, rhythm, and repetition to make the communication of that narrative visually dynamic;
- fully explore the possibilities of multiple 3D media; and
- learn basic methods of stop-motion animation and how to use the appropriate technology.

COMMUNITY ENGAGEMENT OUTCOMES

Students will
- work effectively in collaborative teams with both campus and non-campus participants;
- engage with technology to communicate effectively with community partners;
- engage in critical reflection to process personal experiences in the broader community;

- "recognize ... the value of the arts as a means of facilitating civic dialogue and engaging diverse constituencies";[9] and
- reflect upon their own learning in order to intentionally practice metacognition.

INFORMATION LITERACY OUTCOMES

Students will

- achieve greater understanding of the community by focusing on data;
- know how to find and discern quality resources and data using Google or other online search engines;
- challenge their current knowledge, thinking, and possible stereotypes about their communities by using the information and data they find;
- investigate the relationship between power and privilege in the information landscape in order to identify underrepresented and disenfranchised populations and their stories;
- use quality resources to inform their ideas and thinking related to their lines of inquiry; and
- find and evaluate other resources found in their own searching using online search engines and the library's catalog.

Informal Learning Outcomes
ART OUTCOMES

Students will

- acknowledge the power of art and words as an effective communication tool;
- prioritize the dialogue between art and communication; and
- understand commonalities and differences spanning generations, culture, and time.

Community Engagement Outcomes

Students will

- gain real-world project management experience;
- respond effectively to unpredictable situations;
- improve problem-solving skills and resiliency;
- develop communication skills while considering varied audiences (instructor, classmates, community partners, campus community); and
- learn about themselves as a whole person, with a focus on holistic approaches to personal development.

Information Literacy Outcomes

Students will
- learn that different kinds of information and data can be used to develop artistic ideas or solve artistic problems;
- develop empathy for others, informed by evidence they discover about their communities;
- utilize search and discovery methods using library and information literacy skills and techniques, sparking the students' curiosity so that they want to delve more deeply into specific issues they encounter; and
- learn transferable search techniques and research skills to use during their course of study at the University.

Curriculum Materials

Early in the process, the authors collaborated to guide students' preparatory research, exploring the value of the arts, the arts as citizenship, and the local community/collaborating agency. During a hands-on information literacy session, students worked in small groups to consider research questions and analyze sources. This model supports several concepts from the *Framework for Information Literacy in Higher Education* (ACRL, 2015), particularly "authority is constructed and contextual" and "searching as strategic exploration."[10]

As evidenced by faculty and student reflections (see Post-Project Feedback), researching helped students contextualize and conceptualize the project while alleviating their apprehensions about service-learning. Librarians also provided guidance for archiving the final films in the university's institutional repository and provided a venue for a panel discussion and film viewing at the end of the course.

Librarians who are interested in implementing the information literacy component of this project may consider using and modifying the authors' resources, including a course LibGuide and five sets of relevant research questions for students. These materials are described in the Step-by-Step Outline of the Project section below and full versions are included in Appendix Materials: Other Curriculum or Project-Related Materials.

Steps Involved: Prior to the information literacy session, Waseskuk introduced the project to students and described the purpose of the upcoming session. The authors collaborated to create a course LibGuide (see Appendix Materials: Other Curriculum or Project-Related Materials). This research guide included group activity instructions and links, a list of recommended resources for each topic area, advanced Google searching tips, links to subscription resources such as the local newspaper, and the librarians' contact information and office hours.

Gruber and Pratesi also prepared five sets of research questions on broad topics Waseskuk had provided: the value of the arts, arts as citizenship, youth voice, the Cedar Valley area, the Waterloo Writing Project, and writing and public art (see Appendix Materials: Other Curriculum or Project-Related Materials). Waseskuk provided feedback to modify the questions to better meet course goals.

The class met in a library active learning classroom for a research session during course lab time; the room technology enabled each group to wirelessly display their work from library laptops on a TV monitor. The librarians used approximately thirty minutes of the 2.25-hour class session to introduce search techniques and tools. Gruber introduced the small group activity purpose and instructions. Pratesi introduced advanced Google search strategies. For this class, librarians chose to focus on advanced Google searching to complement specific web-based resources that librarians provided on the LibGuide. The instruction session focused on introducing keyword searching strategies, using quotation marks, Boolean operators, limiting by site/domain, and using CTRL+F to search within a document or page.

The remaining forty-five minutes of the class session were then spent with students working in small groups of four or five students each to research and explore resources. Each group was responsible for answering one set of the librarian-provided prompts using a document shared via Google Drive and linked on the LibGuide. They were instructed to use both the suggested resources from the LibGuide and the search strategies Pratesi had introduced. The instructor and library faculty circulated during the research time to assist groups, asking further questions, talking through stumbling blocks, defining unfamiliar concepts students encountered, and suggesting search terms and techniques. After collecting information and answering questions, the students had an opportunity to reflect on what they had learned and think about what they could do next (see the Post-Project Feedback section).

Following the information literacy session, Bruecken and Roberts with WWP visited the 3D Concepts classroom and introduced through PowerPoint some of the young authors they work with followed by a workshopping session with the art students. The session was run similarly to how they would run a WWP session with open-ended prompts, asking the students to write about communities they identify with and reflect on whether those are chosen or given to them because of familial and cultural participation. Time was also included for dialogue and sharing with the group. Bruecken and Roberts concluded the workshop by asking the students to go around in a circle and list two communities they belong to without repeating any answers. This activity was enlightening and empowering as students thought more deeply and shared about their past experiences, identities, and values.

Youth and college students corresponded via Google Drive, with youth authors sharing writings and UNI students responding with questions and encouragement. Electronic methods of communication helped address some of the scheduling and transportation challenges and enabled youth authors to provide writings and have a dialogue with their college-level counterparts.

When beginning development of the film project, Waseskuk introduced concepts and best practices for stop-motion film. Students created storyboards using final writings from youth authors and spent several weeks building props and backdrops for the films. Three days were scheduled in the library for shooting films, and students used Digital Media Hub space and equipment. The students then edited their films. Waterloo Writing Project staff recorded youth authors reading their works, and the art students edited these excerpts into the films as well. The final films were passed along to Arts to End Violence, with youth from that program selecting one for which to create a soundtrack.

There was a joint screening and discussion at Waterloo Writing Project, where youth participants provided feedback on the films to ensure the interpretations were true to their intentions. The project culminated in a public red-carpet premiere and performance at a local arts center. It was important to debut the films in a recognized community space, so it was accessible and open to all. UNI photography students served as "paparazzi" on a red carpet prior to the event, and the photo backdrop the 3D Concepts students had created included the logos of the Waterloo Writing Project, Waterloo Center for the Arts, Arts to End Violence, UNI Art Department, and Rod Library. Youth from both the Waterloo Writing Project and Arts to End Violence performed, WWP directors, ATEV co-director Meacham, and Waseskuk spoke about the project goals and experiences, and all four films were screened.

The UNI students also presented their work to the campus community in the university's library through a panel discussion and film viewing. This was hosted in the ScholarSpace, which is a large meeting room designed for sharing faculty and student scholarship and creative work. This presentation was attended by faculty, staff, students, and several administrators. Waseskuk, Meacham, Bruecken, Roberts, and Gruber introduced aspects of the project and students shared their experiences and responded to audience questions.

Following the conclusion of the semester, digital scholarship staff in Rod Library worked with Waseskuk to add project artifacts to the institutional repository, UNI ScholarWorks (see Appendix Materials: Sample Resulting Projects). This collection falls within the Community Engagement and Service-Learning Institute collections and includes youth writings, the final films, event photographs, and other project artifacts.

Other libraries interested in similar projects might consider starting small by hosting events related to community engagement projects and by creating relevant collections in their institutional repositories to highlight campus work in this area. In terms of information literacy instruction, others might consider modifying the lesson based on discipline, session time, and student level. The authors have adapted this session to a wide variety of disciplines ranging from art history to public administration, and from environmental ethics to first-year composition/rhetoric. They have also offered a similar session in as little as fifty minutes and for classes with students ranging from first-year students to seniors. Regarding student level, an upcoming modification will include questions collaboratively drafted by librarians and the course instructor being further modified by upper-level students themselves in preparation for the activity. A collaborative classroom space would not be required, as this session has been conducted in traditional computer labs, large meeting spaces with a laptop for each group, and other configurations. The lesson plan, though somewhat time-consuming to prepare due to its customized nature, offers flexibility in all aspects.

POST-PROJECT ASSESSMENT

There were several methods of feedback used to measure, assess, and understand the impact and effectiveness of this project, primarily focusing on the university art students.

Methods of Reflection

The art students in Waseskuk's class completed a series of journal assignments answering prompts (See Appendix Materials: The Actual Assignment as Presented to Students for prompts and due dates). She designed the prompts so students had to engage in self-reflective learning practices to assess their own learning throughout the project.

The youth participants' writings served as methods of reflection on their own lives. When meeting with the art students in person and via Google Drive, participants from both groups had to use their personal experiences, body of knowledge, and collaborative skills to create works of art. These processes required a great deal of reflection, though in a manner different from a traditional reflection assignment in a service-learning project. The final products themselves embodied the continuous reflection of participants throughout the project.

Reflection played a key role during the 2.25-hour information literacy session. Art students answered questions like, "In the information you gathered, whose voices are represented only minimally or not at all? Why do you think this is the case? How might you gather information representing these other perspectives?" Gruber added these questions, inspired by the *ACRL Framework for Information Literacy in Higher Education* (2015) in an effort to help students think about the power and privilege issues inherent in the information landscape.

In addition, students engaged in a critical reflection activity called Head-Heart-Hands during the last thirty minutes of the class. Each student verbally shared with the class something they were thinking about (Head), something they were feeling (Heart), and something they wanted to do next as a result of their information gathering (Hands). The reflections, described below, were powerful and at times surprising, though depth and topics of reflection varied. Taking the time to reflect is a critical component of the service-learning process, and including such an activity in the session itself set the stage early on in the semester for further reflection taking place later in the course.

At the end of the semester, the library hosted a panel discussion on campus at the culmination of the project in which students described their experiences in an open-ended format for an audience of faculty, staff, administrators, and WWP coordinators. Each student briefly shared the notable parts of the experience for them and responded to questions from the audience, some of which focused on reflection.

Post-Project Feedback

Community Partners: Waterloo Writing Project facilitators Roberts and Bruecken reflected on the process and described their reactions as follows:

> "Moving Words" treated the voice of students with the sense of importance they deserve. From responding to feedback from college artists, watching their words inspire more art, posing for the cameras on a red carpet, and proudly sitting with a large community of supporters as their collaborations were shared on screen, the authors of the Waterloo Writing Project were able to engage others with their ideas and messages. The entire "Moving Words" project centered on the idea that young authors and artists have much to say about their communities and much that can be learned from others. With an audience, authorship and art can challenge, provoke, and enlighten regardless of age. Each student has something of value to say and each student has the ability to move us.[11]

Students: The UNI art students overall reported very positive reactions. While most students reported being nervous or unsure of what to expect at first, they enjoyed the experience and found it valuable to their learning. This was particularly apparent through students' reflections and their comments during the culminating panel presentation and film viewing on campus. Skills they specifically mentioned developing through the project include technical abilities with stop-animation film, a medium that was new to most of them, as well as teamwork and flexibility. There were many moving pieces and people involved with the project, so the students learned quickly that things may not always go as planned.

The ability to do research to support art creation was also unfamiliar, and they learned advanced web search techniques many students plan to use in future courses. During Head-Heart-Hands verbal reflection at the conclusion of the information literacy session, students shared a wide range of reactions. Some expressed what they saw as a contradiction between the significant economic value of the arts and what they perceived as an unrealistic expectation that artists can make a living in the arts. A few were surprised by a story about a youth-created mural that city officials painted over in Des Moines due to miscommunication. Most of the students found the information literacy session helpful in providing context for the project. For example, one student reflected, "The time in the Library was very informational, I wouldn't really have known how many resources we had at our disposal."[12] Another indicated, "The time that we spent in the library researching really helped me to get a better idea of the Waterloo Writing Project and how exactly we would be collaborating with the students."[13]

Prompted by one of the questions groups explored during the session: "Whose voices were included only minimally or not at all?" several students reflected on issues of power and privilege in the information landscape, which they had previously not considered. There were some humorous moments as well, including when one student mentioned he was thinking about the CTRL+F trick Pratesi had taught. This technique was new to nearly all the students and many followed up saying they felt excited about learning it and planned to use it in the future.

Several students continued to volunteer with WWP following the project. As mentioned previously, one such student even indicated his academic plans changed, as he added a minor in women's studies to his art education major in an effort to experience more coursework to develop his interpersonal skills. Several art education students indicated they hoped to incorporate service-learning into their own art classrooms in the future.

Instructor: As an instructor, Waseskuk found this project addressed some stereotypes she had about the scope of librarians' work and library services. She had previously neither used the Digital Media Hub to check out equipment nor used library spaces for her students' art creation process. The project also addressed some departmental stereotypes about the role of research and community engagement in studio art and gave weight and student accountability to work being done in an introductory-level art course.

During the initial information literacy session, some of the students had remarked how they felt that the reality of being an artist meant a lifetime of financial sacrifices. Through the "Moving Words" project, the students were able to see other ways that art becomes a part of people's lives and can play a significant role in building community and building a life. The myth of the lone starving artist is antiquated and unrealistic, and many art studio students need exposure to other paths in the arts to realize this. Empowerment and confidence in what artists are able to contribute locally and globally and the ways in which they can do this were alluded to through the work with their community partners.

Librarians: While Gruber had previously taught many similar service-learning information literacy sessions, she had never done so in an art course. At first, it was quite challenging to determine questions for the groups. Collaboration with Pratesi and Waseskuk helped address this challenge. The project was also a reminder of the need to customize instruction for various student levels, as Gruber and Pratesi revised some of the first draft questions with the first-year students in mind. With a course of primarily first-year students, providing fairly specific research strategies and ample work time proved important. This course led to several other faculty requests for information literacy sessions focused on service-learning research in the arts, so it has been a learning experience as librarians have customized sessions for various course needs.

Gruber piloted the Head-Heart-Hands reflection model with this course, previously having simply asked students to share one thing they learned. The authors found this reflection prompt worked well to elicit a variety of student responses focused both on content and emotional components of the project; it is also flexible enough that students hesitant to share in-depth or personal reactions could still participate.

The librarians were grateful to have had so much time allocated for the information literacy session, as well as having the convenience to work with a small class size. It was a gift to have 2.25 hours and a class of only sixteen students. Often, IL sessions may feel rushed and reflection must happen at the group level rather than giving each student time to share individually; these corners did not have to be cut for this course because Waseskuk was so generous with her class time. It seemed as though there was more opportunity to develop rapport between the students and librarians as well, aiding in reflection quality.

The librarians were disappointed that some of the technology support provided by a library partner (Digital Media Hub) did not go as expected and worked with the instructor to report the problem in the hopes of avoiding future issues. While Gruber and Pratesi were concerned that the room and equipment schedule conflicts experienced during the project would prevent Waseskuk from collaborating with the library in the future, this has not proved to be the case.

Project Assessment and Reporting Methods

Both art and information literacy skills are difficult to assess because they are so process-oriented. The final outcome may be less important than the process the students followed. In information, as in the arts, a single "right" answer may not exist. Researchers must determine when they have gone far enough in the process to come to a conclusion or final product. Assessing only a final product may be a flawed measure lacking the complexity and nuance necessary to truly evaluate student learning. Incorporating student reflection assisted with this because it allowed the instructor to have project "check-ins" at various points throughout the process in addition to the final film product. In the future, the authors will consider having community partners assist in the assessment of student learning outcomes, particularly those related to community engagement.

Formal assessment relative to the course learning objectives indicated that most students' skills improved in the areas of mastering art-making materials and compositional elements as well as specialized technology use. During the course of the project, students clearly improved in skills related to problem-solving and resilience. Students handled problems that occurred later in the project more smoothly than those that occurred early on. More informally, at the panel discussion, the art students who presented were extremely poised and reflective. While students were not formally assessed on their interactions with community partners, Waseskuk observed the small groups truly listening to the youth authors and seeking to honor the youth authors' voices. In their reflections, students were asked to compare their experiences with those of the youth authors in order to effectively translate the youth writings into film. This allowed Waseskuk to see the depth of students' critical reflection related to the community engagement aspect of the project. In terms of information literacy skills, Pratesi observed the impact in an unexpected way; she had several of the students in another course the following semester and noticed a marked difference in their research abilities when compared with classmates who had not taken 3D Concepts. The students who had research experience through the service-learning project were more proficient in conducting secondary research, especially using the specific search strategies they had previously learned and applying them to next contexts (i.e., a new database). Meanwhile, many of the other students struggled with using effective research strategies.

The primary quantitative measure—the estimated number of student hours dedicated to community engagement activities—was reported as part of the institutional community engagement tracking. The project was also held up as a successful example of external partnerships; community engagement leaders on campus publicized this success story in several ways. Waseskuk's work was highlighted by University Relations on the university's main website as an example of engaged learning.[14] This example was incorporated into efforts to encourage more faculty to use service-learning pedagogies and to better tell the story of community relationships' impact on university partners and students. There may be additional opportunities to share this project and continue similar work as community engagement continues to be elevated on our campus. Faculty feedback has been recorded and reported to library public relations staff for potential use in materials marketing the library's services.

One measure of library impact is the number of collaborations prompted by this course and the library's involvement in the campus Service-Learning Institute. As mentioned previously, half of the faculty participants in the Institute requested information literacy instruction, with Waseskuk the most deeply involved. Waseskuk requested similar instruction in an additional course during the same semester. Beyond that, two more art faculty who attended the panel discussion and film showing requested similar library instruction in their courses, and other faculty who heard about the project have been in communication with librarians about library support for future community engagement projects.

The red-carpet premiere was extremely well-attended, with more than one hundred people, a majority of whom were community members. The panel discussion was attended by about twenty-five UNI faculty/staff/students/administrators, and the discussion was particularly rich. All three authors were struck by the power of having first-year students serve on a panel to discuss their project, including their research. The students were reflective, articulate, and had powerful things to say about the personal impact of the project. While communication skills were only an informal learning objective, students clearly grew in this area, as evidenced by their performance on the panel. Additionally, this experience set a positive precedent for students' academic experience at UNI, modeling and allowing them to practice that they are expected to not only produce scholarship (art in this case) but to share it, discuss it, and expand the reach of their work beyond the classroom.

To continue sharing the story and encourage support of this and similar projects in the future, library staff collaborated with Waseskuk to include project artifacts (the films, youth writings, event photographs, etc.) into UNI Scholar-Works, the university's institutional repository. This is an important part of the institutional priorities, to elevate community engagement and share success stories on campus and beyond. This reporting method is vital to provide case studies to others on campus and at other institutions, demonstrating library support for community engagement and deep student learning.

Future Directions

Waseskuk has continued her relationship with the Waterloo Writing Project, working with them the following semester for another course, Two-Dimensional Concepts, in which the youth authors provided stories of their experiences and memories growing up in the Cedar Valley; they were partnered with first-year UNI art students who took inspiration from the authors' writings to create accompanying illustrations. This project is part of the national Facing Project, "a non-profit that connects people through stories to strengthen communities" and provides "tools, a platform, funds, and inspiration so communities can share the stories of citizens through the talent of local writers, artists, and actors."[15] The resulting book, *Running Past the Trees: Facing Childhood and Adolescence in Iowa's Cedar Valley*, is included in the Rod Library print collection as well as in UNI ScholarWorks.[16] Waseskuk has developed partnerships with other organizations with the hope of connecting her students to the community through service-learning in the art curriculum.

Future considerations for Waseskuk include creating a rubric to further formalize assessment in her courses of student-learning objectives related to art, community engagement, and information literacy. She also would like to explore options to incorporate short videos of participants to facilitate conversations between the youth writers and art students. From a library standpoint, Gruber plans to continue collaborating with other librarians and teaching faculty to offer information literacy sessions for service-learning courses across the curriculum. These requests are likely to increase as Gruber continues her involvement with various community engagement efforts on campus. As IT-provided services located in the library continue to change, the authors will need to be flexible regarding spaces and technology access.

Gruber is currently completing a study of faculty perceptions of library's role in service-learning and intends to map this instructional model to the ACRL Framework in a more detailed manner. She would like to connect information literacy to service-learning theories and frameworks, as libraries are only very minimally represented in the community engagement literature to date. Future research could be done to rigorously investigate the impact of hands-on secondary research activities and information literacy instruction on students' engagement with service-learning projects.

Difficulties Encountered

This was a new project with many moving parts, so there were challenges in every step in the process. Attempting to coordinate multiple schedules inside and outside of the university proved a daunting task—one that did not have clear solutions. The community partner, students, and instructor all faced difficulties during the experience, which can serve as lessons moving forward.

Community Partner Issues: Facilitating personal connections between the young authors and the art students presented an initial challenge. Aligning schedules in order to facilitate student relationships was an issue that was never completely resolved. Bruecken, Roberts, and Waseskuk relied on shared Google documents for author-artist communications. This worked but was not ideal, and the group discussed how to use this platform more effectively in the future.

The underestimation of time needed to complete the films became an issue when it came to handing the projects over to the Arts to End Violence youth musicians. Being faced with the task of writing, performing, and recording four new songs in a condensed amount of time proved more daunting and less manageable than when the project was initially discussed. Meacham, ATEV program director, addressed this issue by sharing the four films with the musicians and asking them with which film they felt most connected. They chose the film *Life in Color*. The result was an impressive original song crafted to accompany the film, filled with a powerful narrative that was fitting for the visual narrative. Had they tried to force four new songs to happen, the result would have been superficial. One film already had an original song accompanying it, written and recorded by an author at the WWP. The filmmakers of the remaining two films used royalty free music in their films.

Student Issues: The Waterloo Writing Project met every Sunday afternoon, which was when many of the art students were traveling back to campus or preparing for the week, and Waseskuk's class met on Tuesday and Thursday mornings when the youth authors were usually in school. Bruecken, Roberts, and Waseskuk scheduled WWP sessions that art students could attend; however, it still proved to be a challenge to encourage the art students to take time on their Sunday afternoons to attend. Many of Waseskuk's students were first-year students with limited access to vehicles and were apprehensive using public transportation.

It was not just transportation that kept the art students from engaging with the WWP authors. A Sunday afternoon was scheduled with the Rod Library Digital Media Hub for the WWP authors to visit campus to learn and engage with the library's green screen technology alongside the art students. Even with the WWP coming to campus, only one art student attended. In speaking with her students during the following class period, Waseskuk learned that students encountered barriers such as work schedules, homework, and travel time back to campus after being away for the weekend. The challenge lies in motivating students to overcome these hurdles, to prioritize opportunities for partnering with outside entities, and to value face-to-face time outside of the classroom. Perhaps if a relationship is better nurtured up front, beyond the Google document solution, students will be more apt to prioritize time in their schedules to connect with the youth personally.

Instructor Issues: In addition to the challenges of facilitating student schedules, Waseskuk had to navigate a lack of clear communication with the Digital Media Hub staff. Room and equipment access became an issue when the art students began shooting their short films but rooms and cameras Waseskuk had reserved were not available. While this created some frustrations for Waseskuk and the art students, these experiences allowed students to develop skills in problem-solving in a real-world setting. Despite the challenges, Waseskuk has continued to incorporate service-learning into her courses.

Conclusion

This creative collaboration has supported student learning in the arts and has helped position the library as a key contributor to strong campus efforts to enhance community engagement. The instructor, college students, local youth, the university, and the library all benefitted from this partnership. College students became more embedded in the community, which hopefully will help them throughout their college career and encourage them to commit to being engaged citizens following graduation. Exposing area youth to the university and the resources it can offer, including library and technology services, can pay dividends in terms of campus-community relationships. Academic libraries can play an important role in community engagement efforts and projects, further positioning them as vital stakeholders both on campus and in the broader community.

APPENDIX MATERIALS

- Assignment as Presented to Students
- Other Curriculum or Project-Related Materials
- Course Research Guide (LibGuide)
- Sample Resulting Projects

Assignment as Presented to Students
PROJECT CALENDAR

DATE	PROJECT
Th 9/29	Receive rough drafts from writers, begin responding in Google Docs, look at Tiny Circus and Mike Pasley in class
T 10/4	3D small groups receive finished writing from writers, begin storyboarding
Th 10/6	Begin constructing film props (Angela gone to Imagining America conference, but attendance will be taken)
T 10/11	Work
Th 10/13	Work
T 10/18	Work
Th 10/20–S 10/22	Shoot film at Digital Media Hub at Rod Library and ITTC (Bring media, i.e. SD card, external hard drive to store your images and film on!!)
Su 10/23, 4 p.m.–6 p.m.	Writers and musicians will be at the Rod Library green screen production studio
T 10/25–Th 10/27	Film editing

DATE	PROJECT
Su 11/6, 4–6 pm	Filmmakers are invited to a poster making party at the Waterloo Writing Project
T 11/8	Films complete and ready for musicians
Su 11/20	Pre-screening and conversation at the Writing Project
Su 12/4, 3–5 p.m.	Black Tie Movie Premiere at Waterloo Center for the Arts
Th12/8, 3:30–5 p.m.	Presentation at the Rod Library ScholarSpace

PART I: REFLECTIONS

(100 points: equivalent of one project, graded individually). Each of you will write 4 (25 pts each) reflections. One page, typed.

A. Due Oct 11
   a. What do you already feel you understand about the Waterloo Writing Project, the Waterloo Community and the students we will be collaborating with?
   b. Reflect on the time spent with Anne Marie Gruber and Angela Pratesi in the library.
   c. What are your apprehensions going into this project?
   d. What are your goals and expectations for this project?

B. Due Oct 27
   a. Reflect on the collaborative writing process.
   b. What insight did you gain from reading the students' writings?
   c. When were moments you felt you identified with what was written and when was it difficult to connect to the writing?

C. Due Nov 10
   a. How were you able to translate the writers' words into imagery?
   b. What did you gain from working with a group of your peers and what was most difficult about the collaborative process?
   c. Do you feel you were able to convey the spirit of the writings into visual form?
   d. Reflect on the filmmaking process.

D. Due Dec 6
   a. Reflect on the movie premiere.
   b. What would you most like to share with other students and faculty at UNI about your experience with this project?
   c. Final reflection on the entire project.

PART II: FILM

(100 pts, graded as a group)

> You will turn in your storyboard sketches along with the finished film.
>
> A. Craft (25 pts)
>
> B. Ability and willingness to collaborate (25 pts)
>
> C. Integration of your vision with the vision of the writers (25 pts)
>
> D. Visual impact and cohesion (25 pts)
>
> • Your team will need to consider the following formal elements: color, shape, volume, real and implied movement, positive and negative space.
>
> • Your team will need to consider the overall concepts of your film: What is the story being told? Is there room for the viewer to come to their own conclusions? What do you feel when you read the writings and do these feelings come through in your film?

Other Curriculum or Project-Related Materials

> **GROUP 1: DEFINITIONS & THE VALUE OF THE ARTS**
>
> 1. What do the "arts and humanities" departments include at UNI?
> 2. What do statistics show regarding the economic impact of the arts nationally? In Iowa?
> 3. How does participating in the arts (including arts education) influence academic achievement/success for K-12 students?
> 4. Our class is partnering with a non-profit organization that helps youth engage with creative work (writing). Find some examples of how the arts, including creative writing, influence kids/youth.
> 5. How is creative writing connected to literacy for K-12 students?
> 6. What kinds of learning do youth do outside of school? What are they learning and through what sorts of activities?
> 7. (Complete this question after all previous questions for your group.) In the information you gathered, whose voices are represented only minimally or not at all? Why do you think this is the case? How might you gather information representing these other perspectives?
> 8. (Complete this question after all previous questions for your group.) Add at least 3 additional questions. What else do you want to know about the topic?

GROUP 2: THE ARTS AS CITIZENSHIP/YOUTH AS CITIZENS

1. What is civic engagement? Provide some examples of how the arts can contribute to civic engagement.
2. Provide some examples of programs that encourage youth civic engagement. What are the potential impacts?
3. Explain the concept of youth voice. What are the goals of the youth voice movement?
4. Provide some examples of how creative writing and civic engagement are connected.
5. Find some articles about a recent misunderstanding relating to a school project in Des Moines to create a mural. What lessons does this situation illustrate about public art? Non-traditional forms of art? About youth participation in creative expression? Provide some positive examples of similar projects.
6. What are some potential social impacts of the arts? How are these measured?
7. (Complete this question after all previous questions for your group.) In the information you gathered, whose voices are represented only minimally or not at all? Why do you think this is the case? How might you gather information representing these other perspectives?
8. (Complete this question after all previous questions for your group.) Add at least 3 additional questions. What else do you want to know about the topic?

GROUP 3: THE CEDAR VALLEY & WWP

1. Our partner is Waterloo Writing Project. What programs do they offer? Who are the typical participants? (Be sure to use sources in addition to the organization's website. For example, try searching for newspaper articles, videos, etc.).
2. What benefits does participation in Waterloo Writing Project provide? Are there costs or potential barriers to participation?
3. What cultural opportunities are available in the Cedar Valley (Cedar Falls & Waterloo area)?
4. Our class will be partnering with a non-profit agency in Waterloo. What should we know about Waterloo? What is there to do there? Arts venues? Main employers?
5. Are there local organizations that provide arts education in Cedar Falls & Waterloo? For children? For adults? If so, what?

GROUP 3 (CONTINUED)

6. What can you learn about the population of Black Hawk County (where Cedar Falls & Waterloo are located)? Compare population demographics in Waterloo to the hometown of one group member. How do populations compare?
7. (Complete this question after all previous questions for your group.) In the information you gathered, whose voices are represented only minimally or not at all? Why do you think this is the case? How might you gather information representing these other perspectives?
8. (Complete this question after all previous questions for your group.) Add at least 3 additional questions. What else do you want to know about the topic?

GROUP 4: WRITING & PUBLIC ART PROJECTS

1. Provide some examples of how Cedar Falls and Waterloo schools have incorporated writing in creative ways. How is UNI involved?
2. Provide some examples of writing projects involving youth. What are the goals?
3. What is college-ready writing? Why is it important? Do programs that focus on it work?
4. What resources are available for youth filmmakers?
5. What is public art? What forms can it take? Provide some examples of organizations that advance public art. How do they do so? (Think about the ethics of public art.)
6. What are some common barriers to arts attendance/participation?
7. (Complete this question after all previous questions for your group.) In the information you gathered, whose voices are represented only minimally or not at all? Why do you think this is the case? How might you gather information representing these other perspectives?
8. (Complete this question after all previous questions for your group.) Add at least 3 additional questions. What else do you want to know about the topic?

Course Research Guide (LibGuide)

Students used suggested resources in information literacy session and responded to questions, all linked from this guide. Available at: http://guides.lib.uni. edu/3DConcepts.

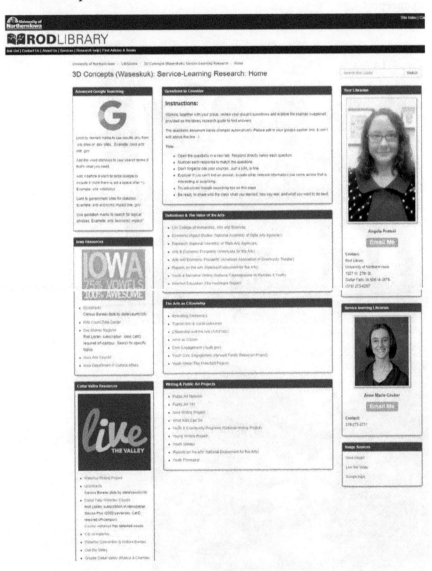

Sample Resulting Projects

Resulting projects, including youth authors' writings and drawings, art students' final films, and photographs from the red-carpet premiere, are all available in the institutional repository, UNI ScholarWorks, at: http://scholarworks.uni.edu/tdconcepts/.

Several representative photographs are included below.

Notes

1. The University of Northern Iowa (UNI) has a long history of strong community engagement, and there is significant synergy and growth on campus about this topic. UNI is one of just 361 institutions nationwide to be awarded The Carnegie Foundation's Community Engagement Classification and has been named to the President's National Community Service Honor Roll six times, each year since the Honor Roll's inception. In that timeframe, 34,308 students served more than 2.3 million reported hours. During the 2015/16 academic year alone, 12,913 UNI students completed 873,891 reported hours. The Honor Roll has also recognized UNI with Distinction twice (2013, 2015), as a finalist twice (2011, 2013), and as the Economic Opportunity Award recipient (2016). Julianne Gassman, e-mail message to Anne Marie Gruber, February 7, 2017.
2. "Iowa Campus Compact (IACC) is a statewide association of college and university presidents providing leadership for the civic mission of higher education. Iowa Campus Compact strengthens the capacity of member colleges and universities to prepare all students to become engaged citizens." "Who We Are," *Campus Compact Iowa*, accessed June 28, 2017, http://iacampuscompact.org/who-we-are/.
3. "2016 UNI Fact Book," *University of Northern Iowa*, accessed February 2, 2017, https://uni.edu/president/sites/default/files/2016-UNI-Factbook.pdf.
4. Mathew Johnson and Donald Levy, "2015 National Assessment of Service and Community Engagement (NASCE)," (report from the Siena College Research Institute, University of Northern Iowa, June 11, 2015).
5. Nick Fisher, "Dear Future Panthers," *Northern Iowan*, November 9, 2015, http://www.northerniowan.com/3072/showcase/dear-future-panthers/.
6. James Wohlpart, "Provost Pens Response on Racial Justice Forum, Black Lives Matter," *Northern Iowan*, November 12, 2015, http://www.northerniowan.com/3088/opinion/provost-pens-response-on-racial-justice-forum-black-lives-matter/.
7. "Waterloo Writing Project," Waterloo Writing Project, accessed June 30, 2017, http://www.waterloowritingproject.com/.
8. Christina Crippes, "Waterloo Writing Project Gives Youths a Voice," *The Courier*, April 17, 2016, http://wcfcourier.com/news/local/education/waterloo-writing-project-gives-youths-a-voice/article_143f99be-b1a1-5238-975f-88117f4a02dd.html.
9. Tufts University, "Student Civic Learning Outcomes," accessed June 30, 2017, http://activecitizen.tufts.edu/wp-content/uploads/learning_outcomes_13.pdf.
10. Association of College and Research Libraries, *Framework for Information Literacy in Higher Education*, accessed March 22, 2017, http://www.ala.org/acrl/sites/ala.org.acrl/files/content/issues/infolit/Framework_ILHE.pdf.
11. Waterloo Writing Project Directors, e-mail message to Angela Waseskuk, April 17, 2017.
12. Student B, "Reflection 1" (student reflection assignment, University of Northern Iowa, October 11, 2016), 1.
13. Student C, "Reflection 1" (student reflection assignment, University of Northern Iowa, 2016), 1.
14. Karlene Izer, "Service Learning in Motion," Office of University Relations, last modified June 5, 2017, https://uni.edu/resources/features/service-learning-motion.
15. "About the Facing Project," The Facing Project, 2017, http://facingproject.com/about/.
16. "Running Past the Trees Project," UNI ScholarWorks, 2017, http://scholarworks.uni.edu/sli_trees/1/.

CHAPTER EIGHT

A Storied Tale:
Melding Digital Storytelling, Service-learning, and Digital and Information Literacy Skills for Pre-Service Teachers

Heather Beirne

Associate University Librarian
Eastern Kentucky University Libraries
heather.beirne@eku.edu

THE ACTIVITY

Description: This chapter explores how an education librarian partnered with an elementary education faculty member at Eastern Kentucky University (EKU) to facilitate digital storytelling-based service-learning in an Introduction to Children's Literature course for pre-service elementary teachers. The librarian supported this course and its service-learning component by collaborating with the faculty member on assignment design and via strategic library instructional support for the digital storytelling service-learning projects assigned. Their long-term goals included instilling competence and confidence in students regarding their own digital and information literacy skills and empowering them to take these skills forward into the field to use in the classroom and share with future K-12 students. Also important was the development of the skill of recognizing school librarians as ideal and strategic partners in information literacy instruction and technology-based pedagogy.

The service-learning projects done by EKU's children's literature students required them to create digital stories with some kind of an impact in the local community. Over the course of several semesters, they included life story video projects for local elderly nursing home residents, horse story video projects about and for use by the Kentucky Horse Park and Central Kentucky Riding for Hope, and video projects about—and for use by—various local historical sites and organizations.

Getting Started: Cultivating meaningful partnerships with faculty is essential in setting up opportunities for academic service-learning. In spring 2012, as a newly minted academic librarian, I was approached by an elementary education faculty member about integrating digital storytelling into her course. The instructors for LIB 301, Children's Literature, were interested in shaking up their assignments and incorporating some technology-based projects and goals into their students' learning. They thought the library could support these goals. Though I didn't know much about digital storytelling at the time, I was eager to please, willing to learn, and wanted to help assist one particular instructor's students with the development of digital book talks, their first digital storytelling assignments. We decided we would learn together, and it was the beginning of a fruitful partnership involving digital storytelling, education students, and the library.

In fall 2012, my College of Education colleague invited me to a meeting with a contact of hers at the Kentucky Horse Park in nearby Lexington, Kentucky, about the possibility of having our students apply their digital storytelling skills to a real-world project there in the park. This resulted in our first collaboration with a third-party organization and marked the beginning of the service-learning era of the Children's Literature course. It was at this point that the goal of their digital storytelling assignments became community-focused rather than specifically book-focused.

That fall, the LIB 301S students assembled into groups, traveled to the Kentucky Horse Park, met, photographed, and filmed some of the equine residents of the park while interviewing their handlers, and then created biographical digital stories starring the horses. Their digital stories, which were geared toward children and highlighted facts about horses, then became digital learning resources for the Kentucky Horse Park to use to educate their young visitors. At the time, the videos were specifically incorporated into the exhibits at the Kentucky Horse Park's Children's Barn; visitors could use a QR code posted on a horse's stall to view the digital story about that horse. Finally, students created a website using Weebly to display their finished projects: http://horseytales.weebly.com/index.html.

Over time, student projects became more complex and varied. Eventually, the course officially became a service-learning course with an "S" designation. After the students had told all the horses' stories and could do no more at the Kentucky Horse Park, my faculty partner and I looked into other local horse-related organizations (this being Kentucky), continuing our work for a few semesters at another organization called Central Kentucky Riding for Hope (CKRH), located in Georgetown, Kentucky. According to their website, CKRH is "dedicated to enriching the community by improving the quality of life and the health of children and adults with special physical, cognitive, emotional and social needs through therapeutic activities with the horse." At CKRH, students were tasked with creating videos that the organization could use to explain and promote what they do, particularly to school-age children, bringing awareness to their organization as well as greater understanding for people with special needs. From that collaboration, our service-learning students produced videos like this one, titled "Dallas the Cowboy" (https://safeshare.tv/x/HMKrhlQwEW), in which students told the story of a young CKRH client from the perspective of his CKRH therapy horse, Kyky.

Each subsequent semester thereafter, the projects have changed and diversified. In spring 2014, groups of EKU students were assigned an elderly resident of Richmond, Kentucky's McCready Manor and directed to tell that person's life story as a digital story. The culminating event of that semester was a "red carpet" premiere in which the students debuted their videos for the residents and their families, many of whom came from out of state. That night, between fifty and sixty people packed into the room to see their loved ones honored. Copies of the videos on DVD-R and thumb drive were highly requested commodities.

Other ongoing projects since then have included work with local historical sites in Richmond, Kentucky, to create history-related promotional and educational videos. For this project, our students found themselves spending a lot of time in the Special Collections & Archives at EKU Libraries, as they researched local primary sources to incorporate into their videos, another layer of information literacy pedagogy.

Motivations: Today's teachers, a diverse body of individuals with a variety of technological backgrounds and skill sets, often find themselves working from a "digital immigrant" perspective. Even pre-service teachers, who may be classified as digital natives, report "strong positive beliefs in technology, yet moderate confidence and reserved attitude in using technology."[1] Lei reports that, though they are often viewed as "innovative users of available technology and eager adopters of new technology,"[2] pre-service teachers are also not utilizing digital technology to its fullest advantage, self-report that they do not feel comfortable with or proficient at the use of higher-level technology, let alone with using it pedagogically, strategically, "critically, wisely, or meaningfully,"[3] and are not aware of the scope of its capabilities, particularly those related to the field of education. Similar studies show pre-service teachers struggle with information literacy topics such as locating, evaluating, and effectively and ethically using and attributing information, particularly for classroom use.[4]

A strategic partnership between the course instructor and myself provided the chance to co-create an authentic, extended, experiential learning opportunity in which students gained practical, teacher-centered technology and information literacy skills while doing good in their community.

Through service-learning, students would be able to combine service with pedagogically useful technology skills and information literacy skills to produce digital videos for an "authentic audience."[5] When students not only create a digital story but create a digital story as an act of service, the authentic audience of those they are serving puts them into true "learn mode." They are called upon to actively synthesize, create, evaluate, locate, and gather information about their subject, amass and organize content, include only copyright-friendly media, and select appropriate content in order to construct meaning for their potential viewers. As they struggle productively through this process and experiment with what works and what doesn't, the act of creating their digital story forces them to become more comfortable with technology.

Regarding designing assignments that take advantage of the "authentic audience" concept, Burns explains, "One of the reasons we want to establish authentic audiences for students is so real people can view and interact with the projects students create. We want to take student work out of a pile of papers (or a hidden digital folder) and place it in the real world. Because when we establish authentic audiences for students, they can see the purpose for their work."[6] Because of this concept of "authentic audience," it is easy to see why digital storytelling is such a perfect match for service-learning.

THE PEOPLE

Library: Eastern Kentucky University Libraries (EKU Libraries) includes the John Grant Crabbe Main Library, the Elizabeth K. Baker Music Library, and the Business Library. It serves Eastern Kentucky University (EKU), a mid-sized, regional, comprehensive, public university located in Richmond, Kentucky, which offers a variety of undergraduate and graduate degrees taught face-to-face at the main campus or at one of its satellite campuses or online.

EKU Libraries' Learning Resources Center (LRC) is EKU's curriculum materials center or education library, located inside the John Grant Crabbe Library. The LRC provides access to materials that are appropriate for use by K-12 students as well as professional materials intended for use by EKU's pre-service teachers. Our collection includes K-12-appropriate books and manipulatives, teaching materials, puppets, games, puzzles, models, kits, textbooks, and many other items for circulation to students, faculty, and staff. The LRC also facilitates access to the library's education databases via online research guides, tutorials, help at our service point, and library instruction, typically performed in one or more one-shot sessions by one of two full-time education librarians (of which I am one). The education librarians provide information literacy instruction for education students at all levels on topics such as using the databases to find articles, evaluating information, and selecting appropriate and relevant K-12 books and materials, both online and physical, for classroom use. We strive to make library instruction sessions as focused on the practical as possible while still tackling big-picture, critical thinking and information literacy concepts relevant to the needs of twenty-first-century teachers.

Instructors: LIB 301S: Children's Literature (with a service-learning component) is taught by an elementary education faculty member in the School of Clinical Educator Preparation, specifically in the Curriculum & Instruction Department. One of two education librarians in EKU Libraries' Learning Resources Center traditionally provides support for the course. This has typically included multiple library instruction sessions on various topics, in addition to a digital storytelling session, reference help, technology support, and an assignment design consultation each semester. In this consultation, the education librarian meets with the faculty member to re-examine and refine the various course assignments so that they most intentionally and strategically incorporate the librarian and best practices in pre-service teacher information literacy.

Students: LIB 301S is required of all elementary education majors and is usually taken sometime between the sophomore and senior year.

Community Partners: Each semester, the course instructor for LIB 301S chooses potential community partners based on a variety of factors. These include personal connections, geographical proximity for ease of travel for students, their ability to accommodate large numbers of students coming and going, the applicability of storytelling and digital storytelling to the nature of their mission and needs, and possible curricular connections to K-12 learning for the purposes of modeling future partnerships for teaching students.

The service-learning projects done by EKU's children's literature students require them to create digital stories with some kind of an impact in the local community. The course instructor chooses and connects with each community partner prior to the semester to focus and structure the digital storytelling assignment around their legitimate needs. However, for the most part, student groups are required to contact the organization to schedule times to visit and conduct their work.

Finding and Working with Partners: In order to initiate and then to sustain a healthy service-learning direction for a course or program, the course instructor and any campus partners must be on the lookout for potential partners and add local contacts to the list of possible community collaborators when the opportunity arises. During a recent semester, after some program changes, the student roster for LIB 301S swelled to four sections with a total of about one hundred students. It can be challenging to always have a nascent project that will accommodate large numbers of students lined up in the pipeline but it is necessary in case a partnership falls through suddenly.

In addition, classes of students may eventually complete a given project, so the prospects for working with that particular community partner will be exhausted and it is necessary to have a new one to replace it. One recommendation for keeping your Rolodex packed with community contacts and fresh project ideas is to present or speak regularly about your service-learning project at regional academic or service-learning conferences, local relevant events, and any other opportunity that presents itself, specifically mentioning your need for a continuous supply of community participants.

Having three or four concurrent service-learning options for students to choose from also helps project coordinators avoid some of the inevitable logistical pitfalls. It is also important to be transparent about logistical issues with students, as teacher candidates will share the struggle of maintaining a steady stream of possibilities as they embark on future K-12 service-learning projects. Facilitating them in making connections in their community now via service-learning is a great way to ensure that they begin forging these connections early, which should help mitigate this issue.

Benefits

Instructor Benefits: The new ACRL Framework calls librarians to be information literacy facilitators, advocates, and partners, collaborating more deeply with faculty and mentoring students as they navigate an information environment that is becoming increasingly participatory and less static and hierarchical.[7] Accordingly, librarians must go above and beyond the one-shot model of library instruction by "creating a new cohesive curriculum for information literacy, and in collaborating more extensively with faculty."[8] Through the intentional, synergetic redesign of instruction, assignments, and courses, librarians will truly and authentically empower students to engage in deep learning about topics in information literacy.[9]

Service-learning provides just such an opportunity for librarians, faculty, and their students to collaborate intentionally for meaningful and engaged learning beyond a single one-hour library instruction session.

The ultimate goal for library instruction in the College of Education, for us, has been to strategically embed library advocacy within our pedagogy. We strive to be "intentional in demonstrating effective pedagogical use of educational technology in a way that cultivates a strong, collegial relationship between teachers and school librarians for years to come,"[10] as "this relationship benefits teachers and librarians, but first and foremost, generations of K-12 students."[11]

Student Benefits: The LRC's mission is to model both the form and function of the school library for College of Education students. The larger goal is to inculcate pre-service teaching students with a fuller understanding of the purpose of school librarians as both competent K-12 teacher colleagues and teacher support professionals whose expertise is not simply limited to the important but conventional role of student literacy support but also includes command of twenty-first-century learning skills instruction for both K-12 students and their teachers. The continuing expansion of information demands that all individuals acquire the thinking skills that will enable lifelong learning. Toward this end, AASL's Standards for the 21st-Century Learner illustrates the ways in which school librarians must "collaborate with others to provide instruction, learning strategies, and practice in using the essential learning skills needed in the 21st century."[12] Imparting twenty-first-century skills to our pre-service teaching students is necessary for their development as teachers, and modeling such skills is essential for teaching teacher candidates how to use the librarians in their lives most optimally for their professional success and the success of their students.

Guiding students toward metacognitive critical thinking and "productive struggle" in instruction sessions is a tall order when divorced from some sort of meaningful context, which service-learning can provide, as it supplies a dynamic opportunity for faculty and librarians to collaborate toward all of these ideals.

Since quality assignments from the faculty member represent step one in the design of a meaningful learning experience for students, it is the job of librarians, where possible, to liaise and collaborate with faculty members to intelligently and purposefully design assignments (perhaps using the ACRL Framework as a starting point) that lead students to meaningfully self-reflect as they seek, evaluate, and communicate information. From there, we can co-design activities for library instruction sessions that hold special relevance, thanks to the service-learning context.

Digital storytelling, a common assignment for pre-service teaching students and, in turn, for K-12 students, is defined by Heo as "a branch of storytelling that uses digital media resources to tell a story,"[13] on virtually any topic or content area that may be "expressed through art, oral history, creative writing, speaking, photographs, music, news clippings, digital videos, the Web, graphic design, sound engineering, or animation, and thus involves multiple modalities" and which "fosters higher order cognition and helps students with various learning styles by utilizing multimedia technology."[14] Digital storytelling can take endless shapes and dynamically apply to just about any subject or student age group. For example, it could take the shape of a tutorial in which students explain a concept they have learned about (such as a math concept), a digital show-and-tell or family tree project (social studies), a digital manifestation of a story or poem a student has written or a digital book talk or book trailer (language arts), a digital story that creatively and/or narratively teaches a natural process, such as the water cycle or a historical event (science or social studies, respectively). The pedagogical possibilities are endless.

Learning about digital storytelling tools and their classroom applications boosts self-efficacy in student teachers and helps them think pedagogically with the help of librarians.

Partner Benefits: Through the service-learning experience, future teachers (many of whom will practice in their hometown and in their home state of Kentucky) learn about community service organizations in their area and make local connections that they might be able to use again as teachers in their own classrooms. The whole process is designed to model a service-learning activity, or perhaps simply a field trip, that they might arrange for their own future elementary school students. Service-learning helps EKU's pre-service teachers build a foundation and a culture of real-world, locally aware, empathy-based pedagogy from which community partners will continue to derive benefits.

Institutional Benefits: Incorporating service-learning into LIB 301S has many benefits for Eastern Kentucky University. Service-learning aligns with EKU's Strategic Plan, specifically Strategic Goal #6, Service to Communities and Region. According to Goal # 6, "We will create a culture of outreach and engagement through innovative teaching and scholarship, as well as valuing engagement with our communities and regional partners. By applying our academic and professional expertise to collaborations with community stakeholders, we will improve the quality of life for the communities we serve."[15] The plan goes on to state that "engagement in our region allows us to use our skills and resources in collaboration with the community to benefit both the university and our community partners. Our outreach and engagement through enhanced communication and deeper relationships will promote an improved quality of life for all community members" and will help us "bring EKU to our Service Region" so that our Service Region will come to us (6.3).[16] In addition, Strategic Goal 1.2.2 directs that we will "focus on involving students in decision-making, research, and creative activities with faculty, scholarship, service-learning, international education, co-op, and internships." Such activities provide meaningful learning experiences for students so that they are more likely to be retained, to graduate, and, in turn, garner positive and productive attention for the university.

THE PROCESS
Expected Learning Outcomes

No matter the specific service-learning application, general expected learning outcomes for completing digital storytelling projects in support of students' service-learning goals included the following (created as a result of collaboration between the faculty member teaching the course and myself):

- Critical thinking, metacognition, and pedagogy:
  - o Students will engage in metacognitive and critical thinking as they create a digital story to engage an authentic audience.
  - o Students will understand and extrapolate the pedagogical value of digital storytelling in their future K-12 classroom.
  - o Students will understand and extrapolate the pedagogical value of service-learning in their K-12 classroom.
  - o Students will reflect metacognitively upon the service-learning and digital storytelling experience via reflective journal entries.

- Productive struggle:
  - o Students will learn the necessity of keeping up with educational technology, which is constantly changing.
  - o Students will become more comfortable with technology but, more importantly, with the feeling of powering through the discomfort associated with productive technology struggle, thus fostering a "growth mindset" around technology.[17]
  - o Students will learn to solve problems, particularly technological problems that will inevitably arise.
  - o Students will learn coping skills for problem-solving.
  - o Students will understand how, when, and whom to ask for help (professor, librarian, community partner) as they productively struggle with their digital storytelling assignment.
- Building connections and community:
  - o Students will build valuable local connections with community organizations which they can draw upon for their own K-12 service-learning endeavors in the future if they teach in the area.
  - o Students will learn how to work effectively and efficiently as a team within their groups.
  - o Students will learn about civic responsibility.
  - o Students will gain insight into global understanding, empathy, and citizenship.
- Information literacy/digital literacy/technology literacy:
  - o Students will select, evaluate, and implement appropriate information resources, technology, and tools.
  - o Students will demonstrate a concern for selecting appropriate materials (including digital tools) that meet the needs of children with diverse cultural backgrounds.
  - o Students will understand the valuable role school librarians have as technology and information literacy support professionals for K-12 teachers.
  - o Students will synthesize and communicate knowledge via their digital story product and will understand the value of the digital story as a tool for their own future K-12 students to communicate their knowledge.
  - o Students will learn how to use information ethically as they gather appropriate multimedia from the web (photos, music, video, etc.) to synthesize with media they create themselves while interviewing and interacting with their subjects.
  - o Students will form a foundational understanding copyright, particularly in creating digital learning objects such as their digital stories.

- o Students will begin to understand the importance of digital citizenship and the importance of passing on these lessons to their students, particularly with regard to evaluating, proper sharing, and proper attribution of multimedia materials, specifically using Creative Commons.
- Research skills:
  - o Students will understand the difference between primary sources and secondary sources, and when and where to use them (in applicable projects), and will gain a foundational understanding of how and why to teach them in the K-12 classroom.
  - o Students will understand the valuable role school librarians have as information literacy support professionals for K-12 teachers.
- Children's literature:
  - o Students will learn and apply the principles of storytelling to the digital story project.
  - o Students will understand digital storytelling as a means for promoting literacy through technology (particularly when creating booktalks, etc.).

Curriculum Materials

Before students could get out into the "field" and create digital stories about horses, nursing home residents, or local history, they needed some foundational instruction. This included content and experience that would to enable them to gain a basic understanding of the technology they could use to craft their work, and concepts such as copyright and general ethical sharing and use of multimedia found on the web for incorporation into their work, as well as general principles of designing aesthetically pleasing, well-made videos, etc. These are concepts that an information-literate individual in the twenty-first century needs to know, and they are concepts that it would be important for these future teachers to impart to their own K-12 students. Listed in the Appendix Materials at the end of the chapter, you will find

- links to Librarian-Created LibGuide and YouTube tutorials on free or cloud-based video editing application(s) and Creative Commons used to walk students through making their videos;
- an assignment description created by the course instructor; and
- a Digital Storytelling Evaluation Rubric

Steps Involved

1. **Library instruction.** Each semester, after students have been given their service-learning/digital storytelling assignment, but before students go out to their service-learning sites, I facilitate a library instruction session designed to give students a foundation in these concepts while simultaneously making a concerted effort to avoid handholding. In fact, I deliberately don't actually use class time to teach them the "point here, click here" aspects of using free or cloud-based video editing application(s); of their choosing that provide the ability to include a narrative voiceover, music, images and/or video, and a credits slide, the only required elements of the project). Instead, I strategically flip the classroom, using the class Blackboard site (in which I am embedded) to push custom-made YouTube tutorials (included in the Appendix Materials at the end of the chapter) on using free or cloud-based video editing application(s) to create a digital story for them prior to the library instruction session. The value of this is that they can also refer back to the video later when they have technological questions during their actual work process, rather than trying to force students to remember all of it before they have a frame of reference for it. In the session itself, we then engage in more meaningful, abstract thinking about best practices in synthesizing multimedia to create a polished product, and how teaching with digital storytelling benefits them and their students. Typically, we engage in four activities during class time which are built around four questions:

2. *Why is digital storytelling a relevant and constructive activity for students?* To answer this question, students view a video which demonstrates what digital storytelling looks like in practice in the elementary school classroom,[18] then do a think/pair/share activity wherein they journal about the benefits and skills they see students gaining from engaging in digital storytelling, then share with a partner, and then with the class.

3. *What makes for a "good" digital story?* To answer this question for themselves, students view digital storytelling examples created by LIB 301S students in previous semesters (approved in advance), then do another think/pair/share activity wherein they journal about improvements they would suggest that the author of the video make, as well as things they found to be effective about the video. These responses usually end up corresponding with the University of Houston's "The 7 Elements of Digital Storytelling,"[19] which breaks down many of the best practices in creating good digital stories (this page also includes examples and other extremely helpful resources), which I show the students and share with them as a resource which they can refer to as they go through the

process. Such best practices include good grammar and language usage, appropriate pacing, economy of detail, clarity of voice (and not reading from a script), use of an appropriate, meaningful, and copyright-friendly musical soundtrack, and content choice.[20]

4. *What does copyright have to do with all this?* Third, I lead students in a discussion about copyright, engaging them in a third think/pair/share about what they think teachers should know about copyright and what role they think copyright might play in their classroom when facilitating multimedia projects or otherwise. This usually leads to a lively full-class discussion as students grapple with ideas about whether they should be allowed to show Disney films in class, etc. We then talk about the role copyright plays in this assignment and why it's an important skill they and their students might gain from creating digital stories. I follow this up with a demonstration of Creative Commons Search, a site which allows the user to search sites like Google Images, Flickr, Soundcloud, Jamendo, and others for copyright-friendly multimedia to use in projects such as this one.[21] It is imperative that students understand that although Creative Commons (CC) is a good starting point, they still need to take certain steps to find CC licensing information and thus verify and interpret it.

5. *Where do I start on my digital story?* Finally, students use class time to begin storyboarding their digital story, identifying relevant copyright-friendly media to potentially use, and brainstorming with their group members about how they might start on the assignment. This gives them dedicated time with me to begin asking questions they have, also, though most often, the questions do not come until they are deep into their work.

Intentionally refraining from coddling students at this point in the process is crucial. It is important for the librarian to give them enough information to get started and contextualize the significance of the assignment, but which will then let them struggle productively as they move into the beginning stages of their work, as this helps contribute to a student growth mindset around technology.

1. **Productive struggle/work begins.** Students go out to work with their community partners and begin creating their digital story. At this stage, students often express anxiety and feelings of being overwhelmed. Typically, students approach me or their instructor and worriedly express self-doubt about having to use technology for a grade. Because the service-learning component of the assignment has, of course, been introduced at this point in the semester, they also tend to declare misgivings about that as well. Having never completed such a multi-faceted, meaningful assignment that also happens to involve technology, students are apprehensive about their ability to do what is asked of them; they are

very much in a "fixed mindset" mode (avoiding challenges and struggles, giving up easily when confronted with obstacles to success, etc.) as they begin to ponder leaving their comfort zones.[22]

2. **Required librarian meetings.** I usually end the required class session with a plug for our libraries' Ask Us service, being sure to communicate to them that struggle (technological and otherwise) is inevitable with this assignment, and that it's okay and even expected. I let them know that it's okay to feel overwhelmed; when they sit down to work and the questions come, they can seek me out for an appointment, e-mail consultation, or for assignment-related technology assistance. I also make a point of mentioning that everything I do for them is what their future school librarian will do for them when they assign a similar project to their own students. During some semesters, we required students to meet with me about their project at least once during the semester, and I felt that this really helped students and drove home my purpose as a librarian in supporting them.

3. **End-of-semester presentations.** Students present their digital stories to the class. It is kind of like a "red carpet" event; the feeling is very laid-back, and students bring snacks to share. At various points in the history of the assignment, the instructor has had students give peer feedback, and then groups of students may be given a final chance to fix any issues they may be having before they officially turn in their work for the last time. In the past, students have also presented their final videos in a service-learning community-specific setting, such as a red carpet event at the local nursing home, where the videos were shown for the movies' subjects and copies of the videos were ceremoniously presented to their family members in attendance.

POST-PROJECT ASSESSMENT
Methods of Reflection

LIB 301S students have been, up to this point, assessed qualitatively and informally on their digital storytelling service-learning projects. A rubric created by the instructor provided a means for scoring their final videos. As mentioned previously, regular, spontaneous reflections in the form of journal entries provided a way for students to formatively assess themselves (and for the instructor to do so as well) and self-monitor throughout the semester. Students were also asked to reflect on their experiences as part of their final examinations. In the future, our goal is to make assessment more formal, evidence-based, and meaningful in order to better gauge the impact that service-learning and digital storytelling are having on the desired learning outcomes.

Post-Project Feedback

Though assessment up to this point has been largely qualitative and informal, student reflections and feedback collected at various points throughout the semester, including the final exam, have shown that students do experience personal transformation in the process of creating their digital stories and participating in service-learning. In their various reflections, including several on their final exams, students were asked questions like, What did you learn? What was a surprise to you? What didn't surprise you? What three things did you not know about children that you learned? What did you learn about storytelling to children? What did you learn from working with the LRC staff? What tidbits did you take away about how a library runs that will help you in the future? What was the most moving thing that happened to you during your service-learning time? The value of service-learning is_____?

Many of the statements made by the students in their resulting reflections reflect the expected learning outcomes:

- Critical thinking, metacognition, and pedagogy:
    - o   "I learned that children love to be read to. They also love being a part of making something. If you involve them in the process they will learn more. Storytelling with kids is great.... A story can be in many different forms. It can be read aloud to them, in a digital form, or even just in pictures. They will listen and learn any way they can as long as they are engaged."
    - o   "Through my service-learning project I have learned that using digital stories and interrelated technology can deeply enhance the impact that my lessons have on my future students."
    - o   "In my future classroom I could have my students make their own digital stories to tell either their own story or about a person from history, a person they have made up, a place, and many other topics. They could use them as tools to help other children learn and it could be something they could show their parents or guardians with pride."
- Productive struggle:
    - o   "Getting positive feedback from children was really empowering. I was actually surprised at the ending product; I did not realize that putting a digital story together was something that I was able to do. It had me thinking about my future students who may also struggle with their reading; I think that this would be a great way for them to work on their skills in reading, writing, communication, and organization.... I hope to show them that they can create something that is worth being shared with other students, thus empowering them and showing them that they

can succeed in academic [sic] far better than they may have thought."

o "When I first looked at the assignment I was nervous and a little apprehensive. After completing it I was rather proud of how it looked and worked."

o "Doing my digital story was a little frustrating; I had a hard time getting the photos that I wanted. After I finally got some photos I had a lot of fun putting it together, and I found that I could see how it would be more interesting for a student to watch a quick video than read a textbook. The images if paired well could help a student link the images to the information and give them a way to read it more effectively."

- Building connections and community:

    o "Based on my service experience and the knowledge that I have gained in LIB 301, I feel that teachers can address community needs in various ways. First of all, teachers can create assignments in which the students will be serving their community. For instance, students could create digital stories or graphic novels on topics concerning their community or state, like we created the stories on the horses."

    o "I think that teachers can use the creativity and abilities of their students to address community needs. Just like we created something that will aid in a better Children's Barn at the Kentucky Horse Park, a teacher's students could do anything to help raise awareness of or raise money for anything the community may need."

    o "I learned that the Horse Park had far more to offer to its visitors than just a beautiful view and a chance to see some magnificent horses. There is a lot of information about horses, of course, but there was also a lot of valuable information about Kentucky, history, geology, and people. This gave me a chance to rethink some of the ideas I had for field trips and what I would want my students to take away from them."

    o "The Children's Barn [at the Kentucky Horse Park] is a very interesting place for children to explore and I was honored to have made something that could have a home there."

    o "As a teacher, I can increase the service-learning components and collaboration in my classroom by providing my students with the opportunity to go visit places and make their own creations."

    o "I feel that by participating in these activities I have learned how to incorporate technology and service-learning into my lessons more easily. I learned how to use software I had never seen before that I can pass on to my students."

- Information literacy/digital literacy/technology literacy:
  - "I was surprised at first because I didn't know there would be assignments. I thought it was going to be more like a guided tour of the LRC and really getting to know each part of the library and what it can do for you. I know a lot about the LRC and that is a great thing."
  - "The staff taught me through the assignments. I learned to really use all my resources. In the process of doing the core content assignment I found a way to use it in my Music for Teachers class. It all just started to click in my head."
  - "I can use the up and coming ways of technology to teach the children and pair it with the old school books. The future is changing and teachers have to learn to adapt to their environment. They need to teach children in the best way they can learn."
  - "With Heather's classes, she showed us a variety of ways to do projects. This will come in handy for my own classroom."
  - "I learned through the EKU LRC that the school librarian can be a great connection to have, and my classroom will benefit by using the library resources."
  - "I also began to think of the different activities [my students] could do to show what they have learned and ways that they could share their newly learned knowledge with their fellow students, giving them the chance to share their thoughts, and the new information."
  - "After taking this course, I feel that teachers would benefit immensely from forming a relationship with their public and school libraries. Learn what other teachers or schools are doing, and they could share ideas. The librarian may know of books or websites that fit the teacher's lesson they are planning. The librarian may learn of books that need to be purchased for the library to make them readily available."
  - "[The project] is real practice for what is to come.... The most valuable thing I learned is just to seek the resources that are available to me, use the library and the library staff as much as possible, and to provide students [with] first-hand, memorable assignments that will stick with them."
  - "When I get a teaching position I will definitely need to create a close working relationship with the staff at both my local public library and the school's library."
  - "I learned so much throughout this course. The biggest surprise was how easy and effective it is to incorporate technology in the classroom.... It was great working with the LRC staff and having a connection in such a resourceful part of the library. I am now

able to find my way through the LRC and can use its tools like the catalog and professional section to help make me a better teacher candidate."

o "The library resource personnel within the school I teach at is going to be an asset to me while I work. There are so many great tools and resources that I look forward to using in my classroom."

o "I will establish a personal relationship with librarians and let them know I am open to their assistance in teaching about books and libraries."

o "I can ask librarians to visit my classroom, talk to my students, order magazines and books, and help me find resources as well."

o "The digital booktalk really helped me realize the importance of teaching with technology and how to do that. In my classroom I want to allow my students to explore different ways to present information that interests them and the knowledge I have gained has really allowed me to broaden my ways in doing this."

Project Assessment and Reporting Methods

Though no formal assessment was done, it was clear that as students worked through the process of creating their digital stories for their particular service audiences, they honed lifelong information literacy and digital literacy skills. Over time, they also built up so-called "soft" social-emotional skills (such as empathy, collaboration, time management, etc.) and took advantage of the opportunity to build valuable community connections for their own future K-12 service-learning and information literacy- and digital literacy-related projects. This is demonstrated in the responses given by the students in their post-project reflections (detailed later in the chapter). Finally, the experience modeled important pedagogical strategies for meaningful and authentic service-learning as pre-service teaching students prepare to enter the classroom, including the benefit of collaboration with a school librarian. In the future, we have plans to assess these outcomes more quantifiably.

Difficulties Encountered

Instructor Issues: For librarians, one of the most difficult hurdles in becoming involved with a service-learning endeavor is simply initiating partnerships with faculty members. For those who teach a for-credit information literacy course, this might not be as much of an issue, but for those of us without regular, sustained ownership over a semester-long, captive group of students, becoming involved with a service-learning project means working closely with faculty members, and often it can take time and effort to establish these partnerships.

Suggestions for actualizing such relationships are similar to typical suggestions and best practices for building faculty-librarian relationships in general. First, use the ACRL Framework as a discussion tool with faculty. As previously stated, getting full value out of the framework requires deep collaboration between faculty and librarians, and service-learning provides such an opportunity. The framework, which is marketable to faculty because of its scholarly language and promotion of a research orientation beyond simple "library skills," provides an excellent starting point for faculty-librarian conversation and collaboration around information literacy. The framework gives us a common language and common goals that we can all use to productively partner with faculty.

In addition, attending regional, local, and campus professional development gatherings (conferences, workshops, or even department meetings) that are geared toward faculty, particularly when they center around the scholarship of teaching and learning, may present opportunities not only to learn about how you may be able to better serve your faculty in general but may also reveal possibilities for service-learning or digital storytelling-based collaborations with faculty. Most faculty would not automatically think of librarians as partners in service-learning endeavors, as many are unaware of the many facets of information literacy, digital literacy, instructional support, and technology support with which we are capable of furnishing them and their students. Presenting at scholarly functions your faculty will be attending provides a good chance to sell the framework and communicate with faculty about how librarians support student learning, specifically through service-learning, digital storytelling, a combination of the two, or a similar project. Once you have some experience with service-learning or digital storytelling or both, presenting about your work helps spread the word about potential librarian-faculty partnerships of all types and all the potential student benefits thereof. In my experience, word spreads quickly around campus, and the possibilities for joint interdisciplinary projects grow exponentially over time. In addition to working with education students, I have been asked more frequently to provide instruction and consult with faculty about their assignments in departments such as engineering (students made a how-to video for how to build a device they invented to solve a problem) and anthropology (students visiting Peru on a study abroad trip made a video synthesizing what they learned on their trip and how it changed their views).

Student Issues: Surprisingly, education students—even traditional students—often show an extraordinary amount of reticence and fear surrounding technology use. Regarding the importance of a positive instructor attitude and with respect to technology in particular, it is crucial not to reflect students' growing pains or negativity with respect to technology and an unfamiliar learning mode back to them, and that is often easier said than done. It is the librarian's job (and one to which we are accustomed and which comes naturally to us) to encourage students to ask for help and to always make students feel safe and unjudged when they seek help. Again, learning how to forge a good relationship with their librarian is especially consequential for education students as we are teaching them how to use library professionals to their maximum advantage as their careers progress.

In addition, librarians and instructors must demonstrate a growth mindset for students.[23] McGuire suggests that all instructors "create a supportive learning environment for …students by setting a clear positive tone," making yourself as approachable as possible by sharing personal, humanizing details about yourself whenever possible.[24] She goes on to explain that "because students so often think that we are omniscient automatons placed in their lives to make them feel inferior, why not share past academic struggles with them? Make it clear that you were not always the thinker and scholar that you are today and that you believe they can make a similar journey…. Students *want* to know that you have the same challenges that they do"[25] and this "immediately relaxes …students and allows them to focus on learning."[26]

Community Partner Issues: It can be difficult identifying a community partner who will accommodate the schedules of so many students (sometimes, between all of the sections in a given semester, there have been around one hundred students) descending upon them over the course of the semester. Grouping the students helps with the load for community partners, and it also helps to be honest with them about the kind of undertaking they face by taking on student service-learning. Often, the hassle of dealing with these students can outweigh the potential benefits, so it is good to be open, flexible, understanding, and willing to move on to other partner options if things don't work out with the organization you would like to work with.

Conclusion

The projects described in this chapter represent one possibility for meaningful and powerful service-learning. It was intentionally constructed to help LIB 301S students forge meaningful community connections that they might draw upon as future elementary school classroom teachers, learn the value of K-12 service-learning, gain valuable, pedagogically-based educational technology skills, become comfortable with the productive struggle of constantly keeping up with new technologies, develop some digital and information literacy skills (both general and education-specific), metacognitively learn about storytelling as a pedagogical tool, and grow their understanding of the purpose of libraries and librarians and their role in supporting teachers and students beyond traditional literacy facilitation. It truly speaks to the effectiveness of service-learning that we were able to utilize it as a means for guiding students toward so many varied student learning outcomes.

APPENDIX MATERIALS

- Links to Librarian-Created YouTube Tutorials and LibGuide
- Assignment Description
- Digital Storytelling Rubric
- Digital Story Images

Links to Librarian-Created YouTube Tutorials and LibGuide

- http://libguides.eku.edu/digitalstorytellingandbooktalking
- http://tiny.cc/lib301creativecommons
- http://tiny.cc/lib301moviemaker

Assignment Description
DIGITAL STORY ASSIGNMENT

Assignment: Create a Digital Story

The following websites will help you to develop a successful digital story. You will also receive instruction from one of the EKU LRC staff using digital storytelling websites and software during a class session. To begin your assignment, I suggest that you search the following website for information.

Your story will be four minutes in length and will be graded on the components of a good digital story. These include images, music, story plot, hook, pacing voice quality, dramatic question, emotional quality, economy, and point of view.

Steps:

1. Begin this assignment by perusing the EKU Libraries LibGuide (http://libguides.eku.edu/digitalstorytellingandbooktalking).
2. Then find, read, and learn about the "7 Elements of Digital Storytelling." The elements are incorporated into the rubric for this assignment.
3. After learning what the seven elements are, you will need to learn the differences between a digital story and a digital booktalk (use the tabs to find this information).
4. Watch the videos in the About Digital Storytelling box?
5. Watch the How-To Videos located under the How-To Videos tab to learn about copyright and free or cloud-based video editing application(s).
6. View some of the examples from previous students that are located on the page.
7. Next, go to the websites listed on the LibGuide to find copyright-free music and images to use for your digital story.

8. Next, I have attached a storyboard for you use as a guide for constructing your storyboard: http://tiny.cc/noelstudiostoryboard.
9. You will be using YouTube to share your digital booktalk. Instructions can be found here: http://tiny.cc/lib301youtube.
10. Finally, once you have created your video, you will then post the URL link on Blackboard. Please use as your title last name_first name_title of your digital booktalk.
11. Be sure to save your work in multiple locations. It is technology and it does crash.
12. Happy developing your digital story!

Digital Storytelling Rubric

CATEGORY	ABOVE TARGET	TARGET	TARGET/ PROFICIENT	BELOW TARGET
Points	4	3	2	1
Images 10 points	Images create a distinct atmosphere or tone that matches different parts of the story. Images may communicate symbolism and/or metaphors.	Images create a distinct atmosphere or tone that matches some parts of the story. Images may communicate symbolism and/or metaphors.	An attempt was made to use images to create an atmosphere/ tone but needs more work. Image choice is logical.	Little or no attempt to use images to create an appropriate atmosphere/ tone.
Soundtrack – Emotion 10 points	Music stirs a rich emotional response that matches the storyline.	Music stirs a rich emotional response that somewhat matches the storyline.	Music is ok and not distracting but it does not add much to the story.	Music is distracting, inappropriate, or was not used.
Duration of presentation 10 points	Length of presentation was four minutes.	Length of presentation was three minutes.	Length of presentation was two minutes.	Presentation was less than two minutes long or more than four minutes.

CATEGORY	ABOVE TARGET	TARGET	TARGET/ PROFICIENT	BELOW TARGET
Points	4	3	2	1
Voice – Pacing 15 points	The pace (rhythm and voice punctuation) fits the story and helps the audience "get into" the story. Appropriate voice volume.	Occasionally speaks too fast or too slowly for the storyline. The pacing (rhythm and voice punctuation) is relatively engaging for the audience. Good voice volume.	Tries to use pacing (rhythm and voice punctuation) but is often noticeable that the pacing does not fit the storyline. Appropriate voice volume needs attention.	No attempt to match the pace of the storytelling to the storyline or the audience. Appropriate voice volume cannot be heard or is too loud.
Dramatic question 10 points	All questions will be developed and answered completely by the end of the story.	All questions will be developed and answered by the end of the story.	All questions will be somewhat developed and answered by the end of the story.	All questions will not be developed and answered by the end of the story.
Emotional Content 15 points	The content that is addressed or issue speaks to the audience in a very personal, clear, precise, and powerful way.	The content that is addressed or issue speaks to the audience in a personal and clear way.	The content that is addressed or issue somewhat speaks to us in a very personal way.	The content does not speak to us in a personal way.

CATEGORY	ABOVE TARGET	TARGET	TARGET/ PROFICIENT	BELOW TARGET
Points	4	3	2	1
Economy

15 points | There is appropriate amount of content to tell the story without overloading the viewer with too much or without giving enough information. | There is sufficient content to tell the story without overloading the viewer. | There is an okay amount of content to tell the story; however, there may be gaps in the story. | There is too much or too little content to tell the story without it interrupting the message. |
| Point of View – Purpose

10 points | Establishes a purpose early on and maintains a clear focus throughout. | Establishes a purpose early on and maintains focus for most of the presentation. | There are a few lapses in focus but the purpose is fairly clear. | It is difficult to figure out the purpose of the presentation. |
| Digital Story on YouTube

15 points | Digital Story placed successfully on YouTube. A CD copy of the story is required. | Digital Story placed successfully on YouTube. No CD copy. | Digital Story unsuccessfully or not placed on YouTube. Has CD copy of the digital story. | Digital Story unsuccessfully or not placed on YouTube. No CD copy of the digital story. |
| Self-Reflections,

Peers Reflections

20 points | Successfully completed all the self/peer assessments and service-learning reflections. Evidence of self-reflection and critical thinking. | Completed the self/peer assessments and service-learning reflections. Good evidence of self-reflection and critical thinking. | Completed most of the self/peer assessments and service-learning reflections. Some evidence of self-reflection and critical thinking. | Did not complete the self and peer assessments and self-reflections with little if any evidence of critical thinking. |

CATEGORY	ABOVE TARGET	TARGET	TARGET/ PROFICIENT	BELOW TARGET
Points	4	3	2	1
Service-learning Collaborative work

20 points | Collaborated with service-learning partners and was able to successfully produce a digital story. Met with the service-learning partner on a routine basis. | Collaborated with service-learning partners and was able to produce the digital story. Met with the service-learning partner. | Collaborated with service-learning partners somewhat and produced the digital story. Met occasionally with the service-learning partner. | Did not collaborate with service-learning partner and was not able to produce the digital story. Did not meet with the service-learning partner. |
| Total:

____/150 | | | | |

Digital Story Images

Notes

1. Jing Lei, "Digital Natives as Preservice Teachers: What Technology Preparation Is Needed?" *Journal of Computing in Teacher Education* 25, no. 3 (2009): 87.
2. Ibid., 88.
3. Ibid.
4. Elizabeth Lee, Brenda Reed, and Corinne Laverty, "Preservice Teachers' Knowledge of

Information Literacy and Their Perceptions of the School Library Program," *Behavioral & Social Sciences Librarian* 31, no. 1 (January 2012): 6.

5. Peggi E. Hunter and Nisha D. Botchwey, "Partnerships in Learning: A Collaborative Project between Higher Education Students and Elementary School Students," *Innovative Higher Education* 42, no. 1 (2016): 86.

6. Monica Burns, "The Value of an Authentic Audience," *Edutopia*, November 15, 2016, https://www.edutopia.org/article/value-of-authentic-audience-monica-burns.

7. "Framework for Information Literacy for Higher Education," Association of College and Research Libraries, 2015, http://www.ala.org/acrl/standards/ilframework.

8. Ibid.

9. Ibid.

10. Heather Beirne and Cindy Judd, "Tech Training and Library Advocacy: Linking the Academic Library with the School Library and Turning Pre-Service Teachers into Lifelong Library Users," in *Teaching Technology in Libraries: Creative Ideas for Training Staff, Patrons, and Students*, ed. Carol Smallwood and Lura Sanborn, (North Carolina: McFarland, 2016), 211.

11. Ibid., 212.

12. "Standards for the 21st-Century Learner," American Association of School Librarians, 2007, http://standards.aasl.org/

13. Misook Heo, "Improving Technology Competency and Disposition of Beginning Pre-Service Teachers with Digital Storytelling," *Journal of Educational Multimedia and Hypermedia* 20, no. 1 (2011): 64.

14. Ibid.

15. "Make No Little Plans: A Vision for 2020," Eastern Kentucky University, http://strategicplanning.eku.edu/vision.

16. Ibid.

17. Carol S. Dweck, *Mindset: The New Psychology of Success* (New York: Random House, 2016), 8.

18. "Free Online Resources Engage Elementary Kids (Tech2Learn Series)," *Edutopia*, June 13, 2012, https://www.edutopia.org/tech-to-learn-free-online-resources-video.

19. "The 7 Elements of Digital Storytelling," Educational Uses of Digital Storytelling. University of Houston, 2017, https://digitalstorytelling.coe.uh.edu/page.cfm?id=27&cid=27&sublinkid=31.

20. Ibid.

21. "CC Search," CC Search, 2017, https://search.creativecommons.org/.

22. Dweck, *Mindset*, 200.

23. Ibid.

24. Saundra Yancy McGuire, *Teach Students How to Learn: Strategies You Can Incorporate into Any Course to Improve Student Metacognition, Study Skills, and Motivation*, Stylus Publishing, LLC, 2015, 82.

25. Ibid.

26. Ibid.

CHAPTER NINE

Public History Service Projects to Prepare Future Public Historians

Dr. Jeanine Mazak-Kahne

Associate Professor of History
Indiana University of Pennsylvania
jeanine.mazak-kahne@iup.edu

Dr. Theresa McDevitt

Government Information/Outreach Librarian,
Indiana University of Pennsylvania Libraries
mcdevitt@iup.edu

THE ACTIVITY

Description: Coursework that engages students with real-world assignments and helps them prepare for future careers is valued by most disciplines in higher education today and is recognized as a hallmark of quality teaching. Public History is an applied branch of historical study that has emphasized work place readiness as well as civic engagement and where "history is put into the world."[1] Best practices in training public historians call for a curriculum that goes beyond teaching theory to providing opportunities in experiential and service-learning as well as forming community partnerships.[2] The best public history programs provide students with experiences that will enable them to apply what they have learned to authentic projects. Such projects also foster the development of twenty-first-century skills, including collaboration, communication, and critical thinking, which leave them better prepared for their future careers.

For this service-based learning activity, Indiana University of Pennsylvania (IUP) Public History students were asked to work in teams to learn about—and help others learn about—a topic related to a decade in their university's history. They formulated a research question, investigated it, and found, evaluated, and eventually chose the most appropriate information resources to help answer the question, including consideration of primary sources available through the university archives. As they did their investigations, they were asked to develop lists of sources that they believed would be useful to future researchers who might wish to investigate similar topics and to make the source lists available through a topical LibGuide. Finally, they were asked to prepare presentations that introduced others to the topic. These presentations were also made available online through the same LibGuide. Thus, this assignment allowed students to share what they learned and provide advice to future researchers to help them better understand the history of their institution and get started in their own research. They also assisted the university archives in promoting their collections. This assignment has been refined over a number of years and used with both graduate and undergraduate history students.

Getting Started: In 2009, Dr. McDevitt, the humanities and social sciences bibliographer, met Dr. Mazak-Kahne, a new instructor in the History Department. Dr. Mazak-Kahne invited Dr. McDevitt to work with her in developing information literacy-related activities and assignments related to doing historical research in the university archives for her Public History classes.

The earliest research projects carried out in Mazak-Kahne's Public History classes related to the redevelopment of historic campus tours and the documentation of a building soon to be razed for new construction. Such assignments provided students with ideal public history-focused learning and aided in developing Mazak-Kahne as a teacher-scholar. The students taking the classes enjoyed and learned from these early assignments. However valuable these learning experiences were to the professor and students, the service element of the experience was limited. When the semester was over, the projects were filed away and the potential of such projects to assist future researchers, enrich alumni, and build community was left unrealized. The decision to use a LibGuide to make student work available online to the public allowed the projects to reach a broader audience and gave students a sense of the importance of their efforts to future students and researchers.

Also, the decision was made to include more frequent reflective activities in the class to increase the potential for deeper learning on the part of students and faculty and help the instructor better understand the totality of student experiences in order to build a better course for future students. This assignment has been used in undergraduate and graduate classes. Successful in both, it was particularly useful in the graduate course where the emphasis on experiential and collaborative learning takes on different and perhaps more significant meaning.

Motivations: Public History instruction cannot be properly done without a commitment to service-learning and community engagement. A public historian not only preserves and presents the past for the public but serves as a bridge between academic and popular audiences. Students must learn early on that their chosen career path is a vocation dedicated to lifelong learning and teaching with the public as the main audience. By engaging service-based learning throughout the formal educational process, the vocational purpose is clear.

The instructor regards this type of collaborative learning as invaluable, not only for practical hands-on student learning experience but also because it instills in students a sense of professional and personal commitment to the communities in which they work and live. It is often said that all history is local, and the preservation of local history is arguably one of the most valuable professional activities in which public historians can engage. Professionals and scholars in the field underscore the value of identifying, preserving, and presenting the past for not only public consumption but also to help shape, grow, and in some cases reinforce a community's collective identity. This project serves as the centerpiece of a course with the above philosophy driving instructional design.

The librarian working with the instructor in this class served as the university archivist at one time and was aware of the sorts of questions that those researching university history usually had. A paucity of available secondary source material related to university history often made it difficult for researchers to make sense of primary source materials available in the archives. Often it seemed as if each new researcher was re-inventing the wheel. She felt that student projects and relevant source lists prepared by them would benefit future researchers. Making their projects and lists of sources consulted more permanent and accessible would ease the research process for many and possibly lead to a better understanding of the history of the period. As added benefits, the students would also have a link to include in their CV and gain satisfaction from doing something that would have lasting benefit.

THE PEOPLE

Libraries: Indiana University of Pennsylvania (IUP) is a public university in southwestern Pennsylvania that serves approximately 13,000 graduate and undergraduate students in undergraduate, masters, and doctoral degree programs. The History Department has had a master's degree with a concentration in public history education since the 1970s and has recently developed an undergraduate certificate in this area. When creating the certificate, the faculty working group followed the National Council on Public History's "Best Practices in Public History" for developing undergraduate public history programs. In addition to the standard emphasis on public history coursework, career introductions, and internship experiences, faculty paid specific attention to finding tight relationships between an emphasis on "training in History basics," "grounding in historical content" and the aforementioned service-learning and community partnerships.[3]

Coursework in research methods, historiography, and solid US survey courses provide the foundation upon which local history service-learning projects are based. Engagement in such experiential learning fosters the further development of research skills and allows students to make connections between the local and national narratives of our collective past. The 2016–2017 academic year marked the first full year of the certificate program. The certificate is open to any major at the university but has drawn from students in history, anthropology, and even interior design.

The university library has a large Special Collections and Archives Department, which has grown through the years with assistance from history faculty and student interns, so there is a close relationship between the two groups. Given the nature of historical research, the library, and particularly the Special Collections and Archives Department, are seen by history faculty as laboratories for their students. Librarians are frequently called upon to help students formulate research inquires, find appropriate sources for their research, help professors to develop assignments related to library collections and research, and visit classes to provide library- and research-related instruction.

Instructors: This activity was developed by a public history professor and a librarian. Dr. Mazak-Kahne is the history instructor. Her teaching specialty is public history. She serves as the coordinator of the History department's undergraduate certificate and master's programs and as one of the primary public history instructors. She teaches public history courses to graduate and undergraduate students as well as classes in archival studies and museum methods.

Prior to becoming a history professor, she worked as a university archivist with special projects and outreach at a large midwestern university. There, she did her doctoral work in a program which valued a student-centered approach to student learning and training future educators in the scholarship of teaching and learning.

The librarian involved is the subject bibliographer for the humanities and social sciences, has served as university archivist, and has carried out her own historical research on university history-related topics. She also serves as a co-director for the Center for Teaching Excellence's Reflective Practice Faculty Development Project.

Courses: This assignment was used in History 420 and 605, both titled "Introduction to Public History." These courses are designed around hands-on projects to complement readings and shorter activities that introduce students to public history and the role public historians play as community preservationists and activists. History 420 and 605 are the required introductory courses to both the undergraduate certificate and graduate master's programs. The purpose of these courses is to provide the foundation upon which all other program skills are based. Here, instructors outline philosophies and general practices, such as shared authority and the value of collaboration, which are carried through all other public history courses.

Students: Students enrolled in these classes are typically students in history or anthropology or have a minor in history with an interest in careers in public history. At the undergraduate level, they are in a certificate program that emphasizes experiential learning in coursework coupled with practical experience in an internship. A number of the undergraduates continue to pursue graduate studies in a public history or related field.

Community Partners: IUP Libraries' Special Collections and Archives Department is the community partner for this assignment. This office collects, arranges, preserves, and makes accessible the permanent records of the university and other unique collections and cultural heritage materials related to the history of the institution and the region. In this way, it supports teaching, research, and other educational endeavors of the university and local community. Central to their mission are reference and outreach services that make the collections available to scholarly and community researchers and support research, teaching, and lifelong learning. This assignment could also easily be used with a local historical society as a partner. These organizations have many of the same missions and concerns as university-related archives and are often even more in need of assistance in making their resources more accessible to the public.

Finding and Working with Partners: While public history instructors might create simulations of actual practice, authentic experiences are preferable for a number of reasons. Non-profit organizations that are dedicated to preserving local history and helping their community members find information on historical topics can benefit from student research and projects. They are natural partners for quality public history programs.

Instructors may also utilize resources from their home institution. Engaging other parts of the university provides students with a familiar setting, one with which they share a common identity and one where they are most comfortable. Student ties to the institution they have chosen are an interesting starting point for understanding collective identity. It is also a natural fit for exploring the idea that "all history is local."

This project is designed to assist the University Archives by making it easier for their clients, the university, and the larger community to use their collections and to learn about university history and the history of the region. Students' projects are designed to help future investigators and researchers learn about the history of the university and begin their research. Emphasizing how this project helps the archives do its work is useful in finding partners for this assignment.

Benefits

Instructor Benefits: The local history research/LibGuide project serves as the "major" graded project for the course. Service-learning and civic engagement are central to the mission of the History department's undergraduate certificate and M.A. in Public History programs. The collaboration with the library is one of the most critical partnerships for the program. We work with regional institutions to provide similar class-focused experiences, specifically with our archives, museum, and oral history courses. However, the LibGuide project is the first introduction students have to service-learning, civic engagement, the practice of public history, and the value of working with the public.

Students Benefits: By working with an IUP-related topic, students in the public history courses work within their own community—the university—with which they have shared as well as with varying connections. They work in a controlled, welcoming environment on a subject with which they already have a curiosity. Students learn how to use primary source-driven research. Even though they have separate topics, they learn to work collaboratively as they use similar sources, and often their research uncovers materials that span multiple student interests. In essence, they learn how to be public historians through individual effort and community dialogue.

Community Partner Benefits: The Special Collections and Archives Department benefits from this student experience and resulting projects in a number of ways. Online student projects assist future researchers in getting started, increase awareness of what they do, increase use of their collections, and perhaps even increase donations. Though the department's more than three hundred record and manuscript groups are arranged and inventoried, using these primary sources is still a challenge to researchers who do not have enough background in local history to make sense of them. Ease of use of the collections is enhanced by the independent investigations of student researchers who create accessible secondary source introductions to historical topics and tips on how to best investigate them.

Integrating archival collections into the curriculum increases use of materials for this course and makes it more likely that students will use the archives in the future or lead them to volunteer there. Though the archivist is already familiar with the collections, students' research often uncovers interesting and significant documents on historic topics that he may not have been aware of, enhancing his knowledge and ability to assist users.

Researchers who are also owners of potentially useful primary source material may find the projects online, use them to understand what they have, and may even become interested in donating documents or scans of documents to the Department. The result is increased relevant documentation in the collections to help make even better sense of the past.

Institutional Benefits: The institution benefits from quality instruction, improved student outcomes and career potential, improved understanding of university history, and improved community engagement.

THE PROCESS
Expected Learning Outcomes

Students who complete this course should be able to

- develop significant historical questions relating to one period of university history;
- develop a deeper understanding of the value of local history and the importance of the preservation of the past for use of a larger public audience;
- investigate a unique historical topic using appropriate primary and secondary sources, including developing skills in finding information in archival collections;
- prepare a presentation that shares findings of historical inquiry based on their research;
- provide lists of primary and secondary source materials related to the historical question investigated and suggestions for further research designed to enhance the accessibility of collection for future researchers;
- increase understanding of the importance of collective memory/identity;
- collaborate with peers in both small group and full class environments; and
- make a presentation and finding aids available to the general public through a course LibGuide.

Curriculum Materials

The class deals with theory and method of public history. Students read a variety of sources related to the practice of public history and do hands-on assignments that require them to apply theory to authentic tasks.

Readings vary from semester to semester and between undergraduate and graduate classes. Texts provide general background on public history as a field, examples of how a community creates and engages its past and shared identity, and offer manuals for "doing" public history and the professional role of the public historian.

Three textbooks used and the reasons for using them are listed below:

- Thomas Cauvin, *Public History: A Textbook of Practice*.[4] This standard introductory text introduces varying professions within the field and emphasizes the concept of "shared authority," the understanding that there is a multiplicity of voices involved with the preservation and presentation of the past.

- David Kyvig and Myron Marty, *Nearby History*.[5] Provides a practical guide on how to conduct research and serves as a manual for locating, evaluating, and interpreting primary and secondary sources.
- Carolyn Kitch, *Pennsylvania in Public Memory*.[6] Illustrates how communities preserve their past in a multitude of ways and how those actions contribute to collective memory and identity in a state with which all students are familiar; a number of her examples are concrete to students' personal experiences.

Steps Involved

This assignment was used in undergraduate and graduate courses that are designed to introduce students to theory and practice of public history. It can be assumed that students in the classes are upper-level or graduate students who come to the class with some background in historical method or research practices in anthropology or museum studies.

- Students are introduced to the class and the assignment during the first class meeting of the semester. When the assignment is introduced, it is important to emphasize to the students the connection between this assignment and their future careers in public history, the service nature of the assignment (i.e., that their efforts will result in something that will help future local history researchers at all levels), and that their research projects and help guides will continue to be available in the future, even after the class is completed.
- During the first week, the instructor provides an overview of the historical period. A guest speaker who is an expert on the local history of the period visits the class and provides more context. By the end of the first week, students are expected to pick a general topic for investigation. Though the topics will shift and focus in the course of the semester, the instructor encourages students to stay with the topic chosen for the rest of the semester.
- In the first few weeks, students are asked to complete two assignments designed to introduce them to how material is organized in an archive and the challenges inherent in finding information there. It also helps them understand the difficulties local history researchers experience when they attempt to find information on public history topics. The assignments are the Inventory Investigation and a History Detective scavenger hunt.
    - o Inventory Investigation. After students have decided upon a general topic to investigate, they are asked to examine archival collection descriptions (inventories) to assess their value for doing research

on the historical topics chosen by them or their classmates. They then write up their analysis and post to the class learning management system forum. Discussion follows completion of the inventory investigation assignment, including taking note of which inventories/collections are most significant for their research and would be most valuable to someone else who might want to investigate a similar topic. Some discussion of the difficulties working with these finding tools and primary source materials presents, and how what they are doing mirrors the research process of the professional historian, is also invited.

- o   History Detective. The History Detective scavenger hunt assignment asks students to search for basic information on university history, such as the name of the yearbook or how many students were on campus during a specific time period. The final questions on the scavenger hunt are reflective and ask students to consider the difficulty of finding information on university history. These are designed to lead them to consider how this can be made easier for users.

- After students complete this assignment, the instructor and librarian lead a large group discussion on what answers students found or were unable to find, what their search process was, and what difficulties they encountered as they did their research. Finally, they considered the authority and appropriateness of the information located. During the discussion, the librarian gathers lists of useful search tools and resources that are mentioned. These are used to begin the university history LibGuide.

- Students begin working on their projects early on in the semester and are given some time during regularly scheduled class periods to visit Special Collections and Archives to work on research. The librarian stops by during these class periods to ask if they have any questions and ask how things are going.

- At the midpoint of the semester, students are given a reflective prompt about how their research is going and how they feel about doing it.

- Two-thirds of the way through the semester, students are asked to provide a full description of their topic, a historical image that represents it, and an annotated bibliography of primary and secondary sources that they will be using to do their research. They also make an appointment to meet with the librarian so she can work with them to build the LibGuide pages for each of their topics.

- When they have completed their research project, students are asked to complete a final personal reflective essay where they reflect upon their service-learning and research experience.

- On the final day of class, students provide a PowerPoint presentation outlining their findings. Any local history experts brought in during the course of the semester and the librarian collaborator are invited to attend the presentations. Discussion of what they felt were the benefits of the assignment to them and future researchers and things that were good about, or could be improved in the way the course was offered, occurs during this class session.
- Completed presentations and resource lists are made available through course LibGuide.

POST PROJECT ASSESSMENT
Methods of Reflection

Students reflected upon the service-learning aspects of this course on many occasions in the course of the semester in both large group discussions and as part of other assignments. At the beginning of the semester, they reflected on the connection between their assignments, professional practice of public history, and their feelings about making a lasting contribution to assisting future researchers. At the midpoint of the semester, they reflected on their learning experience so far and how the course might be improved for future students. In the course of the semester, students were also prompted to share their projects' progress and relevant materials they felt would help other students in class discussion and in the class learning management system discussion board. This allowed not only for the instructor to monitor the work done outside of the class period but also provided a forum for student communication and a vehicle for them to help their classmates. At the end of the semester, students were required to write a multi-page reflection covering not only what they learned about their project but reflect upon the research process, what it means to be a public historian, and how this project shaped their understanding of public history.

Post-Project Feedback

Student response to the project was overwhelmingly positive. They spoke to the value of archival research and the application of classroom research skills in the archival setting. They found the History Detectives assignment to be a gateway to the project, helping them to apply what they learned in class readings and underscoring the idea that local history is important. Students noted their appreciation for the challenges of collaborative learning and working with outside partners; as one noted, "public history is about collaborating with professionals" and the project demanded this. Many emphasized their growth as researchers and that the "fluidity" of the project demanded not only organizational skills but helped them grow in their decision-making processes about what was and was not relevant. They reflected on the value of their work; as one noted, "[this project was] hands-on learning that I can give back to the public."

Project Assessment and Reporting

The instructor and librarian met after classes were over and discussed the information available through student-written and oral reflections and the resulting projects. Generally, they concluded that students had had a good learning experience and that the increased availability of historical resources (student projects) was a positive outcome of the class.

Another positive outcome of the project was an improved connection between the Public History academic department and the campus communications office that prepares articles for alumni publications. Employees in the communications area were pleased to see the student projects and felt that they might be very useful both in terms of inspiring future articles and in finding resources to pursue the topics. Also, some of the images and documents located by the students in their research illuminated aspects of university's history that were not known. The librarian involved in the project shared these with offices of diversity and student affairs and they were excited to get them. This highlighted the value of the library's collections and the work of the public history instructor and students.

Though working with local history projects can be fascinating for all involved, and allowing students to choose their own topics to research within a particular timeframe is likely to produce stronger projects, it also may lead to unanticipated frustrations and unequal project results. While some students may find a rich collection of materials to support their research, others may find much less and request topic changes much later in the semester than is desirable. In spite of this downside, the instructor and librarian partner expect to continue this collaboration in the coming semester. They are eager to see if projects and reference lists now available will make it easier for students in future classes to choose researchable topics, and if students in future classes will be able to go further in research, given that they will have had a head start.

Difficulties Encountered

Student Issues: Students expressed anxiety about the project for a number of reasons. By design, the project was open-ended and students were presented with a broad set of guidelines. This is a departure from traditional assignments in other history courses. Students were to learn that sources often drive the direction of public history and therefore do not often follow set rules. Undergraduates were assigned collaborative work within assigned two-person groups. Coordinating schedules for group work proved challenging at times. Graduate students, specifically those in their first semester, found difficulty balancing heavy workloads among other courses and graduate assistantship requirements. Deadlines were fluid and set as benchmarks to keep them more on task. Finally, the authenticity of the task, writing about local history, was challenging. Being asked to do research projects related to topics where there is little secondary literature available to guide students was new to the majority of the students. The difficulty of finding resources in archival collections which use provenance rather than the subject as the arrangement method was also a challenge. Students often found themselves getting "lost" or following unrewarding tangents. When students remark on such topics, the instructor might take the opportunity to point out to them that this is the same experience that untrained researchers have and that is why the work they have done will be important in the future.

Instructor Issues: The use of fluid benchmarks often leads to uneven quality in resulting presentations. If this is disturbing to instructors, they may wish to design more formal benchmarks to guide students' progress, like those in a more formal history course or bi-weekly group conversations, and "check-ins" might be developed.

Students seemed to need contextual instruction to help them anchor their work in a larger picture, but there is often limited secondary source material available on local history topics. An emeritus history faculty member writing a university history lectured the classes on their given periods and assisted them in developing research topics but they seemed to need more context. In the future, the instructor will identify an applicable monograph and assign that for each course and provide formal lectures on the broad strokes of American society in the given period. Corresponding reflective writing and class discussion will also be implemented. The instructor may also have to work around limited hours of availability of archives or local historical societies.

Community Partner Issues: Archives and local historical societies often have staffing and preservation concerns that lead them to be reluctant to invite large groups of students to use invaluable and irreplaceable collections. Stressing the lasting value to the organization in terms of increased use statistics, more accessible collections, and the potential for increased donations to the archives in addition to improved student's outcomes may assist in getting them on board.

Conclusion

Public history instructors at IUP have worked with their librarians and archivists to create authentic and service-based learning experiences for both undergraduate and graduate students that prepare them for work in the field, assist future researchers, and contribute to the formation of community identity without going far from home. By investigating topics of their choosing relating to university history, contributing to resource guides designed to help other researchers, and preparing accessible presentations, students gain skills that prepare them for their future careers, even as they assist others.

APPENDIX MATERIALS

- Final Project Description
- Inventory Investigation Assignment
- History Detective Assignment
- Final Reflection Paper

Final Project Description

To introduce ourselves to this practice, we will engage in a project collecting our past as a university community to share with the public. Our tentative topic is "IUP in the Sixties: A Decade of Revolutions?" We will work on this project in phases with multiple public service outcomes. We will be working with Dr. Theresa McDevitt of the IUP Library. First, we will engage in a "scavenger hunt" of appropriate resources on the subject. Then we will determine categories for further group research. In your group work, you will research your category further. This is more than mere internet research; it will involve books and the library and its archive and maybe even the Indiana Historical Society! You will then take this research and contribute content to a library guide that will make your research available on the IUP Library website for future researchers.

You will be expected to regularly chronicle your research experience on a D2L research forum and write a three- to four-page paper in which you reflect upon your experience which will be collected by the end of class.

You will create a PowerPoint "exhibit" utilizing text and images to appropriate standards.

Finally, your group will present your work to an audience of the public! We will discuss this project in stages as we move through the course.

INTRODUCTION TO THE REFLECTIVE NATURE OF THE ASSIGNMENT

The work of a public historian (and all categories of historians really) is incredibly organic—fluid, so to speak. It changes constantly depending upon sources, time, and public demands. Therefore, we need to be flexible and adapt when and where necessary. Consequently, our assignments are very open-ended by design. We will constantly check in and reflect upon our work, adapting and making changes where necessary. Public history is also a very collaborative endeavor. It demands that you communicate effectively and work well with others. You carry a good amount of responsibility—if you falter, those around you are affected. It is expected that you treat each other in a fair and collegial manner. It is expected that you conduct yourself in a professional manner—in class and in public—when you gather your research and when you present it. Finally, a good public historian is a good writer. Take care with all of your writing.

Inventory Investigation Assignment

Now that tentative topics have been determined, you will now move on to assessing which University Archives collections may be valuable to your and your classmates' research. Collection finding aids will be as evenly divided among all students. You are to carefully review each finding aid, thoroughly reading histories and scope and content notes, as well as the container lists. For each finding aid, write a two- to three-sentence summary followed by a brief assessment as to whether or not this collection may be valuable to you or your classmates for their research. Please post your findings to the Inventory Investigation discussion thread on D2L so that all of your classmates will have access to your assessment. Please post up your findings by the Thursday before class. We will discuss our findings in Friday's class.

History Detective Assignment

In public history, professionals are called upon to be history detectives. Just as detectives investigate mysteries and try to find the answers, historians investigate interesting historical topics, find the most accurate information they can in books, articles, and websites, and use this information to make history come alive. To begin the class, you will be asked to put yourself in the place of a university history researcher and find the answers to questions relating to Indiana in the 1960s. Please work in groups of two or three to attempt to answer the following questions. Because finding the best information is also important, you will be asked to include your analysis of whether the source and information you located is trustworthy enough to be included in a historical exhibit, website, or article, or if you think further verification is necessary. You will also be asked to share the bibliographic information for the source, so others will be able to find the information again.

Find as much information as you can, but if you can't find the answers, please provide a description of how you went about looking for the information. That is important, too.

Good places to begin looking for information are the IUP History LibGuide include: http://libraryguides.lib.iup.edu/c.php?g=60459, the IUP Special Collections and Archives Web page (http://www.iup.edu/archives/), and feel free to contact Theresa McDevitt, mcdevitt@iup.edu if you want some help.

Please answer the questions listed below as thoroughly as possible:

- Indiana University of Pennsylvania had a number of names throughout its history. What was Indiana University of Pennsylvania called during the 1960s? In the space below, provide your answer to the question, plus: Where did you find the answer? State your opinion on whether the source of this information is trustworthy. Why or why not?
- Who was (or were) the presidents of IUP during the 1960s? In the space below, provide your answer to the question, plus: Where did you find the answer? State your opinion on whether the source of this information is trustworthy. Why or why not?
- What was the name of the yearbook of the school during the 1960s? (Can you find the full-text of it on the internet?) In the space below, provide your answer to the question, plus: Where did you find the answer? State your opinion on whether the source of this information is trustworthy. Why or why not?
- What was the name of their student handbook during the 1960s? In the space below, provide your answer to the question, plus: Where did you find the answer? State your opinion on whether the source of this information is trustworthy. Why or why not?
- What was the name of the library during the 1960s? In the space below, provide your answer to the question, plus: Where did you find the answer? State your opinion on whether the source of this information is trustworthy. Why or why not?
- What was the number of students on campus during the 1960s? In the space below, provide your answer to the question, plus: Where did you find the answer? State your opinion on whether the source of this information is trustworthy. Why or why not?
- What was the women's housing policy for female undergraduates between 1961 and 1963? In the space below, provide your answer to the question, plus: Where did you find the answer? State your opinion on whether the source of this information is trustworthy. Why or why not?
- What was the name of the town's newspaper in the 1960s? How can you get access to its contents from the period? In the space below, provide your answer to the question, plus: Where did you find the answer? State your opinion on whether the source of this information is trustworthy. Why or why not?
- What was the name of the school newspaper during the 1960s? How can you get access to its contents from the period? In the space below, provide your answer to the question, plus: Where did you find the answer? State your opinion on whether the source of this information is trustworthy. Why or why not?

- Has anyone written a history of IUP? Is so, write the title and location information for the history below.
- As you attempted to answer these questions, broadly explain what your research method was. Were there any web pages, search tools, books, articles, or individuals that were particularly useful to you as you did your research?
- How difficult did you find it to find the answers to these questions?
- How easy do you think it would be for a beginning researcher to find answers to these questions?
- How might the researcher's task be made easier by the public historian who attempts to make history more available to the public?

Final Reflection Paper

Once you have completed your project, you are to write a three- to five-page paper reflecting on the total of your class experience. Explain your research process and strategies. Discuss your successes and challenges during the research process. Note what you learned from working alone and working in groups. Explore the experience crafting the content for the LibGuide as well as your final presentation. After you have done this, step back and reflect on what you learned in course readings and discussion about the field of public history and the role of the public historian in society. How does what you did in class fit? What is the role of the public historian? What are the roles and responsibilities? This is due both to the D2L Dropbox as well as a hard copy to the instructor. This is due by noon on final exam day.

Notes

1.   John Dichtl and Nicholas Sacco, "'Putting History to Work in the World': the National Council on Public History," last modified April 4, 2014, https://scholarworks.iupui.edu/handle/1805/5269.
2.   "Best Practices in Public History," NCPH Curriculum and Training Committee, last modified February 2016, http://ncph.org/wp-content/uploads/2016/02/Best-Practices-for-Establishing-and-Developing-a-Public-History-Program.pdf.
3.   Ibid.
4.   Thomas Cauvin, *Public History: A Textbook of Practice* (Abingdon, United Kingdom: Routledge, 2016).
5.   David E. Kyvig and Myron A. Marty, *Nearby History: Exploring the Past around You* (Lanham, MD Rowman & Littlefield, 2000).
6.   Carolyn L. Kitch, *Pennsylvania in Public Memory: Reclaiming the Industrial Past* (State College: Penn State Press, 2012).

CHAPTER TEN

Fostering Community Engagement through Intentionality and Faculty-Librarian Partnerships

Tracy Lassiter, PhD
Assistant English Professor
University of New Mexico-Gallup
tlassiter@unm.edu

James Fisk, MLS
Research Librarian
University of New Mexico-Gallup
fiskj@unm.edu

THE ACTIVITY

Description: An English professor based her research-writing course around the topic "Solving a Community Problem," allowing students to conceive the term "community" broadly. She and a campus-based research librarian employed the concept of *intentionality* in order to construct a scaffolded syllabus that would support the students throughout the research and writing process. Working together, the faculty member and the librarian ensured that all library-related materials, workshops, and resources were tailored specifically to the course. Ultimately, the students saw how the research and writing process could benefit them and their community and potentially result in lasting change. This effort and the collected resources for it turned a basic research-writing course into one with a service and community engagement aspect.

Getting Started: In August 2016, Lassiter began her faculty position as an Assistant Professor of English at the University of New Mexico-Gallup (UNM-G). Her course load that semester included two sections of English 120 ("Composition III"), which Lassiter envisioned as a research-based writing course. While she hoped eventually to turn her sections of English 120 into a service-learning class where the students performed work with community partners, she didn't have time to establish the necessary connections before the start of the fall semester. Instead, she viewed this first term as an opportunity to learn about local organizations and issues that could inform future collaborative service-learning opportunities. She constructed the course around the topic "Solving a Community Problem," allowing students to have wide latitude in how they conceived the term "community" based on her earlier experience using multimodal conceptual maps.[1]

Since she intended the course to emphasize research, she sought librarian Jim Fisk for his advice and ideas about regional issues and resources to include in the syllabus. First, he gave her a library tour. After this introductory conversation, they arranged to meet at different times early in the semester to coordinate the materials for her English 120 class and to plan workshops for Lassiter's other courses. Fisk, also fairly new to the UNM-G campus, was eager for the opportunity to support Lassiter in her course and to help students with their research and information literacy skills. Lassiter mentioned a few general research topics but admitted she knew little about the critical local issues students would likely write about. During her conversations with Fisk, she mentioned the types of student-centered learning activities she usually employed in her classes, and she and Fisk discussed ways they could enhance the students' research and information literacy skills. There are benefits and precedence to such collaboration. As scholars Debra Hoffmann and Amy Wallace state, "We believe that is it our responsibility as librarians and faculty to provide [students] with an educational experience and opportunities that challenge them to reflect, engage, and act."[2]

As a result of their conversations, Fisk and Lassiter decided to focus on the recently added ACRL framework "Research as Inquiry"[3]; their pedagogical approach combined student-centered learning with *intentionality*. They used the concept of intentionality first in the way Bereiter and Scardamalia defined it in 1989: "Intentional learning refers to the cognitive processes that have learning as a goal rather than an incidental outcome."[4] Lassiter and Fisk further were informed by Maybee, Bruce, Lupton, and Rebmann, who cite Lupton, stating, "Recent research suggests that in learning contexts, where using information is experienced simultaneously with curricular content, participants may use information with more sophistication."[5] Therefore, a faculty-librarian partnership founded in intentionality is a vital mix for students to attain a range of desired learning outcomes.

Motivations: Lassiter advocates for service opportunities for two main reasons. First, she has participated in various kinds of international, community, professional, and campus-based service, and she recognizes how important this work is. It is important for the organizations who need members to carry out their various activities, but community engagement can be revelatory for the student. Participants can network, gain work skills, or even become inspired to seek a vocation based on the service work they perform.

Second, she thinks service-learning is important because it is one way for students to see the value of their classroom learning. When students research a topic they feel strongly about, the research process becomes less a chore and more a discovery. If students can apply what they are learning to a "real world" situation, they are more likely to take to heart what the instructor emphasizes in the classroom. For example, during the Solving a Community Problem course, students learned about MLA and APA style, academic formatting, and other standards. One course assignment asked students to write a letter about their research topic to the editor of a local publication they selected. They had to adhere to that publication's submission and word count guidelines if they wished to see their letter in print. These learners were less resistant to discussions of standardization because they saw how adherence to guidelines could lead to a positive result.

Additionally, Fisk viewed this collaboration as an opportunity to observe the students' use of information literacy throughout their research process. He wanted to track what they learned from their attendance at an initial library presentation through to their final product. He noted that, generally, once the one-shot Introduction to the Library workshop has ended, whether or not students achieve intended learning outcomes becomes a mystery to the librarian.

In a 182-page report prepared by Megan Oakleaf for the Association of College and Research Libraries,[6] she argues that the value and relevance of the academic library are made most apparent by the support it contributes to the institution's mission. Furthermore, according to W. Lee Hisle, "we [librarians] must find ways to promote the values, expertise, and leadership of the profession throughout the campus to ensure appreciation for the roles librarians do and can play. Though access to information is increasingly decentralized, and computer labs now compete with libraries as campus gathering points, librarians must demonstrate to the campus community that the library remains central to academic effort."[7] Lassiter's assignments and her collaborative engagement with Fisk provided him a way, during his one-shot workshop, to showcase library resources and services; it was an opportunity for the library to "show its stuff."

THE PEOPLE

Library: The Zollinger Library serves the campus and the community at large. This is reflected in its collection of bestsellers, academic titles, young adult literature titles of regional interests, and an assortment of documentary and popular film titles. Online resources include an EBSCOhost suite of products, InfoTrac titles, and a collection ProQuest products. Additionally, when the main campus in Albuquerque negotiates licensing terms for online resources, it includes branch campuses in its discussions. These efforts are typically successful in providing Gallup and other branch campuses a host of materials.

The building is light, airy, and inviting. Built-in study carrels line the east wall and offer a beautiful view of the Zuni Mountains and the red rock formations of Gallup. It offers conference and study rooms. Although a computer lab of twenty-eight stations shares the space, it is separate and removed from main library area. Most recently, the library opened a lower level that is designated as a quiet area.

Instructors: Lassiter came to UNM-G three years after completing her PhD in Indiana University of Pennsylvania's (IUP) English Literature and Criticism program. She had many years of teaching experience, including five years at a community college in southeastern Arizona. She also taught as a temporary professor for IUP and as an adjunct at other two-year colleges.

Fisk joined the faculty at UNM-G in the fall of 2015 as a public services librarian. He came to Gallup after a twelve-year stint at Morningside College, a private liberal arts institution in Sioux City, Iowa. He began there as a reference and instructional services librarian and later was appointed to the position of college librarian. He received his MLS from Emporia State University in 2001.

Course: For that semester's five-course load, Lassiter had two sections of English 120, or Composition III, which Lassiter envisioned as a research-based writing course. Students have to pass prerequisite composition courses in order to enroll in English 120. Approximately fifty-two students attended the two sections of Lassiter's course. Each semester runs for sixteen weeks.

The Students: Since UNM-G operates as a community college, the students range widely in age. UNM-G has a partnership with a local charter high school with an enrollment cap of one hundred students, so roughly 4 percent of the campus enrollment are students from that school. However, about 25 percent of Lassiter's class enrollment came from the charter high school and a local career and tech program from other area high schools, combined. Several other UNM-G students were nontraditional learners entering or returning to college after other experiences such as military service, parenthood, or previous careers. The campus's enrollment is approximately 79 percent Native American, primarily Navajo and Zuni, but also with a large number of Laguna and Hopi students, along with many from Gallup's Muslim and Filipino communities. Most students live on or near a reservation and focus their research on topics related to issues they encounter there.

Community Partners: The greater Gallup community was involved in this course indirectly. Since this instructor was new to the region when she was designing this course, she did not contact any community organizations in order to establish a service-learning opportunity whereby the students worked in partnership with them. Yet, "the community" was the focus of the course, as students had to address a local problem. For this course's purposes, "community" could be a reservation, the city of Gallup, the UNM-G campus, or any other defined population, such as fellow veterans, an artists' collective, or concerned parents. Lassiter encouraged her students to interview members of the community as part of their research process. Lassiter is networking now with local organizations and fellow faculty members to coordinate service-learning opportunities for an upcoming academic year; however, perhaps the students' experience with the inaugural English 120 course means they already understand how important local problem-solving is and will engage in community activities in the near future.

Finding and Working with Partners: Since the initial design of Solving a Community Problem course, Lassiter has learned more about the region, its organizations, and its resources. Her involvement with a local recycling non-profit has allowed her to meet members of other organizations, including, for example, an employee of the Zuni Environmental Protection Program. She also spoke to colleagues who are interested in teaming up so that their courses have a similar theme or service-learning component in each of their disciplines. She and they are meeting currently to address the logistics of such collaboration.

Another way Lassiter located potential community partners was through participation in other service-oriented activities. For example, as part of a Women's HERstory Month series hosted at UNM-G, Lassiter helped to coordinate a resource fair that invited various local and regional organizations to the UNM-G campus. These organizations addressed needs in health and child care, domestic violence, educational or employment opportunities, social services, philanthropy, and more. Lassiter was able to use the event to share with these groups her ideas for her class and to determine preliminary interest in collaborating in a service-learning opportunity. Based on this experience and her conversations with UNM colleagues, she is considering a service-learning course focused on farming and food. At first, the collaboration would be considered an exercise in "coordinated curricula." If successful, in the long term, she and her UNM-G colleagues, including Fisk, ideally would like to see such efforts become campus-wide practice, particularly since service-learning is recognized as an AACU High Impact Practice (see the link provided in the Practice Bibliography).

During that first semester, Lassiter also attended a service-learning workshop held at UNM-Albuquerque that described how to find and foster relationships with community organizations. The workshop organizer, Monica Kowal, Associate Dean of the Office of Community Engaged Learning and Research, made the community organizations the primary focus of consideration; that is, she indicated that a service-learning course is more likely to be successful if the community partner's needs are prominent. For example, Kowal stated that it might be difficult for some organizations to train and orient a new pack of students every semester for them to only work for approximately six to ten weeks each term. She advises the faculty member and organization representative to have upfront, detailed conversations about expectations, time commitments, student learning outcomes, and similar matters before each agrees to a service-learning partnership. The information Kowal provided will be pivotal to how Lassiter develops the more engaged service-learning component she envisions for this course.

Benefits

Instructor Benefits: Lassiter has viewed this course as an opportunity to get to know well her new community, its people, and its myriad challenges. She appreciates the opportunity to meet and work with so many other residents, faculty, and staff who wish to contribute to positive community change and growth.

This collaborative effort created an opening to increase Fisk's presence on campus. Lassiter kindly "promoted" his skills and collegiality to colleagues. In part, as a result, his number of workshops nearly doubled from his first year on the Gallup campus. In addition, he made other connections and facilitated library participation in campus-wide events such as Women's HERstory Month.

Student Benefits: The students have gained from this foray into community problem-solving. While the course was not a service-learning course where they interacted with organizations or their constituencies, the learners recognized that their proposed solutions to a community problem actually could come to pass if they chose to implement them. (Some barriers to this implementation are discussed below under "Difficulties Encountered.") As part of their research process, Lassiter encouraged students to interview experts, organization leaders, and stakeholders for their insights. One nontraditional student from Zuni recalled her grandfather talking to about a farming method known as "waffle gardens." Youth on the Zuni reservation no longer learn this method, so she developed a survey and, with permission, presented it to students and a principal from a Zuni school in order to gauge their interest in having waffle gardens become part of their curriculum. Another student proposed a student ambassador program at the UNM-G campus to help new or returning students transition more easily into college life. Currently, a university administrator, whom this student interviewed, is starting a piloted mentoring program through the campus's TRiO program.

Beyond their own learning, students also value knowledge by sharing with others what they learned from their research process. That is, after the students attended Fisk's workshop, Lassiter gave them an assignment requiring them to find an article on their topic and write a summary of it. The students had to draw upon the information literacy skills they gleaned from Fisk's workshop, plus draw upon classroom instruction that distinguished between quoting, paraphrasing, and summarizing. Aside from receiving their grade on the summary, the students knew these articles would contribute to a class resource file that future English 120 students would consult, so they provided citation information on the printouts. Lassiter then organized the articles topically to make it easier for upcoming students to find ideas or resources for their own projects.

Community Partner Benefits: Lassiter and Fisk don't have data that reflect benefits to community partners, but they hope student interest is piqued enough that they will see increased involvement and support as a result of this course.

Institutional Benefits: Collaborative activity benefits the library as an institution. According to the Ethnographic Research in Illinois Academic Libraries (ERIAL) study, faculty colleagues are in a position to broker library services. In other words, "Students routinely learn about librarians and library services directly from a professor's recommendation, or through librarians' in-class information sessions.... Professors therefore act as gatekeepers who mediate when and how students contact with librarian[s] as they are working on research assignments. In this way, the attitude of professors towards librarians is a key determining factor in developing student/librarian relationships."[8] The collaborative relationship that Fisk and Lassiter share fits this model.

Service-learning projects, in particular, facilitate opportunities for academic librarians "to get serious" about implementing the *Framework* for *Information Literacy* for Higher Education. The framework, rather than focusing on a set of skills associated with information gathering, looks upon research as a process of open-ended investigation. In particular, the framework especially identifies desirable learner dispositions relative to research, many of which may be counted as student learning outcomes in and of themselves. For example, when considering research as inquiry, learners shall "value intellectual curiosity in developing questions and learning new investigative methods," or when viewing research as strategic exploration, learners shall "recognize the value of browsing and other serendipitous methods of information gathering." These understandings can clearly inform new pedagogies of the one-shot library presentation.[9]

THE PROCESS
Expected Learning Outcomes

The University of New Mexico spells out its expected student learning outcomes for its English courses on its website.[10] Notably, these outcomes include considering "Writing as a Social Act," where students should recognize "the role of discourse communities at the local, national, and international level." Turning a composition class into one dedicated to community problem-solving helps locate student writing and engagement as such a form of social act.

While appreciating these academic standards, less formally, Lassiter hopes students recognize that research and writing are important processes with implications and applications beyond the English classroom walls. She hopes they understand that reliable resources come in various forms (interviews, archival documents, film, government studies, maps, and more), and that a university library is a vital place to begin research exploration. Finally, she hopes her students gain confidence not only in their writing skills but in their potential to be community and tribal leaders down the line.

Fisk has particular expectations with respect to students' information literacy. He notes that the one-shot, fifty-five-minute library session is the core of library instruction on many campuses. It may be the one opportunity the library has to market to first-year students its portfolio of services, to offer some basic skills training, and—in the spirit of the ACRL framework—to encourage students to understand research as a dynamic *process* of developing and articulating a succinct and meaningful research question. It provides a chance for students to recognize they can change course or re-articulate the research question if search results are unsatisfactory, to narrow or broaden their search strategies, to build upon initial search results to locate other sources, and to develop a vocabulary germane to their research question. These sessions are most effective if they can be held in a computer lab setting that facilitates an active-learning experience, one timed to match the introduction of the assignment and providing content related to the assignment prompt. According to Angela Weiler, including hands-on activities increases retention, particularly if the task meets a need—that is, is related to the assignment.[11] The library workshop may represent many students' first visit to the library. A guided and prompt-driven assignment is given to reinforce the hands-on lab experience and to document the intentionality of the process.

The desired student learning outcomes from the workshop include: becoming familiar with library resources, especially online databases and librarian-created resources such as LibGuides; recognizing the library as an inviting place to learn; and fostering a willingness to develop collaborative relationships with classmates, instructors, and library staff. Furthermore, he hopes students will learn to conduct successful searches using the EBSCOhost advanced search interface in order to address the requirements of their assignment.

Curriculum Materials

In designing the course, Lassiter drew upon previous experiences designing research writing courses. Because she intends to turn the class into a more student-engaged service-learning opportunity one day, she built in assignments that support that goal. She also asked Fisk for ideas for community and library resources the students could refer to.

Early in the term, then, Fisk offered a workshop to familiarize the students with research strategies and database hunts. Prior to the start of his instruction, Fisk conducts a brief and informal needs assessment and student survey. Generally, the survey solicits responses relative to student attitudes about library research and their experience doing said research. Of particular interest to Fisk is the learners' relative lack of any experience using online databases. Of the twenty-four students who completed the survey, only six students reported using these tools. To the question, however, regarding their Internet use, nineteen of the twenty-four reported "Yes." Not surprisingly, these results reflect a 2012 Pew study entitled "How Teens Do Research in a Digital World."[12] In the study, when asked about their students' research strategy preferences, teachers reported that 94 percent of these students most likely used search engines (i.e., Google) as compared to online databases (17 percent). Fisk presented a complete-the-sentence prompt, asking Lassiter's students, "When given a difficult assignment requiring research, I…" Only five of Lassiter's students included consulting a librarian as one of their help-seeking choices. Similarly, in the Pew Study, just 16 percent of the survey participants viewed librarians as a probable "go-to" student resource. Interested to see how Lassiter's students compared to other UNM-G first-year students, Fisk compared her students' responses to his prompt to those of students in two other sections of English 120; those results were very similar.

The materials Fisk creates result from the workshops he offers and are tailored to Lassiter's course. Students leave his initial workshop session with a number of resources. His PowerPoint guides students through catalog and database searches and serves as an "instruction manual" students can use for their subsequent independent research. The presentation handout includes diagrammed sample search strategies including interfaces, sequenced instructions, and callouts. Since the students are fully engaged during the session, they are prepared to complete the hands-on activity that follows the workshop, and from there they have the confidence to begin their research project.

Fisk also prepared a LibGuide especially for the class.[13] He also suggested three additional LibGuides, "Citation Help for MLA,"[14] "Citation Help for APA,"[15] and "Current Issues in the News"[16] as helpful and relevant to Lassiter's students. These LibGuides are available on the UNM-G library home page for further review.

Finally, throughout the semester, Fisk was available to Lassiter's students if they had questions as they completed various assignments related to research, information literacy, and citation. A selection of both Lassiter's and Fisk's materials are attached, roughly in the order in which they would have been assigned during the term.

Steps Involved

On the first day of the semester, Lassiter begins the class by playing Michael Jackson's *Man in the Mirror* on YouTube and then initiating a discussion of the issues Jackson sings about. She then engages students in discussing what they feel are contemporary social problems. Following that, she reminds them of Jackson's message that change begins with the individual and asks them to think right away about changes they can make to help their community. She tells them their research paper will present a solution they realistically could implement to solve that problem. Only after this introduction does she review the syllabus and refer them to the course text, *A Writer's Reference* by Diana Hacker and Nancy Sommers. On the second day of class, she shares with them an article Fisk located about students on a service-learning trip to South America and the challenges they faced that they hadn't anticipated. Following this reading and discussion, she introduces them to the multimodal concept drawing activity (referenced earlier) based on the word "community." If the student groups don't finish these posters during this class, they are able to complete them at the end of a later class when time permits.

Students begin their library exploration in the second week, where each student is assigned a library section and must answer questions related to that section. The class meets at the library and, for each area, the student assigned that section has to lead the tour, using their answers to the questions as the basis of their explanation. After this physical orientation, during the next week they take the first of Fisk's workshops, which introduces them to the library's catalog and databases, and how they can conduct information literacy searches.

Lassiter also assigns the students a field observation activity. Students visit various locations around the campus to discover services, organizations, and information available about the campus and the region. Students are required to answer questions on everything from room numbers to kiosk-posted fliers to data found in pamphlets and other handouts. This activity alerts students to resources they weren't aware of and/or gives them research topic ideas. It also reinforces the idea that observation can serve as a kind of reliable evidence, and so can citing experts—through interviewing—including those they might first meet during their field observation. Later, between both a class lecture and another of Fisk's workshops, students learn how to integrate and properly cite, in either MLA or APA style, these various research sources.

During week 6, students receive the research paper assignment and a set of research proposal guidelines that asks them to prepare a summary of their topic, tentative thesis, and a preliminary list of reliable sources. During week 8 (mid-semester), students meet with Lassiter for at least fifteen-minute conferences in lieu of class. She uses this time to ensure students are on the right track with focused solutions and specific sources. If need be, she helps them locate sources during this brief conference; if students need more in-depth assistance in tracking down materials, she steers them to Fisk, who serves as a kind of *de facto* embedded librarian for the course. During the next class meeting following conferences, Lassiter assigns a concession/refutation assignment based on student use of the Opposing Viewpoints "Topics in Context" database. By this time, students have a sense of the gaps in their research, and the Opposing Viewpoints database provides them with an array of material to fill those holes.

During week 11 of the semester, students have started their papers sufficiently that they have a coherent grasp of their topic and solution. The class resource file provides copies of various local newspapers and magazines, ranging from the student newspaper the *Daily Lobo* to the regional *Navajo Times*, and more. Students choose a periodical and then must locate the editor's name and its submission guidelines in order to prepare a letter to the editor. Due to safety and other concerns, students are not required to submit their letter, but they could receive extra credit for doing so. However, they are graded on writing a summative letter that meets the publication's requirements. Besides any bonus points, students have the satisfaction of seeing their name in print related to a cause they care about.

Students submit their final research papers by the end of week 15 of the semester so Lassiter has time to grade and return them before final exams. Students briefly share with classmates their topic, solution, and any other information they learned during the research and writing process.

POST-PROJECT FEEDBACK
Methods of Reflection

Throughout the semester, students have opportunities to consider their topics, receive feedback from classmates and instructors, and anticipate challenges to their proposed solutions. This feedback allows them to reflect on their research process and resource list, and it shapes their paper into one that creates as sound a rhetorical argument as possible.

As mentioned, students use the field observation and the class resource file to become aware of issues and organizations that could inform their topic or source list. Lassiter uses that resource file also as part of an in-class MLA/APA citation practice exercise so students engage with these materials closely. Lassiter also uses class time to offer "round robin" opportunities for students to receive peer feedback on their preliminary topic ideas and to discover whether anyone else in the class can suggest experts or other sources they can pursue. After the paper-drafting process has begun, students post their topic and solution on sheets of poster paper, which are hung around the room. The class engages in a "gallery walk" where they read and comment on each poster, posing potential counterarguments or other concerns the writer might want to include in his or her research paper. Finally, the students receive individualized feedback on their topics, solutions, and resources during their conference with Lassiter. Fisk also provides feedback when he assists students in locating materials—for example, when he helps them come up with related subject terms or points them to government documents or other materials they hadn't considered.

As a way to assess student "take-away" from his information literacy workshops, Fisk asked Lassiter to share her students' final "sources cited" pages so he could informally evaluate student research associated with their projects. Additionally, Fisk tracked the information literacy component with respect to the types of resources students cited. One of the dispositions identified in the Research as Inquiry framework is a demonstrated "understanding that information sources vary greatly in content and format and have varying relevance and value, depending on the needs and nature of the search."[17] The citation analysis was an opportunity for Fisk to "close the loop"; in other words, he could determine whether his instruction influenced student research and whether students used a variety of resources. A cursory analysis of twenty-seven student "sources cited" pages (158 citations) revealed a good mix of materials that are not necessarily typical of UNM-Gallup student papers. Of note, of the 158 citations, students cited thirty-one peer-reviewed articles, twenty-nine resources from local, social service/nonprofit organizations, eighteen regional news stories, twenty government sources, and eight personal interviews. These results show the students knew the value of citing peer-reviewed journal articles and could locate them. Importantly, it showed they recognize the myriad kinds of materials that could constitute research sources. Lassiter and Fisk expect the students took these skills and ideas forward into their other college classes.

Post-Project Feedback

The students themselves indicated they benefitted from the research-writing process. One student, whose topic was recycling on the Navajo reservation, said, "I could not have completed my paper without an interview from ...the Navajo Nation EPA.... I felt that it was important to be able to include comments from [the] EPA. Thank you. I learned so much from writing this paper as far as research and writing for effectiveness." (Due to FERPA laws, students' names herein are withheld.) Another student sent a gleeful e-mail reporting "I found it! My letter to the editor was published in the *Gallup Independent*!" Another student commented anonymously in the course's student evaluations: "As a returning student coming back to school after a 20-year break, it was nice to have the Library tours and tutorials that Dr. Lassiter [and Mr. Fisk] offered at the beginning of the course. Our final paper required a lot of research and she did a good job of making sure we were familiar with all the various resources and digital tools at our fingertips." In fact, one of the resources the student mentioned was a LibGuide Fisk wrote specifically for the course theme. (See the printout of basic LibGuide in Appendix Materials).

Project Assessment and Reporting

Lassiter and Fisk believe students have gained from this foray into community problem-solving. While the course did not engage students into regularly-scheduled community service, students recognized that their proposed solutions to a local problem actually could come to pass if they chose to implement them. Some barriers to this implementation are discussed below.

Difficulties Encountered

Student Issues: As Koval recommended, attention to community partners' needs in the planning stages could help stave off the more traditional challenges emerging from service-learning courses. However, Lassiter anticipates that she will have to address separate challenges that perhaps don't face many instructors who organize a service-learning course. That is, she believes there are particular concerns to address specific to working with at-risk populations.

For example, many students lack reliable transportation; this is one of the most persistent problems at the UNM-G campus, where students have been known to hitchhike to campus even from the Arizona border. Community organizations reasonably expect service-learning participants to arrive on time and as scheduled, so any collaboration would have to provide options that allow students to perform service work from home or campus and not at the organization's site. Students who are parents also struggle to find consistent child care. Absenteeism and tardiness regularly occur in classes because these learners cannot find consistent care for their children. In order to best serve community organizations, Lassiter will have to work closely with their administrators and her students to find opportunities that do not require child care considerations or to locate service volunteers for whom child care is not a concern.

At the same time, some locations on the reservations have poor infrastructure, resulting in impassable roads during inclement weather or spotty-at-best Internet service. These challenges further dampen students' ability either to report to a service site on time or perform work (such as website updates) from their home. This is why Lassiter expects that, when she offers a service-learning component, it necessarily will have to be a course *option* and not a requirement. Students without any added challenges, such as those described above, could take advantage of the service-learning aspect if they wished, but for those for whom service-learning would be a burden, she will offer the traditional research writing option that emphasizes community engagement.

Conclusion: Both Lassiter and Fisk hope their ongoing collaboration will support student interest in community engagement and expect their efforts will provide additional service opportunities in the near future. They cite Kissel, et al. who state, "The work of the community of practice is not yet complete. But this work has opened a new conversation shared by librarians, faculty, and administration …a conversation that will help lead students to become confident users of the complicated contemporary world of information."[18] To that, Fisk and Lassiter would add, "and help students to become confident leaders in an increasingly complicated contemporary world."

APPENDIX MATERIALS

- English 120 – Research Paper Guidelines
- Getting to Know You Exercise
- English 120 – Research Proposal
- English 120 – Letters to the Editor Assignment

English 120 – Research Paper Guidelines

Our major assignment this semester is a minimum five-page research paper. In this paper, you will come up with a solution to a problem in your community. We spent some time in class talking about how you might define "community": the UNM-Gallup campus, Gallup, or your hometown, for example. But we also considered community from the standpoint of other definitions, such as the "community of local musicians," tribal nations, or other categorizations.

Once you have decided on a community and a problem you'd like to address, you'll need to come up with a research proposal and a list of potential resources for you to start gathering quotes and data. As you begin these steps, consider including the following elements for your paper. You do not have to follow this model, but you might find it useful. You can use these main idea topics to guide your research and help you meet the length requirement:

- catchy introduction, leading to your point, or thesis
- a history or background information on the problem
- the current state/status of the issue you want to address or an explanation of why this topic is important
- other solutions to the problem that have been tried or suggested, and perhaps an explanation of why those other solutions didn't or wouldn't work
- your solution to the problem and your arguments/evidence supporting why you think it would be effective
- anticipated counter-argument to your solution and your rebuttal to those arguments
- a conclusion that restates your earlier point and ends on a strong note
- (Separate page at the end—the Works Cited or References page—this doesn't count as part of the five pages of writing.) You'll draw from at least five sources, only two of which can be "pure Internet" sources.

You will cite your paper according to MLA or APA format, depending on which style your major uses. Don't use a cover page, but you could consider including tables, graphs, maps, or other appended items that support your paper.

Getting to Know You Exercise

Getting to Know You: Course Name: _____

Instructor: _____

1. In high school or before enrolling at UNMG, were you expected to write a paper requiring research at the library, on the Internet and/or from a library database?
   Library: ❑ YES ❑ NO
   Internet: ❑ YES ❑ NO
   Library databases: ❑ YES ❑ NO

2. Which library databases have you used? Check those that apply.

   ❑ EBSCO ❑ ProQuest ❑ InfoTrac (Gale) ❑ From El Portal—State Library of New Mexico ❑ Other (Identify one) _____

3. Generally, my experience has shown me that librarians are friendly and helpful. (Check which answer applies).

   ❑ Strongly Agree ❑ Agree ❑ Not sure ❑ Disagree ❑ Strongly disagree

4. When I do go to the library or search for information online, I find what I need. (Check which answer applies).

   ❑ Strongly Agree ❑ Agree ❑ Not sure ❑ Disagree ❑ Strongly disagree

5. Generally speaking, a person can rely on the reliability, credibility, and objectivity of information found on the World Wide Web.

   ❑ Strongly Agree ❑ Agree ❑ Not sure ❑ Disagree ❑ Strongly disagree

6. When using the Internet, I am confident that I can differentiate information that is of good quality from what is poor quality.

   ❑ Strongly Agree ❑ Agree ❑ Not sure ❑ Disagree ❑ Strongly disagree

7. When given a difficult assignment requiring research.... Check responses that apply
   ❑ I generally try to figure it out myself
   ❑ I ask for assistance from my professor
   ❑ I ask a friend for help
   ❑ I ask a librarian for help
   ❑ I panic

8. If you were doing a paper about adults who have Attention Deficit Hyperactivity Disorder (ADHD), what search strategy would probably be best?
    a. ADHD and Adults _____
    b. "Information about ADHD" _____
    c. ADHD or Adults_____
    d. Adults who deal with Attention Deficit Hyperactivity disorder _____

English 120 – Research Proposal

When we meet for mid-semester conferences, you'll bring your research proposal so we can go over it and make sure you're on the right track with your paper. Your proposal should be typed, double-spaced, and either in MLA or APA format. You'll include the following information:

1. The working title of your paper
2. Your tentative thesis
3. A 5-6 sentence minimum summary of what you'd like to do. What problem are you addressing? Why is it important? What solution are you suggesting? Why does it interest you?
4. Provide a preliminary list of five sources you intend to use in your paper. Don't just say: "I'm going to use two Internet sources, a library book, and two database articles." Identify authors, titles, URLs, expert names, etc. We'll have started learning MLA/APA style by the time this is due, so do your best to put this in the proper citation style (and then you'll be ahead as you start to put your paper together!).
5. Let me know about any research or writing problems you have encountered so far so we can talk about them during our conference.

English 120 – Letters to the Editor Assignment

We will spend some time in class today going through different local/regional newspapers and magazines. After we conduct a brief analysis of the publication, you will select one to direct a letter to the editor to. In your letter, you will write about your research paper topic and your proposed solution. Your letter must be addressed to the publication's editor and conform to that publication's word count and other submission guidelines.

While you are not required to actually submit your letter to the publication you've chosen, you are encouraged to do so. One of the hallmarks of a free press in a democratic society is the opportunity to have your voice heard and considered in the community. Please consider taking advantage of this opportunity to exercise this right.

For our class's purposes, your letter must be typed in a 12-pt. font and conform to standard letter setup. This means using an inside address, mailing address, salutation, and closing. See sample on page 65 ("C" tab) of *A Writer's Reference*, the link provided in our UNM-Learn site to the Purdue OWL, and the student samples in Course Information for examples of setup and content.

Notes

1.   Ann Amicucci and Tracy Lassiter, "Multimodal Concept Drawings: Engaging EALs in Brainstorming about Course Terms," *TESOL Journal*, Special Topics Issue: "Critical Crossroads: Investigating Nonnativeness, Race, Class, Gender and Sexuality in an Era of World Englishes" 5 (2014): 523–31, doi: 10.1002/tesj.161.

2.   Debra Hoffmann and Amy Wallace, "Intentional Informationists: Re-envisioning Information Literacy and Re-designing Instructional Programs Around Faculty Librarians' Strengths as Campus Connectors, Information Professionals, and Course Designers," *The Journal of Academic Librarianship* 39, no. 6 (November 2013): 1.

3.   Association of College and Research Libraries, "Research as Inquiry," *Framework for Information Literacy in Higher Education*, http://www.ala.org/acrl/standards/ilframework#inquiry.

4.   Carl Bereiter and Marlene Scardamalia, "Intentional Learning as a Goal of Instruction," *Knowing, Learning, and Instruction: Essays in Honor of Robert Glaser*, last modified 1989, http://www.ikit.org/fulltext/1989intentional.pdf.

5.   Clarence Maybee, et al., "Designing Rich Information Experiences to Shape Learning Outcomes," *Libraries Faculty and Staff Scholarship and Research. Paper 129*: 13, last modified 2016, https://docs.lib.purdue.edu/cgi/viewcontent.cgi?article=1136&context=lib_fsdocs.

6.   Megan Oakleaf, *The Value of Academic Libraries: A Comprehensive Research Review and Report* (Chicago: American College and Research Libraries, 2010), last modified September 2010, http://www.ala.org/acrl/sites/ala.org.acrl/files/content/issues/value/val_report.pdf.

7.   W. Lee Hisle, "Top Issues Facing Academic Libraries: A Report of the Focus on the Future Task Force," *College and Research Libraries News* 63, no. 10 (2002): 714–715.

8.   Andrew Asher, Lynda Duke, and David Green, "The ERIAL project: Ethnographic Research in Illinois Academic Libraries," *Academic Commons* 13 (2010), http://www.erialproject.org/wpcontent/uploads/2010/03/NITLE_summit_presentation__final_3_22_10.pdf.

9.   ACRL, "Framework for Information Literacy in Higher Education."

10.   University of New Mexico, "Student Learning Outcomes," http://english-old.unm.edu/corecourses/student-learning-outcomes.html.

11.   Angela Weiler, "Information-Seeking Behavior in Generation Y Students: Motivation, Critical Thinking, and Learning Theory," *The Journal of Academic Librarianship*, 31, no. 1 (2005): 46–53.

12.   Kristen Purcell, et al., "How Teens Do Research in a Digital World" (Pew Research Center, 2012), http://www.pewinternet.org/2012/11/01/how-teens-do-research-in-the-digital-world/.

13. Jim Fisk, "Student Civic Engagement and Voluntarism," University of New Mexico Zollinger Library, http://unmgallup.libguides.com/c.php?g=591904.

14. Jim Fisk, "Citation Help for MLA," University of New Mexico Zollinger Library, http://unmgallup.libguides.com/c.php?g=591884.

15. Jim Fisk, "Citation Help for APA," University of New Mexico Zollinger Library, http://unmgallup.libguides.com/c.php?g=591885.

16. Jim Fisk, "Current Issues in the News," University of New Mexico Zollinger Library, http://unmgallup.libguides.com/current_issues.

17. ACRL, "Framework for Information Literacy in Higher Education."

18. Francia Kissel, Melvin R. Wininger, Scott R. Weeden, Patricia A. Wittberg, Randall S. Halverson, Meagan Lacy, and Rhonda K. Huisman, "Bridging the Gaps: Collaboration in a Faculty and Librarian Community of Practice on Information Literacy" (Fort Collins, CO: University of Colorado Press, 2017), 428, https://wac.colostate.edu/books/infolit/chapter20.pdf.

CHAPTER ELEVEN

Generating Buzz on Campus about Fair Trade through the Writing for Public Relations Course

Jen Jones, PhD

Associate Professor and Department Coordinator, Communication
Seton Hill University
jjones@setonhill.edu

Amy Podoletz

Senior Communication Major
Communication Department
Seton Hill University
a.podoletz@setonhill.edu

THE ACTIVITY

Description: Writing in Public Relations is a writing-intensive course. In this case, the project refines researching and writing skills through the process of planning and promoting a fair trade event on campus. In order to gain knowledge and critically evaluate the practice of fair trade, students read course materials and do independent research through library databases on that topic. After gaining an in-depth understanding of fair trade, students utilize this research to develop written assignments to connect with their peers and foster constructive conversations about fair trade. Some of the events students developed included showing a fair trade documentary on campus with a panel discussion, selling fair trade items at a holiday sale, bringing an expert on fair trade to speak on campus, identifying fair trade items in the cafeteria, providing information tables on fair trade, offering fair trade gift basket raffles at athletic events, and hosting fair trade coffee, tea, and chocolate tastings. This project provides the essential research and integrative work necessary for a successful event, while at the same time practicing the university's mission of transforming the world.

Getting Started: I was initially inspired for this service-learning project through a conversation with a colleague at a conference about how to get students to think critically about humanistic aspects of the marketplace. I was inspired further by witnessing a Fair Trade Holiday Market at the Duquesne University Student Union. A vital aspect of getting started with this fair trade service-learning project is support from university leadership. Leaders of Seton Hill support our involvement with fair trade due to its strong connection to the university's mission, history with the Sisters of Charity, and Catholic Social Teaching (CST). A Seton Hill librarian developed an extensive LibGuide for CST, which grounds the practice of CST on campus and affirms the university's commitment to it.[1] Faculty members are encouraged to integrate CST into their coursework, so this LibGuide is particularly helpful. The university also provides instruction and mentoring for faculty on CST. Additionally, Catholic Relief Services offers support for faculty on the topic of fair trade and other social issues. Also important to acknowledge is Seton Hill's commitment to be a welcoming community to people of all faith traditions and non-faith perspectives. Integrating a CST pedagogy is an orientation of social justice and commitment to the poor.[2] As such, regardless of religious background, we are all called to value others with human dignity. Thus, the CST LibGuide spurred the idea of creating a LibGuide for the fair trade project, which also helped the students see connections to CST and academic sources that ground fair trade.

Motivations: I have found that the current generation of college students is very socially minded and eager to learn and practice corporate social responsibility. Engaging them in a service-learning project on the topic of fair trade suits this mindset as well as aligns with the university's commitment to social justice and Catholic Social Teaching. Students within the Communication major expect to be involved in service-learning and enjoy this pedagogical approach. When students complete assignments for a real-world project, they have greater buy-in and commitment to doing good work. Furthermore, they find that this service-learning project gives them a sense of meaning and purpose since their efforts may contribute to a positive impact on society. I was pleasantly surprised by the students' suggestion to visit a Ten Thousand Villages store to learn even more about fair trade. The students discovered that the store was hosting a fashion event to introduce new clothing lines. Attending the event fostered greater motivation and insight into event planning. The University Board of Trustees also provides motivation for this project. When I presented this project to them, they were delighted to see the spirit of the Sisters of Charity alive in the students' work. One of the trustees shared her involvement with the organization Human Thread[3] and followed up with me later with additional resources.

THE PEOPLE

Libraries: The recently renovated Reeves Memorial Library and Learning Commons houses library services for the university as well as the Writing Center, the Solutions Center (Information Technology), Career and Professional Development, and Instructional Design. The library is a valued division for its support of the university's reputation for academic distinction and an Apple Distinguished institution, and it has established and promotes information fluency standards for students. Librarians participate in monthly school meetings to discuss new and discontinued resources, share analysis of information fluency in student research, answer faculty members' questions, and provide any other information relevant to the group. Librarians serve on many university committees. The library also offers an annual student research award, which is highly competitive and includes a monetary award.

Founded in 1883 by the Sisters of Charity, Seton Hill University (SHU) is a private Catholic liberal arts university in southwestern Pennsylvania with approximately 1,700 undergraduate students and offers graduate programs in business, physician assistant, and orthodontics. The faculty to student ratio is 14:1 and the majority of classes have fewer than twenty students. It is a mission-driven institution, which provides a common center for a collaborative community.[4] The university's mission states: "Seton Hill is a Catholic university rooted in Judeo-Christian values. In the tradition of Elizabeth Ann Seton, we educate students to think and act critically, creatively, and ethically as productive members of society committed to transforming the world."[5]

Instructor: I am an associate professor of Communication at Seton Hill. I teach the three-credit writing-intensive Writing in Public Relations (SCA251) course that is required for communication majors. Aligned with the mission of the university, all communication courses integrate critical, creative, and ethical thinking and acting. Prior to teaching in an academic setting, I was a corporate trainer in the areas of team building, communication, and leadership. I translate this type of activity-based learning into my approach teaching college students and utilize academic resources to further develop this pedagogical approach.

Course: The Writing in Public Relations course provides a transition from the 100-level Communication Theory course where, in addition to reading a textbook, students also read *Search Inside Yourself: The Unexpected Path to Achieving Success, Happiness, and World Peace*[6] to the 300-level Corporate Ethics and Social Responsibility course where they read *Firms of Endearment: How World-class Companies Profit from Passion and Purpose.*[7] As such, the coursework is integrated so students are able to make connections among their courses while building upon previous knowledge.

Students: Students in this class are in their second year of study. In this writing-intensive course, students gain written communication skills that are necessary for their progressive coursework. A majority of students in the class are communication majors and take the class as a requirement; however, English and business students also take the course as an elective.

Community Partners: Our primary partner is Fair Trade Campaigns (FTC), which describes itself as "a powerful grassroots movement mobilizing Fair Trade consumers and advocates across the US to increase the availability of Fair Trade products."[8] The website is organized into segments, Fair Trade Universities, Towns, Congregations, and Schools. Fair Trade Campaigns provides unique guidance for each segment to work toward passing a resolution to become designated with fair trade status. Through resources and webinars, Fair Trade Campaigns introduced us to the myriad of partners who produce the fair trade products. Some of the major fair trade organizations involved are Divine Chocolate, Equal Exchange, Alta Gracia, Laughing Man, Patagonia, and Ten Thousand Villages.

Finding Partners and Working with Partners: I found the organization Fair Trade Campaigns by reading the *Beginner's Guide to Fair Trade.*[9] I spoke with the National Organizer of Fair Trade Colleges and Universities, who was incredibly helpful sharing information about fair trade on campuses, resources available to us, and how to get started initiating a fair trade campaign at Seton Hill.

I also attended a faculty information session with Catholic Relief Services (CRS) to learn about faculty curriculum resources on the topic of fair trade and other social issues. Additionally, the students connected with the Fairtrade Foundation because they chose to donate money raised in a raffle to this organization. They found this organization in the text and performed further research on it while developing resources for the LibGuide. Another partner identified in the text is Ten Thousand Villages. A Ten Thousand Villages store is located in Pittsburgh, and the students found events there through the app Eventbrite.

The information from CRS was helpful for students' research and the information from FTC beneficial for the events students coordinated. Additionally, FTC provides a webpage for a registered college/university campaign where campaign activity can be logged. This activity includes organizing a team of students committed to the campaign, working with campus vendors to carry fair trade products, hosting fair trade events and meetings, and serving fair trade products at events and meetings. FTC offers additional support with videos, fliers, and other resources, along with providing free samples of fair trade products and promotional materials for students to distribute at their events. Students become easily oriented to FTC through the webinars it offers and by signing up for email updates and the newsletter. We also work with the production studios that produce fair trade documentaries to secure the rights to show films on campus.

Benefits

Instructor Benefits: Incorporating this service-learning project in the course has brought me great joy, particularly because of the students' commitment to doing well for their own sake and not just for a grade. As such, they also experience the spirit of a liberal arts education, which the university defines as "The Liberal Arts Curriculum equips students with ideas, knowledge and skills, leads them toward wisdom and inspires their service to the common good. It forms graduates who consider diverse ideas and ways of being, who bring passion to life and work, creating a world of justice and compassion."[10] Along with the Mission of the University and a description of Catholic Social Teaching, I list the definition of liberal arts on all my syllabi as well. When the students read this information on syllabi for every class I teach, they gain an understanding of how these approaches are integrated into their courses and they come to embody them in their attitude toward learning. In addition to this philosophical perspective, from a practical point-of-view, students become more self-directed, accountable, and creative, which are necessary skills in the workplace. Employers have shared with me that too often interns and new hires want to be told exactly what they are supposed to do, so they can deliver accordingly, as if a manager should provide an assignment and rubric, so the employee can check boxes and earn an "A" for their work. Service-learning helps to extend students' thinking about the meaning of professional excellence and success and to achieve this for their own purpose, not just to please the professor. I am beyond pleased with my students' intellectual maturity and work ethic.

    Students' Benefits: Students receive multiple benefits from this service-learning project that include gaining practical experience in the field, living the Mission of the University, and garnering an awareness about global social issues in the marketplace. Employers seek graduates with strong written and verbal communication skills, so this project helps students hone these skills while also gaining an understanding of writing and presenting for various audiences. At the end of the semester, students have a digital portfolio and professional report to share with potential employers, which may give them an advantage in the employment process. This course project is memorable for the students and will be memorable with an interviewer. Additionally, students can share that they have experience working in a team to accomplish goals.[11]

Throughout the Communication curriculum, students learn about the importance of mission for the success of any organization. They learn that though all organizations, including universities, may have a nicely framed mission statement hanging on a wall somewhere, few organizations actually embody that mission. The service-learning project helps students learn about the university mission by living it. Moreover, students also acquire perspective on global social issues, which makes them more conscious about purchasing products and the impact business has on human life. In addition, following the initiation of the fair trade campaign on campus, two honors students have taken up the subject for their senior honors projects. Thus, the students in the service-learning project are making a positive impact on their peers while shaping the campus culture to be oriented toward social justice.

Community Partners Benefits: A recent account of the Fair Trade Campaigns organization shows the following statistics for Universities: 123 Active Campaigns; 807 Advocates; 500 Fair Trade Retailers; 43 Resources; and 47 Resolutions Passed.[12] The SHU Fair Trade Campaign was very active this semester to contribute to these statistics. Moreover, Seton Hill is the only campus campaign on the western side of the state of Pennsylvania and one of only seven in the entire state. Activities the students coordinate are shared on social media, which provides Fair Trade Campaigns with information to repost and share within its network and larger audience. Ultimately, the local initiatives on campus make a positive global impact with the fair trade organizations that Fair Trade Campaigns supports.

Institutional Benefits: A component of the university's strategic plan is community engagement, so this service-learning project makes a valuable contribution. During the semester, our director of media relations reached out to me asking if I would be interested in being interviewed by a regional newspaper reporter. The reporter saw my tweets about the fair trade campaign, which sparked her interest for a story. A news story on the project affirms and celebrates the students' good work, fosters positive relations with the community, builds the reputation of the university, and extends the idea of fair trade beyond the campus. Additionally, when prospective students talk with current students, they are excited to hear their enthusiasm in stories of service-learning. Thus, a course project like this may make a positive impact on recruitment, retention, and reputation.

THE PROCESS

Expected Learning Outcomes: The expected learning outcomes of this course include course objectives, Catholic Social Teaching, and information fluency. Based on how other universities are oriented, they can be modified for other religious and secular ethics. Through a service-learning approach, students will gain knowledge and expertise developing, editing, and producing varied written public relations pieces for an experiential-learning goal of fair trade. This course is designed to introduce students to the principles and tenets of writing in a professional setting, develop correct writing of communication documents, practice writing skills, and receive feedback to help students grow as public relations communication professionals.

Upon successfully completing this course, communication students should be able to

- define and demonstrate effective public relations writing;
- understand ethical and dialogic considerations with engaged publics;
- understand and practice active listening;
- explain basic principles of professional writing;
- articulate informational and persuasive writing approaches;
- conduct the process of researching, obtaining and creating, organizing, and publishing information about an idea, product, service, individual, or organization;
- evaluate sources and resources for credibility and appropriateness;
- explain the basic concepts, style, and terminology associated with corporate and organizational writing;
- demonstrate writing skill in multiple media and formats utilized to communicate information and ideas to multiple audiences in a variety of mediums and media;
- demonstrate appropriate presentation modes for a variety of venues and audiences;
- demonstrate skill in drafting, revising, editing, and presenting written assignments;
- utilize a budget for implementation of the service-learning project; and
- understand strategic planning and project management involved in a public relations project.

Catholic Social Teaching Learning Objectives

Throughout the course students will practice each of the key principles of Catholic Social Teaching:

- **Human dignity**: The principle of human dignity is found in the communication theories of persuasive ethos and dialogic theory, which will be implemented in a service-learning project of fair trade that recognizes and supports human dignity in food and goods production.
- **Community and the common good**: In this course, public relations is positioned with attention to "otherness" and the positive impact public relations may offer to social change. The course reorients the idea of firm-centric "target audience" to a conception of the common good in "engaged publics."

- **Rights and responsibilities:** The goal of fair trade and fair food is fundamentally about uplifting workers' rights and responsible participation in the marketplace.
- **Option for the poor and vulnerable:** Public relations writing for fair trade raises consciousness about those who are poor and vulnerable in regard to both producer and consumer. Fair trade is explicitly oriented toward people living in the peripheral margins of society.
- **Participation:** The service-learning approach of the course initiates students' awareness about fair trade with a move toward thoughtful action. Through the service-learning project, students will understand communicative practices of and participation in the economic, political, and cultural life of society.
- **Stewardship of creation:** Public relations writing for fair trade acknowledges responsibility and care of materials as gifts from God and fosters sustainable practices for human development and the environment.
- **Global solidarity:** The idea of "think globally, act locally" is integral to the fair trade movement. Through public relations writing, students will garner a greater understanding of where and how food and goods are produced and share their knowledge with the larger university community.
- **Constructive role for government:** Students will explore regulatory issues in public relations writing and critically reflect on the role of government in global marketplaces.
- **Promotion of peace:** Ultimately, communication is about building positive relationships, which involves an attitude of mutual respect and the actions of dialogue and collaboration directed toward peace and justice.

Expected Learning Outcomes for Information Fluency

Our Library defines information-fluent students as those who, upon graduation, will possess the ability to combine all forms of literacy in order to master a chosen topic. Students who develop information fluency skills will successfully

- critically analyze appropriate topics;
- conceptualize the parameters of the topic;
- locate and access relevant information in all forms;
- competently evaluate information;
- understand practical, legal, and social issues related to the information;
- interact with faculty and staff in a manner evident of the development of superior research skills; and
- synthesize diverse types of information into a comprehensive and coherent work.

Curriculum Materials

- Zappala, Joseph M., and Ann R. Carden. *Public Relations Writing Worktext: A Practical Guide for the Profession.*[13]
- DeCarlo, Jacqueline. *Fair Trade: A Beginner's Guide.* Oneworld Publications.[14]
- Students also watch a fair trade documentary such as *Dukale's Dream* or *The True Cost.*[15]
- Students complete a digital portfolio, an extensive grammar assessment, and other writing assignments derived from the textbook. These assignments include:
  - o fair trade book chapter presentation
  - o white paper/backgrounder and LibGuide
  - o project management plan
  - o flier
  - o memo/letter/email
  - o press release
  - o proposal report
  - o final project presentation

Steps Involved

- The course begins with viewing a movie about fair trade such as *Dukale's Dream*[16] or *The True Cost.*[17] Students then attend a webinar about fair trade through the Fair Trade Campaigns organization. Since this webinar takes place outside of normal class time, I provide fair trade snacks for the students, such as coffee, tea, and toaster pastries. It involves me bringing in my toaster and coffee maker from home but is worth the inconvenience with how much excitement it adds to the event. Students have also offered to share their own teapots and fair trade tea. The webinars offered from Fair Trade Campaigns vary every year but are always relevant. The webinars allow speakers from fair trade organizations to present and respond to questions through video conferencing. Speakers in the past have included the owner of AltaGracia, a manufacturer of fair trade college apparel, and an executive from Patagonia, an outdoor clothing company committed to environmental sustainability, and a senior marketing manager for Divine Chocolate, a fair trade cocoa cooperative. Other webinars are offered throughout the semester, which provide additional information and support.
- After watching the movie and webinar, students read the book *Fair Trade: A Beginner's Guide.* In groups, students develop a PowerPoint presentation on two of the chapters and incorporate secondary sources from the library's databases. Therefore, the first half of the semester is devoted to

the students formulating an understanding of the fair trade industry and its history, practices, critiques, and future directions. During their reading, students identify fair trade organizations cited within the chapters and collect them into a comprehensive list. Additionally, they identify key terms from the chapter and perform academic research utilizing the library's databases to collect scholarly articles on these related terms. Amy Podoletz, one of the students in this class and co-author of this chapter, coordinated this collaborative research with her peers to organize the sources and resources into a Fair Trade LibGuide for the university's website.[18] While it is not necessary to create a LibGuide specific for a project such as this, it is beneficial to the students in the class and to future classes. While our research librarian would have created the LibGuide for us, having the students involved with Amy leading them provided enhanced learning as well as greater depth and breadth for the LibGuide.

- Each group then uses this research to formulate a modified backgrounder/white paper to respond to the question, "What is fair trade?" This document is then used as a reference for subsequent writing assignments that support the fair trade event, including a project plan, social media, promotional piece, letter, email, speech pitch, media release, report, and final presentation.

- This service-learning project is an example of "big teaching."[19] Small teaching involves creating short, in-class activities independent of one another. Conversely, big teaching involves a comprehensive semester-long project. While big teaching is often associated with requiring greater faculty involvement and planning with the accompanying time commitment, I do not find this assertion to be the case with the fair trade service-learning project. The increase in students' motivation and engagement leads to their ownership and commitment to the work. My role has become more of a facilitator, directing them to partners and helping them navigate logistics. Working on this project helps students to connect with others on campus, which fosters a feeling of being a part of a learning community rather than taking classes in isolation of student life. Moreover, I have found that students feel energized by this collaborative experience and become even more involved in other university initiatives after having these connections established.

- The fair trade project involves working with partners on and off campus. Having partners support the project is necessary for its success. The following list identifies key partners and their involvement with the project.

  o   Research librarian—works with the students to develop a LibGuide on fair trade. Once the LibGuide is created, the research librarian works with students in successive courses to update the LibGuide and works with students on how to use it for their research. Students in successive courses will work with the research librarian to revise and update the LibGuide. Also, the research librarian works with students to host fair trade events in the Learning Commons.

o Student affairs staff—meets with the students, brainstorms ideas for events, and assists students with the implementation and promotion of their events. Student affairs also secures the rights to host movie screening events.

o Service outreach coordinator—invited to class to brainstorm ideas with the students, discuss how their service is important for the university's mission, and share experiences with similar service experiences.

o Bookstore manager—talks with students about fair trade items in the store and the possibility of adding more fair trade items to the assortment.

o Athletics—either works directly with students if a fair trade event will be incorporated into an athletic event or works indirectly by encouraging student-athletes to participate in events.

o Solutions center—provides technology for showing movies.

o Food service—coordinates with students for varying needs, such as holding an event in the cafeteria, providing barista service for fair trade coffee, or adding fair trade food items to the cafeteria and other food outlets on campus.

o Marketing/alumni relations—shares students' initiatives with local press and alumni newsletter.

o Fair Trade Campaigns—provides webinars and resources on fair trade event planning, promotional materials and samples of fair trade products, and a webpage for the campus campaign.

o Ten Thousand Villages—provides a tour of the store and background on the organization. Visits campus for information sessions and sale of fair trade items.

- Specific steps of the fair trade campaign:

o The class was introduced to the book store manager and toured the bookstore to locate fair trade items and discuss the adoption of attritional fair trade goods.

o The class watched a fair trade documentary as an introduction to fair trade.

o Students read the text *Fair Trade: A Beginners Guide* and worked in groups to present certain chapters to the class, which included additional sources found in library databases.

o Students created a backgrounder/white paper by researching additional scholarly sources and then shared them with their peers and the research librarian to develop the LibGuide.

o   During class, students discussed how to plan an event and created a project management plan.

o   Once the students decided on what kind of event they wanted to do, they discussed and determined how they wanted to promote the events. This work met writing assignment criteria.

o   Once the advertisements were distributed to the community to see, the class took the time to write a letter to deans, the university's president, and the *Setonian*, the university's magazine.

o   The class brainstormed for a hashtag to use for social media when going live during the event: #SHUdents4good.

o   After the events, students wrote a report proposal that shared their research, reflection on their involvement with the service-learning project, and recommendations for continued involvement with the fair trade campaign on campus.

POST-PROJECT ASSESSMENT
Methods of Reflection

Students reflect on their experiences through in-class discussion, reflections on their digital portfolio websites, and class presentations. I also ask students to reflect on the work of others. For example, throughout the semester, students not only submit assignments but also share them with the class. We call this component of small teaching "SHU's Got Talent Moments," where the class and I express strong aspects of their work as well as areas that could be improved. In addition to the technical features, students share their feelings about doing the work and the impact they have. Students find the digital portfolio assignment a creative opportunity to showcase their work and involvement while reflecting on these experiences. Presentations also offer a venue for students to share their work and express their thoughts. All of these methods of reflection provide ways for students to contemplate their learning throughout the service-learning project and gain a comprehensive understanding of the integrated its aspects.

Post Project Feedback

•   At the end of the semester course evaluations, students have indicated the benefits they received through the service-learning project.

o   "Continue to use the Fair Trade theme for the class, I didn't realize it until the final portfolio assignment, but having a theme really helps me to understand PR writing better."

       o   "We had many real assignments, as opposed to hypothetical ones. I thought that helped me grow as a student, and as a communication professional."

       o   "The hands on assignments were great!"

       o   "I contributed to my own learning by doing personal research and being granted creative liberty."

- Amy interviewed students currently enrolled in the course as well as from a previous course. Amy also shares her own experience as a student in the course and her additional contribution working with a research librarian to develop the fair trade LibGuide. Thus, Amy shares the following:

       o   "As an undergraduate student, my experience with the fair trade campaign project has been very positive. I learned how to create a LibGuide, develop a whitepaper/backgrounder, and coordinate an event on campus. Creating the Fair Trade LibGuide was my favorite part of the entire experience. It allowed me to be creative, organized, and intellectually stimulated. The other students in my Writing in Public Relations class helped me find sources from a database and identify websites from different fair trade organizations. From there, I created the LibGuide with the collection, books and e-books, which we had in our library and libraries around the area. The students informed me that the LibGuide was very helpful in finding sources for their whitepaper/backgrounder assignment."

       o   "While doing this project, there were a lot of things that I have never done before; the LibGuide being one. When creating the whitepaper/backgrounder, I wasn't sure what I was doing. As my group and I looked at the description for the project, we were intimidated and confused about what it was actually supposed to look like. Thankfully, we were given examples from our professor about what we were supposed to do. My group and I noticed that it was an essay that incorporated visual elements. With this understanding, we were able to create something that was truly educational and fun to make. Many of my classmates said that this project really gave them the sense of a real-world experience and will add this experience to their resumes and digital portfolios. The students also mentioned that they could see the growth from when they first started the project in early September, until now, late October. One student said, 'It was really interesting to learn about something so relevant and modern. While researching, I found old articles, new articles, and many different organizations that made it easier to understand and learn more about the issue.' A student from the course a previous semester shared, 'It felt really good to not only make a campaign, but plan the actual event as well.' Other students agreed that having the opportunity to be creative was the most empowering aspect for them. Overall, the student experience was positive with some minor difficulties."

- University leaders remarks:
  - o Amy spoke with primary leaders on campus affiliated with the fair trade campaign. She writes: "I had the great opportunity to work with the community partners that we have both on-campus and off-campus. The Vice President of Student Affairs, and the Coordinator of Service Outreach, are great on-campus community partners who were more than happy to talk to me about the experiences they have when working with students on social justice issues like fair trade. They both agreed that being able to come to a class, speak about an important issue, and see that the students understand and want to do something about it, is the most rewarding. The VP of Student Affairs said, 'It is so rewarding to share with college students the potential they have to make real change, to lead initiatives, and to be educated about people on the margins.' They also agreed that it is difficult to show students the injustice when it is not right in front of them, but knowing that there are movies, images, and other resources out there can foster a greater understanding of how important this issue is in our world. The Coordinator of Service Outreach said, 'We may have a negative view of people, but when I go into a class and find students passionate about relevant issues, it gives me hope for humanity. I want the students to be aware of injustice in the community, and want them to address that injustice.' Amy Biller, our school Bookstore manager said 'I am so glad that the students are able to do events and projects like this, to make a difference. I hope that President Finger sees your proposals and your work and will think about putting more fair trade products in the school. Or will at least be aware of the issue and will be more open-minded about it.'"
- Community partner remarks:
  - o Amy continues, "I also had the great opportunity to talk with the National Organizer for Fair Trade Colleges & Universities. She explained that working with the students is the best part of her job. She enjoys seeing students in colleges and universities grow by being a part of the fair trade campaign. She conveyed that working with Seton Hill University has been very rewarding. Seton Hill University has shown great support of the Fair Trade Movement along with other colleges and universities that are trying to be a fair trade designated school. She hopes that Seton Hill will share the Fair Trade project that they are doing on their fair trade campaign

website and those involved with the movement. While talking to the community partners, they have expressed great interest in the learning of students and want to see them do more for their community and for important issues in our world today."

Project Assessment and Reporting Methods

- The instructor had the opportunity to present this project to the University Board of Trustees, who found great interest in it and offered their accolades for continuing the fair trade campaign and shared this course project in a campus-wide Teach & Learn session with faculty and administrators.
- The students chose to do an extra fair trade event during finals week on their own.
- Students have often contacted the instructor later about news and products related to fair trade.
- Two students started their own business selling fair trade items and met with representatives from the Home Shopping Network.
- During the Fair Trade Week, students engaged social media prior to and during the events. During and after the events, many people were posting about how well it went. Someone posted a video of the Griffin mascot chasing someone down the hall to the Ten Thousand Villages winter sale. Everyone really got into it and the class ended feeling proud of what they accomplished.
- When I first taught the course, none of the students had heard of fair trade, and when I taught the course a second time, all of the students were, at the least, aware of the term.

Difficulties Encountered

Student Issues: Amy Podoletz talked with current and past students in the course about difficulties they encountered and found that their primary issues were related to the research process and using library databases to find sources to address a continually evolving topic. Students mentioned a variety of issues, such as difficulties in understanding the arcane organization of library databases, with "finding good articles," with locating the full-text of an article or book as opposed to an abstract, finding current information and that "perfect" source, or using interlibrary loan. They also noted that the class text seemed somewhat outdated, though still useful. While students found these issues challenging, they will encounter similar issues when they do research for their future careers, so the experiences will help them succeed. The instructor will discuss this issue with the librarian to provide an introduction to database searching early in the semester and perform more work with library databases in 100-level courses.

Students who took the class the first time it was offered felt that the later classes benefited from the addition of the fair trade LibGuide resource because it was much harder for them to find sources for the project. While students did not report feeling intimidated to take on a project at the beginning, at the end of the semester, they learned that they were too confident at first, which prevented them from paying more attention to detail and allowed errors to occur. For example, the students did not follow up with Student Affairs to ensure the fair trade documentary video had been purchased. On the day of the event, they realized a miscommunication had occurred and the DVD had not arrived. They immediately felt the anxiety of dealing with a crisis management situation and found a way to stream the movie instead. Another group that offered a ticket raffle for a fair trade gift basket did not think about needing a cash box to make change. They also had to think quickly to resolve the situation. While these issues could have been prevented with more careful planning, they proved to be some of the best learning moments for the students despite the anxiety they produced.

Instructor Issues: Maintaining the Fair Trade Campaigns webpage is an easy task, but I wasn't able to update it as much as I would have liked. In the future, I will delegate this task to a student. Since the writing assignments were for a real audience, including the president of the university, my feedback on student work needed to be meticulous and rechecked before sending. While the students found the fair trade text helpful, they also noted that it is outdated. I am considering adopting a recently published text, *Sewing Hope: How One Factory Challenges the Apparel Industry's Sweatshops*.[20] The students did a good job utilizing social media to promote their events and share information during the events; however, we should have been more deliberate tagging the Fair Trade Campaigns organization.

Community Partner Issues: Since Fair Trade Campaigns collects data on campaign activity, they also would have liked me to update the campaign webpage more often. Fair Trade Campaigns sets goals for each campus campaign, including hosting events and educational sessions and adopting fair trade items in campus outlets, such as dining services and the bookstore. While the university leadership is supportive of promoting fair trade on campus, the dining service is run by an outside company, making it difficult for fair trade items to be offered. Also, the campus bookstore is run by a large corporation, which limits the bookstore manager's product decisions. However, having the students' support helped acquire an additional fair trade product in the store.

Conclusion

As I continue to use this service-learning project each year, I become more comfortable and confident leading the students in this endeavor. Correspondingly, the students' enthusiasm to engage this project grows each year. The students now call me, endearingly, "The Fair Trade Queen" and with the buzz this project creates on campus, first-year students look forward to their opportunity to take this project on in their second year of study. Also, some of the more successful events, such as the Ten Thousand Villages Holiday sale, are now requested each year and will become part of the university's traditions. I will continue to offer the fair trade service-learning project for the many wins it creates. Students gain researching and writing skills, contribute to the cultural ethos on campus, and embody the university's mission to transform the world. In addition, Ten Thousand Villages offers a fundraising component for selling items on campus. Since the sales were a great success and we received a percentage of those sales, the students and I discussed putting this money toward attending the Fair Trade Campaigns National Conference. In the future, I would like to extend this project even further by taking students abroad to visit fair trade organizations. If anyone reading this chapter is interested in collaborating on this initiative, please feel free to contact me.

APPENDIX MATERIALS

- Fair Trade Book Chapter Presentation Assignment
- White Paper/Backgrounder Assignment
- Proposal Report Assignment.

Fair Trade Book Chapter Presentation Assignment

Your team is tasked with creating a presentation (PowerPoint, Google Slides, Prezi, etc.) on chapters from the fair trade text (approximately twenty minutes). Use the textbook and checklist for guidelines on professional presentations. You will be evaluated based on content and style.

Content: Share major ideas and resources from the reading. Use these major ideas as key terms to search the library databases for supporting secondary sources. You should identify at least three secondary sources. Scholarly peer-reviewed journal articles are a priority, followed by trade periodicals and newspaper articles. One slide needs to connect the reading to Catholic Social Teaching (CST). Use the CST LibGuide to identify a source that relates to the reading. If specific organizations are listed in the reading, look at their corresponding websites and share what you find. Develop a quiz or interactive exercise at the end of the presentation to evaluate the audience's understanding/comprehension of the material. The final slide should provide a bibliography using a citing style of your choice (APA, MLA, and Chicago). Make sure content is cited within/throughout the presentation and the citing style is consistent.

Style: Please make sure that all team members' names are on the first slide. Use an appropriate theme and color scheme. Limit the amount of text on slides and include effective visuals. Include a video clip that is embedded in the presentation (not linked). All members of the team should speak during the presentation and refrain from using notes except to provide source citations. Dress is business casual. Speakers should utilize effective public speaking skills.

White Paper/Backgrounder Assignment

While the work may be divided among group members, the submitted white paper/backgrounder needs to be a cohesive document. Also, each member should proof and edit others' writing. Finally, every group member needs to contribute to the assignment equitably.

DELIVERABLE DESCRIPTION

A white paper is an informative, comprehensive piece drawing on multiple sources to help the audience understand a particular topic or issue. Further description of white papers can be found using this link to the Online Writing Lab at Purdue University: https://owl.english.purdue.edu/owl/owlprint/546/.

While white papers are written for an external audience, backgrounders are often used to assist writers preparing other public relations pieces. They are also less standard than a white paper, ranging from fact sheets to multiple-page briefings. Further description of backgrounders can be found in the textbook. White papers and backgrounders are shorter than a report but share similar organizational structures.

ASSIGNMENT DETAILS

Now that you have finished reading *Fair Trade: A Beginner's Guide*, you will develop a white paper/backgrounder on fair trade. Additionally, you will include other sources and resources identified within the book and related to topics in the book. Based on your reading and class presentations, you will provide an organized synopsis of the book highlighting the most important information for the SHU Fair Trade Campaign and your team project. The additional **sources** you incorporate throughout the report add depth, and the **resources** you highlight add breadth to the white paper/backgrounder. **Check your sources and resources.**
- Is it honest, credible, and unbiased?
- What is the source's purpose?
- Where does the material originate?
- Can you verify it?
- Is it current and complete?

Begin by summarizing the book and organizing the material into sections based on the topics/chapter titles in the book. You may organize and change titles within your paper. Thus, the section titles do not need to follow the same order as the book or share the chapter titles. Make decisions on the organization and section titles based on what you believe to be the most appropriate and relatable to the reader. Very important: one section needs to be on Catholic Social Teaching that draws from and connects to ideas from all of the sections. Use the Catholic Social Teaching LibGuide to define terms and discuss the relationship between fair trade and CST. Next, incorporate additional sources (scholarly articles)* and resources (organizations) that correlate to the sections of the paper. Then add aesthetic elements of design to the paper with graphics, images, and infographics. Finally, review the paper for typos, grammar errors, and layout.

Sources should be cited with footnotes or endnotes. Include a bibliography page.

You may also want to incorporate appendices of organizations' websites or other relevant material that is too large to be within the document. Print a black and white copy of the white paper/backgrounder to submit in class. A cover page should be visually appealing and include group member names in alphabetical order.

Proposal Report Assignment

1. Determine purpose
- What are you trying to convey?
    - o   Analyze a situation or a new idea
    - o   Provide recommendations
2. Determine content
- Which format of report do you need?
    - o   Proposal
3. Determine audience
- Is the audience internal or external?
    - o   Internal
4. Develop the proposal report
- Think about the appearance of your report (professional and attractive)
- Avoid switching tenses in the report
- Use headings and subheadings (lower-level headings)
- Use transitions, previews, and reviews

Proposal Report Outline: Your report will be graded on content and style
1. Title Page (outside cover)—needs to be aesthetically appealing (graphics and color)
    - o   title of the report
    - o   date submitted
    - o   authors listed in alphabetical order

2. Table of Contents—list of headings and subheadings throughout the report with page numbers
3. Table of Figures—list of images, charts, graphs, and other figures throughout the report with page numbers (can be on the same page as the Table of Contents or a separate page)
4. Executive Summary—an overview of the report in one paragraph. Ask yourself, if the President only read the executive summary, would she have a good understanding of the report's contents? Would it entice her to look at the report?
5. Body (use headings and subheadings)—remember to cite information, Chicago style, within the text (you may include full title pages for each section to differentiate them)
   o Introduction to Fair Trade (use information from white paper/backgrounder)
   o Fair Trade Campaign 2017 (what you did, include pictures)
   o Recommendations for future students participating in the fair trade campaign
   o Recommendations to become a Fair Trade Campus
6. References—in Chicago format, heading should be "Bibliography"
7. Appendices—include a copy of all course assignments (Fair Trade Book Chapter Presentation; Project Management Plan; Flier; Memo/Letter; Press Release). Include source material as you see fit (websites, articles, other).

Page numbering:
- Make sure that pages are numbered.
- The title page should not be numbered, but it is understood to be page i.
- The table of contents is page ii and the number is put on the page. The table of figures can be (begin) on the same page as the table of contents.
- The executive summary follows the table of contents and is numbered in lower case roman numerals (e.g., iv).
- All other pages through the end of the reference page are numbered sequentially, starting with the stakeholder commitment as page 1.
- You do not need to number the appendices, but provide a separator page, which is numbered so it may be referenced in the table of contents.

Style:
- Review the aesthetics of each page. Do not let the end of a sentence of a paragraph go to the next page. Use headings and subheadings (may be different sized font). Use consistent graphics and fonts. Include pictures. Use a page header with logo. Proof for spelling, typos, grammar, and syntax. Use third-person voice. Print in color and professionally bind. Needs to

be a cohesive document (not pieced together by different people). Needs to be completed equitably.

You will use the information in the proposal report for your Final Project Presentation assignment.

Notes

1. "LibGuides: Catholic Social Teaching: Home," Home—Catholic Social Teaching—LibGuides at Seton Hill University, accessed December 14, 2017, https://setonhill.libguides.com/Catholic_Social_Teaching.

2.   Erin M. Brigham, *See, Judge, Act: Catholic Social Teaching and Service Learning* (Winona:. Anselm Academic, Christian Brothers Publications, 2013); Susan Crawford Sullivan, *A Vision of Justice: Engaging Catholic Social Teaching on the College Campus* (Eldoret, Kenya: AMECEA Gaba Publ., 2014).

3.   The Human Thread, accessed December 14, 2017, https://www.humanthreadcampaign.org/.

4.   Susan Van Zanten, *Joining the Mission: A Guide for (mainly) New College Faculty*, (Grand Rapids (US): William B. Eerdmans, 2011).

5.   "Mission Statement," Seton Hill University, accessed December 14, 2017, https://www.setonhill.edu/who-we-are/mission-statement/.

6.   Chade-Meng Tan, *Search Inside Yourself: The Unexpected Path to Achieving Success, Happiness (and World Peace)* (New York, NY: HarperOne, 2014).

7.   Rajendra Sisodia, David B. Wolfe, and Jagdish N. Sheth, *Firms of Endearment: How World-class Companies Profit from Passion and Purpose* (Upper Saddle River: Pearson Education, 2014).

8.   "Grow the Fair Trade Movement in Your Community," Fair Trade Campaigns, accessed December 14, 2017, http://fairtradecampaigns.org/.

9.   Jacqueline DeCarlo. *Fair Trade: A Beginner's Guide* (Oxford: Oneworld, 2010).

10.   "Liberal Arts Curriculum Handbook," Seton Hill University Documents, accessed December 14, 2017, https://griffinslair.setonhill.edu/documents/getfile.cfm?DocID=2830.

11.   Diana Whitney, Amanda Trosten-Bloom, Jay Cherney, and Ron Fry, *Appreciative Team Building: Positive Questions to Bring Out the Best of Your Team* (New York: iUniverse, Inc., 2004).

12.   "Fair Trade Campaigns Website," accessed December 14, 2017, http://fairtradecampaigns.org/.

13.   Joseph M. Zappala and Ann R. Carden, *Public Relations Writing Worktext: A Practical Guide for the Profession* (New York, NY: Routledge, 2010).

14.   Jacqueline DeCarlo, *Fair Trade: A Beginner's Guide* (London: Oneworld Publications, 2007).

15.   "Dukale's Dream Movie, Hugh Jackman coffee documentary," Splash | Dukale's Dream Movie | Hugh Jackman Coffee Documentary, accessed December 14, 2017, http://dukalesdream.com/.

16.   Ibid.

17.   "The True Cost," accessed December 14, 2017, https://truecostmovie.com/.

18.   "LibGuides: Fair Trade: Home," Home—Fair Trade—LibGuides at Seton Hill University, accessed December 14, 2017, http://setonhill.LibGuides.com/FairTrade.

19.   James M. Lang, *Small Teaching: Everyday Lessons from the Science of Learning* (San Francisco: Jossey-Bass, 2016).

20.   Sarah Adler-Milstein and John M. Kline. *Sewing Hope: How One Factory Challenges the Apparel Industry's Sweatshops* (Oakland, CA: University of California Press, 2017).

CHAPTER TWELVE

Integrating Library Research and Information Literacy into Archaeological Service-learning

Lara Homsey-Messer
Associate Professor, Department of Anthropology
Indiana University of Pennsylvania
lmesser@iup.edu

THE ACTIVITY

Description: In the fall of 2012, the Public Archaeology class at Murray State University (MSU) conducted archaeological testing of the historic Canton site as part of a semester-long community service-learning project. The historic town of Canton, located at the confluence of Hopson Creek and Lake Barkley in western Kentucky, consists of several archaeological sites and historic properties. The particular site involved in this project is listed by the Kentucky State Historic Preservation Office as 15Tr477.[1] Our community partner was the United States Army Corps of Engineers (USACE), Nashville District. The USACE, like all federal agencies, is mandated to manage and protect historic properties from any and all "adverse effects," be they man-made, such as looting or Army activity, or natural, such as erosion. In order to comply with these federal regulations, USACE contracted with New South Associates, a CRM firm headquartered in Stone Mountain, Georgia, to conduct an archaeological survey along the Cumberland River.[2] 15Tr477 was identified at this time but was considered to lack enough significance to garner protection under the National Historic Preservation Act (NHPA). However, because two historic coffins were soon after reported to have eroded out of the bank along the site's northern edge, New South recommended further work at the site in order to determine whether more graves were present. As a result, the Nashville District put out a request for proposals to undertake the additional testing (hereafter referred to as "Phase II testing"). Serendipitously, the author just so happened to contact USACE staff archaeologist Valerie McCormick to see if the Corps was interested in partnering with MSU for the training of undergraduate students in the archaeology program. The Corps readily agreed to have MSU conduct the Phase II testing as a service-learning project. McCormick's immediate concern was to determine whether or not additional burials were present at the site, and, if so, if they were at risk of eroding out of the cut bank and would therefore require reburial and/or stabilization of the cut bank to prevent further loss, a management effort funded by taxpayer dollars.

It was immediately apparent that on-the-ground fieldwork alone would be insufficient to answer these questions and provide the necessary data for the USACE to determine whether the site warranted protection under the NHPA. A great deal of library, archival, and internet research would also be necessary. Library-based methods included (1) USACE historic maps and real estate records, (2) US census records, (3) oral histories and modern cemetery surveys, and (4) internet research to identify and date maker marks from diagnostic artifacts. During one class period, the class visited the Pogue Special Collections Library at Murray State University in order to find historic maps of the area. There, staff introduced students to the range of materials available and gave them a tour of the map room containing historic and rare maps of western Kentucky. With their help, we identified two maps of interest, one a 1930 TVA map showing the area prior to impoundment (Figure 1c), and another from the 1895 Kentucky Atlas showing the location of Canton in Trigg County (see Figure 1b). During another class period, we met with USACE librarian Tammy Kirk. Kirk was invaluable in helping us identify cemetery and archival records for the region as well as retrieving USACE real estate records. In fact, it was Kirk who tracked down local historian and genealogist David Sumner's cemetery survey, *Cemeteries of Cadiz and Trigg County, Kentucky,* a publication that proved invaluable but which is not readily available outside the USACE-Nashville district office and local historical society. Finally, we spent two class periods becoming familiar with and utilizing web-based resources to find National Register nominations, census records, and dates for maker's marks appearing on bricks and pottery recovered from the site. The results of these resources are described below, but it is worth noting here that prior to this work, over 80 percent of the students admitted to not being familiar with all or most of these kinds of resources.

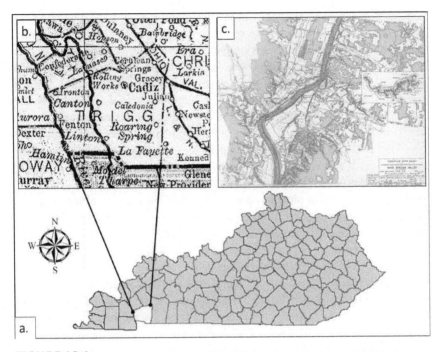

FIGURE 12.1
Location of Trigg County in Kentucky (a); location of Canton Site as recorded in the 1895 Kentucky Atlas (b), and location of Canton Site with reference to USACE 1930 map of the Main Stream Valley (c).

Getting Started: Because archaeology is an applied field that is best learned experientially, it is ideally suited to integrating community service-learning (CSL) into its curriculum. And yet, as Nassaney[3] has recently noted, archaeological pedagogy has changed little since the 1960s. The lack of pedagogical reform within the discipline has received significant criticism in the last decade. For example, Fagan[4] has argued that it is no longer acceptable "for an archaeologist to be trained in purely academic and fieldwork skills," and Bender and Smith[5] have called on professional archaeologists to reevaluate the college curriculum in which we train students to enter the profession. Their volume offers numerous avenues for redirecting curricula, but despite archaeology's natural fit, CSL is surprisingly not among them. Nassaney and Levine's recent volume, *Archaeology and Community Service-learning*, seeks to remedy this oversight and provides numerous case studies detailing the benefits of integrating service-learning in archaeological curricula.[6] This paper seeks to add to the emerging literature on this topic by illustrating the ways in which archaeology students can benefit from integrating not just CSL but also library research and information literacy into the curriculum.

Such pedagogical transformations are more crucial given the significant changes that the field of archaeology has undergone since the 1960s, including preservation legislation and the widespread growth in the cultural resource management (CRM) sector. Unlike traditional "academic" archaeology, CRM is focused on the *management* and *preservation* of cultural resources. For example, the National Historic Preservation Act of 1966 mandates that federal agencies "take into account the effect of their undertakings" on historic properties that are included or eligible for inclusion in the National Register of Historic Places (NRHP). Section 106 of NHPA stipulates a three-phase process wherein cultural resources must be identified (Phase 1), evaluated for NRHP eligibility (Phase 2), and mitigated (Phase 3) any time federal land, permits, or funds are involved in a project, such as road or pipeline construction. Section 110 further mandates that federal agencies proactively monitor, manage, and preserve all cultural resources under their purview if they are eligible for the NRHP. These and other influential cultural resources laws ushered in the era of CRM that today employs nearly three-quarters of all archaeologists in the US.

Motivations: At the heart of CRM is determining whether or not an archaeological site (referred to as an "historic property" in NHPA language) is eligible for inclusion on the National Register of Historic Places, the official list of the nation's properties deemed worthy of preservation and maintained by the Department of Interior. Eligibility determination is a somewhat equivocal skill for which many students struggle to gain competency. NRHP eligibility hinges on a site meeting two important criteria. First, a property must have "integrity," meaning that it must be well preserved, intact, and undisturbed by erosion, looting, etc. Second, and more ambiguously, a property must have "significance," meaning that it falls under one of four categories in which it (1) is associated with the events of national, regional, or local history (criteria A); (2) is associated with individuals important to national, regional, or local history (criteria B); (3) represents a distinct architectural style, time period, or the work of a master (criteria C); or (4) has the potential to yield data important to understanding broad historical or prehistoric trends (criteria D). For historic-period resources, the artefactual record itself is rarely enough; often, in-depth historic and archival research is necessary to determine whether a site is truly "significant" or not.

Unfortunately, despite this need, many graduating archaeology students just entering the profession have been poorly or minimally trained in library and information-based skills, the latter which are more commonly employed by historians. Yet, more and more, CRM practitioners are being called upon to broaden their archaeological skill set to include library-based research and information literacy. The following case study of an archaeological survey at the historic site of Canton, Kentucky, illustrates how library instruction and information literacy can be built into an archaeological service-learning project and how such information is crucial to informing a sound determination of site significance, and, by extension, NRHP eligibility.

THE PEOPLE

The Libraries: We utilized two libraries during this project. First, we visited the Pogue Library on the campus of Murray State University, which houses the university's special collections, genealogies, university archives, and historic maps. The Special Collections Department was established in 1968 to serve the needs of its patrons by acquiring and providing access to information about the cultural history of the Jackson Purchase area of southwestern Kentucky and northwestern Tennessee. Published and printed regional and county histories, manuscript materials, oral histories, and other significantly unique items that support the curriculum of Murray State University are acquired and made available for use by students and researchers. The special collections staff at Pogue Library provided assistance in archival research and historic map interpretation. The second library utilized was the USACE library, which contains an archival record of the Corps' past and current civil engineering projects, cemetery relocation reports, real estate acquisition reports and maps, historic flood information, and photographs. Since much of this information is of public interest, the library welcomes requests for information from the general public. Although much of their collection is print-based and not open to the public, items may be borrowed via interlibrary loan or photocopied by staff librarians. Although we were unable to coordinate a site visit with the library due to time constraints, USACE staff librarian Tammy Kirk worked with students via email and telephone to track down local genealogies and cemetery inventories, as well as Corps real estate records going back into the 1940s.

Instructors: The instructor for the course was Lara Homsey-Messer, associate professor of archaeology in the Geosciences Department at Murray State University. Homsey-Messer additionally served as the university-wide coordinator for the Office of Service-learning and Civic Engagement at Murray State University. Other contributors were invaluable in conducting this project. Corps archaeologist Valerie McCormick introduced students to the project areas and gave them an overview of CRM within the context of federal agency management. Lake Barkley Park Ranger Rich Rice and Resource Manager Mike Looney met us in the field in order to coordinate access to the archaeological survey area and provide information regarding the location of the eroded graves in 2010. Finally, several Murray State University offices provided logistical and financial support, including the Office of Service-learning, which provide grant money to purchase equipment necessary to complete the project, the Mid-American Remote-sensing Center, which provided equipment and transportation, and the Department of Geosciences, which provided financial and purchasing assistance.

The Course: The course was ARC 350, Public Archaeology, a three-credit elective for students in the geoarchaeology major and anthropology minor at Murray State University. The course consists of an introduction to the philosophy and mechanics of modern cultural resource management, primarily from an archaeological perspective. Emphasis is placed on gaining a practical working knowledge of CRM legislation, regulation, and process, as well as balancing business, legal, ethical, and public interest issues. The class was a traditional face-to-face course lasting an entire semester and meet for three hours one day a week; the course length was designed to allow time to get to and from the field and/or library, depending on the course content for the week. Students additionally had to devote three Saturdays to fieldwork and ten hours of documented independent library, archival, and/or internet research.

The Students: As a mid-level course, most students were junior and senior geoarchaeology majors and anthropology minors focused on going on to graduate school in applied archaeology (i.e., CRM or other related field such as historic preservation and museum studies) or seeking employment in CRM directly upon graduation. The course often draws students from related disciplines, including history, sociology, and geography/Earth sciences.

The Community Partner: Our community partner was the United States Corps of Engineers, Nashville District. Under section 101 of the National Historic Preservation Act, all federal agencies, such as USACE, are required to identify, monitor, and protect cultural resources on federal property. Given that only two archaeologists are on staff to monitor hundreds of archaeological sites distributed over nearly 60,000 square acres, complying with this federal mandate is difficult at best. Partnering with such agencies provides students with real-world experience in all facets of archaeological management while providing USACE with much-needed labor and resources.

Connecting and Working with Community Partners: Faculty at Murray State University often seek out community partners on their own through various professional and local research networks, or they seek help from the Office of Service-learning and Civic Engagement (OSLCE). In this case, I identified a community partner through my professional networks. Because federal agencies (and state and local agencies when they have federal permits or funds) are mandated by law to inventory and monitor archaeological and historic resources threatened by development and infrastructure projects, identifying potential partners who need assistance complying with these laws is a fairly easy task. Previous agencies which have partnered with the Public Archaeology class include the City of Murray, the Fulton County Economic Development Partnership, and Calloway County Parks and Recreation. It helped that in many of these instances Murray State University alumni worked within the agency and therefore already had a desire to partner with their alma mater and to provide students with real-world experience, something many of them told me they wished they had had while in college.

Benefits

Instructor Benefits: The public archaeology students were not just introduced to unfamiliar library and web-based resources, they also met with librarians and other information experts who guided them in learning to use the resource, thereby expanding the content expertise of the instructor and demonstrating the inherent interdisciplinary and collaborative nature of today's applied archaeology. Other benefits include expanding instructors' professional networks outside of the traditional academic setting. In some cases, the community partners I have worked with have sought me out years later to conduct additional (paid) archaeological consulting work, some of which brought income into the university to purchase archaeological equipment, educational instrumentation, and materials, and to employ students.

Student Benefits: Few archaeology classes build in background archival and library research in a systematic or meaningful way, focusing instead (and understandably) on field and laboratory methods. In the study presented here, students were not just introduced to unfamiliar library and web-based resources, they also met with librarians and other information experts who guided them in learning to use the resource. As noted above, this expansion of key content areas demonstrated for students the interdisciplinary and collaborative nature of today's applied archaeology in a proactive way that simply telling them passively cannot. The CRM careers that archaeology students are likely to be employed in upon graduation in the next decade will necessarily require these kinds of information literacy skills in addition to the more traditional skill set. Thus, gaining familiarity and fluency in this skill set will not only make students more marketable but also give them a greater sense of confidence once they find themselves undertaking CRM projects after graduation.

Partner Benefits: As previously noted, with only two archaeologists available to monitor hundreds of archaeological sites, complying with federal cultural resources mandates is difficult at best. While multiple federal laws require identifying and proactively managing cultural resources, very little money is invested in this effort at the federal level. Thus, partnering with such agencies provides students with real-world experience in all facets of archaeological management while providing USACE with much-needed labor and resources. Finally, an unexpected benefit consisted of improved relations between the USACE and the local community and historical society. When the Tennessee Valley Authority dammed the Tennessee River to form Lake Barkley to create hydroelectric power and the Land Between the Lakes (LBL) recreation area, numerous small towns, such as historic Canton, were inundated and/or abandoned. Between 1960 and 1966, when inundation was completed, Trigg County lost nearly 28,000 acres and saw the displacement of more than 300 residents. Among those displaced were several property owners in Canton. Today, many of these former residents, some of whom we spoke to while working at the site, are still angry about the creation of the LBL. Many believe that the federal government has removed family cemetery plots or hidden them, a belief—while not true—that continues to create animosity between the descendants of displaced residents and the Army Corps of Engineers. But after visiting the site and realizing that we were there on behalf of the Corps in order to investigate and preserve a cemetery site, several residents expressed relief that the Corps was "finally" (in their words) doing something to right a wrong. Service-learning projects such as these will enable federal agencies to do more such work and hopefully begin to repair some of the division between government and citizens in some parts of the country.

THE PROCESS
Expected Learning Outcomes

This service-learning project utilized traditional archaeological methods coupled with extensive archival research and library- and web-based historical research. The overarching pedagogical goal was to train students in both traditional archaeological field and laboratory methods but also to familiarize them with the range of historic and archival materials typically utilized in a CRM project, including historic maps, oral histories, and census records. Student learning outcomes for the course include the following:

- Demonstrate a working knowledge of federal and Kentucky cultural resource management laws and their requirements.
- Conduct a Phase I or II cultural resource assessment in compliance with state and federal directives.
- Complete a Kentucky state site form and determine Section 106 site significance.
- Effectively integrate historic archival and library research into standard archaeological practice in order to make informed National Register eligibility determinations.
- Balance the business, legal, ethical, and research issues embedded in contemporary CRM.

Our project-specific goals were twofold: (1) assess the likelihood of additional graves at the Canton site and (2) re-evaluate its eligibility for the National Register of Historic Places in light of any new information discovered during the course of fieldwork and historic research.

Curriculum Materials: The students in this course completed a variety of assignments associated with the service-learning project and which were completed during class periods when we were not in the field or visiting the libraries. These exercises include developing a scope of work (i.e., research plan and design), obtaining environmental and cultural background for the project area, completing a Kentucky state archaeological site form, and maintaining a field book of all archaeological excavation, site observations, library and web-based research, and artifact analyses—all of which CRM practitioners must do on a regular basis. All these exercises were compiled into a required project portfolio. The portfolio additionally consisted of a personal reflection essay with the general prompts of: "Reflect on how this course impacted your understanding of archaeology research in general, how we get data, and how we share that with the public" and "Discuss how this course may alter your career goals and/or your curriculum plans here at IUP, graduate school, or internships/employment." Finally, students had to complete an exit survey evaluating both the course in general and the service-learning project specifically. These results were designed to produce both qualitative assessments of students' engagement in the project as well as quantitative data regarding their perceptions of various course components. The portfolio assignment and the grading rubric are included under Appendix Materials at the end of this chapter.

Steps Involved

The project proceeded in three phases. Phase One consisted of archaeological fieldwork (Figure 2). Archaeological methods conformed to the Kentucky State Historic Preservation Office criteria set forth in *Specifications for Archaeological Fieldwork and Assessment Reports.*[7]

FIGURE 12.2.
Students excavating STPs at 15Tr477 (a, b), view of a typical STP (c), and student conducting a walk-over reconnaissance on the beach.

Phase Two of the project consisted of artifact analysis (Figure 3) and relevant library and archival research of the artifacts recovered. The vast majority of artifacts were bottle glass dating to 1850–1920 and "Type B" machine-cut nails, produced between 1820 and 1900. Two of the ceramic sherds had makers' marks: an Edwin Knowles Creamlace dating to 1929–1939 and a Homer Laughlin Empress dating to 1910–1920. Several bricks were marked "S.P. & Co." A thorough internet search allowed us to identify this abbreviation as the mark of the Smith Porter & Company, a nineteenth-century brick manufacturer located in New Cumberland, West Virginia.[8] These sources, including advertisements in the 1890s journal *Paving and Municipal Engineering* (a monthly magazine self-proclaimed to be "dedicated to the improvement of cites"), coupled with email communications with an historic brick collector/buyer,[9] further refined the company's operations to between 1869 through 1894. Collectively, the historic artifact assemblage suggests a likely date of occupation between 1820 and 1900, with a possible later occupation into the 1920s.

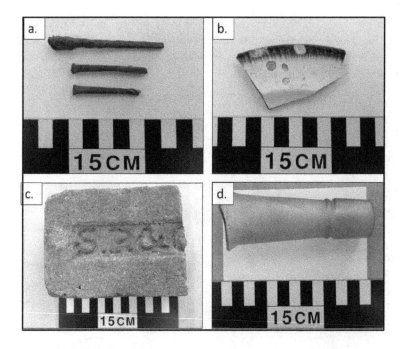

FIGURE 12.3.
Representative artifacts: type B machine-cut nails, c. 1820–1900 (a); blue-edged whiteware (b); S.P. & Co. brick, ca. 1869–1894 (c); and amethyst bottle glass, ca. 1890s (d).

Finally, Phase Three consisted of historic archival and web-based research to contextualize the tombstones recorded at the site (Figure 4). The USACE Library was a key source of this information; indeed, without the assistance of staff librarian Tammy Kirk, we would not have been able to discover who the two families were that lived at the site, nor would we have been able to advise the USACE on the likelihood of additional burials. Historical sources included census records, USACE real estate records, oral histories, and county cemetery surveys conducted by local genealogists David Sumner and Charles Morris.[10] The cemetery book (*Cemeteries of Cadiz and Trigg Counties*) we discovered in talking to Kirk, who, through a mutual connection at the Canton Historical Society, was able to put us directly in contact with Morris. During research for the book, Morris interviewed local residents who are descended from some of the original landowners in Canton. Local residents noted that four tombstones (but not the coffins) located at 15Tr477 were relocated to their current position in 2001 by the Canton Historical Society, which wished to salvage them from eroding into Lake Barkley. They further note that two of these graves washed into Lake Barkley on May 7, 2001, while the other two remained intact near the water's edge. The latter are likely the two that LBL Park Rangers witnessed eroding out of the bank in 2010. Although the graves themselves are gone, the three remaining tombstones were fortunately in good enough condition to be recorded. Once we had family names, we were then able to discover more about them through online census records[11,12] and several volumes documenting the history of Trigg County.[13–16] The stones turned out to belong to just two families: the Grace and Trice families, who were prominent families in the Canton area.

FIGURE 12.4.
Relocated tombstones from the 15TR477 site.

POST-PROJECT ASSESSMENT
Methods of Reflection

Students participated in three types of reflection. First, they were required to maintain a portfolio of relevant research and notes throughout the project (see Appendix Materials). These included their field notes and observations (standard archaeological practice), artifact analysis summaries, and results of their independent historical and web-based research. Students were additionally required to prepare a résumé and cover letter reflecting the fieldwork, laboratory work, and relevant skills acquired during this project. These they submitted in a three-ring binder at the end of the semester as part of their final assessment. Second, the students were assigned sections of the resulting technical report (required by state law to be submitted to the Kentucky State Historic and Preservation Office following all archaeological assessments) to write. They were then assigned two "peer-reviewers" (me plus one student) who provided feedback on both the content and format. Finally, students had to write a three-page personal reflection essay at the end of the semester (see Appendix Materials).

Post-Project Feedback

One student notably wrote: "As an undergrad, field experiences are often limited and it was valuable [to me] to handle an actual project …. We were able to participate in every step of the process which gave me an idea what our future careers could possibly be like." Another student wrote, "Before class began when you told us what we'd be doing, I sort [of] panicked. But now that I see everything together, [I] realize it was mostly just figuring out where to look for stuff." This student was referring to the historical research, which most students admitted to being intimidated by. These results are not surprising since such library and web-based information literacy is rarely incorporated into archaeology curriculums. Only one student (Table 1) felt the project did not benefit them and this may well be the one history major taking the class (archaeology minor) who had previously taken a course in Museum Studies and Archival Research at the same university.

Post-Project Assessment

In this archaeological service-learning project, students actively collaborated with their teachers, each other, and community members. Such collaborative research raised important ethical issues pertaining to representation, ownership, preservation, and stewardship. In a traditional classroom, such ethical issues can be raised but learning shifts from passive to active when students discover these issues themselves through the course of their engagement in various aspects of the project and their interaction with community members. During this project, students are challenged to think about why sites are threatened, how sites can be protected, and whose stories get preserved in the process. The collaborative nature of CSL fundamentally alters the traditional teacher-student relationship since emphasis is shifted from passive teaching to active learning. It also allows students to realize that learning occurs not just in the classroom from a teacher but in the real world from non-academics, including local landowners, residents, municipal leaders and workers, and indigenous communities, to name a few.

For students, applying what they learned in the classroom to a real project makes them feel like emerging professionals in the discipline. Students participating in the projects demonstrated genuine enthusiasm for all of the activities associated with the projects. Unlike the traditional classroom, every student engaged in the project, most with great vigor. In an attempt to quantify some of these subjective observations, students exiting the class completed an anonymous survey to rate various aspects of the course on a scale of 1 (very poor) to 5 (excellent) (Table 1). In response to the question "the [CSL] project enhanced student learning and interest in subject material," 100 percent of students responded with a 4 or a 5. In response to the question "the project helped me identify a need in the community," 100 percent of students responded with a 4 or a 5. These responses quantitatively confirm our observation of student behavior. From a more practical perspective, students gained confidence in field techniques and course content. In response to the questions "the project helped me gain practical hands-on skills" and "I feel better prepared for a career in applied archaeology/CRM," 100 percent of students responded with a 4 or a 5.

TABLE 12.1.
Selected end-of-semester survey questions and student responses.

THE CSL PROJECT...	% OF STUDENTS (N=6) RESPONDING:					AVERAGE RATING
	Very Poor (1)	Poor (2)	Fair (3)	Good (4)	Excellent (5)	
...enhanced student learning & interest	0	0	0	17	83	**4.83**
...made the class more practical and interesting	0	0	0	33	67	**4.67**
...helped me to identify a need in the community	0	0	0	33	67	**4.67**
...successfully met a community need	0	0	0	33	67	**4.67**

THE CSL PROJECT...	% OF STUDENTS (N=6) RESPONDING:					AVERAGE RATING
	Very Poor (1)	Poor (2)	Fair (3)	Good (4)	Excellent (5)	
...helped me gain practical, hands-on skills	0	0	0	33	67	**4.67**
...better prepared me for a career in CRM and/or archaeology	0	0	0	33	67	**4.67**
...helped me appreciate the interdisciplinary nature of archaeology	0	0	0	0	100	**5.00**
...made me aware of resources I was previously unaware of	0	0	17	0	83	**4.83**

Effectively locating and integrating archival and library research into the standard archaeological testing of 15Tr477 resulted in several important findings that greatly expand the knowledge gained by New South's original survey. These findings allowed us to refine the occupation of this site to between 1840 and 1890 (with a possible later occupation in the 1920s–1930s), as well as to enable archaeological and management professionals at USACE to make a more informed decision regarding NRHP eligibility and site management. Historic and library-based research confirmed archaeological evidence for a second homestead existing at 15Tr477 which was not originally identified. Historical research not only supports the field evidence but also puts a name to the families—something that an archaeological survey alone cannot do. If Sumner's cemetery survey and oral history are correct and only four graves ever existed here, this cemetery is likely a family plot only rather than an open cemetery. Based on the location of homesteads to the west and south, it is likely that this cemetery existed in the northeast portion of the site, which is where Park Rangers remembered having found the coffins eroding from the cut bank. Indeed, today there exist numerous concrete pieces with reverse imprinting on them and evidence of rebar. It is unknown what these belong to but may have once been part of a wall around what was left of the cemetery (Figure 5). If this is indeed the location of the cemetery, heavy erosion along the northwest bank has likely obliterated any remaining graves.

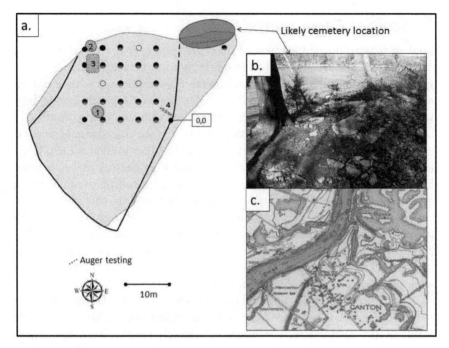

FIGURE 12.5.
Likely location of the Trice Cemetery (a); modern view of the likely location (b); and 1930 USACE map showing site at the bend in the Cumberland River (c).

The Trice and Grace families were clearly prominent members of society in pre-Civil War Trigg County. As such, 15TR477 is associated with people important to local and regional history. Such significance would normally make this site eligible for inclusion in the NRHP under criterion A and B. Unfortunately, it did not meet the integrity criterion due to rapid erosion of the bank into Lake Barkley. Erosion is greatest where the Trice Cemetery was located. It is likely that whatever remained of the cemetery when Sumner and Morris interviewed local residents in 2001 has since washed into Lake Barkley. Thus, there are unlikely to be additional graves; rip-rapping the bank to prevent further graves from washing away would be an unproductive use of taxpayer funds by USACE. That said, were the site to have had better integrity, it would have been eligible for the NRHP. But the association with the Trice and Grace families is what makes it significant, an association we only know about now thanks to extensive library and web-based research, not due to the archaeological work alone.

Difficulties Encountered

Student issues: The development of a service-learning course or project, while clearly beneficial to students and communities, is not without its challenges. A service-learning project requires, first and foremost, a commitment of time and energy from both students and faculty.[17] Since these projects typically involve field-work, data analysis, and/or significant engagement with community members, a large portion of the work must be conducted outside of the classroom and on weekends or evenings. Upon hearing how many Saturdays they would have to give up, two students dropped my course in the first week—not because they didn't care but due to work obligations. With more and more college students needing to work off campus in order to finance rapidly increasing tuition costs, this may be an increasing problem. In an attempt to mitigate this problem, Murray State University began listing service-learning classes with the section designation "S" (e.g., ARC 350-S-01) so students know ahead of time which classes will entail service outside of regular class hours. A final issue is class size. In this case, six students was not quite enough personnel to complete the work and I relied on volunteers (including my family) to complete the project in time. In other years, the class enrolled eight to twelve students, which enabled us to do more field work and historic research. Similarly, if the class size exceeds twelve, archaeological service-learning—including the information literacy and library component—becomes difficult to manage. An MSU colleague undertaking a similar project a year later had difficulty keeping his sixteen students occupied and on task. Unfortunately, it can be hard to predict how large a class will be from year to year, nor were we able to "cherry pick" the right project for the right class size as we'd ideally like to.

Instructor issues: An additional challenge for instructors is that they must be able to change the project as unanticipated circumstances dictate; the course cannot be planned or structured in any great detail but rather must be fluid in order to adapt to the nature of the project. This was the case for our project, particularly since it frequently took a long time to track down historical resources and local informants. A final challenge—one that the author felt acutely in this particular project—is the need to step outside of one's zone of comfort. In my case, as a prehistoric archaeologist who had heretofore only worked with the archaeological record prior to written history, I had to make use of historic maps, census data, and web-based research sites with which I had little to no familiarity. This is where our community partners became indispensable. Without the help of Corps librarian Tammie Kirk, we would not have known about the Sumner's cemetery survey work, which painstakingly recorded cemeteries LBL and collected oral histories of local residents whose ancestors lived in LBL prior to TVA flooding of the rivers. Second, the Special Collections library staff at Murray State University enabled us to locate the historic maps of the region, which in turn allowed us to understand why the site had so little geologic integrity.

Community Partner issues: As previously discussed, partnering with a university can greatly benefit an agency that is underfunded and understaffed. That said, taking time to meet with students requires extra time in an already overloaded schedule. In this particular case, archaeologist Valerie McCormick met with the class after hours on her own time because management initially failed to see the benefits of spending some initial time up front in order to save time and resources down the road. Thus, it is imperative that instructors work with their community partner at all levels in order to make clear the full benefit of the project.

Conclusions

Despite the increasing need for archaeology students to be trained for careers in Cultural Resource Management, few archaeology courses utilize service-learning as a primary pedagogical tool. While field and laboratory work are standard, archaeology classes rarely take on a project from beginning to end, such that students are involved in *all* aspects of the project, not just the fieldwork or artifact analysis. Even fewer classes build in the background archival and library research in a systematic or meaningful way. In the study presented here, students were not just introduced to unfamiliar library and web-based resources, they also met with librarians and other information experts who guided them in learning to use the resource, thereby expanding the content expertise of the instructor and demonstrating the inherent interdisciplinary and collaborative nature of today's applied archaeology. The CRM careers that archaeology students are likely to be employed in upon graduation in the next decade will necessarily require these kinds of information literacy skills in addition to the more traditional skill set. Thus, gaining familiarity and fluency in this skill set will not only make students more marketable but also give them a greater sense of confidence once they find themselves undertaking CRM projects such as the case study presented here. At 15Tr477, the archaeology alone would not have been enough to illustrate the historical significance of the Trice and Grace homesteads. Only by spending the extra time to use historic maps, seek out oral histories by local informants, and delve into nineteenth-century census and cemetery records were we able to document the exact families who lived on this plot of land just outside Canton—families that become very real for the six students in the Public Archaeology class. Thus, integrating library and information literacy components into archaeological research, particularly historic archaeology, is crucial to telling the entire story of an archaeological site, and, by extension, making sound NRHP eligibility determinations and management decisions, the cornerstones of Cultural Resource Management.

APPENDIX MATERIALS

- Portfolio Checklist and Personal Reflection Guideline
- Grading Rubric for ARC 350 Portfolio
- Course and Project Exit Surveys

Portfolio Checklist and Personal Reflection Guidelines

Please hand in a *hard copy* at the *final exam*. Portfolios must be collated in a 1" 3-ring binder. The following must be included:

- ❑ **Exit Survey** *(course & SL evaluation evals, print p. 3–4 and put at end of portfolio)*
- ❑ **Field Notes** *(place field book in front pocket)*
- ❑ **Exercise 1** *(Request for Proposal)*
- ❑ **Exercise 2** *(Scope of Work)*
- ❑ **Exercise 3** *(Project Background info)*
- ❑ **Exercise 4** *(completed KY state site form)*
- ❑ **Exercise 5** *(peer-reviewed section of technical report—must show comments)*
- ❑ **Personal Reflection Essay**
  - o 2–3 pages, TYPED, double-spaced, 12 pt. font, 1" margins
  - o Describe your career goals and how this course prepared you (or not prepare you).
  - o What skills were most applicable to your career goal(s) & which were least applicable?
  - o Which skills were easiest and/or most enjoyable for you? Which were the most difficult and/or least enjoyable for you? Why? *(e.g., Have you had, or are you missing, relevant course work? Do you excel at or despise, math? Do you prefer lab vs. fieldwork (or vice versa) and if so why? Had you never used a compass? etc.)*
  - o Reflect on how this course impacted your understanding of archaeology research in general, how we get data, and how we share that with the public. (And has your view of who "the public" is changed at all in this course?)
  - o Discuss how this course may alter your career goals and/or your curriculum plans here at IUP, graduate school, or internships/employment. What are your summer and/or post-graduation plans—how will your knowledge of applied archaeology (CRM) influence these plans?
  - o Feel free to include other thoughts or comments—this is YOUR reflection!
- ❑ **1-page résumé** *(see templates on Canvas)*
- ❑ **Cover letter** *(must be for a current job listing on archaeologyfieldwork.com)*

Grading Rubric for ARC 350 Portfolio

COMPONENT	FAILS EXPECTATIONS/ NOT PROFICIENT	UNSATISFACTORY/ LACKING PROFICIENCY	SATISFACTORY/ PROFICIENT	EXCELLENT/MASTERY
Participation, Initiative & Engagement during Fieldwork: (from participation rubric)	(<15) Misses many classes, poor participation or poor attitude; lack of engagement or cannot undertake majority of skills.	(15–19) Misses several classes and/or relies on class-mates to do work or participates only at urging of instructor. Ability to undertake most skills (e.g., Shovel testing, pacing) requires guidance.	(20–23) Attends most classes; participates but sometimes side-tracked by non-class distractions or waits to be told how to use class time. Able to do most skills (e.g., pacing) with little guidance.	(24–25) Attends all classes and uses class time effectively, doesn't wait to be told how to use class time & is actively engaged in & focused on project. Able to undertake all skills (e.g., pacing) with no or minimal guidance.
Exit Survey:	(<5) incomplete			(5) complete
Reflection Essay: describes how class impacted your understanding of CRM & public archaeology	(<20) Fails to answer most of required elements.	(20–21) Fails to answer 2 or more required elements, not within page requirements, or answers are very vague or cliché.	(22–23) Answers all required elements but lacking in page limit, detail, or with vague references to career goals.	(24–25) Answers all required elements & some of your own in detail and with obvious thought and reflection regarding relation to your career goals.
Résumé + Cover Letter:	(<12) Messy, doesn't follow template, hurriedly put together.	(12–14) Not neat, hard to follow, awkward flow and/ or use of white space, not career-specific & doesn't reflect cover letter.	(15–18) Generally neat (min. typos), follows a general template, moderate reflection of career goals & cover letter.	(19–20) Professional, neat, no typos, uses template well, excellent reflection of career goals & cover letter.
Overall Portfolio Usability	(<20) Missing required elements. Exercises incomplete or not turned in. Fails to meet federal & KY SHPO standards.	(20–21) Disorganized & difficult to find info for future use. Some exercises incomplete and/or not corrected. Fails to meet federal & KY SHPO standards.	(22–23) Generally easy to find info for future use. Exercise complete and corrected, and field notes meet federal and KY SHPO standards.	(24–25) Goes above and beyond expectations with additional information, handouts, and resources. Exceeds federal and KY SHPO standards.
				Total = _____ / 100

Additional Instructor Comments:

Course and Project Exit Surveys

ARC 350 Course Evaluation *(to be placed at the end of your portfolio)*: On a scale of 1 (not at all) to 5 (very), how competent/comfortable do you feel with the following CRM skills?

Knowing where to find jobs	1	2	3	4	5
Writing a résumé/cover letter	1	2	3	4	5
Familiar with most CRM laws (e.g., NHPA)	1	2	3	4	5
Applying NR criteria for significance	1	2	3	4	5
Applying creative strategies to Section 106	1	2	3	4	5
Shovel testing	1	2	3	4	5
Reading a compass/sighting a transect	1	2	3	4	5
Pacing along a transect	1	2	3	4	5
Reading topographic maps	1	2	3	4	5
Making a map in National Map Viewer or equivalent	1	2	3	4	5
Making an artifact density map	1	2	3	4	5
Interpreting cultural resources for the public	1	2	3	4	5
Describing the basic soil profile	1	2	3	4	5
Getting data from the Web Soil Survey	1	2	3	4	5
Tailoring a cover letter to a particular job	1	2	3	4	5
Knowing what goes into a SOW	1	2	3	4	5
Knowing what goes into a budget	1	2	3	4	5
Surveying using transects	1	2	3	4	5
Surveying using sampling strategies	1	2	3	4	5

ARC 350 Service-learning Project Evaluation *(to be placed at the end of your portfolio)*: Please rate the following aspects of our Service-learning Project with the Corps of Engineers: VP=very poor; P=poor; F=fair; G=good, E=excellent

	VP	P	F	G	E
The service project as a whole was	1	2	3	4	5
The project helped me identify a need in the community	1	2	3	4	5
The project successfully met a community need	1	2	3	4	5
The project helped me gain practical, hands-on skills	1	2	3	4	5
I feel better prepared for a career in CRM/archaeology	1	2	3	4	5

The project was well designed	1	2	3	4	5
The project was broken down into reasonable sections	1	2	3	4	5
The project made the class more practical and interesting	1	2	3	4	5
Student requirements/responsibilities were clear	1	2	3	4	5
Use of class time to complete the project was adequate	1	2	3	4	5
Time spent in field was reasonable	1	2	3	4	5
The project made use of concepts learned in lecture	1	2	3	4	5
The project enhanced student learning	1	2	3	4	5
The project enhanced student interest in archaeology	1	2	3	4	5
The project made me more aware of resources I was previously unaware of	1	2	3	4	5
The project made me more aware of the interdisciplinary nature of archaeology/cultural resource management	1	2	3	4	5

What aspect of the service-learning project was most useful and why? What aspect was the least useful and why? Please be constructive:

Notes

1. Site numbers are based on the Smithsonian Institution's trinomial system in which the 15 stands for Kentucky (e.g., 15th alphabetically), Tr stands for Trigg County, and 477 means that it is the 477th site identified in the Trigg County.
2. Danny Gregory, *Cultural Resource Investigations and Geophysical Survey along the Cumberland River, Lyon, Russell, and Trigg Counties, Kentucky; Cheatham, Steward, and Sumner Counties, Tennessee*, Technical Report No. 32, American Recovery and Reinvestment Act of 2009, Section 110 Compliance Report for the U.S. Army Corps of Engineers, Nashville District (Stone Mountain: New South Associates, 2011).
3. Michael S. Nassaney, "The Reform of Archaeological Pedagogy and Practice through Community Service Learning," in *Archaeology and Community Service Learning*, ed. Michael Nassaney and Mary Ann Levine (Gainesville: University Press of Florida, 2010), 3–35.
4. Brian M. Fagan, "Epilogue," in *The Public Benefits of Archaeology*, ed. B. J. Little (Gainesville: University Press of Florida, 2002), 253–260.
5. Susan J. Bender and George S. Smith, *Teaching Archaeology in the Twenty-first Century*. (Washington D.C.: Society for American Archaeology, 2000).
6. Mary Ann Levine and James A. Delle, "Archaeology and Community Service Learning at the Thaddeus Stevens and Lydia Hamilton Smith Site, Lancaster, Pennsylvania," in *Archaeology and Community Service Learning*, ed. Michael Nassaney and Mary Ann Levine (Gainesville: University Press of Florida, 2010), 83–109.
7. Kentucky State Historic Preservation Office, *Specifications for Archaeological Fieldwork and Assessment Reports*, Kentucky State Historic Preservation Office (Frankfort: Kentucky Heritage Council, 2011).
8. J. H. Newton, *History of the Panhandle: Historical Collections of the Counties of Ohio, Brooke, Marshall, and Hancock* (Wheeling: J. A. Cadwell, 1879), 432.9.

9. Jim Graves, email message to author, November, 2013.

10. David Sumner, Kim Fortner, Pam Metts, and Charles Morris, *Cemeteries of Cadiz and Trigg County, Kentucky* (Cadiz: Sumforme Publishing, 2008), 341.

11. Betty Sellers, transcriber. n.d. 1850 Census of Trigg County, Kentucky, USGenWeb Archives, accessed February 6, 2013, www.westernkyhistory.org/trigg/census/1850_Trigg_Census.html.

12. Betty Sellers, transcriber. n.d. 1880 Census of Trigg County, Kentucky, USGenWeb Archives, accessed February 6, 2013, www.westernkyhistory.org/trigg/census/1880_Trigg_Census.html.

13. William Henry Perrin, *Counties of Christian and Trigg, Kentucky: Historical and Biographical* (Louisville: F. A. Battey Publishing Company, 1884).

14. Trigg County Historical and Preservation Society (TCHPS), *Trigg County History.* (Dallas: Taylor Publishing Company, 1986).

15. Trigg County Historical and Preservation Society (TCHPS), *Trigg County Veterans: Lest We Forget* (Paducah: Turner Publishing Company, 2002).

16. Trigg County Historical and Preservation Society (TCHPS), *Canton on the Cumberland.* (Cadiz: Trigg County Historical and Preservation Society, 2007).

17. Lara K. Homsey, Anthony L. Ortmann, and Kit W. Wesler, "Integrating Community Service Learning into the Murray State University Archaeology Curriculum," *Journal of Kentucky Archaeology* 1, no. 2 (2012): 39–51.

CHAPTER THIRTEEN

How to Succeed in International Business (With a Lot of Trying)

Russell A. Hall

Associate Librarian
Penn State Behrend
rah29@psu.edu

Mark Bestoso

Lecturer in Management
Penn State Behrend
mwb5@psu.edu

THE ACTIVITY

Description: Workplace information literacy is a burgeoning field of study in the library world. Information literacy needs vary based on the context in which the person finds him or herself. In academic libraries, we tend to only teach to the scholarly environment. A good way to avoid that and bridge the gap from college to the workplace is to get involved with authentic learning experiences. The service-based activity described here is a collaboration between a librarian and a business instructor to help students get experience with the types of information problems that businesses face while also assisting local companies. The librarian acted as an "information consultant" to the groups of students as they attempted to fill the information needs of their partner companies.

This chapter describes the steps taken to complete the semester-long projects. Most importantly, it portrays a situation where a librarian was able to work with upper-level students and engage them on broader and deeper levels of information literacy with a particular focus on the workplace. In workplace information literacy, the context of the information environment is paramount and, therefore, many of the traditional "higher education approved" sources, such as peer-reviewed journal articles, while perhaps useful, are not mandated. In fact, going beyond the bounds of "approved" information resources was critical to student success in this service-learning project.

Getting Started: This project got off the ground by way of serendipity. Mark, the instructor, was going to be teaching a freshman seminar for the first time in a long while and he wanted to brush up on library databases and services. During that meeting, the librarian mentioned his research interest in workplace information literacy. In the course of that discussion, the instructor mentioned that his international management class might align neatly with the librarian's interests.

Motivations: Service learning is a win-win situation for the students and the outside organizations. The organizations get intelligent, motivated students to study a problem for them and give them advice on how to solve it. The students get an opportunity for authentic learning by working with an actual company on an authentic problem the company is grappling with. In service-based experiential learning, students tend to be more invested in the activity. To this point, Andy Spackman writes, "Experiential learners are motivated because they are working for real clients on actual projects that are similar to the work they expect to do after graduation."[1] Students also can make contacts that they might use in their later careers. It's also a great experience for them to talk about in their job and internship hunts.

For Russ, the librarian in this chapter, several endeavors by Project Information Literacy (PIL), led by Alison Head, served as a motivation to get involved in this type of project. PIL "is a large-scale, national study about college students and how they find, evaluate, and select information for use in their courses and for solving information problems in everyday life."[2] In some of PIL's work, the group investigated how recent college graduates were using information in their workplaces and contrasted that with how their employers felt they were handling information.[3] One study in particular found a gap between what employers wanted and what the newer employees were delivering. In that study, Head, et al. found that "information competencies for today require the ability to locate information in multiple formats and synthesize diverse viewpoints, by taking a flexible, critical, and iterative approach to solving workplace information problems." However, the participants in that study seemed to place a "premium ...on finding the answer as quickly as possible" and to have a low tolerance for ambiguity about their assignment and did not adopt a "strategy that imagines all possible answers."[4] It was from this that Russ felt that experiential learning might be a way to counter this problem being found among the new graduates in the workplace. In working directly with local companies, students would actively be involved in information situations where they would need to function in an ambiguous information environment and consider a multiplicity of possible answers to the problems posed to them.

For Mark, the impetus for this fall 2015 class project in MGMT 461 (International Management) revolved around his annual review and a key mission statement theme. The Black School of Business at Penn State Behrend is preparing for renewal of AACSB accreditation with an AACSB accreditation team visit scheduled for spring 2018. A relatively new school director (dean) identified three themes to more aggressively steer our school toward Penn State's historic land-grant mission: "Thinking across boundaries—Learning by doing—Innovating through collaboration." A number of initiatives directed at these three themes became the school's priority, and faculty annual reviews were adjusted to align with the increased emphasis on these themes. Mark's annual review with the director was held in June and he expected the usual "you are doing a fine job; however, you might want to…" but instead the director ignored his teaching evaluations altogether and challenged him to introduce a "learning by doing" project into his fall MGMT 461 class. As this was not something he had ever done in his classes, Mark was somewhat apprehensive and had no idea where to start. However, he also was intrigued by the opportunity for change as he has been teaching for twenty-five years and felt he was losing his enthusiasm for teaching and his classes seemed stale. Mark said he would look into it and would get back to him with what he might do to meet the director's challenge.

THE PEOPLE

Library: The John M. Lilley Library at Penn State Behrend in Erie, Pennsylvania, serves approximately 4,400 full-time students. The staff includes a director, three reference and instruction librarians, three full-time paraprofessionals, two part-time paraprofessionals, and numerous student workers. Russ is the reference and instruction librarian who is the liaison to the business department and was the only librarian involved in this project. Given the small size of the staff, Russ, while having specific liaison duties, is also very much a generalist. As such, time pressures prevented him from being as fully embedded in this project as he would have liked.

Instructor: Russell Hall is a reference and instruction librarian at Penn State, where he has worked for the past fifteen years. His interests are in information literacy, specifically in how college graduates carry their information literacy skills and mindsets from college into the workplace. Mark Bestoso recently retired from Penn State after teaching management for twenty-six years. His work and teaching focused on management, international business, and data analysis.

Course: This project was part of the MGMT 461, International Management, course. According to Penn State's course catalog, MGMT 461 (International Management) "[e]xamines issues of nations and cultures including motivation, communication, negotiation, leadership, ethics and social responsibility, and women in management."[5] The course is designed to give a broader context for business and management than what might be found in the rest of the curriculum.

Students: The class consisted of forty students, most of whom were senior business administration students, with some juniors comprising the rest of the class.

Community Partners: The community partners were local industrial firms that had already established an international presence. These partners were looking to expand their business in markets where they had an existing presence, though some were looking to invest in new markets. A similar assignment could be accomplished with other community partners, such as non-profits, particularly if they were reaching out to international audiences. An immediate example from our local area is a refugee resettlement organization. Clearly, work could be done to help understand the culture and the communities, as well as the terrors that these refugees are leaving behind in order to create a better, more welcoming environment for them here.

Finding and Working with Partners: One of Mark's favorite sayings is that "jobs difficult by design prove easy in performance." Peoples' first reaction when faced with a seemingly difficult challenge is to perceive it as impossible. But once you move beyond the negative and focus on steps to meet the challenge, the obstacles disappear and a path to success becomes clear. The first challenge—and the one Mark needed to attack to clear the path—was finding corporate partners. Fortunately, he had good social contacts in upper-level corporate positions, and in his role as associate chair of Recruitment, Retention and Career Advancement, he routinely interacts with managers recruiting our students. Mark's first call was to a neighbor who happened to be a vice president at a major manufacturing company in Erie who headed a team focused on developing the locomotive business in Eastern Europe. She canvassed her team after he requested her help and one of the product managers enthusiastically agreed to work with the class and to mentor two student teams. Two teams down, six to go.

Mark also happens to be a member of a wine club. One of the wine club members is the VP of sales and principal owner of a local manufacturer which has operations in many parts of the world. Mark emailed him as to whether he could find someone who would be willing to work with student teams on some issue related to international business. The senior manager of exports for the firm agreed to work with two teams as well. Four down, four to go.

Mark then contacted a very successful entrepreneur in Erie who founded an up-and-coming global logistics company. He is a very dynamic leader who Mark used a number of times as a class speaker. This entrepreneur too agreed to work with two teams.

Mark then contacted the plant supply chain manager for a unit of an engineering and manufacturing company who he had assisted in securing a business intern and, again, this manager was very enthusiastic and accommodating. The final two teams were paired with a firm!

It is important to mention that Mark was turned down on two separate occasions during this process, so it was quite a relief when all the corporate sponsors were secured. Business managers tend to be overworked in many cases, so taking on a project like this is not something they take lightly due to the added demands on their time.

The next step was to set up meetings with the company representatives to delineate what the teams would work on that would reflect the content of the course. Over a period of a few weeks in late summer, Mark met with each company sponsor. Interestingly, three of the four firms were being battered by the steep drop in the price of oil and its significant impact on their businesses. The major manufacturer was suffering from a steep drop in orders for their heavy-duty locomotives that were used to transport oil across Russia and the Eastern European countries in that region. The local manufacturer, much smaller and less diversified than the major manufacturer, was also being hammered by the low price of oil and other commodities as their core business revolves around separation technologies for the oil and mining industries. They wanted teams assigned to them to identify new markets in Colombia and Peru so they could diversify into selling separation technology to food, coffee, and pharmaceutical firms to offset the precipitous loss of orders from their core industrial customers. Finally, the engineering and manufacturing firm's core market is the oil industry and orders were way down for them. The plant manager wanted us to research the African market that China was aggressively targeting to see if there might be growth opportunities to offset the fall in business in their traditional country markets.

Two teams each (five students) were assigned to conduct research for four local firms relative to countries of interest to each. Countries studied were Colombia and Peru, Ghana and Nigeria, the Commonwealth of Independent States Region and Mongolia, and Libya and Angola. Three of the firms involved were facing a similar challenge: how to adjust to the tremendous fall in commodities as they are all tied closely to such industries. The logistics company was looking for research into targeted countries to determine when or if it would be viable to open sales offices in those countries now or at some point in the near future.

All of the teams (with exception of those assigned to the major manufacturer) toured the firms' local facilities, and all four of the firm representatives visited Behrend to present to the class as a whole while taking end-of-class time to meet with their teams separately to further refine the assignment. Additionally, Mark mandated that each team meet with Russ, the business librarian, to identify research resources.

Deliverables included three reports and an oral presentation delivered to their business clients. The first report was on the company and industry. The second report was on the economic and political environments as well as current events. The final report was to synthesize the first two reports and present specific recommendations addressing original respective problems as framed by the corporate clients.

The assignments coming from these businesses posed authentic questions to the students. This is the sort of work they might be tackling in the "real world." This real-world impact is what gives service-learning so much of its value. As Alon notes, "Loosely structured experiential activities have been shown to increase student enthusiasm and satisfaction, grades, and the perceived value of education."[6]

Benefits

Instructor Benefits: The library recognized several benefits from this project. First, it deepened our relationship with our business department. For example, this project directly led to another opportunity where Russ and another librarian worked with the Integrated Business and Engineering students who were working their year-long capstone project. Russ will be looking for more opportunities like this in the future. Second, it allowed the library to expand its information literacy mission. This assignment carried the librarian and the students well past the one-shot library session. This is a clear need talked about a great deal in librarian circles in recent years. The more in-depth experience with the students allows more opportunities to engage them in critical thinking and information literacy skills that may just be glossed over in a traditional one-shot.

Student Benefits: The students received multiple benefits as well. First, they had the chance to work with an actual company, which is something that can potentially look good on a résumé as well as creating a more interesting and engaging assignment. The audience for the project is no longer the professor, as it is with so many classes. This makes for a more meaningful learning experience. Second, the students are exposed to an array of information problems they may not have encountered previously. A "regular" class assignment might be to write a paper on how a major corporation conducts international business in a given country and use at least three peer-reviewed journal articles and no web sources. This type of paper may have its uses but it makes for a dry and uninspiring assignment. In actual companies and organizations, workers don't have those sorts of restrictions on what types of information to use and it's unlikely that the students would be given that type of assignment in their future job. With this experiential learning project, the students get a chance to get their hands dirty and work on actual research and produce a report that a real company is interested in. Finally, the students have the benefit of having a librarian available to them who is deeply immersed in these projects. Having the librarian as an "information consultant" allows the students to have some guidance through these uncharted information waters.

Community Partner Benefits: The participating companies receive the benefit of having motivated upperclassmen work on a project for them. It helps them perhaps take a look at the information they have with a fresh set of eyes, as well as an alternative analysis that might be informed by information they didn't know existed. The companies also benefit by discovering talented students that they might want to work for them after graduation.

Institutional Benefits: Workplace information literacy ties neatly to Penn State University's land-grant outreach mission.

THE PROCESS
Expected Learning Outcomes

Students who complete this assignment will

- get real-world experience working with actual businesses in order to increase their perceived relevance and therefore increase their course engagement;
- learn how information problems are structured differently in business in order to see how this differs from the college context;
- experience the complex nature of real-world business issues in order to recognize that these issues are often not as clear-cut as in college; and
- utilize a wide variety of information resources to solve these real-world problems in order to increase the flexibility of their thinking about information resources.

Curriculum Materials

The information literacy instruction took place in multiple ways and at multiple times. First, Russ presented a lecture to the entire class. The first lecture was a refresher on what the library has to offer and what business databases they might find useful. The second lecture was presented to the smaller groups and focused on what those teams might want to investigate for the industries and countries they were assigned. However, the most fruitful learning likely happened once the students delved into their research and came up with their own questions and realized that this kind of "real world" research isn't as easy as they had originally anticipated. The real success in this story involves these follow up meetings, as we will see below. Please see the Appendix Materials for the actual assignment details.

Steps Involved

- All of the teams had to start by getting background information on the countries they were going to be studying as well as business information. One cannot make solid business judgments without understanding at least some of the culture, government, history, politics, and vital statistics of the country in which you are planning to do business. The librarian introduced the student groups to many resources they were not aware of, such as the US government's Export.gov site, Michigan State's GlobalEDGE, data from the Organization for Economic Co-Operation and Development (OECD), and the old reliable CIA World Factbook. The students also used information sources they were already familiar with, such as EBSCOHost and ProQuest products to enhance their knowledge of current events in their country of study. Russ often gave the students advice during group and individual conferences on how to get deeper into industry information by looking for organizations such as commerce groups in the country of study, industry groups (a fictitious example might be the Soybean Growers Council), and government agencies in charge of foreign investment.

- The groups, or representatives from the groups, also met with Russ to discuss specific problems in their research. Often, these dealt with issues of competitive intelligence. There are just some instances where you cannot get the information you need without paying large sums of money for it, and sometimes not even then. Companies are rightfully loathe to give away the names of partnering companies or organizations, let alone vendor names. And trade secrets are clearly just that, secrets. However, many of the specific questions were answerable with the application of critical thinking on the part of the students and the librarian. But it should be stressed that these were not "traditional" reference questions. These were questions that had application to real-world problems and were often quite thorny. Often, email questions would come from members of the group, and sometimes Russ and the group would have to meet a couple of times to work through a problem and find a sufficient solution (because, as a colleague of mine often says, "In order for there to be statistics, someone has to collect the data. No data, then no statistics"). The students, as groups and individuals, struggled with this research, but it was clear that the learning only came with the struggle. As much as they wanted to just get "the answer" and move on, many students had a "light bulb" moment of discovery when they figured out a new information source or a new angle to attack an information problem.

POST-PROJECT ASSESSMENT

Methods of Reflection: Mark and Russ did not build in any formal reflective practice for this project. The reason for this is that we were both completely new to the idea of service-based experiential learning. Simply put, we were ignorant of the established practice. We regret it thoroughly because it is clear how much learning could have been expressed through required reflective assignments.

Students informally expressed reflective concerns to Mark and Russ on occasion, both for positive and negative reasons. Often, they felt overburdened by the assignment and the requests of their community partners. They also stated that sometimes the community partners were hindering their work because they were not forthcoming with information that would have helped their group do their project better. Clearly, the partners have a right to value their proprietary information (such as vendors, clients, sales data, etc.) but they also need to realize that this will affect the ability of the students to complete the assignment.

Students also expressed to Russ that they wished they had encountered many of the libraries resources earlier in their academic careers. While this was a hopeful note for the juniors in the class, it was a missed opportunity for the seniors. The library obviously should look to partner more with faculty in these innovative assignments so that our students do not fail to take advantage of all of our offerings.

Also, though they did not express it in this language, in conversation with Russ, the students were quite happy to be working with an expanded definition of acceptable sources. They felt liberated from the constraints of having to use peer-reviewed articles when the information they found elsewhere was as valuable or more valuable to them in the context of their assignment.

Post-Project Feedback: From the students, it was mostly feedback from their faculty evaluation forms as well as the quality of the project they produced. Student feedback was mixed but leaned toward positive. Some select examples follow.

When asked what they liked best about the course:
- "I really like the group project. It's nice to do something meaningful that we know will make a difference to a company and I have learned a lot from doing it."
- "[T]he team projects and working with local businesses in the area."
- "The opportunity to do a project for an actual company was really cool."

When asked what they liked least about the course:
- "I hated the project that we did. Although it was a good experience to have it was very stressful...."
- "The group project is good, but the expectation that it will be the best quality work of a professional is too high."

Project Assessment and Reporting Methods

Students were required to submit interim reports to the instructor to make sure that the groups were on the right track. They also gave final presentations on their research to the class and representatives of the company, and they presented a research portfolio to the instructor and the company representatives.

In the future, we hope to develop a more robust evaluation method and include multiple opportunities for reflection from the students. If and when Russ is able to find a new partner for this endeavor, he will urge the instructor to include multiple modes of assessment for the project.

Mark and Russ were mostly pleased with the results of the student projects. Some reports were, of course, better than others but all projects met the minimum requirements. The projects achieved the goals that were set out, namely to get the students involved with real-world learning and engaging in more sophisticated research with the "training wheels off." The local companies expressed varying degrees of satisfaction with the projects. The ones that did not engage with the students much were the ones that were less pleased with the reports they received. Students expressed frustration throughout the semester that these companies were not very responsive to their inquiries about expectations and requests for data. As with most things, the companies got out of it what they put into it. The companies that were more engaged with the student groups uniformly were, at minimum, satisfied and for the most part pleased with the student projects. As mentioned above, the students also had mixed emotions about the assignment but it's safe to say that they felt it was much more appealing and valuable than a standard term paper.

Difficulties Encountered

Student Issues: As seen above, the students often felt they were being tasked with doing the job of a professional and that asking them to meet that standard was unreasonable. The students also found this project to be difficult, but it was designed to be difficult. The assignment asked them to stretch their learning and apply it. Since service-learning is not a "standard" learning method, it is understandable that the students would be vexed by being forced to work outside their comfort zones.

Instructor Issues: The main difficulties for the instructor and the librarian were time. This sort of project takes a lot of time to lay the groundwork: find partners, find scalable research problems, etc. It also takes a lot of time to consult with the students both in class and out of class. Their research needs are not trivial. It takes a lot of communication to be successful.

Community Partner Issues: Community partners were generally pleased with the results of the projects. As mentioned under the student issues, in some instances the partners keeping proprietary information prevented students from producing the highest quality final project.

Conclusion

This service-based activity had a significant impact because it required students to work with information in a more sophisticated way than they might have in their lower-level classes. Students had to deal with more ambiguity in the information they found and had to evaluate the information without the "training wheels" of approved information (such as the stamp of peer-review as a marker for authority) that is found in most classes. Further, the students had to research both broadly (in terms of the business and political climate of the country) and deeply (in terms of market research in that country for their particular product or service). Perhaps most important, this research also has consequences beyond a grade. The partner companies are truly looking for solid analysis on which to base real economic decisions. In short, this type of engaged scholarship delivers serious impact for learning about information literacy as well as international business.

APPENDIX MATERIALS

- Doing Business in a Selected Country Report Description

Doing Business in a Selected Country Report Description

Your team will conduct research and prepare a written report on the Erie business that you have been assigned that is seeking to expand its market into a prescribed country or region of the world or to respond to a specific request for information from the assigned business contact.

Your research will include attention to the social, political, cultural, and economic environment as well as relevant current events in the assigned country. What you ultimately focus on will be a function of the needs of your assigned firm which will require a meeting of the group with a designee of the firm. All of the assigned firms are US-based, so assume that you are dealing with employees that have a US-based perspective on the world.

Again, the needs of your assigned firm will influence your research and the structure of this report. However, two preliminary reports will be due with a final report consolidating and completing the research that will answer the questions posed by your company contact.

The **first report** will be due on **February 16th.** This report will provide an overview of the assigned firm as well as insights on the industry or key industries in which the firm operates and identification of core customers or customer groups.

The **second report** will focus on the current economic and political environment as well as current events and how these events represent opportunities or threats for your firm. You should also frame for your company contacts (with their assistance) precisely what they are seeking from your team so that you provide something of value to them that is focused and concise. This report will be due **March 30th.**

The consolidated **final report** with recommendations will be due **April 25th.**

Elements of a good paper are as follows:

1.   **Breadth of coverage** (variety of materials from a variety of sources)
2.   **Depth of coverage** (going beyond the superficial to point where you have a meaningful understanding of the topic)
3.   **Appropriateness of coverage** (are materials relevant to topic?)
4.   **Logic of presentation and arguments** (are conclusions justified and well argued?)
5.   **Style of presentation** (is paper easy to read and follow with proper grammar and sentence construction?)

Notes

1.   Andy Spackman, "Client-Based Experiential Learning and the Librarian: Information Literacy for the Real World," *Journal of Business & Finance Librarianship* 21, no. 3–4 (October 2016): 258–73. doi:10.1080/08963568.2016.1226616.
2.   "About," Project Information Literacy, accessed June 13, 2017, http://www.projectinfo-lit.org/about.html.
3.   Alison J. Head, "Learning Curve: How College Graduates Solve Information Problems Once They Join the Workplace," accessed at SSRN 2165031, 2012, http://papers.ssrn.com/sol3/papers.cfm?abstract_id=2165031; Alison J. Head, Michele Van Hoeck, Jordan Eschler, and Sean Fullerton, "What Information Competencies Matter in Today's Workplace?," *Library and Information Research* 37, no. 114 (2013): 74–104; Alison J. Head, "Project Information Literacy's Lifelong Learning Study, Phase One: Interviews with Recent Graduates Research Brief," last modified, August 4, 2014, http://papers.ssrn.com/sol3/papers.cfm?abstract_id=2475974; Alison J. Head, "Project Information Literacy's Research Summary: Lifelong Learning Study, Phase Two and the Online Survey, Phase Two and the Online Survey," modified February 17, 2015, http://papers.ssrn.com/sol3/papers.cfm?abstract_id=2573090.
4.   Head, Van Hoeck, Eschler, and Fullerton, "What Information Competencies Matter," 74–104.
5.   "MGMT 461—International Management," *Penn State University Course Catalog,* accessed January 22, 2018, https://goo.gl/HTwn32.
6.   Ilan Alon, "Experiential Learning in International Business via the World Wide Web," *Journal of Teaching in International Business* 14, no. 2–3 (2003): 79–98.

PART III

Library as Location for Student-Led Educational Outreach Events and Projects

CHAPTER FOURTEEN

Putting Theory into Practice and Promoting Children's Literacy through Service-Learning

Janet Pinkley

Associate Librarian
California State University Channel Islands,
janet.pinkley@csuci.edu

THE ACTIVITY

Description: The Children's Reading Celebration and Young Author's Fair (CRC & YAF) is an annual event held at California State University Channel Islands' (CI) John Spoor Broome Library. It is made possible by a partnership between the John Spoor Broome Library, CI's English Program, and the Ventura County Reading Association (VCRA). In addition to these core partners, there have been other partners throughout the years as time and schedule allowed. The CRC goals are to promote literacy, create opportunities for experiential and service-learning, cultivate an appreciation for print culture, and send every family home with a free book to continue fostering a love of reading. Designed to encourage children to think about their favorite stories or imagine their own adventures in creative expression, it includes a variety of activities, such as storytelling, bookmark making, book making, button making, creative writing, and open mic sessions. We have also featured a presentation by the author of the book selected as the book give-away for each family in attendance.

CI's Children's Reading Celebration is a service-learning opportunity for CI students enrolled in the English program to put into practice the theory and principles they are learning in the courses, Introduction to Children's Literature and Adolescent Literature. It allows these students as well as those in CI's senior honors society, the Four Pillars Chapter of Mortar Board, to engage with children from the community and foster a love of reading. The CRC & YAF provides a memorable and enjoyable experience related to books and reading for families and children in attendance and consists of many thoughtfully designed elements that encourages reading and promotes literacy. Such components include spending time in a library, reading aloud to children, fostering respect for books, children reading their favorite books, engaging in conversations about books, and enhancing home libraries with new books.

Getting Started: California State University Channel Islands, opened in 2002, as the twenty-third campus in the California State University system. In 2003, the dean of the library was interested in building partnerships with campus programs to support student learning and looking for ways to engage the local community. Concurrently, Dr. Claudia Reder, an English professor who taught English 212: Introduction to Children's Literature, was seeking opportunities for her students where they could work with children first hand and utilize the techniques taught in the class.

As a result of this shared interest, the Children's Reading Celebration began in 2004 as a festival to celebrate reading children's books and promote literacy to the surrounding community. The first year, the event was modest with about thirty attendees. At first, the event only offered one activity, which was storytelling by CI students. In 2005, the event added additional activities to increase ways to engage families—and it doubled in attendance.

In 2006, CI was approached by VCRA who was interested in combining their event with the Children's Reading Celebration. They had been hosting a Young Author's Fair in the county for twenty-seven years; the event encouraged the creation of books in the classroom and provided a venue to display and celebrate young authorship. It was also a place for teachers to attend and display works from students in their classes and serve as inspiration to one another. The two events were both designed to support literacy among children and families throughout Ventura County, so it seemed a natural fit. Combining the two events would allow us to attract more participants and reach out to more Ventura County families. As the event continued to grow, we increased our outreach efforts, generating bilingual promotional materials and targeting First 5, a California program that provides support resources for parents of young children. These efforts were in addition to a press release provided to the local newspapers and flyers sent home to K-8 students.

Motivations: The mission statement of California State University Channel Islands is "Placing students at the center of the educational experience, California State University Channel Islands provides undergraduate and graduate education that facilitates learning within and across disciplines through integrative approaches, emphasizes experiential and service-learning, and graduates students with multicultural and international perspectives."[1]

As part of our mission, service-learning is an integral part of the campus and is talked about frequently. As a young campus just starting out, the library was interested in ways to engage the community while serving a student need at the same time.

THE PEOPLE

Library: California State University Channel Islands opened in 2002 in the facility that was previously Camarillo State Hospital. On April 4, 2008, the John Spoor Broome Library, a new 137, 000-square-foot library facility designed by Lord Norman Foster, opened its doors to the campus community.

The library's mission is to enhance the CI mission of interdisciplinary, international, multicultural, and service-learning. This is achieved through active collaboration with students, faculty, and staff to plan, implement, promote, and access the use of collections and services and support student learning via its robust information literacy program. When Dr. Reder approached the library about the possibility of the literacy event, there was never a question of if we wanted to do this. It seemed like a natural way to support students participating in service-learning.

Instructors: Our primary partner for the event was Dr. Claudia Reder, the instructor of ENG 212: Introduction to Children's Literature. Dr. Reder received her PhD in storytelling from New York University. Dr. Reder will tell you that working in children's literature allows her to share her love of folklore, storytelling, poetry, and service-learning with others.

Courses: Students in English 212: Introduction to Children's Literature have participated on an annual basis and provided some of the core activities for the event. Some years, students from English 477: Young Adult Literature participated and hosted Reader's Theater for the older children in attendance. In 2011, when CI established the Four Pillars Chapter of Mortar Board, part of the Mortar Board National senior honor society, student members became involved. As part of Mortar Board's national project, the "Reading is Leading" initiative, students in CI's local chapter felt that they could provide meaningful service by participating in the Children's Reading Celebration and promoting literacy to their local community.

Students: CI's student population continues to change and evolve. Initially, the campus was considered an extension of CSU Northridge, so the first students were students that were attending CSU Northridge at Channel Islands. Once CI became its own unique campus, a growth plan was implemented with steady growth that has brought CI's current enrollment to 6,611. In 2010, CI was designated a federal Hispanic Serving Institution (HSI); our number of Hispanic students has grown since this time with our current enrollment at 48 percent. In addition to this, 59 percent of our students are first-generation college students.

Community Partners: This event began as a joint endeavor between the John Spoor Broome Library and the CI English Program. Ventura County Reading Association (VCRA) is the primary outside community partner for this activity.

Finding and Working with Community Partners. The initial partnership with the CI English Program allowed Broome Library to support student learning in a meaningful context. Working with VCRA resulted in a mutually beneficial partnership that helped CI draw a broader community audience while strengthening logistical support for VCRA's long-time event, the Young Author's Fair. These two primary partnerships solidified the core of the event and allowed us the flexibility to include and remove additional partners year-to-year as their interest and schedule permitted. For example, due to spring breaks the AVID middle school groups were not able to participate every year, but this did not affect event logistics because we had a strong core.

It was essential to identify who would be responsible for what aspect of the event to ensure everything went smoothly the day of the event. For example, VCRA had strong ties to the author community and so they are responsible for securing the author, but Broome Library paid a small honorarium to the author. There are many considerations for an event this size, including promotion to the community, parking, event signage, logistics in the event space, supplies for the event, directing student volunteers, and much more. These things go a lot more smoothly when it is identified well ahead of time who will be handling what. This may require several meetings ahead of time but will pay off with clear responsibility and less confusion later.

Benefits

Library Benefits: Ultimately, this event allowed the Broome Library to fulfill a core part of its mission by supporting students who are engaged in service-learning. This allowed us the opportunity to collaborate with faculty in the design of the event and create a space for students to put what they learned in their course into practice. It strengthened our community partnerships with Ventura County Reading Association and the Ventura County Office of Education as we worked collaboratively to combine our events. It also allowed the library to offer something back to the local community through an event where families could come out and enjoy a day at the University.

Instructor Benefits: For the instructors, the partnership formed through the Children's Reading Celebration provided them with a space for their students' service-learning. One of the most challenging parts for instructors for something of this magnitude is the logistics. Reserving space, securing funding, ordering and organizing supplies, and coordinating the participation of external partners are all logistical things that can become roadblocks in pursuing an event of this size. With the library handling these aspects of the event, it allowed the faculty to focus on their curriculum and prepare their students to engage in service-learning.

Student Benefits: Students reveled in the experience to put theory into practice! The set-up of the event allowed for students with different personalities, strengths, and comfort levels to participate in different ways. The more outgoing students loved the freedom they were given to select texts for their own story times, to bring props to decorate their storytelling area, and to engage children at this level. Students who were reluctant to have such a visible role, preferred working one-on-one with the children in creative writing or bookmark making, supporting literacy in a different way.

Partner Benefits: Combining our events allowed the Ventura County Reading Association to continue their long-time event of the Young Author's Fair while minimizing the logistics involved in supporting the event. As a volunteer organization, event logistics take a lot of time and commitment from members that could be refocused on other organizational goals, like supporting classroom teachers, if the logistics were handled for them.

THE PROCESS
Expected Learning Outcome

There are multiple components to this event, each with their own outcomes identified by the partner responsible for that aspect of the event. The overall outcomes for the Children's Reading Celebration are to

- prepare CI students to become engaged citizens in the community via service-learning;
- expose children to a college campus early in the hopes to inspire them to attend university;
- provide a venue for CI and K-12 students to have experiential learning opportunities;
- promote literacy and foster appreciation for print culture to underserved populations; and
- cultivate current and new community partnerships through the continued success of the event.

Students enrolled in courses at CI who participated in service-learning at the event had learning outcomes for their course, but these are designated by the professor in support of the broader course curriculum.

Curriculum Materials

This aspect of the program was handled by the Dr. Reder, professor of English 212. The learning outcomes for the course are to

- study and examine a variety of genres within children's literature, including picture books, folktales, myth, modern fantasy, poetry, contemporary fiction, historical fiction, and nonfiction biographies and informational books;
- conduct literary analysis on a variety of children's literature genres, focusing specifically on plot, settings, characterization, theme, style, and point of view;
- examine children's literature as sources of cognitive and social development of children and adolescents of diverse backgrounds;
- apply effective techniques for reading aloud to children in school settings; and
- utilize technology via the use of electronic research tools.

The Children's Reading Celebration was incorporated into her syllabus as a required event. Students who were unable to attend the event were required to notify her ahead of time and serve as volunteers in the weeks before the event to prepare supplies for activities and to help set up for the event. Students did receive credit for their participation, resulting in greater number of students engaged in the event.

Steps Involved

Initially, this event was simply a joint endeavor between the John Spoor Broome Library and the CI English Program. In 2006, The Ventura County Reading Association partnered with CI and added in their Young Author's Fair, and the event formally became the Children's Reading Celebration and Young Author's Fair. Broome Library, the CI English Program, and VCRA were the core and consistent partners for the event. Other campus and community partners for the event varied over the years.

In 2009, after the event was in place for about five years the dust began to settle, and it was apparent that there was a need a clearer vision of what the event should be. In the early years, we tried different activities to draw attendees, such as paint-by-number with an artist, reading to therapy dogs, and other activities with a "wow" factor. However, what we discovered was that all of these things were taking away from one of our primary reasons for starting the event: service-learning. While the attendees were really attracted to these exciting offerings, it meant that the focus of the event was not on the storytelling and activities that were actually provided by CI students. As a result, we eliminated most everything that was not student-run or student-driven, with the exception of the Author Presentation and the Young Author's Fair.

We refocused the event to align with CI's mission of placing students at the center of the educational experience by providing experiential and service-learning opportunities for our university students as well as K-12 students in local school districts. During the event, CI students in ENG 212: Introduction to Children's Literature are engaged and empowered by leading activities and hosting areas where they serve as "storytellers" and "artists." All CI service-learning students are self-directed at their rotating stations. The storytellers select the books ahead of time and conduct "read alouds" to the families and children in attendance. The artists cultivate an appreciation for print culture with bookmark making and concertina or non-adhesive book making. Students in Mortar Board serve as "imagineers" where they facilitate creative writing and the writing process, encourage children to draw interpretations of a favorite story, have their illustrations made into buttons, and host an open-mic area where children share items they made in the creative writing area or books they created for the Young Author's Fair. In 2015, another class was seeking a service-learning opportunity, so students in ENG 477: Adolescent Literature hosted a Reader's Theater used materials from Gary Soto's *Baseball in April* to engage older children in attendance at the event. They created scripts, worked with older children to prepare a reader's theater, and facilitated the performance of the reader's theater to event attendees.

In keeping with the spirit of celebrating young authorship and reading and literacy for Ventura County's children, we continued to provide attendees with the opportunity to meet a well-known children's author or illustrator. Each year we had a featured author or illustrator; some of the past participating authors and illustrators include such acclaimed writers as Ellen Kelley, author of *Buckamoo Girls*, Lee Wardlaw, author of *101 Ways to Bug Your Parents*, Barbara Jean Hicks, author of *Jitterbug Jam*, R. L. LaFevers, author of *Werewolf Rising*, Dan Hanna, illustrator of *The Pout Pout Fish*, Alexis O'Neill, author of *The Recess Queen*, Kristine O'Connell George, poet and author of *Old Elm Speaks*, and Tina Coury Nichols, author of *Hanging Off Jefferson's Nose: Growing Up On Mount Rushmore*. All featured authors and illustrators are also local residents of Ventura, Santa Barbara, and Los Angeles Counties. The author presentation was the culmination of the day, with the author presentation taking place after all other stations were shut down. This both ensured that it did not take away from the service-learning opportunity for students and also allowed CI students to attend the author presentation. Starting in 2009, we wanted to find a way to support family literacy and help parents continue fostering reading at home, so a signed copy of the featured author or illustrator's book was given to each family in attendance.

In addition to these activities, VCRA also hosted their Young Author's Fair. On average, thirteen local school districts were represented with approximately 1,500 books displayed that were created by local children. Children who participate in this aspect of the event acquire a greater respect and appreciation for books, as they learn how to make books themselves. Through sharing their books with their peers, they realize that books are valuable tools in learning about each other and serve as an expression of themselves. These young authors are absolutely delighted when they see other people read their books.

Throughout the years, we have also cultivated a partnership with students in the Advancement Via Individual Determination (AVID) program from Frank Intermediate School (2014, 2013, 2012, and 2011) and Ocean View Junior High (2010). AVID programs are dedicated to closing the achievement gaps and preparing students for college. The AVID teachers were seeking meaningful ways to expose their students to a college campus, where they could see students like themselves engaged in learning and see a future for themselves. AVID students worked in pairs to support CSUCI service-learning students by replenishing supplies, directing families, giving children stickers on their activity passports at the completion of activities, helping with breakdown, and, of course, promoting literacy to other children.

The campus of CI is set outside of Camarillo, CA, about four miles from the city, making it somewhat isolated. There is a small residential community attached to the university that houses both community members as well as staff and faculty. We hoped to provide a service to draw attendees from this community as well as draw community members from the surrounding cities out to the campus. We also wanted to reach out to a broader population, so in later years we began generating bilingual promotional materials and sending out flyers to K-8 students throughout the county.

POST-PROJECT FEEDBACK
Methods of Reflection

Dr. Reder had a follow-up assignment for students that was a one-page reflection on the event. She then utilized information from this assignment to provide the library with feedback.

Post Project Feedback

Some years, we received internal funding for Instructionally Related Activities. This is a student fee that students pay to support activities that enhance their curriculum. There is a committee that reviews applications for these funds and selects who will receive money. As a condition of funding, we were required to solicit feedback from students who participated with a simple fill-in-the-blank form that had three questions:

Here are a few examples of comments we received on these forms:

- "Children loved making the bookmarks, they talked about the books they enjoy and which book they are going to use their bookmark for!"
- "It [the event] helped children feel more excited about reading and what types of books they enjoy reading."
- "This course focuses on children's literature. By being able to read to the children we were able to practice what we have learned in class."
- "Through reading books I was able to work with children in another language. It is so true if you validate a child's culture they will open up in a variety of ways."

Project/Program Assessment and Reporting Methods

We have counted attendees and the number of books distributed in order to have some metric, but it only reflected the number of attendees and not an assessment of the programming. We also conducted a short event survey for parents one of the years but it had a less than a 10 percent response rate.

Difficulties Encountered

Library Issues: Ensuring there was adequate funding in order to provide a book to every family in attendance and purchase all necessary supplies was something that had to be planned for well ahead of time. This required seeking both external funding opportunities as well as internal funding sources. Much of the funding received required applications by a certain deadline as well as defined reporting after the event, so it was imperative that it was considered as part of the broader planning process. For several years, we received an Early Childhood Literacy grant from the Target Foundation that allowed us to purchase the books to give away. We also sought a variety of internal funds that varied in their availability from year to year, including: the Provost Faculty Resource Fund, which aimed at supporting faculty research or service; Instructionally Related Activities funds, which were to support educational activities; and lottery funding, which could be applied for to support activities that had a direct impact on student learning. Along with this, we tried to purchase supplies that could be reused from year to year to help control the costs.

Partnering with volunteer-based organizations always comes with a unique set of challenges. It is important to keep communication open and continuous with the organization. As members and leadership within the organization change, diligence and gentle reminders may be required to ensure that they are aware of their commitment to the event.

It took many years for us to refine the book giveaway process and get it right. The first year we gave away books, we did not have the author sign ahead of time. This resulted in very long lines and waiting for families who wanted their book signed. This was very hard for the children in attendance! We learned from this and began having the author sign the books prior to the event (one of the many benefits of using a local author). People who were interested in a more personalized greeting with their signature had the opportunity for this after the book giveaway if they wanted. We also ran into the challenge that many people just wanted their free book and to not really stay and participate in the event. As a result, we came up with an activity passport that the children found to be rather fun. The passport had a space for each activity, including the book giveaway and the time it would be offered. After participating in the activity, the child would get a sticker on that activity's space. Along with this, when children picked up their passport at the beginning of the event, we gave parents a ticket for the book. The books were limited to one per family, so we collected the ticket at book giveaway time. Tickets were counted out ahead of time so we could ensure that we only handed out enough tickets for the number of books available. We had a lot of trial and error on where to set up and how to distribute books but the passport/ticket system seemed the best. We also moved the giveaway location so that it was near the main library exit. Although some attendees were still upset when we wouldn't give them a book ahead of time, it really was the best way to approach it to be fair and ensure participation in the event.

The biggest challenge for this event was that as it grew it became harder to ensure that our student's service-learning objectives were being met. In recent years, we had up to 450 attendees—a far cry from the modest beginnings of thirty attendees. It also became challenging in more recent years to balance differing objectives of the different partners involved. For example, we had partners trying to provide guidance to CI students without understanding the curricular objectives that were put in place by the professor. The professor was always in attendance and very involved with the students throughout the event, so not only was the direction inappropriate, it was off-putting to the professor and left students confused. Serving as the primary coordinator required some patience and politeness to remind partners of their responsibility in the broader scheme of things.

Conclusion

In the most recent CRC & YAF, we had about 450 attendees, gave books away to 180 Ventura County families in attendance, distributed 250 creative writing journals for children, and provided service-learning opportunities for over sixty-five students. Despite the challenges that the event offered, creating the opportunity for students to engage in the joy of reading and support literacy among children and families was worth the effort.

Notes

1.   "CI Mission Statement," accessed January 17, 2018, https://www.csuci.edu/about/mission.htm.

CHAPTER FIFTEEN

Promoting Scholarly Conversations through an Undergraduate Research Conference in the Library:

A Communication Class Project

Jen Jones, PhD
Associate Professor, Communication Department
Seton Hill University
jjones@setonhill.edu

THE ACTIVITY

Description: More and more colleges and universities are promoting oppor-tunities for students to participate in undergraduate research and to share their work through undergraduate research conferences. At Seton Hill University, the Undergraduate Research Conference (URC) is a campus-wide celebration of our community of learning that provides an opportunity for students in all majors to gain experience presenting research in an academic conference setting, boosting student learning outcomes, and supporting the library's goals and the university's mission.

Originally, the conference was developed and run by a single faculty member. In the spring of 2016, the event was transformed into a student-led endeavor by making the planning, organizing, and facilitating of the event a service-based assignment for a communication class. The URC orients students to the manner in which conferences are conducted, including a conference theme, call for proposals, anonymous review, and panel and poster sessions. After students became involved, the number of participants doubled.

While this service-learning project is conducted within a communication course, faculty members in any discipline or librarians may adopt it. The project could also be utilized outside of a course as a fieldwork experience.[1] This chapter provides a practical guide for faculty members and librarians interested in getting students involved in hosting an undergraduate research conference on their campuses.

Getting Started: The URC at my university began as a small conference within the School of the Humanities and was run entirely by one faculty member. When this faculty member asked me if I would like to take it over, I had the idea of integrating it into the Communication Research class as a semester-long service-learning project. Having a group of students involved relieved the burden of one individual handling all of the conference responsibilities and allowed the conference to extend to a campus-wide initiative. As such, the conference has grown significantly and has become a distinctive event for the university. The conference also promotes co-curricular communication among faculty, administrators, and staff, which enhances the collaborative culture on campus.

The URC involves regular communication and cooperation. My campus already has a collaborative culture, which makes the process and implementation of the URC run much more smoothly and effectively. At a large institution, or even a small one that does not have such a culture, I recommend starting small, in one department or college, and allowing small successes propel the conference forward by building momentum, credibility, and buy-in from future partners who will want to be involved rather than feeling like they are being asked to do yet more service for the university.

Motivations: Service-learning is implemented throughout students' academic career in communication coursework. By the time they take the Communication Research course, they have an understanding of and value this approach to learning. The stated goal of the Communication Department emphasizes service-learning: "to create experiential learning environments in which students have opportunity to learn theory and investigate theoretical constructs, develop skills and abilities through practical management of learned theories, and resolve communication problems through the application of established knowledge, good judgment, collaboration, and exploration." Having ten-years' experience in marketing and management, service-learning takes me back to this role and exposes students to a professional atmosphere that they will experience in their careers. Students find their service-learning experiences significantly impactful and memorable. Alumni have contacted me to express even greater appreciation of service-learning "retroactively" after being able to make connections to their work or graduate school experiences.

The library director enthusiastically supports the URC for its connection to the library's strategic goals. Not only does the conference energize the space of the Learning Commons, it also, and more importantly, supports the library's goal to enhance information fluency and the quality of student research. Additionally, the renewal of library databases is determined by their use, so the URC helps librarians evaluate which resources are the most viable and substantiated.

THE PEOPLE

Library: Founded in 1883 by the Sisters of Charity, Seton Hill University (SHU) is a private Catholic liberal arts university in southwestern Pennsylvania with approximately 1,700 undergraduate students and offers graduate programs in business, physician assistant, and orthodontics. The faculty to student ratio is 14:1 and the majority of classes have fewer than twenty students. It is a mission-driven institution described as "a Catholic university rooted in Judeo-Christian values. In the tradition of Elizabeth Ann Seton, we educate students to think and act critically, creatively, and ethically as productive members of society committed to transforming the world."[2] All areas of the university base their work on this mission. The library makes a significant impact toward fulfilling the mission by providing resources and helping students use those resources effectively to engage in critical, creative, and ethical thinking and writing. Librarians embody the "Setonian Spirit" by working positively and graciously with students, faculty, and administrators. They are vital to our students' success in transforming the world.

The university is teacher-scholar oriented. The provost holds an event every year for faculty to share their most recent research, which usually showcases collaborative research projects with students as well. The university also offers multiple teach-and-learn sessions where faculty members share ideas and experiences with innovative pedagogy. Along with scholarship and teaching, faculty members are highly engaged in service, such as accompanying students to conferences and professional development events, serving local non-profits and charities alongside students, and integrating service and experiential learning into clubs and classes.

Instructor: I am an associate professor and department coordinator of communication at Seton Hill. I teach the three-credit, upper-level Communication Research course that is required for communication majors. On one hand, students at this level are ready to handle the responsibility of the URC, while on the other hand, it also challenges them and gets them out of their comfort zones.[3] They experience a healthy level of anxiety that I monitor, which transforms into a sense of accomplishment and pride with the success of the conference. Throughout their study in the major, students read and learn about the field of communication; the URC project adds a service element where they engage in theory experientially.

Course: This project is utilized in the Communication Research Course, which is rigorous with the demands of researching and writing a presentation-worthy paper and coordinating all aspects of the Undergraduate Research Conference. The small class size is conducive for a writing-intensive course and the URC service-learning component.

Students: Students are third-year level and enrollment is typically fifteen students. Students are encouraged to take the course in their third year so they can submit their papers to the Pennsylvania Communication Association Conference, which takes place the following fall semester. Thus, the URC prepares students for this next level of scholarly activity.

Community Partners: The URC primarily serves the library through this project as it encourages the development of undergraduate research and celebrates the work done by students as demonstrated in the conference. Libraries have always been the place where pre-existing knowledge is gathered and new knowledge is developed and shared. Hence, the library is the perfect venue for such an event. Holding the URC at the Learning Commons of our library communicates to the campus community that the library is at the heart of the university's intellectual tradition, and is committed to the university's foundational pillars of welcoming, learning, serving, and celebrating. Librarians visit classes to assist students with the research process and respond to questions about students' particular needs in various disciplines. As such, librarians are exemplar mentors who help students create quality scholarly work.[4] The conference incentivizes students to utilize library resources and to hone their research skills by meeting with librarians. In an electronic age, where libraries are becoming devalued as mere gathering spaces, the students working on the URC uphold the integrity of the library by engaging their peers to fully utilize all the many facets it has to offer for the development of their academic acumen.

Finding and Working with Partners: I was only in my second year of teaching at Seton Hill when I implemented the URC as a service-learning project. I invited the faculty member who previously coordinated the conference to my class so he could talk with the students and me about his prior work with the conference. He helped the students make connections with partners and offered his support and encouragement. Through this conversation, the students gained an understanding that the URC was *their* primary responsibility to help their peers value and celebrate academic research and that I performed the role of empowering and supporting them to orchestrate the conference. A librarian also met with the students during a class session to discuss information fluency and the research process. She asked the students to complete an online form about their research interests, additional questions they had, and to set up a time to meet individually about their papers. The students also performed a walk-through with the library director to discuss all aspects of planning the event (e.g., technology, presentation space, registration, and refreshments). Through the service-learning experience, students in the Communication Research course provide an enriched learning opportunity for their peers, support the goals of the library, and contribute to the university's reputation for academic distinction.

Benefits

Instructor Benefits: Working with the students on the URC gave me great satisfaction in my vocation as an educator. I thoroughly enjoy the collaborative effort of this project. Too often, faculty and administrators remain in distinct silos, as do faculty from different departments or colleges. The URC offers an opportunity for everyone to work together on a project and celebrate its success. The URC has helped me know people on campus. I find greater reward in shared accomplishment rather than individual accomplishment. I also feel assured that I am providing my students with an experience that will benefit their lives beyond college. My university values teaching at 50 percent and scholarship and service at 50 percent. The URC is a significant component of my professional development plan that elucidates my commitment to teaching and service. The success of the URC made a major positive impact on my promotion application.

    Students' Benefits: Even though students are familiar with other disciplines by taking liberal arts and elective courses, students have shared that they enjoy getting to know faculty, staff, and administrators in multiple areas on campus even more through the URC. Moreover, the URC contributes to their experience of community on campus along with learning about the importance of social capital.[5] While information fluency is integrated throughout their coursework, the URC exposes them to various approaches to research along with the corresponding methodologies, source credibility, and evaluative criteria. Furthermore, they gain an understanding of peer reviews and the publication process. The URC prepares students for the next level of graduate study and contributes to their intellectual growth.[6] Students have shared that the URC also generated their interest in graduate work, which would otherwise not have occurred. From the practitioner point-of-view, students who have gone on to professional careers have shared that running the URC prepared them for project management, event planning, teamwork, and relationship building in their careers. Yet, even those not implementing their learning in such a direct fashion gain an understanding of breaking down silos and communicating collaboratively and positively with partners, which are vital skills for any career.

Community Partners' Benefits: The atmosphere of the URC is filled with shared affirmation and appreciation among faculty members, administrators, and staff. Hosting the conference at the library sends a message to our campus community that it is a space for learning and academic rigor. Our librarians deal with the common occurrence of tight and reduced budgets. The URC showcases the profound importance of our library resources—database usage, assistance finding the strongest sources, technology, and the physical space. Our library recently went through a major renovation, and events like the URC showcase the importance of this vital resource and the need to allocate funds accordingly. Additionally, the submissions from the URC provide librarians with material to evaluate information fluency. Librarians compare research from first-year students in the Celebration of Writing, another event held in the learning commons, to research from third- and fourth-year students in the URC. Faculty members from multiple disciplines have expressed their fulfillment in getting to learn about research from other areas. We intrinsically know our colleagues are doing good work with their students, and the URC is an opportunity to see it first-hand. Additionally, with more students utilizing the Writing Center, administrators are able to quantitatively demonstrate the usage of this important campus resource. The URC also helps first- and second-year students learn about the kind of work they will be doing in their upper-level courses.

Institutional Benefits: The liberal arts and Catholic intellectual traditions compel our university to be distinctive in academic rigor. The URC is representative of the distinguishing education the university seeks to maintain. Moreover, the URC benefits the university as student participants go on to become successful alumni. Employers often seek students with written communication and speaking skills, so the URC experience gives our students an advantage during the job application process. The URC is an important event to highlight on the university's website, which also gives the admissions team information to share with potential future students and their parents.

THE PROCESS
Expected Learning Outcomes

Learning outcomes for this course include:
- Define scholarly investigation as qualitative and quantitative.
- Identify a question that guides inquiry and formulates an argument.
- Utilize information fluency skills to acquire scholarly sources.
- Develop an understanding of the research process.
- Recognize significant scholars and philosophers in the field of communication in book/text and article publications.
- Employ APA format for in-text citations, reference page, and paper format.

- Differentiate and organize primary and secondary sources into an established frame of academic writing including an introduction, question, literature review, implications, and conclusion.
- Apply communication theory in various case study contexts to foster continued questioning as a professional or scholar.
- Conduct a peer review and perform editing.
- Present ideas and issues to a public audience and respond thoughtfully to questioning.
- Understand and implement all aspects of conference planning, organizing, and facilitating.
- Work collaboratively as a team (small and large group) and communicate effectively with campus partners.

Expected Learning Outcomes for Information Fluency

The library defines information-fluent students as those who, upon graduation, will possess the ability to combine all forms of literacy in order to master a chosen topic. Students who develop information fluency skills will successfully

- critically analyze appropriate topics;
- conceptualize the parameters of the topic;
- locate and access relevant information in all forms;
- competently evaluate information;
- understand practical, legal, and social issues related to the information;
- interact with faculty and staff in a manner evident of the development of superior research skills; and
- synthesize diverse types of information into a comprehensive and coherent work.

Curriculum Materials

The main assignment in this class is to write a "presentable or publishable" research paper. Students engage in a research process throughout the semester to develop their papers. The students conduct interpretive research in philosophy of communication. They also learn about other qualitative and quantitative research approaches. The secondary assignment is the URC. Conducting their own research and learning about other research methods provides them with an understanding and appreciation of the multiple types of research projects presented at the URC in panels and poster sessions.

To gain an understanding of the type of research they will conduct along with the research process, the students read and respond to the following articles and book chapter. These articles also challenge them to read at the graduate level.

- Arnett, Ronald C., "Interpretive Inquiry as Qualitative Communication Research." *Qualitative Research Reports in Communication* 8, no. 1 (2007): 29–35.
- Arnett, Ronald. C., "Defining Philosophy of Communication: Difference and Identity." *Qualitative Research Reports in Communication,* 11, no. 1(2010): 57–62.
- Arnett, Ronald. C., "Philosophy of Communication: Qualitative Research, Questions in Action." *Qualitative Research Reports in Communication,* 17, no. 1 (2016): 1–6.
- Prellwitz, John. H., "Dialogic Meeting: A Constructive Rhetorical Approach to Contemporary Public Relations." In *Philosophies of Communication: Implications for Everyday Experience,* eds. M. A. Cook & A. M. Holba (New York, NY: Peter Lang, 2008): 79–94.

Students generally have no prior experience with academic or professional conferences. To help them become more familiar with academic conferences, students look at programs from conferences I have attended, along with current conference calls and programs for organizations in my field. This practice also helps them to become familiar with the various interest groups within communication. Their research papers engage theory from one of these areas along with a philosopher of communication. The following are organizations that students evaluate to learn more about the field and their respective conferences:

- Pennsylvania Communication Association
- Eastern Communication Association
- National Communication Association
- International Communication Association

Assignments used specifically for the URC component in the class may be found at the end of this chapter include:

- URC project management
- peer evaluation
- cover letter

Steps Involved

- Students work in dyads (pairs) of their choosing based on their shared interest in a project management area.[7] Students work well in dyads and have reported that they enjoy this format. In dyads, they share the workload, brainstorm ideas, proof/edit work, hold each other responsible, and celebrate successes. It is also easier to coordinate schedules for meetings

and simplify communication. During class time, they provide progress reports and receive feedback from the larger group and the instructor. Students also conduct a peer performance evaluation at midterm and at the
end of the semester. While students often shy away from delivering constructive feedback to their peers, conducting a performance evaluation
mitigates issues and prepares students for expectations in a professional
career. At the end of the semester, they also write a professional cover
letter detailing their involvement and learning from the URC. While not
a requirement for the course, students are highly encouraged to submit
their final papers to the Pennsylvania Communication Association Undergraduate Research Award Competition and conference. The university
library also offers a research award that includes a monetary component,
so I also encourage them to submit their papers to this competition.

- The students and I work collaboratively with a number of faculty, administrators, and staff on campus. The following identify co-curricular partnerships with others on campus, which are vital to the success of the URC. It
  is important to establish contact with these individuals and maintain regular communication with them throughout the planning of the conference.

    o   Provost—provides funding for conference expenses (food, pro-
        motional materials, printing, etc.); places the conference on the
        Academic Calendar.

    o   Library director—reserves all of the space in the Learning
        Commons where the conference takes place and consults on the
        conference layout.

    o   Librarians—visit classrooms to discuss library resources, infor-
        mation fluency, and the research process; conduct evaluations of
        the quality of student research; chair panels and facilitate poster
        sessions; promote the conference; serve on the URC Committee.

    o   Faculty members—promote the conference and encourage
        students to submit the conference; build the conference into their
        syllabi; serve on the URC Committee; work the registration table;
        chair panels and facilitate poster sessions.

    o   URC Committee—group of faculty members and librarians
        responsible for promoting the conference with their colleagues,
        review submissions, communicate accept/reject/revise decisions
        and other conference correspondence with conference partici-
        pants.

    o   Writing Center—meets with students about editing and revising
        their research papers; offers their space in the Learning Commons
        for the conference.

    o   Student Affairs—helps promote the conference through social
        media, residence halls, and flyers on campus.

o   Marketing and Media Relations—sends press releases to the local newspaper, invites reporters to the event, promotes the event on the website and social media, and takes pictures during the event.

o   Food service director—provides refreshments for the conference.

o   Solutions Center—makes sure that all technology is functioning properly and has staff available to troubleshoot during the conference; they also set up a conference specific email account.

o   Xerox copy center—prints flyers and programs.

o   Campus newspaper—prints conference advertisement, sends student reporter to the event, and publishes a story on the event.

The Undergraduate Research Conference involves the following tasks throughout the semester, which is organized by the students into project management specific areas.

1. Communicate with partners.
   a. Establish a URC committee.
   b. Talk with faculty members about building the URC into their syllabi, especially for research classes where students will submit to the conference, but also to faculty who will encourage or give credit to students to attend the conference.
2. Develop the call for papers/panels.
   a. Review past conference information and numbers, and establish goals for the current conference.
   b. Decide on theme, date, time, location, directions/deadline for submitting, technology needs.
   c. Create a logo for the conference.
   d. Create an email account for the conference.
   e. Create an ad for the University newspaper.
   f. Create a Google Form to collect submissions.
3. Send out the call.
   a. Email campus-wide and announce at faculty senate meeting.
   b. Alert campus newspaper, media relations, and Student Affairs.
4. Plan logistics.
   a. Reserve meeting room space, communicate with administrators near the site (e.g., library, administration), order food, and create an event on the university calendar.
   b. Collaborate with all co-curricular partners.
5. Send submissions to reviewers.
   a. Email reviewers papers (made anonymous by removing names), set a deadline for returning reviews.
6. Create conference program.

    a.   Email decisions to submitters (accept/reject/revise).

    b.   Decide on panel organization.

    c.   Design program, include thank you section to supporters.

    d.   Decide on social media, hashtag, etc.

7. Promote the conference.

    a.   Email presenters with conference information/length of time to present and encourage them to promote the conference.

    b.   Encourage students, faculty, and administers to attend the conference.

    c.   Design flyers, get them approved to display.

    d.   Announce at faculty senate meeting.

    e.   Send direct emails to college deans.

    f.   Send faculty calendar meeting invitation.

    g.   Solicit faculty to chair panels, host poster sessions, and register participants.

    h.   Send personal invitations to the university president and provost.

    i.   Utilize social media.

8. Pre-plan the conference.

    a.   Complete a walk-through of the conference space with the library director. Identify where panels and poster sessions will be held and during what timeframe. Decide where the registration table and refreshments will be placed.

    b.   Create and print signs.

    c.   Create and print directions for participants and volunteers.

9. Facilitate the conference.

    a.   Place signage: registration banner, directions, posters, and panels.

    b.   Provide directions for time-keepers, registration table, and photographers.

    c.   Check on food order.

    d.   Check technology.

    e.   Prepare registration table: tablecloth, printed sign-in sheet (presenting/attending).

    f.   Utilize social media.

10. After the conference.

    a.   Send thank you notes to partners.

    b.   Debrief with students.

    c.   Debrief with URC committee.

At the beginning of the semester, student dyad teams will choose a project management area and then identify tasks associated with the theme from the listing above and any other task that may emerge. Students may choose titles related to the areas. For example, a title associated with the corresponding area may be "communication director." The project management areas include:

- designing
- writing
- proofing/editing
- organizing
- promoting/social media
- presenting
- corresponding

POST-PROJECT ASSESSMENT
Methods of Reflection

- Students have reported on benefits they received from this project. In addition to gaining an in-depth understanding of the philosophy of communication and communication theory, they also appreciate the "real-world" experience of orchestrating an entire conference. They have expressed that employers and graduate schools are particularly interested in the work they did with the conference.
- At the end of the semester, students are required to develop a "cover letter" addressed to me that details their involvement with the conference and reflection on their conference experience. This format is also experiential because they obtain practice writing in a professional context.

Project Feedback

- Quotes from this assignment are provided below:
    - o "Organizing the Undergraduate Research Conference taught me a lot about event planning and promotion skills. While I've planned events in the past, I had never planned a conference and learning about what goes into one is great experience that I can take with me into the future."
    - o "I would like to express my gratitude for the professional development experience and the opportunity to refine my communications skills. It has proven to be an extremely beneficial experience at Seton Hill University and one I will remember. I found it was an opportunity to refine my skills that I have acquired through my involvement with Seton Hill University. I believe I demonstrated professional level presentation skills as well as demonstrating my ability to be a team player."
    - o "Presenting the paper in front of my peers and professors really showed me that I knew what I was talking about and this gave me confidence for future presentations. The planning for this event

also gave me a glimpse of the workings behind a conference and showed me how much effort is needed in order to pull off an event of this size. This class really taught me a lot and I am happy that I was able to write a large-scale research paper and help plan an event all in one class."

o "Through this process I learned the importance of repetitiveness and making sure all of the text on every flyer, program and poster stayed consistent. I also developed better professional digital communication. In the world we live in now digital communication is essential and throughout this entire process I found that skill improving greatly."

o "This whole process planning and facilitating the Undergraduate Research Conference was definitely an enlightening experience that I value. The process allowed me to expand my professional skills additional to taking part in creating another opportunity where our Seton Hill community can celebrate the accomplishments of another. The facilitation allowed me to witness the incredible diversity of the student body on an academic level. I was truly amazed overall by the quality of work and professionalism of my fellow classmates and student body."

o "I believe that this conference was very beneficial and educational for everyone that was involved. This was the first time ever participating in a research conference, and I believe that I learned a lot. By designing the theme, logo, conference flyers, and planning the event it was an unforgettable experience. I worked independently on the research for the paper, but also on a team for the panel presentation of the conference. This was an unforgettable experience to participate and to listen to others at this event. I hope to participate in many other research conferences held in this future. This event was a huge success."

o "While being involved in this process I learned what all goes into planning a conference. Each of us had to speak to other classes about the conference and just by doing that I realized so much more of what the conference was going to entail. It took teamwork and attentiveness to plan this conference. Professionalism was one of the most important aspects to planning because we were not students we were being communication professionals. I tried to be as involved as possible and work with my classmates to plan a successful undergraduate research conference."

o "The Undergraduate Research Conference at Seton Hill was a crucial part of this year's communication research course, which provided upperclassmen an opportunity to display their work to the academic community. In addition to sharing various research projects, underclassmen were also provided an opportunity to investigate the work of their peers and ponder the future research possibilities lying before them. Playing a role in planning and facilitating the conference was not only beneficial for experience, but it was an honor to put on such a rewarding academic experience at our home campus. Reflecting on this year's Undergraduate Research Conference, I've learned that successful events are nearly impossible to plan alone. When a group collaborates, diverse perspectives combine, creating an experience that is truly more than the sum of its parts. I am very proud to have been a part of planning and executing this conference, but I am even gladder that this conference will continue to become a Seton Hill academic tradition that brings all members of the SHU community together for intellectual discussion and reflection."

o   "I learned many different lessons through this process of developing the URC. I learned amount the time and effort it takes to create an event like this. I learned the many different moving parts that all have to align perfectly to create a fully functioning event. I realized the amount of time and pressure that presenters feel when presenting their work at a conference."

o   "From this conference, I have expanded my knowledge on certain topics and feel more inclined to share the information. I have also learned that details matter when planning an event. Think about all aspects and fewer issues with arise."

o   "I believe that the Undergraduate Research Conference was planned and executed very well by our Communication Research class. We had a very good group of students with some different educational goals which made the conference that much more diverse and creative."

o   "My involvement in the Undergraduate Research Conference at Seton Hill University was a very fulfilling and professional experience. Seton Hill, as an institution, has a lot to offer its students. Students are able to recognize this and show initiative to partake in things offered and take steps to go give back to this great school and the students who gain an education here. The URC was another way for me to get involved in the school."

o   "This was the first time I have participated and assisted in planning a conference and it is safe to say that I have learned quite a bit. From understanding the graphic design and written elements that go into advertising to the actual 'making it happen' takes a lot of hard, thoughtful work. We well achieved our goal regarding the outcome of participants. Through this opportunity and experience came a lot of knowledge and understanding in planning and presenting at a research conference. Without the participation and work the rest of my classmates and peers put into this event, it would not have been possible. Teamwork is incredibly important. Solid effort and time are also huge factors that play a role in the planning and facilitation, as well as respect and compassion for all members involved."

- Community partner remarks:
  - o Faculty email: "I wanted to thank you for all of the work that you put into the undergrad research conference. I'm sure there was a tremendous amount of planning that went into the logistics of the conference, and from an outsider's perspective at least, it seemed to go really smoothly. I was happy to see all of the students who presented—and happier to see the faculty support—and I know participating in this process was a great experience for all of the presenters. Congrats!"
  - o Faculty email: "I love how excited everyone is for this, you're really doing a great job with it."
  - o Dean comments: "The Undergraduate research conference was particularly noteworthy. The students organized the entire event, providing all the support for a large campus research celebration involving more than 80 student presenters."
  - o Dean comments: "The event had been held under various auspices for several years, but never as successfully or with as much community involvement and support. Kudos on reinvigorating to this essential campus experience!"
  - o Lots of faculty members and administrators expressed appreciation and accolades directly to me during the conference.

Project Assessment and Reporting Methods

- The URC Committee reported on the high quality of submissions received and chairs of panels and poster sessions reported on the high quality of student presentations.
- Communication students have consecutively received awards from the Pennsylvania Communication Association Undergraduate Research Competition—awarded to only three students in the entire state of Pennsylvania—and one of my students had her paper published in an academic journal.
- The conference has grown every year. The first year had nineteen presenters, the second year twenty-five, and the third year sixty. Some faculty

members have talked about expanding the conference by inviting students from other colleges and universities in the area.

- Our librarians complete an assessment of information fluency advancement from first to fourth year by evaluating URC papers and comparing them to the work first-year students who present their work at the Celebration of Writing event.

- After the most recent conference, the career and professional development director inquired about the possibility of inviting graduate school representatives and employers to the URC to recruit student participants. She would also like to add a panel session for students to share their internship, fieldwork, and practicum experiences.

- During a conference debriefing session, another faculty member discussed the possibility of publishing online conference proceedings to provide an additional vita/résumé line for conference participants.

Difficulties Encountered

Student Issues: The rigor and demands of this course are great. Students must balance completing their own research while orchestrating the conference, which adds another learning element of time management. However, students often struggle with time management, even at this level of their coursework. Some students have a history of procrastination and writing papers over a weekend, which is not a viable option for this course. Additionally, I often have to remind students that writing a research paper is a process and they will become frustrated with the process at various times throughout the semester. None of their work with the paper or conference can really be "made up" if they fall behind.

A common issue among students involves justice and fairness working in teams. Some students are more committed to their work than others. Meta-communication, or communicating about communicating, is necessary to mitigate this issue. We explicitly discuss the benefits and drawbacks of working in teams, the necessity to develop strong teamwork skills, and the importance of positive and constructive feedback. I talk with them about the problems with the type of student who thinks he or she has to do everything as well as the student who rides the coattails of others. Working in dyads and performing peer performance evaluation reduces the frequency of either negative phenomenon, but they may still occur.

Another issue is students' lack of knowledge about academic conferences. I have spent more time in class talking about conferences, having the students look at conference calls and programs (online and hard copy) and encouraging questions about conferences. It is a challenge to have students orchestrate a conference when nearly all of them have never attended a conference. To prime future students involved with the URC, when I am teaching lower-level courses, I have been more deliberate talking about the conferences I attend. The provost is very generous in funding students to attend the Pennsylvania Communication Association Conference so they can support their upper-class peers presenting at the conference while also learning about how conferences work. Also, I need to implement another service-learning activity in these courses where first- and second-year students are required to attend the URC and reflect on their experience. I have also invited fourth-year students and alumni who were in the Communication Research course previously to visit my current class and offer advice.

Instructor Issues: Even with student involvement, this URC demands significant involvement and oversight by several faculty members and librarians who comprise the URC committee. Involvement with the URC is time-consuming, which increases with the growth of the conference. Yet, I keep in mind that the benefits outweigh the stress associated with inevitable challenges and issues that emerge. This work is recognized as teaching and service for professional development, so it creates a win-win for both students and faculty. For those planning to initiate a URC on their campus, I recommend incorporating it into their professional development plan and annual review.

Since the service-learning experience is a "learning" experience for the students, it is inappropriate to expect event planning and project management to be at the level of what a professional in the field would do. Oversight is necessary to review student work with the URC, but errors still occur. Thus, grace is needed to avoid "should" comments, such as "I should have read that email more closely before it was sent" or "the students should know they ought to attend panel sessions, not just show up to present." Additionally, sometimes students make plans or do something without talking with appropriate partners. While the instructor is very involved, not all missteps or miscommunication can be predicted; therefore, grace, on the part of the instructor, students, and partners is needed. Grace is an understanding that everyone is trying their best, and when things go wrong, rather than blame and judge, compassion, kindness, and forgiveness are better responses to help resolve issues and move forward.

Community Partner Issues: The Library Learning Commons is an excellent space for the conference but we are close to outgrowing it. Graduate students were upset that the area for collaborative study was disrupted or unavailable for such a long period of time. We need to do a better job communicating with them about when the conference is taking place. We learned that the food for the event needed to be guarded because non-conference attendees were helping themselves to the refreshments. Moving the refreshment table beside registration and placing signs on the table helped to resolve this issue.

Other instructors who encourage their students to submit to the conference may not realize their students' lack of knowledge about conferences. We often receive submissions missing the title of the paper or not listing others on the panel. We have learned to request that faculty educate students on proper submission procedures, conference etiquette and attire, and how a conference works. Using a Google Form instead of email for submissions greatly reduces missing or incorrect information and helps organize submissions.

The participants at the conference attend other poster and panel sessions but we had difficulty getting non-participant attendees. Some of the presenters had friends attend, which was the most effective way to solicit attendees. We would like to see faculty members bring their entire class to the conference or offer incentives to their students to attend. Also, the last session wasn't as well attended as the first, so we need to work on ways to keep people at the conference.

Getting all members of the URC committee to attend a monthly meeting was difficult due to the immense teaching, scholarship, and service load our faculty members and librarians maintain. Reviewing all of the submissions was a challenge for the faculty committee. Members of the committee, along with other faculty volunteers, ran the registration table, chaired panels, and facilitated poster sessions. Getting people to serve in these roles was not difficult at my university but I could imagine that it could be a challenge. After the conference, we discussed what went well and what could have gone better, and a common concern was the budget. The conference runs on approximately $500 to cover refreshments and supplies. We did not adequately account for how much food was required and ran out of food at the last conference, even while monitoring the table for non-participants.

Conclusion

The interest and excitement for the URC necessitate its continuation, and I am happy to be at its helm. I anticipate its continued growth, and some of my colleagues have suggested extending it to include other universities and colleges in the area. If it would become a regional conference, I would move this course project to a course in event planning, where the entire focus of the course could be on the conference. Also, we have also discussed offering monetary research awards and possibly bring in a guest speaker in the future. As the conference grows, budgetary considerations will be paramount. I am grateful to be involved in a campus-wide initiative that has the potential to become part of the intellectual tradition at Seton Hill.

APPENDIX MATERIALS

- Undergraduate Research Conference (URC) Project Management Assignment
- Project Management Peer Performance Evaluation
- URC Cover Letter Assignment
- URC Sample Conference Call

Undergraduate Research Conference (URC) Project Management Assignment

Prospective employers and graduate schools view students who possess skills in project management and experience in academic conferences more favorably. This assignment also engages your practice of positive communication, relationship building, and leadership, which are also important and necessary capabilities for your professional or academic pursuits after graduation. Your involvement in the URC contributes to the university's reputation as a distinctive institution for academic rigor. Your involvement also enhances the sense of community on campus and supports the university's mission and Catholic identity. Thus, the URC project is a culminating praxis experience of theory-informed action where you will implement your acquired knowledge in communication to manage all aspects of a campus-wide undergraduate research conference.

This assignment requires you to identify an area of project management that is most aligned with your professional interests. You will work in a dyad (pair) to collaborate and complete project management tasks for the conference in your respective area. Project management areas include:

- designing
- writing
- proofing/editing
- organizing
- promoting/social media
- presenting
- corresponding

After selecting an area, you will review the conference timeline (below) with your partner and the large group class to identify tasks related to your project management area. Students may also assign titles for their respective roles such as "Chief Designer" or "Communication Director" and should view their role reporting to the URC Vice President (the instructor).

1. Communicate with partners.
    a. Establish a URC committee.
    b. Talk with faculty members about building the URC into their syllabi, especially for research classes where students will submit to the conference, but also to faculty who will encourage or give credit to students to attend the conference.
2. Develop the call for papers/panels.
    a. Review past conference information and numbers, and establish goals for the current conference.
    b. Decide on theme, date, time, location, directions/deadline for submitting, technology needs.
    c. Create a logo for the conference.

       d.   Create an email account for the conference.

       e.   Create an ad for the University newspaper.

       f.   Create a Google Form to collect submissions.

3.   Send out the call.

       a.   Email campus-wide and announce at faculty senate meeting.

       b.   Alert campus newspaper, Media Relations, and Student Affairs.

4.   Plan logistics.

       a.   Reserve meeting room space, communicate with administrators near the site (e.g., library, administration), order food, and create an event on the University calendar.

       b.   Collaborate with all co-curricular partners.

5.   Send submissions to reviewers.

       a.   Email reviewers papers (made anonymous by removing names), set a deadline for returning reviews.

6.   Create conference program.

       a.   Email decisions to submitters (accept/reject/revise).

       b.   Decide on panel organization.

       c.   Design program, include thank you section to supporters.

       d.   Decide on social media, hashtag, etc.

7.   Promote the conference.

       a.   Email presenters with conference information/length of time to present and encourage them to promote the conference.

       b.   Encourage students, faculty, and administers to attend the conference.

       c.   Design flyers, get them approved to display.

       d.   Announce at faculty Senate meeting.

       e.   Send direct emails to college deans.

       f.   Send faculty calendar meeting invitation.

       g.   Solicit faculty to chair panels, host poster sessions, and register participants.

       h.   Send personal invitations to the university president and provost.

       i.   Utilize social media.

8.   Pre-plan the conference.

       a.   Complete a walk-through of the conference space with the library director. Identify where panels and poster sessions will be held and during what timeframe. Decide where the registration table and refreshments will be placed.

       b.   Create and print signs.

       c.   Create and print directions for participants and volunteers.

9.   Facilitate the conference.

       a.   Place signage: registration banner, directions, posters, and panels.

       b.   Provide directions for time-keepers, registration table, and photographers.

      c.   Check on food order.

      d.   Check technology.

      e.   Prepare registration table: tablecloth, printed sign-in sheet (presenting/attending).

      f.   Utilize social media.

10. After the conference.

      a.   Send thank you notes to partners.

      b.   Debrief with students.

      c.   Debrief with URC committee.

Once specific tasks are identified, your dyad will create a project management plan in a Google Sheet and share it with the instructor. The project management plan will include the following categories.

- task
- deadline
- assigned dyad member
- progress notes
- complete/incomplete
- evaluation

The dyad team will decide on evaluative criteria for the tasks, which will be used for the instructor to grade.

Class time will be allocated for dyads to consult on their tasks, work on tasks, and provide progress reports to the class and the instructor.

Project Management Peer Performance Evaluation

Working successfully in a project management team requires you to excel along two primary dimensions: task (getting things done well) and people (communicating and building positive relationships). Striving to excel in both of these areas will benefit your personal development, relationship with your peer, and success in this class and beyond. Since we are unable to see ourselves from an outside perspective, receiving feedback (feed forward) from others is vital for self-awareness and development. The assignment challenges you to acknowledge the areas where your peer excels and where your peer could improve. The assignment also challenges you to welcome constructive feedback from others, reflect on the feedback, and make changes to your approach to tasks and people. You will receive evaluations in the workplace, so this assignment offers great practice. You will share your evaluation with your peer during one of our conference labs.

Please rate your peer on a 0-5 scale where 0 is never and 5 are always. After each rating, please provide reasons (with examples) for the rating you assigned.

1. My peer provides me with encouragement and is interested in my ideas for the project.
2. My peer is dedicated to accomplishing project tasks.
3. My peer is keenly aware of deadlines and completes tasks on time or early.
4. My peer holds me accountable for my project management responsibilities.
5. My peer enjoys tackling challenging tasks.
6. My peer encourages me to be creative.
7. My peer is very detail-oriented.
8. My peer is able to manage multiple tasks at the same time.
9. My peer strives to be a good leader and cares about leadership development.
10. My peer is comfortable confronting me to address issues.
11. My peer is self-motivated and displays energy and enthusiasm.
12. My peer enjoys sharing details of our tasks during reporting update meetings.
13. My peer is accomplished at breaking our project management area into tasks.
14. My peer makes a concerted effort to make our dyad a strong team.
15. My peer enjoys analyzing problems.
16. My peer does not micro-manage me and is nonjudgmental.
17. My peer communicates positively with classmates, community partners, and me.
18. My peer values this project for professional development and contribution to the campus community.

URC Cover Letter Assignment

Written communication skill is the primary capability employers and graduate programs seek. The Cover Letter Assignment provides you with an opportunity to practice your writing while reflecting on your experience with the URC.

You will write a cover letter to your professor detailing your involvement in the conference and reflecting on what you learned from it. Also, discuss the relationship with your dyad partner. Finally, reflect on how this experience will benefit your future career or application to graduate school. Conclude your letter by discussing your thoughts on doing a service-learning project and what advice you would offer to future students coordinating the URC. The cover letter should be one page in block format. It should not contain typos, grammar, spelling, or syntax errors.

URC Sample Conference Call

 *Undergraduate Research Conference 2017*

"Multiple Voices: Interdisciplinary Research to Overcome the Single Story"

Date: Monday, April 24, 2017 3-6 p.m.
Location: Reeves Learning Commons

Submission Details:
Deadline to submit: April 1, 2017 to
shu.submissions@gmail.com
We welcome scholarly submissions in the form of a 250-word
abstract (a brief summary) of your research project.
Please identify whether you would like to present on a panel or
poster session. If you would like to submit a panel of presentations,
please provide abstracts for each paper and the proposed title of your
panel session.

*Please provide name(s) of the author(s) of the project, email address(es), major, and year of
study. Also, if this project was developed in a particular course, please provide the name of
the course and the professor.

Conference Theme:
The conference showcases student projects from multiple
disciplines rooted in interpretive, quantitative, qualitative, and
practitioner research approaches. The conference theme calls
for an analysis of and exposure to a wide range of cultures,
areas of study, and backgrounds to foster a community of
celebrated diversity, radical empathy, and empowerment through
our shared human experiences. Projects engage critical,
creative, and ethical thinking, which contributes to students'
respective fields and inspires life-long dialogic learning.

Notes

1. See also, Cory L. Pedersen, Jocelyn Lymburner, Jordan I. Ali, and Patricia I. Coburn, "Organizing an Undergraduate Psychology Conference: The Successes and Challenges of Employing a Student-Led Approach," *Psychology Learning and Teaching* 12, no. 1 (2013): 83–91.

2. Seton Hill Catholic Identity, https://www.setonhill.edu/who-we-are/identity-traditions/.

3. Marcia Reynolds, *The Discomfort Zone: How Leaders Turn Difficult Conversations into Breakthroughs* (San Francisco: Berrett-Koehler Publishers, 2014).

4. Jon R. Hufford, "Librarians as Mentors in an Undergraduate Research Program," *Journal of Library Administration* 57, no. 7 (October 2017): 776–88; Anthony Stamatoplos, "The Role of Academic Libraries in Mentored Undergraduate Research: A Model of Engagement in the Academic Community," *College & Research Libraries* 70, no. 3 (2009): 235–49.
5. Robert Putnam, *Bowling Alone: The Collapse and Revival of American Community* (New York: Simon & Schuster, 2000).
6. Sharyn J. Potter, et al., "Intellectual Growth for Undergraduate Students: Evaluation Results from an Undergraduate Research Conference," *Journal of College Teaching & Learning* 7, no. 2 (February 1, 2010): 25–34.
7. Betsy Polk and Maggie Ellis Chotas, *The Power of Partnership: How Women Lead Better Together* (San Francisco: Berrett-Koehler Publishers, 2014).

CHAPTER SIXTEEN

Banned Books and Dangerous Fictions:
Co-Creating an Annual Banned Books Read Out

Tanya Heflin

Associate Professor of English
Indiana University of Pennsylvania
heflin@iup.edu

THE ACTIVITY

Description: For each of the past six years, students from the Department of English at Indiana University of Pennsylvania (IUP) have co-coordinated an annual Banned Books Read Out, a lively hour-long "slam"-style public reading of excerpts from books that have been banned or challenged in recent years. Coinciding with the American Library Association's Banned Books Week celebration that takes place during the last week in September each year, IUP's Banned Books Read Out event is sponsored by the Department of English in partnership with the IUP Libraries, the College of Humanities and Social Sciences, and the English Graduate Organization. Our Read Out event is the centerpiece of a full week of up to five events designed to foster the joy of reading and highlight the dangers of censorship. Each year, the week's slate of events varies based on student and faculty offerings but the constant every year is the Read Out, which will be the focus of the following piece.

Getting Started: Our first Banned Books Read Out developed organically as one of three service-learning options in my course for English majors, ENGL 340 The Novel. As a newly hired faculty member first entering the campus community, I was looking for ways to make my first semester's courses shine, so I had

301

themed my version of this standard course on the novel as "Banned Books and Dangerous Fictions," hoping that the slight edginess of the theme would pique student interest. I designed this upper division course for juniors and seniors with a focus on covering the history and genre of the novel by way of reading texts that had been viewed as banned, challenged, controversial, or otherwise "dangerous" in their time. As part of all my courses, I require a "scholar-in-society" component, typically worth 10 percent of the final grade. During class, we discuss the objective of this component as being to seek new ways for sharing the pleasures of studying literature in a college classroom with a larger community in some creative fashion.[1] That course's scholar-in-society project was titled "The Novel Communities Project," and it gave three offerings from which students could choose: (1) to organize a Banned Books Read Out in September/October;[2] (2) to participate in a NaNoWriMo novel-writing group throughout November;[3] or (3) to get involved in the departmental Book Club, which happened to be reading a challenged novel that semester. Of the twenty-four students in this course, six chose to organize a Banned Books Read Out, and the original plan that they devised during their month of collaboration formed the nucleus of what has become an ongoing annual event.

Motivations: My pedagogical motivation for assigning a scholar-in-society project for all my literature courses is centered in my commitments (1) to expanding literature far beyond the classroom walls and (2) to helping my students, most of whom will go on to teach at the primary, high school, or university levels, find innovative ways of sharing their joy of reading with their students. With that as a foundation, our shared motivations for the first event was very simply to share our love of great literature with a wider audience by designing an hour-long "happening" to take the form of a lively "poetry slam" that would get students and others across campus excited about reading.

The American Library Association has a thirty-five-year history of celebrating Banned Books Week, which was devised in 1982 with the purpose of responding "to a sudden surge in the number of challenges to books in schools, bookstores and libraries."[4] One aspect of its purpose is to bring awareness to the many challenges that are brought in communities across the US each year. According to Robert P. Doyle in *Banned Books: Defending Our Freedom to Read*, the annual challenges are immense: "In 2016, the American Library Association's Office for Intellectual Freedom recorded 323 reported challenges, which include not only challenges to materials like books and magazines, but also challenges involving issues such as Internet access, invited speakers, and social media posts. However, research shows that between 82 percent and 97 percent of all challenges are never reported—meaning that nearly 11,000 challenges and/or banning could be happening nationwide each year."[5]

As the event has developed at IUP over the years, it has grown from being a single class's optional assignment to being co-coordinated by undergraduate and graduate student service groups. Likewise, as it has grown each year, it has attracted additional institutional sponsors and new motivations have emerged: for the Department of English, the annual event has become a core part of our recruitment efforts; for the student service groups, involvement in the event serves as a public showcase for their creativity and engagement; and for IUP Libraries, the annual event draws people into the library and demonstrates our library's ongoing core value of freedom of access to information.

THE PEOPLE

Libraries: IUP Libraries is located in a beautiful building at the center of campus and serves a vibrant regional comprehensive university with holdings of 486,000 books, more than 250,000 electronic books, more than 350 full-text electronic databases, a coffeehouse, and ample study space for students and the local community. The IUP Libraries facility offers a windowed casual reading nook across from its coffee shop, and the library takes on the ordering and arrangement of the podium, microphone and speakers, extra seating, and all the physical needs for hosting the event. In addition, librarians coordinate closely with students to decorate a Banned Books Week display window each year for the week prior and Banned Books Week itself, and they pull a cart of frequently banned/challenged books to have available for checkout at the event.

Instructors: Dr. Tanya Heflin, associate professor of English and College of Humanities & Social Sciences dean's associate. My research and teaching have centered on women's and multiethnic literature of the US from 1848 to the present with a particular focus on recovering voices that have been underexplored or hidden from readers in various ways. Aligning myself with the American Library Association's well-established Banned Books celebration has provided a strategic venue for broadening my own commitment to expanding the reading of little-known writers by connecting with other avid readers on campus as we work together to reach a rather wide campus and the local community.

Courses: ENGL 340: The Novel. The first iteration of this event grew organically from a "scholar-in-society" project option for my class on the novel, which I had themed to focus on banned and challenged novels. Later iterations became service projects for English Department student groups, including the English Graduate Organization and Sigma Tau Delta.

Students: Many dozens of students have had the opportunity to get involved as coordinators, MCs, readers, and volunteers over the six years of the Read Outs. The originating group during the first year consisted of six highly motivated junior and senior English majors who selected the Read Out as their "scholar-in-society" project for the class. In later years, the coordinators were typically drawn from ranks of first- and second-year candidates in the Literature & Criticism doctoral program; MCs were drawn from past presidents of our student organizations or other senior doctoral candidates; and readers and other volunteers stepped up from across the department from the ranks of undergraduate students, graduate students, and faculty, as well as administration and members from across the campus community.

Community Partners: Because it originated as part of a course for English majors, IUP's Banned Books Read Out has been sponsored financially by the Department of English and has relied on the work product of undergraduate and graduate student service groups affiliated with the Department of English. IUP Libraries has served as host in a beautiful reading nook of the library and university officials from across campus have given ongoing support through their attendance and lively participation as readers.

The Department of English at IUP is a large and multifaceted department offering several tracks of undergraduate majors, as well as MA and PhD programs in literature/criticism and composition/TESOL. The multifaceted nature of the department fosters a need for numerous opportunities for students to get involved, so each year we have a between ten and twenty students who take part in everything from selecting and preparing reading passages to serving as co-coordinators and MCs for the event. In addition, the department contributes funds to purchase refreshments and giveaways (which we have come to call the "Banned Books swag") from the American Library Association, whose online store offers annual themed posters, buttons, field reports, bookmarks, gift bags, and other items. These visually eye-catching items are used to promote the event, given away to all attendees, and grouped into "Book-Lover Reading Kits" which are awarded to three lucky winners of a drawing held to close the Read Out.

One important factor in the success of the event has been the annual participation of high-level administrators, including the university president and provost, as well as the dean of the College of Humanities and Social Sciences and the dean of the libraries. Each of these administrators has shown high levels of enthusiasm for the project by gamely standing up to "read out" from their favorite books. For example, it has become an amusing tradition for the university president to read in a deadpan fashion from the frequently challenged *Captain Underpants* series, a spectacle enjoyed by students and faculty alike.

Finding and Working with Partners: The most important aspect of finding partners has been simply to communicate enthusiasm about the project and to emphasize its student-led nature. In truth, the Read Out is such a lively, fun event with obvious benefit to the community that finding partners has been quite easy at our institution. It is such a natural fit for both libraries and English departments that finding partners from both centers would be beneficial virtually anywhere. For libraries, the event is housed and promoted by the American Library Association and Banned Books Week Coalition, both of which offer numerous free resources to support the event. Partnerships with English departments are likewise a natural fit as they are the centers for literary study and frequently face pressure to build major and minor enrollments, which can be enhanced by the public exposure brought by this Read Out and other associated Banned Books Week events.

Benefits: Benefits of the project are shared between many stakeholders and have easily justified the time involved in preparing for the event.

Instructor Benefits: While the event began as a fairly simple "scholar-in-society" service-learning project for an undergraduate course on the novel, it has expanded both into faculty service work in advising student organizations and into a very well-received, graduate-level seminar. Titled ENGL 983: Hidden Voices: Suppressed, Contested, and Recovered Texts in American Literature, the fall seminar began with a four-week sequence that delved deeply into the history of bans and challenges in American literature, then expanded into a six-week sequence that focused on recovering suppressed or otherwise "hidden" archival texts in need of recovery scholarship. Ultimately, this graduate seminar resulted not only in several students' engagement in academic service for independently developed a well-attended panel discussion on graphic novels and pop culture but it has also resulted in external conference presentations and dissertation chapters for students who made this topic core to their scholarship.

Student Benefits: Students are involved in all aspects of the planning for the event—from the prosaic ordering of catering to the intellectually demanding culling of reading passages. Benefits include the surprisingly detailed work of finding brief, three-minute passages that will serve simultaneously to convey a text's essence while being interesting to audience members who have not read the full book. Further, students conduct research to find instances when each book has been banned or challenged, opening their eyes to ongoing issues of censorship attempts in US libraries, schools, and communities. Additional benefits include building collaborative teamwork skills, building writing and proofreading skills, building skills in event promotion via social media and news media, and building skills in overall event planning. I encourage the primary team leaders each year to include co-coordination of the event in the service area of their CVs.

Partner/Community Benefits: This is a brief, one-hour, "slam"-style, lively event. We publicize it heavily on campus, communicate with the event planners of the local community library, hold it in the lobby of the campus library (which has a central location on campus), offer refreshments, hold it during the lunch hour, and make available pre-selected three-minute passages for readers. All of these details make it very convenient for all members of the local and campus community to get involved, either as listeners or readers. While it started as a one-time class-based event, it has become an annual tradition because the community enjoys and benefits from the connections it fosters.

The Banned Books Read Out itself is an excellent event to draw people into the library, and the liveliness and fun of the "slam"-style event—while sometimes noisy and boisterous—shows the energy that a shared love of reading can bring.

Depending upon the institution, other benefits may include closer collaboration with academic departments, particularly English or associated humanities departments, and positive public exposure via student newspaper articles and social media items. (For example, our newspaper runs an annual story publicizing the event, including some years featuring opinion pieces about censorship, and our librarians and student groups have participated in extensive social media campaigns via Facebook and Twitter.)

Department/Institution Benefits: In addition to providing ample exposure for the Department of English and enhancing our recruitment efforts, the involvement in recent years of undergraduate and graduate student organizations has helped to define the scope and mission for those organizations as they function within the larger department. In addition, it has strengthened ties between the English Department and the library, and it has provided an annual forum for all members of the campus community—students, staff, faculty, and administration—to reiterate annually our commitments to both the joys of reading and to the foundational principles of academic freedom itself.

THE PROCESS
Expected Learning Outcomes

The course objectives for the original section of ENGL 340 were defined as follows:

By the end of our semester together, students will have developed the following crucial skills:

1. To understand aesthetic and imaginative facets of human experience by being able to
   o   discuss the purposes and functions of literature within society;
   o   recognize the power of finely controlled language beyond its informational dimension; and
   o   appreciate the ways in which one text can form the basis for multiple, sometimes competing interpretations.
2. To demonstrate critical and reflective thinking skills by being able to
   o   articulate and effectively communicate how a text has become meaningful;
   o   formulate questions appropriate to the understanding of literary texts;
   o   develop interpretations of literary texts that are grounded in careful reading strategies and in any of many literary or theoretical approaches; and
   o   understand literature as a reflection of or challenge to the culture and time in which it was produced.

The Banned Books Read Out, as one of three options for the Novel Communities Project, was evaluated based on their final presentation to the class and a reflective report about the project, which was worth 10 percent of their final grade. (See Appendix Materials.)

Curriculum and Event Material

Included in the appendices are the original assignment sheets for the classroom context, samples of our publicity materials, passages, context introductions, etc. Included in the resource bibliography are print and online resources that we use throughout the month to prepare students as they work toward developing their version of the event.

Steps Involved

While the first iteration of the IUP Banned Books Read Out was developed within the context of a course for English majors, in later years it has been developed as a stand-alone project for student service groups instead, and it has likewise undergone some streamlining for the planning stages. In this step-by-step outline, I will focus on the pre-event preparation as it has developed in recent years.

- First, identify the one or two students who wish to serve as primary student co-coordinators for the project. A fairly high number of small tasks are required, so identifying a student-level project manager to help the faculty member or librarian oversee the details is useful. (In the context of student service organizations, the person or people filling this role are encouraged to put this significant service on their CVs.) Working with the student co-coordinator(s), determine the roles of all students involved. For our institution, this is typically between ten to fifteen student volunteers.
- Preparatory duties include the following, which range from prosaic event planning to intense intellectual work:
    - o **Budget:** Secure the budget from partners. Budgeted items for our event include refreshments and themed banned books "swag" ordered from the American Library Association.
    - o **Venue:** Secure the location and coordinate with the library for work orders for a podium, AV equipment, chairs, etc.
    - o **Catering:** Decide upon refreshments and place the catering order with campus food service.
    - o **Theme:** Study the annual theme, which is announced by the American Library Association and the Banned Books Week Coalition over the summer. Sample themes include "Words Have Pow-

er" (2017) and "Stand Up for Your Right to Read" (2016). Some years focus on specializations within literature, such as Graphic Novels or Young Adult Fiction, and we typically incorporate these specializations into our selection of passages.

o **Banned Books "Swag":** Several weeks prior to the event, develop a wish list of banned books items to publicize and give away at the event. These include posters, bookmarks, buttons, field reports, and gift bag items. If possible, share these widely beforehand with faculty to give out in classes, with library patrons, and with audience members at the event itself. In addition, we have an annual "Book Lovers Reader Kit" prize drawing, where three lucky book lovers will win the drawing for the annual themed Banned Books book bag filled with several banned/challenged books, pens and notepads from the Department of English and College of Humanities and Social Science, and other items of interest to "Book Lovers." In order to ensure delivery, ordering this material should take place early in the planning process.

o **Author List:** Begin to determine which forty to fifty texts and authors to highlight for the Read Out. Students select these texts based on the annual theme with attention paid to favorite new texts they have encountered during their coursework during the year. In developing the author list, pay close attention to representing diverse perspectives, cultures, genders, sexuality, genre, and time period. (See Appendix Materials.)

o **Passages for Readers:** Student volunteers sign up to curate a set of forty to fifty passages from banned or challenged books, and these pre-curated passages will be on hand for readers to select on the day of the event itself. Passages should be short enough to be read aloud in three minutes, should somehow reflect the overall spirit of the book from which they are drawn, and should be accessible and pleasurable to novice audience members who may not have read the book themselves. Over the years, we have found these criteria to foster a successful Read Out event, yet it can be surprisingly challenging to find short passages that fit the bill. This aspect of the preparation requires more time than any other, so it should be started early. The time spent here is well-rewarded, however, in that it makes it very easy for undergraduates and non-majors to take part in the Read Out with great confidence. Readers are also encouraged to bring their own three-minute passages, but having well-selected passages on hand contributes immensely to our success in having a high degree of audience participation. Once students have submitted their passages, co-coordinators alphabetize and collate all passages into a single document, designed with Banned Books imagery and printed one per page to have on hand for selection at the Read Out selection table. (See Appendix Materials.)

o **Book Context Introductions:** Once the author list and passages are developed, students identify two or three specific instances in which the book has been banned or challenged. Resources for these challenges are collected by the Banned Books Week Coalition[6] and are available online or in the ALA's resource guide *Banned Books: Defending Our Freedom to Read.*[7] Once compiled, print these context introductions as one per page for easy re-ordering as speakers are assigned their reading number the Read Out. (See Appendix Materials.)

o **Event MCs:** Identify two to four students to serve as MCs for the event. These students will be responsible for introducing each reader and passage and for providing the context of the book's banning as part of the reader introduction. Our method for selecting MCs has been to honor the past presidents of the student service organizations, taking care to represent gender equity in our invitations each year. This role is the most public face of the student involvement, and every year feedback comes back as to how much audience members have especially enjoyed and been impressed by the enthusiasm of our MCs.

o **Publicity:** Create fliers, images for campus display screens, and press releases to publicize the Read Out throughout the campus and larger community. (See Appendix Materials.) On our campus, the student newspaper typically runs a story and IUP librarians or student groups frequently run social media campaigns. The Banned Books Week Coalition maintains a list of Banned Books events by state, so the people assigned publicity may wish to have your event listed there.

o **Decoration:** In the two or three weeks prior to the event, students decorate departmental and building bulletin boards with fliers, images of banned books, and generous amounts of yellow caution tape as a method of building interest for the event. One very special annual feature at IUP Libraries has been having librarians and students working together to create a beautiful Banned Books display in the prominent glass case at the entrance of the library.

o **Community VIPs:** Identify a few "VIPs" in the community whose support would help to publicize and elevate the event. Campuses and communities may vary in the support offered by campus officials. If you are fortunate, as we are, to have the strong support of our upper administration, invite them to Read Out at your event. Because time is limited and because we emphasize that this event is designed for student involvement, we keep our VIPs to the same three-minute limit as all our readers, and the response from those who participate has been consistently positive.

o **Associated Banned Books Week Events:** On our campus, student and faculty groups frequently organize up to five events that take place across the week, which co-coordinators help to publicize. Recent associated events have included, for example, a campus-wide panel series on "The First Amendment in the Digital Age," developed by faculty members; a Banned Books themed colloquium presentation on "Popular Culture and the Power of Words," developed by a graduate student group; and a very lively debate over a faculty request to remove plagiarized books from the library, developed by librarians in partnership with the requesting faculty member. These events may require advisement but primary planning for them should remain with the student or faculty group proposing them.

o **Table Coordination:** When the day of the Read Out arrives, we anticipate a scramble at the sign-up table in the thirty minutes before the event and during the event itself. Designate one or two well-organized students (including the student co-coordinator who has overseen the passage collection and is therefore most familiar with the author list) to oversee the sign-up of readers on a first-come, first-served basis. The sign-up table is a busy place as readers look through passages, make their selections, and sign up, and we place our sign-up table adjacent to the refreshments table at the entrance of the library's reading nook, which is the farthest point from the podium. At our events, all readers receive a small thank-you gift made up of a special themed button attached to a Banned Book bookmark or the like.

o **Location Set-up:** On the morning of the event, students gather to finalize the library space for the event. The podium, AV, and chairs need to be checked and repositioned. Students enjoy decorating this space liberally with posters, fliers, and yellow caution tape. They distribute bookmarks, field guides, READ pens, and the like throughout the chairs and side tables in the reading area. Our librarians will have pulled a cart of frequently banned/challenged books from ALA's annual list, and students distribute these books decoratively around the space to encourage patrons to check them out at the close of the event.

Finally, on the day of the event itself, our program follows a fairly tight format each year:

12:00	Brief introductory remarks relating the history of the Banned Books Week, encouraging readers to sign up, introducing the student co-coordinators and MCs, encouraging audience members to fill out drawing slips, and introducing the first reader, who is usually the university president or other campus official.
12:05	Readers "read out" their three-minute passages with gusto. In the background, the table organizer and MCs are ordering the passages and work together to introduce each reader, selection, and context for banning, after which the reader gets up to "read out." Expect this time to be lively, funny, and chaotic. For our events, we typically can host approximately fifteen readers during this forty-minute timeframe.
12:45	Remind people to fill out a slip for their drawing and introduce our final reader. In our case, this position has historically been occupied by the chair of the English Department, who typically reads entertainingly from a graphic novel and makes a gentle pitch to students to consider becoming an English major or minor.
12:50	The student co-coordinator(s) and MCs conduct the much-anticipated drawing for the "Book-Lovers Reading Kit" by selecting three slips at random out of the hat and reading the winners' names and favorite books. (See Appendix Materials.)
12:57	We wrap up the event by thanking our readers and partners and encouraging attendance at our associated events. Depending upon the time available, I typically like to end with a word about the importance of protecting our libraries and books—and an exhortation to seek out and enjoy books from diverse authors and to join us again to "read out" next year.

POST PROJECT FEEDBACK
Methods of Reflection

For the initial classroom-based iteration of this event, significant reflection was built into the project in that students completed the assignment by preparing a reflective presentation to be delivered to the class, as well as a reflective writing assignment that asked students to outline their work and reflect upon their experience in some detail. (See Appendix Materials.)

Post-Project Feedback

Feedback for the event has remained strongly positive and has been gathered both formally through feedback slips collected immediately after the event and informally through email and other feedback from readers and audience members commenting on their experience. Other informal indications of positive feedback include offers by our sponsors to expand the budget each year, requests from students and faculty to host an associated Banned Books Week event, and our observations that the popularity of the event has grown each year. Because it has had the effect of bringing the community together for an hour each fall during which we simply enjoy the pleasures of "reading out" from wonderfully diverse books that celebrate the fullest range of human experience, the IUP Banned Books Read Out has become a valued annual tradition and, we hope, it has served increased the number of "book lovers" in our community.

Difficulties Encountered

With strong support and engaged partners in place, I feel fortunate to report that our difficulties have been minimal. Our primary difficulty has been simply a race against time. Because the national Banned Books Week events occur during the last week of September and our fall semester classes begin in late August, the time available to prepare is short. While the event itself is a "happening" of only one hour, it requires significant work on the part of the co-coordinators as they study, write, edit, publicize, place orders, and handle all the preparation in a three- to four-week window. That said, given some organization, the clear time constraints make it possible for coordinators to launch a major, visible, campus-wide event within a bounded timeframe, an investment of energy that has proved itself to be well worth the resources engaged.

APPENDIX MATERIALS

- Assignment Sheet for "Novel Communities Project" (2012)
- Sample Publicity Fliers for 2017 Banned Books Read Out and Associated Events
- Sample Event Materials from 2017 Banned Books Read Out
- Demonstrated Outcomes: Images from the 2015 Banned Books Read Out

Assignment Sheet for "Novel Communities Project" (2012)

ENGL 340: The Novel
Novel Communities Project @ Final Exam Session

Due: At exam session: Wednesday, December 12, 8-10am in LEO 118.

As part of your semester engagement with the novel, you have taken part in your choice of "Novel Communities" project in order to connect with a larger community of novel-readers and novel-writers beyond our classroom. At the beginning of the semester, three primary options were suggested:

     a. Banned Books Week "Read-Out" and other local and online events
     b. NaNoWriMo, or National Novel Writing Month
     c. IUP English Department Book Club, discussing *Ender's Game*

In addition, some of you had in mind alternate activities (e.g., additional book clubs, etc.) to compete this portion of the course.

For your final terminating activity for the semester, you will reflect on your participation in this activity, and you will articulate your experience in two parts:

Part A: Develop a brief oral and/or multimedia presentation relating your experience for the class. With an eye to engaging us viewers, give us a sense of your engagement with a larger community and what it taught you about the ways people consume and produce novels. Creative possibilities for this portion include readings of produced writings, multimedia images of public events, etc.

For Part A, you're encouraged to work with other students with whom you participated in this project to develop a presentation. Due to time constraints, your presentation should last no more than 3-5 minutes per student. (That is, more time total is available if you combine your overall presentation with one or more students.)

Part B: Detail your participation in this project in a brief narrative of two engaging pages. Discuss the factual details of what it was that you did, as well as the impressions you developed of the ways that the larger community approaches novel-reading and/or novel-writing.

This reflection on your engagement in the project should be fun to put together—enjoy!

Sample Publicity Flyers for 2017 Banned Books Read Out and Associated Events

Sample Event Materials from 2017 Banned Books Read Out

Sample Passage to be Selected by Readers

Toni Morrison: Nobel Prize Winner; American novelist whose books are subject to frequent bans and challenges

Excerpt from "Peril": the introduction to her edited collection called *Burn This Book: Notes on Literature and Engagement*

I have been told that there are two human responses to the perception of chaos: naming and violence. When the chaos is simply the unknown, the naming can be accomplished effortlessly—a new species, star, formula, equation, prognosis. There is also mapping, charting, or devising proper nouns for unnamed or stripped-of-names geography, landscape, or population. When chaos resists, either by reforming itself or by rebelling against imposed order, violence is understood to be the most frequent response and the most rational when confronting the unknown, the catastrophic, the wild, wanton, or incorrigible. Rational responses may be censure, incarceration in holding camps, prisons, or death, singly or in war. There is however a third response to chaos, which I have not heard about, which is stillness. Stillness can be passivity and dumbfoundedness; it can be paralytic fear. But it can also be art. Those writers plying their craft near to or far from the throne of raw power, of military power, of empire building and countinghouses, writers who construct meaning in the face of chaos must be nurtured, protected. And it is right that such protection be initiated by other writers. And it is imperative not only to save the besieged writers but to save ourselves. The thought that leads me to contemplate with dread the erasure of other voices, of unwritten novels, poems whispered or swallowed for fear of being overheard by the wrong people, outlawed languages flourishing underground, essayists' questions challenging authority never being posed, unstaged plays, canceled films—that thought is a nightmare. As though a whole universe is being described in invisible ink.

Certain kinds of trauma visited on people are so deep, so cruel, that unlike money, unlike vengeance, even unlike justice, or rights, or the goodwill of others, only writers can translate such trauma and turn sorrow into meaning, sharpening the moral imagination.

A writer's life and work are not a gift to mankind; they are its necessity.

Sample Context for Introductions

Toni Morrison: excerpt from "Peril" the introduction to her edited collection called *Burn This Book: Notes on Literature and Engagement*

Morrison's books are subject to frequent bans and challenges

Example:
2013: Morrison's *The Bluest Eye* was challenged on a suggested reading list for Columbus high school students (2013)
  - One of many challenges that year
  - Complaints: inappropriate and book has "underlying socialist-communist agenda"

Book-Lover Drawing Entry form

**Enter to win a
Book-Lovers gift pack!**

FOSTER EMPATHY ENGAGE READERS HEAL
CHALLENGE BUILD COMMUNITIES
CENSORSHIP OPEN DOORS TO
UNITE EDUCATE LITERARY
WORLD
WORDS HAVE POWER READ A BANNED BOOK
ENCOURAGE ADVOCATE
CONVERSATION INFORM
CHANGE LIVES EMPOWER
INSPIRE CREATIVITY ENLIGHTEN MINDS

Banned Books Read-Out

Name: _____

Department: _____

Favorite Book: _____

I read some banned books!

Demonstrated Outcomes: Images from the 2015 Banned Books Read Out

Event images (photo credit: Kyle Richter)

Notes

1. Bruce Robbins, "Epilogue: The Scholar in Society," in *Introduction to Scholarship in Modern Language and Literatures,* 3rd Edition, edited by David G. Nicholls (New York: Modern Language Association, 2015), 312–30.
2. Banned Books Week Coalition, "Updates," accessed February 7, 2018, www.banned-booksweek.org.

3. "National Novel Writing Month," National Novel Writing Month, "Ready to Write a Novel?," accessed February 7, 2018, https://nanowrimo.org.
4. Banned Books Week Coalition, "About," accessed February 7, 2018, http://www.bannedbooksweek.org/about.
5. Robert P. Doyle, Robert P. *Banned Books: Defending Our Freedom to Read* (Chicago: American Library Association, 2017), 14.
6. Banned Books Week Coalition, "About."
7. Doyle, *Banned Books*.

CHAPTER SEVENTEEN

Facets of Fashion:
Utilizing Library Display Windows to Apply Visual Merchandising Techniques

Janet A. Blood, PhD

Associate Professor
Indiana University of Pennsylvania
janet.blood@iup.edu

THE ACTIVITY

Description: Visual merchandising is a creative form of communication. Merchants use visual merchandising techniques to promote products to sell, to call attention to specific promotional events, to decorate and arrange interior selling spaces, to direct consumers, and to provide atmospherics, or sensory experiences, for their customers. Display windows, in particular, draw in potential customers to a retail space from the street or mall with the latest styles and colors or an elaborate visual scene that shows the store's brand image and appeals to one's aesthetics.[1]

One type, called an *institutional* window, goes beyond a decorative composition of display elements. According to Diamond and Diamond, "A store may develop display themes based on the organization's interests, activities, and image rather than built around certain merchandise."[2] Institutional windows take on the task of educating the public about local government activities, community involvement opportunities, news events, humanitarian concerns, or other topics of interest. Therefore "institutional windows are devoted to intangible ideas and causes and promote an image for the store as an institution rather than featuring merchandise."[3]

Local community- and university-sponsored libraries have been historically architected with display windows integrated throughout. Filled with artifacts from special collections, newly released books, or the handiwork of a local community member, these institutional displays, although not connected with a for-profit merchandiser, communicate visually what is new, interesting, or significant to the library community at large. As such, they offer a unique opportunity for students studying visual merchandising to actively apply concepts and skills learned in the classroom when access to display windows are limited in academic buildings.

Such a situation is what prompted looking elsewhere on campus for display window opportunities for a Visual Merchandising course at Indiana University of Pennsylvania (IUP). As only one display window was available in the academic building where the course was housed, the instructor took advantage of the available resources at the university library, namely a medium-sized display window, to showcase course projects focused on the various aspects of the field of fashion. The goal of the Facets of Fashion project was for students to apply learned visual merchandising techniques while working together in small groups in order to design and install an attractive institutional display that would educate the university public on an aspect of fashion (either a career or another fashion-related topic). In addition, the students were required to integrate library resources within their display related to their chosen fashion theme in order to recognize library as host.

Getting Started

Motivations: The course, offered by the Fashion Merchandising program IUP, is popular with students because of its creative, hands-on nature. A challenge, however, is the lack of viable display spaces within the academic building in which the Fashion Merchandising program is housed. A happenstance meeting, however, held within IUP's Stapleton Library complex, revealed that our campus library was rich with an array of display windows. Through contact with our department's librarian, a mid-size display window on the ground floor of the library in a high-traffic area close to the main stairwell was secured for use during the spring 2015 and spring 2016 semesters. This opportunity allowed students to broaden their experiences in visual merchandising, which is so valuable for a future apparel industry professional. Not only were they able to work with a large, room-sized window and a table-top display housed within the Fashion Merchandising program, but they now had the additional opportunity of working in an unfamiliar space that held special challenges, thus refining their professional skills further.

The development of the Facets of Fashion theme of the library window was directed by many factors. First, the specifications of two group display projects for the course had already been established: for the large, room-sized window, students chose from a list of themes and were to creatively compose a vignette that would attract potential consumers and make them stop and look; the table top display, including signage, was to showcase a category of products for sale. Second, the size of the library display window, lighting, and shelving options were a large influence on the overall theme. The elevated, front-opening glass window (13.5" deep, 45" high, and 68" wide) was only equipped with overhead fluorescent lighting and adjustable plate glass shelves. These limitations would prevent students from putting large objects into the display, such as mannequins or other full-sized objects unless they were miniaturized or shallow. Third, as the library was generously allowing the use of their display case, promotion of library resources was deemed appropriate as part of the window content. Finally, this was an obvious opportunity to inform the university community and beyond about the fashion industry, careers, and the Fashion Merchandising program at IUP, lending further to the overall institutional display window genre. Given these considerations, the Facets of Fashion theme emerged as a viable focus for the display in which the students' goal would be to educate and promote a career or aspect of the fashion industry to help the public understand more fully its multi-dimensional nature by using props, signage, and related elements available at the library.

THE PEOPLE

Libraries: IUP Libraries offers resources, spaces, and services specifically designed to support the informational needs of members of the IUP community. A popular gathering place for students, faculty, and community members, it encourages the use of its spaces for educational programing, particularly for course-related activities. Large display windows on all of its four floors are attractive and well-placed to offer high visibility for educational displays. They are frequently used to highlight valuable library collections but are also open for use of student, faculty, and community groups interested in increasing awareness of educational, cultural, intellectual, or charitable activities.

Each discipline has a subject librarian who works closely with faculty to choose subject-related information resources to support research and study in that discipline and to design instructional activities to support the development of students' information literacy skills. The department in which the Fashion Merchandising program is housed is comprised of four majors, including Child and Family Studies, Family and Consumer Science Education, and Interior Design. The departmental library liaison works closely with the subject bibliographer librarian in procuring new books, videos, and other resources as needed by each of the four unique content areas within the department.

Instructor: Janet A. Blood, PhD has worked at Indiana University of Pennsylvania since 2004 in the Fashion Merchandising program and is an associate professor. With a background in apparel design and education, Dr. Blood strives to bring out the creative side of her merchandising students with active learning activities and projects. She has won multiple education and design awards and seeks to be a lifelong learner through her own experimentation of new technologies and techniques that can be integrated into the classroom curriculum.

Course: This activity was integrated into FSMR 303: Visual Merchandising. This course tends to be a very popular class; when offered, it tends to fill fast. The goal of this class is to introduce students to the multiple dimensions of the visual merchandising career within the fashion industry. This includes designing and installing store displays, including mannequin, table-top, and window displays as well as exploring store layout, signage, and lighting techniques and strategies. Common themes woven throughout the course are recognizing the wants and needs of consumers and the use of the elements and principles of design in the planning, installing, and evaluation of visual displays. Visual Merchandiser is generally an entry-level position in which energetic, creative individuals can work to advance within a company, making it a viable career path for new fashion graduates.

Students: The Fashion Merchandising students who enrolled in FSMR 303: Visual Merchandising at Indiana University of Pennsylvania during the spring semesters of 2015 and 2016 were the primary individuals involved. Most were either freshmen or seniors, and because there was no prerequisite for the course, freshmen who registered first were able to get first pick of the course followed by the seniors. Students who enroll generally enjoy hands-on learning and being creative. They also see visual merchandising as an attractive career path in the fashion industry after graduation.

Community Partners: IUP Libraries is the partner served by this activity. Other parties involved include those who are consumers of the library, including current IUP students and members of the surrounding community who utilize the library.

Finding and Working with Partners: As stated earlier, contact was made between the librarian who oversees the content area related to fashion and the instructor as part of their discipline-related materials discussions. This librarian just happened to have management of the display windows in the library as one of her job responsibilities. Librarians frequently interact with instructors in collection development and instructional design matters. These occasions are excellent opportunities to suggest the use of library display or community spaces for class-related assignments and activities.

Benefits

Instructor Benefits: The main benefit for the instructor was to have an additional opportunity for the students to apply what they were learning in the classroom in a real-world setting. Another benefit was that the library staff managed access to the window, and this partnership carried over to the following spring semester so the project could be repeated.

Student Benefits: Student benefits were many. Having an additional display window allowed them to further develop their skills in a real-world setting in close proximity to the academic building in which their course was housed. Without this project site, students would lose an opportunity to actively apply learned knowledge in a group setting while working with enthusiastic library staff eager to help. By working off-site in another academic building, students also had to manage their time and work with different stakeholders who were expecting quality work worthy of showing to the public. Furthermore, the project pictures and final *planogram* of the display added to their professional portfolio and could be used later in seeking employment in the fashion industry.

Community Partner Benefits: The educational and aesthetically pleasing exhibits offer the libraries high-quality, passive programs to educate their visitors at no cost to them. The inclusion of library materials increases awareness of library resources, and the assignment that familiarizes visual merchandising students with the building and brings students in close contact with the subject librarian makes it more likely that the same students will use the library in the future and consult the librarian at their point-of-need in future research projects. Finally, contributing to the installation of the institutional library windows provided further, unexpected educational benefits to library patrons that hopefully caused them to stop, look, and enjoy.

Institutional Benefits: The benefits of this connection with the library and the surrounding community was multifold. First, having access to a display window expanded the students' opportunities to actively apply the concepts and skills they were learning in the classroom to a real-world assignment, improving student learning outcomes and enhancing their career potential—points specifically mentioned in the university's strategic plan. Also, since the display window was located in a high-traffic area of the library, promotion of the Fashion Merchandising program was easy in order to attract students looking to change their major or those who have ulterior interests in fashion.

THE PROCESS
Expected Learning Outcomes

The course description and learning objectives for FSMR 303: Visual Merchandising as per the course syllabus are as follows:

> Design and arrange display and selling areas in relationship to merchandising trends and consumer demands. Emphasis on promotion techniques and merchandise sales through effective use of space, design, and color.

At the end of this course, the student will be able to
1. define and utilize visual merchandising vocabulary;
2. identify different visual merchandising trade organizations and publications;

3. identify the different types of visual merchandising organizations/departments;
4. identify basic elements and principles of design as they relate to visual merchandising;
5. execute displays using the appropriate elements and principles of design;
6. evaluate merchandising selling area layouts;
7. develop and analyze promotional plans, including theme, visual displays, signage, advertisements, mailings, and special events;
8. evaluate visual work using the critique process; and
9. analyze visual merchandising projects in relation to store image and store philosophy.

Specifically, Course Objectives 4, 5, 7, and 8 relate to the Facets of Fashion display project. In other words, the desired learning outcomes were that the students create an attractive display window utilizing the elements and principles of design to promote a career or aspect of fashion that will also educate the public and highlight the library's holdings of related materials. Once the display was completed, the work was presented by the student group and critiqued and evaluated by their fellow students and the instructor.

Curriculum Materials

Silent Selling: Best Practices and Effective Strategies in Visual Merchandising (Fourth Edition) by Judy Bell and Kate Ternus was the assigned textbook for the course; students were assigned readings and quizzes from this text. Other curriculum materials for the course were also provided to the students as needed via an online learning management system. The appendices contain not only a copy of the project specifications but also the grading rubric used to evaluate each group's performance on this project; this was provided to the students before the first round of displays were due so they could use the rubric as a guide throughout the process.

Steps Involved

The project was introduced on the first day of the course as part of reviewing the syllabus information. This was to immediately initiate the creative process in relation to the overall course objectives. The project description the students were presented within the 2015 course syllabus was as follows:

> Each group will have access to the medium-sized window located in the basement of Stapleton Library at the base of the main stairwell to create an institutional display focusing on one facet of the field of fashion. Emphasis should be placed on using

the window as a PROMOTIONAL tool for exciting the viewer about a potential fashion career and should include appropriate promotional signage. Furthermore, as part of the display, students should incorporate elements such as books, magazines, and journals found in the library that support the facet they are focusing their window on. Each group will present their display to the class for critique and final evaluation. A detailed computer-generated planogram of the display will then be created by the group and turned in for evaluation no later than one week after presentation.

In spring 2016, the assignment was expanded in order to not duplicate the concepts of the previous year as well as to educate the community audience further. Therefore, the second sentence of the project description was modified as follows:

Emphasis should be placed on using the window as a PROMO-TIONAL/EDUCATIONAL tool for exciting the viewer about an aspect of fashion that he/she may not be aware. (For example, groups may choose to highlight the life/career of a key figure in fashion or educate on how to tie a scarf or necktie.)

Student groups of three students were formed early on in the semester; the class enrollment was capped at twenty-seven students in order to have nine student groups total. This allowed for a regular rotation among the three display projects throughout the semester, but the finished displays could only be left in place for a few days before the next group needed to use the display space. Groups were formed by the instructor in order to mix upper and underclassmen; this was done for the upperclassmen to serve as mentors as well as to assist in any transportation or resource needs the group may have that the underclassmen may be unaware or have access. The older students also had additional fashion knowledge gleaned from other courses they took as part of the Fashion Merchandising curriculum, which they could use to more effectively guide the younger students in the conceptualization and execution of the display projects.

Students were provided a copy of the *Display Specifications* handout which was also posted to the course online learning management system (see the Appendix Materials for a copy). This document spanned the requirements and expectations for all three group display projects, referring students back to the information contained in their course syllabus for each thematic focus. It should be noted that as a class, these specifications were gone over in detail, expectations clarified, and questions answered. Also, students were informed that if they felt that any group member was not doing their fair share of the work that they should notify the instructor immediately in order to remedy the situation. As a further incentive, 25 points for the course would be determined from an average score awarded by their group members in regard to their participation and contribution to the overall success of the projects.

Soon after, one class period was devoted to visiting the location of the Facets of Fashion window in the library and meeting with our library representative in this regard. Students were encouraged to take pictures and dimensions of the window for future planning purposes. Our library representative discussed all essential information in regard to when students could work on the window, who to locate within the library to obtain the window key, and where to obtain other props or fixtures that the library had for them to use. A particular point of note was the handling of the plate glass shelving if the students wished to use them; being that they were several decades old and becoming brittle, student safety was a concern.

Discussion of the elements and principles of design in relation to getting consumer attention was a primary focus and was introduced early on in the course. Beyond the traditional art elements and principles of design, visual merchandisers also use surprise, lighting, motion, and other sensory experiences such as music and scent to draw in consumers. The concept of the *focal point* was also stressed in which the eye needs a place to initially focus then later rest after being led throughout a visual display (Diamond & Diamond, 2011).[4] After this introduction, students were exposed to images of professional displays utilizing the various elements and principles for illustration and inspiration. The hope was to motivate students to think about their group display projects in a practical yet creative manner in that using the elements and principles of design in a simplistic way can make a greater statement than an elaborate display that contains too much "stuff."

The critique process was introduced next and included showing pictures of prior student displays. The students then were instructed to analyze each for use of the elements and principles of design besides having them identify what they felt was successful and unsuccessful about each and why. From this discussion, suggestions and solutions were brainstormed on how the display could have been made more effective and why. It was the goal of the instructor to get the students to think about *why* they liked or didn't like an aspect of the display. In this way, they would become more reflective throughout the planning and execution of their own display projects, and when their own displays were critiqued in the same manner, they would be more prepared for such discussions.

The instructor encouraged the exploration of a variety of ideas before settling on a final theme or approach by sketching their ideas. It was also important that students thought logically about what resources were available to them in terms of display fixtures, time, manpower, and budget considerations. Students were expected to use the elements and principles of design as well as a focal point in their final composition, and the instructor provided input as needed in this regard.

Student preparation and display installation happened outside of class time. Efficient groups would prepare as much as they could prior to gaining access to the actual window. In this way, they could quickly install their display soon after the previous group had vacated the space, leaving extra time to fuss with the final positioning of objects or polishing the overall look. The students were encouraged to take multiple pictures of their display for portfolio purposes as well as to use as a reference when creating their final computer-generated display planogram—essentially a map of the final display showing all components and including special directions. These are extensively used in the retail industry to easily set up the same visual display in other locales. According to Bell & Ternus (2012), "...well-drawn or photographed planograms guide merchandisers to present fashion uniformly.... A good corporate planogram can be an efficient long-distance teaching tool as well."[5] (A step-by-step outline of the Facets of Fashion project can be found in the Appendix Materials).

POST-PROJECT FEEDBACK
Methods of Reflection

Full class periods were scheduled for display presentations and critiques throughout the semester. On these days, the instructor took pictures of the finished student displays, including the Facets of Fashion window at the library prior to the start of class; the pictures were then projected in the classroom throughout the group presentation and critique process. For the other two display projects housed within the Fashion Merchandising program, students were instructed to observe the displays in person as would a consumer.

Prior to each group presenting, idea sketches were submitted to the instructor as part of the evaluation process (see Appendix Materials). They each then took turns presenting the information in regard to their creative process as specified in Step 9 of the Student Display Project Specifications (see Appendix Materials). This included such information as their display concept, including what facet of fashion they focused on, challenges and how they sought to overcome them, perceived successes, and the like. After the presentation, the remaining class members (considered to be the *consumers*), were given an opportunity to ask the group questions about the display, including where they obtained certain props or how they created a particular effect.

Group members at this point were given the opportunity to stay in the classroom during the critique process or leave. If they chose to stay, the group members were instructed to remain quiet unless questioned as the rest of the class gave their impressions of and suggestions for the display. If the group members chose to leave, they were instructed to stay close to the classroom so they could be easily summoned back when needed. Also, if the group chose to leave, a student was appointed within the class to take detailed notes of the critique discussion that were given to the group as part of the project feedback.

The critique process for the displays proceeded as stated earlier when students were exposed to prior students' display projects. It should be noted that it was stressed to the students that "ugly" or "stupid" were not appropriate adjectives to use, the critique process was a typical aspect of a fashion professional's world, and they were professionals in training and expected to act as such.

The students were then given an initial opportunity to share their initial impressions of the display. If few students shared, the instructor used probing questions such as, "What did they find successful about the display?" and "How did the group use the elements and principles of design to achieve this?" If students stated that they "liked" the display without context, the instructor probed further with "what and why" questions to pinpoint the success being observed. The same process was used to initiate conversation in regard to what could be changed or improved upon always with consideration of budget and space limitations. Again, the elements and principles of design were used as guides in this discussion as well.

The critique continued until all students were given the opportunity to share their thoughts and suggestions. Before moving on to the next group presentation, the students then were asked to participate in the "consumer critique" portion of the assessment rubric (see Appendix Materials). In this way, students were given another opportunity to share their impressions of the group's display success, given the parameters of the project specifications. Through a show of hands, students rated the group on such items as drawing and keeping their attention, appearance, professionalism of signage, incorporating appropriate elements in the display, and the like; the instructor, of course, had the final say on items that divided class opinion. For both the verbal critique process and consumer critique rating, it was obvious that the students were actively reflecting upon what the group's intentions were with the display while taking in consideration the obvious limitations posed to the group before making honest and insightful comments and suggestions. In fact, the students' maturity seemed to grow throughout the semester as more displays were presented and critiques ensued. Although a little scary at first, students realized that after the first round of display critiques, they were able to learn and improve upon their display skills from the constructive feedback gleaned from their peers and instructor.

Project Feedback

A recent open-ended question survey sent to remaining students who were enrolled in FSMR 303: Visual Merchandising during the semesters the Facets of Fashion display project was introduced and implemented revealed an overall positive experience. Students found the library staff to be friendly and helpful and indicated that the library community benefitted from having a different type of window available for the public to view—one that educated about the diversity of the fashion field and informed others what their major was all about. They especially enjoyed having the opportunity to be creative, apply the visual composition techniques they were learning in class, and showing their originality to the university at large. In all, they found this project to be also beneficial to their future career as an apparel industry professional in that they gained more experience working in groups, despite challenges that honed their patience, time management, and teamwork skills. This project also made them mindful of the quality of the project as more than just their classmates and their instructor would be viewing the finished display even if it was for a short amount of time.

Project Assessment and Reporting

From all indications, this project went very well despite some limitations and difficulties reported below. Given the opportunity to teach Visual Merchandising in the future, this project will again be integrated into the course if agreed upon by the library.

Difficulties Encountered

Student Issues: Reported difficulties included those that were logistical as well as those related to creative differences. Some found finding the person with the key to the window a challenge as well as coordinating fellow student schedules' for display work. The window itself being smaller led to the challenge of finding smaller-scale objects to include. The window had a split open front with two glass panels; this caused a central visual barrier that had to be worked around as part of the final composition. In addition to handling the plate glass shelving, the shelving brackets at the back of the display case posed another challenge as to how to disguise them. In terms of creative differences, students acknowledged that their fellow group members sometimes had conflicting visions on how the overall display should look. They also noted the difficulty of having to make decisions as a group in regard to who was going to obtain what components as well as how items were going to be arranged in the final composition. The instructor was heartened to learn of such collaborative challenges as this learning opportunity is what they will be experiencing once they obtain an industry position. Therefore, experiencing the difficulties and working to resolve them in an academic setting will better prepare them as future professionals.

Instructor Issues: Another difficulty encountered was the fact that the window was located off-site from the academic building in which the Fashion Merchandising program is housed. Therefore, on the days the students would present their window, the instructor took digital pictures of the Facets of Fashion library display immediately before the beginning of the class as there was no in-class time for all to walk as a group and critique the window on site. The overhead lighting in front of the case also proved challenging in obtaining suitable pictures to show causing reflections, so many were taken to have a variety to choose from.

Community Partner Issues: While the library was delighted to have the student displays in the library, the same logistical problems that frustrated students were problematic for library staff. The next time the activity is used in a class, the librarian will work with the instructor to develop a means of communicating directly with the students to ease everyone's frustrations.

Conclusion

In all, this project enhanced the course. It gave students another opportunity to apply what they were learning in class in a real-world institutional display setting. It posed challenges to the students that allowed them to use their problem-solving skills as well as hone their abilities to work with one another on a creative endeavor. It also benefitted the library community at large with something new and interesting to view while promoting the expansive field of fashion. If given the opportunity, this project will be integrated into future offerings of this course when taught by this instructor and possibly expanded to include additional library windows, if available, of differing sizes. Without a doubt, this project was a positive experience that should be explored at other institutions, especially those that offer subject matter related to fashion, art, or visual communication.

APPENDIX MATERIALS

- FSMR 303: Visual Merchandising Student Display Project Specifications
- Facets of Fashion Display Project Grading Rubric

FSMR 303: Visual Merchandising Student Display Project Specifications

***Use the information provided to you in your course syllabus in conjunction with the following to plan your student display projects.

For all display projects:

1. As a group, pick a theme (window), aspect of fashion (library window), or product (table-top).
2. Brainstorm ideas using the following as guides:
    o   available materials
    o   available display fixtures
    o   time to complete display
    o   type of store the display would appear
    o   your theme, facet of fashion, or product

o   amount of manpower

o   the elements and principles of design

3. *Everybody* should sketch their ideas!
4. Try to get agreement on one strong idea. Don't decide on a final plan yet.
5. Make lists of things to do, stuff to get.
6. Gather materials, play with possibilities.
7. Decide on the final display idea.
8. For the table-top display, do a few trial runs if time allows.
9. On the display due date, each group will present their displays by

   o   discussing the display concept;

   o   indicating what type of store the display might appear for the theme window and table-top display or why they chose a particular aspect of fashion to focus on;

   o   discussing challenges that needed to be overcome;

   o   indicating the solutions used to overcome those challenges;

   o   discussing the perceived successes of the display;

   o   discussing the areas they would change; and

   o   reporting on each group member's project responsibilities.

   Note: All members of the group should present some part of the above.

10. Group members will have the option to be present or leave temporarily when their display critique ensues.
11. After the critiques are finished, you should take pictures of your display. You will use the pictures to create a final detailed computer-generated planogram. The planogram needs to be turned in within one week of your presentation.
12. Immediately dismantle your displays, clean up, and remove your belongings so the next groups can use the resources and display spaces.

PLACES TO LOOK FOR "STUFF":

- closets
- basements
- garages
- thrift stores
- yard sales
- flea markets
- family members
- friends

GROUP INFORMATION:			
NAMES	EMAIL	CELL	AVAILABILITY

Facets of Fashion Display Project Grading Rubric (75 Points Possible)

IDEA SKETCHES (WORTH 10 POINTS):

1. Idea sketches were turned in from all group members prior to display presentation.

	Unacceptable		Average		Outstanding
	0	1	2	3	4	5

2. The idea sketches illustrated that each group member brainstormed *individual, unique* display possibilities.

0   1   2   3   4   5

Comments:

COMPUTER-GENERATED PLANOGRAM (WORTH 20 POINTS):

1. The planogram was turned in within one week after the group's presentation of the display.

0   1   2   3   4   5

2. The planogram was created using Adobe Illustrator, Sketch-Up, or Microsoft Word.

0   1   2   3   4   5

3. The planogram is complete and includes all objects displayed.

0   1   2   3   4   5

4. The planogram is easy to use—i.e., the objects are easily delineated from one another, parts are labeled, and any special instructions given.

0   1   2   3   4   5

Comments:

PRESENTATION (WORTH 15 POINTS):

_____ The group discussed the concept of their display (2 pts.).

_____ The group indicated why they chose a particular aspect of fashion to focus on (1 pts.).

_____ The group discussed the display challenges that needed to be overcome (2 pts.).

_____ The group indicated what solutions were used to overcome the challenges (2 pts.).

_____ The group discussed the successes of the display (2 pts.).

_____ The group discussed the areas they would change, why and how (2 pts.).

_____ Each group member's responsibilities for the project were reported (2 pts.).

_____ Each group member took a turn in discussing the above information (2 pts.).

Comments:

CONSUMER CRITIQUE (WORTH 30 POINTS OR 3 POINTS EACH):

1. This display immediately captured my attention.

   Strongly Disagree   Neutral   Strongly Agree

   0   1   2   3

2. This display would cause me to stop and look.

   Strongly Disagree   Neutral   Strongly Agree

   0   1   2   3

3. This display contained elements that I found interesting.

   Strongly Disagree   Neutral   Strongly Agree

   0   1   2   3

4. This display kept my attention.

   Strongly Disagree   Neutral   Strongly Agree

   0   1   2   3

5. This display has a neat, clean appearance.

   Strongly Disagree   Neutral   Strongly Agree

   0   1   2   3

6. The promotional signage used in this display is appropriate and professional-looking.

   Strongly Disagree   Neutral   Strongly Agree

   0   1   2   3

7. This display incorporates supporting elements related to the fashion facet that can be found at the library.

Strongly Disagree	Neutral	Strongly Agree
0	1	2	3

8. This display would excite the viewer about a potential career in fashion.

Strongly Disagree	Neutral	Strongly Agree
0	1	2	3

9. This display gives the impression that the group takes pride in their major and wants to promote it to others.

Strongly Disagree	Neutral	Strongly Agree
0	1	2	3

10. Overall, I enjoyed experiencing this display.

Strongly Disagree	Neutral	Strongly Agree
0	1	2	3

Other Consumer Comments:

Total Score:

_____/75

Notes

1. Judy Bell and Kate Ternus, *Silent Selling: Best Practices and Effective Strategies in Visual Merchandising* (New York: Fairchild Books, 2012).
2. Jay Diamond and Ellen Diamond, *Contemporary Visual Merchandising and Environmental Design* (Upper Saddle River, N.J.: Pearson College Division, 2011), 191.
3. Bell and Ternus, *Silent Selling*, 306.
4. Diamond and Diamond, *Contemporary Visual Merchandising*.
5. Bell and Ternus, *Silent Selling*, 152–53.

CHAPTER EIGHTEEN

The Wikipedia Edit-a-Thon for Critical Information Literacy and Public Service

Dr. Matthew A. Vetter

Assistant Professor of English
Indiana University of Pennsylvania
matthew.vetter@iup.edu

Cori Woods

M.A. candidate in Public History
Indiana University of Pennsylvania
c.l.woods2@iup.edu

THE ACTIVITY

Description: Despite an initial negative reception by academics, Wikipedia, the open access encyclopedia created in 2001, is now recognized by many as an extremely successful use of Web 2.0 technology for the production and maintenance of a free and open-source public knowledge project. As of October 2017, the English edition of the encyclopedia contained nearly 5.5 million articles.[1] The encyclopedia continues to expand through the efforts of thousands of volunteer editors.

Wikipedia Edit-a-thons provide opportunities for students and faculty to (1) increase digital writing skills, (2) practice critical thinking and digital engagement surrounding issues related to information literacy and the politics of representation and access in digital spaces, and (3) make improvements to a public knowledge database (Wikipedia) as a public service. This "success story" provides a case study of a recent edit-a-thon held at Indiana University of Pennsylvania Libraries and includes suggestions for running your own edit-a-thon. Edit-a-thons are workshop-style events in which people come together to edit and improve articles on Wikipedia. Typically, participants work on a common goal. In our recent edit-a-thon, we partnered with Art+Feminism, an organization devoted to supporting edit-a-thons that seek to improve the representation of women and art in Wikipedia and address the gender gap.[2] Accordingly, this case study also reflects on the opportunities presented by a project that engages information politics related to gender representation.

A direct response to the encyclopedia's gender gap, a lack in representation of subjects about and related to women, Art+Feminism was founded in 2014. A loose collective of academics, librarians, artists, and students, Art+Feminism participants have worked together to organize more than 280 Wikipedia Edit-a-thons, or hands-on editing workshops, since March of 2014.[3] The organization continues to provide direct support of edit-a-thons through grants provided by the Wikimedia Foundation and was instrumental in the support and planning of our event, which took place on March 8, 2017, at Indiana University of Pennsylvania. Students involved in the activity included the co-author of this chapter, a graduate student working with women and gender studies at IUP who helped plan and lead the editing during the event, and a doctoral student from the English doctoral program in composition and TESOL who helped sign in participants and otherwise helped facilitate the event. Also involved were undergraduate students enrolled in an Introduction to Women's and Gender Studies class, graduate students from English, and undergraduate students working on museum-related internships who participated in the editing process.

Getting Started: Planning and running a Wikipedia Edit-a-thon requires early collaboration, planning, and training. The planning of our own event involved a good deal of email discussion, early planning meetings, and training tutorials three to four months before the event date. We were guided through this planning process, however, by resources and correspondence offered by the Art+Feminism organization. In the early planning period, you should begin by identifying what's known as a "Wikipedia ambassador"—an individual who has experience in Wikipedia editing and who is willing to conduct training tutorials on basic editing skills before and during the event. In the case of our events, that individual was the lead author, who has been teaching with Wikipedia for over five years and has developed an extensive knowledge of the editing practices, policies, and culture of Wikipedia. You should also review the resources offered by Art+Feminism and get in contact with a representative of that organization. Finally, if you have never edited Wikipedia yourself, you should try editing and watch some training videos, available at the Art+Feminism website (artandfeminism.org). The Wiki Education Foundation, an organization devoted to supporting academic engagement in the encyclopedia, also offers a number of training resources (wikiedu.org).

Starting planning for a Wikipedia Edit-a-thon early can help it run smoothly and increase the success of the event and the resulting learning outcomes. If time allows, you may even want to begin building partnerships with specific faculty and students by making the event part of a major course assignment or embedding it in the class schedule. Relevant disciplines for an Art+Feminism Edit-a-thon include art, women's and gender studies, history, digital media, communication, writing, rhetoric, information literacy, and library and information science.

Motivations: Because they enable direct contributions to a public knowledge project, Wikipedia Edit-a-thons provide concrete and high-impact experiential learning opportunities. Edit-a-thons, especially those devoted to closing content gaps related to marginalized identities and topics, can also achieve student learning outcomes related to digital writing and literacy (e.g., encyclopedic editing), critical information literacy, process-based information creation, and research as strategic exploration and inquiry.

THE PEOPLE

Libraries: IUP Libraries promotes the study, research, teaching, and scholarship-related activities of the students and faculty of a mid-sized university that is part of the Pennsylvania State System of Higher Education (PASSHE). It fosters the development of academic activities and communities with spaces and services, including fully equipped computer labs that can be reserved for classes, meetings, or community events, and a full-range of instruction and student engagement opportunities. IUP Libraries supported the edit-a-thon in a number of ways, including providing space and equipment, research resources for editors to draw from as they worked on Wikipedia articles, and support from library staff. Theresa McDevitt, outreach librarian and women's and gender studies bibliographer, also played an influential role in the organization, planning, and promotion of the event.

Instructors: Women's and Gender Studies at IUP co-hosted, planned, and promoted this event as a powerful tool for increasing representation of women in the online encyclopedia. They led the planning of the event, sought collaborators and financial contributions for refreshments from supporters, and promoted the event. The director of women's and gender studies at IUP, Dr. Lynn Botelho, also gave an introductory talk on the importance of this type of work on the day of the event. The Center for Digital Humanities and Culture at IUP also contributed to planning and promotional efforts. Two representatives from the Center (also

English faculty at IUP) presented on the wiki technology and history of Wikipedia as part of the edit-a-thon program. The lead author served as a Wikipedia Ambassador for the planning and execution of this event. He has been teaching with and editing Wikipedia since 2011 and has held at least one edit-a-thon in the past and designed multiple Wikipedia-based assignments in his own classes. An assistant professor in the English department, he specializes in the teaching of writing, rhetoric, and digital humanities. This experience allowed him to lead training tutorials on Wikipedia editing as well as help organize and plan the event.

Courses: This activity was not a required part of any credit-bearing class. However, one section of a women's and gender studies class invited a librarian to provide an introductory discussion on the importance of Wikipedia as an information source and the desirability of improved representation of women in its entries during one of its class sessions. This discussion included an invitation to attend the edit-a-thon activity. A debriefing discussion for participants followed the activity, and students who participated received extra credit in the class for participation in the event. Undergraduate art students doing an internship at the IUP University Museum also participated in the editing event as a part of their internship experience.

Students: Participants at the edit-a-thon included a diverse group of students and faculty from English, art, women's and gender studies, and history, among other disciplines. A graduate assistant in women's and gender studies played a large role in the event by participating in the planning and leading the editing process during the event. A doctoral student from English helped login participants. Other doctoral students in English Composition and TESOL attended as editors.

Community Partners: IUP Libraries, Women's and Gender Studies, and the Center for Digital Humanities and Culture all benefited from this event which created community, increased awareness of the existence and mission of each group, and furthered learning outcomes that they supported.

Finding and Working with Partners: The Art+Feminism Edit-a-thon held at Indiana University of Pennsylvania (IUP) was a collaborative venture between IUP Libraries, Women's and Gender Studies, and the Center for Digital Humanities and Culture. We envisioned an interdisciplinary event and encouraged participation from both students and faculty across campus. Because one of the main goals of the edit-a-thon was to diversify editorship in Wikipedia and help improve representation of women and the arts, we especially encouraged the participation of cis- and transgendered women. Our program lasted three hours and included an introductory talk on the importance of this type of work from the director of women's and gender studies, a talk on the function and history of the wiki and Wikipedia from the co-directors of the Center for Digital Humanities and Culture, a Wikipedia training and practice session, and the introduction of specific reference materials by a library faculty member. These initial segments were followed by a hands-on workshop in which participants worked directly on improving Wikipedia articles related to women and the arts.

Collaboration among the different groups was key to the success of the event, as each group supplied a necessary element. Keeping the shared goals of all involved in the forefront of planning and delivery of the event helped make the collaboration a smooth one.

Benefits

Instructor Benefits: Instructors involved in this event benefitted from the opportunity to embed a high-impact learning experience into their courses and to engage students in digital literacy practices, research, information literacy, and research. Through this event, instructors were also introduced to resources and opportunities provided by the Wiki Education Foundation (wikiedu.org) for integrating Wikipedia-based assignments into their courses. Finally, instructors also gained direct Wikipedia editing practice and learned more about the conventions, values, and processes of the Wikipedia community.

Student Benefits: Graduate student leaders involved gained experience in planning and facilitating events through their participation. Undergraduate students who edited entries gained experience in online editing, improved their understanding of the origin and quality of content found in Wikipedia as well as what gaps exist, and developed an increased awareness of the need to evaluate internet-based information. Student experience with Wikipedia typically ends at online research but this event gave participants an introduction to, and experience with, making online edits. In addition to teaching them an important twenty-first-century skill, it increased their awareness of how easily information can be added to a Wikipedia entry, how dynamic the content is, and how agendas may be promoted through such edits. Such experience positions them to use Wikipedia to better promote topics and causes that they support but also alerted them to biases which may be found in such entries. This event was organized around the theme of Art+Feminism, making it particularly relevant for students in women's and gender studies classes. Increased awareness of the gender gap in Wikipedia editing and content left students better positioned to consider and confront these issues and shape the world in which they live.

Partner Benefits: The edit-a-thon provided opportunities for IUP's Center for Digital Humanities and Culture to foster active interrogation of the cultural politics of digital communities as well as a more nuanced understanding of Wikipedia itself—its history and culture. For IUP's Women's and Gender Studies program, the edit-a-thon was a feminist project that allowed for recognition of the marginalization of women in digital spaces and direct intervention to address that marginalization. Finally, for IUP Libraries, it drew attention to how research and information literacies can allow active engagement with critical social issues in digital cultures.

Institutional Benefits: The collaborative facilitation of this event also meant that we were able to draw participants from a diverse number of disciplines and to build community between those disciplines. Furthermore, the opportunities for learning and engagement made possible by this event benefitted partners and participants in different ways. IUP Libraries considered this both an outreach and information literacy skill-building event. Participants who may not have otherwise visited the library worked in one of the best library spaces, making return visits more likely and making it more likely students will spend more time in what is considered to be a good educational space that supports student retention and success. In addition, participants built important information literacy skills as they used library sources to edit Wikipedia articles and learned how to properly cite those sources using a specific documentation style. For Women's and Gender Studies, this project provided opportunities for critical thinking and social action that resulted in increased representation of subjects related to art and feminism. From the viewpoint of the Center for Digital Humanities and Culture, collaborating partners were able to model how students can play a role in transforming and extending humanities practices in digital spaces. Of course, from a practical standpoint, collaborating with multiple partners also simply makes the event run more smoothly. As the "Wikipedian" on the team, tasked with working out training processes and running the actual workshop, for instance, the lead author was relieved to have help with promotional efforts from Women's and Gender Studies and research resources from the library. The institution benefited overall from increased learning outcomes related to the mission of each partner, but also from unique learning outcomes and connections that resulted from the cross-disciplinary collaborations.

THE PROCESS
Expected Learning Outcomes

The Art+Feminism Wikipedia Edit-a-thon was held on March 8 at IUP Libraries and was guided by the following objectives.

- First, by taking part in the edit-a-thon, participants were able to increase digital writing skills by learning about policies and values of the Wikipedia community and by practicing editing skills in order to add content to Wikipedia articles.
- Next, because this edit-a-thon was designed to tackle content gaps related to Wikipedia's gender gap, participants engaged in critical thinking concerning issues related to information literacy and the politics of representation and access in digital spaces.
- Finally, this project also had a significant service-learning component in that facilitators and participants were motivated by the goals of making

improvements to Wikipedia by expanding its coverage of marginalized topics.

Curriculum Materials

Curricular materials for this event included both digital and print documents, as well as online resources. The following materials were instrumental in the successful facilitation of the edit-a-thon and are provided in the Appendix Materials or are available online.

- Program overview and schedule: The edit-a-thon program overview and schedule guided the activities in the main event, and helped facilitators plan for the event.
- Participant interest survey: Facilitators created a survey using free web-based application Google Forms and distributed it widely two to three weeks before the event. This survey gauged attendance information as well as gathered useful data on participants' inclinations toward certain subject areas or articles in Wikipedia.
- Program dashboard: As a resource, an online application provided by Wikimedia Foundation and supported by Art+Feminism tracked participants' editing activity and helped us establish and record the work we accomplished.
- IUP Libraries Library Guide: A Lib Guide was created to collect all of these materials and relevant links to editorial training resources. This served as a "launchpad" for our program and organized various curricular materials. The Library Guide is accessible online at http://libraryguides.lib.iup.edu/.

Steps Involved

Planning the edit-a-thon was two- to three-month-long process during which the facilitators and partners took the following steps.

- Identified a Wikipedia ambassador (the lead author), an individual who has experience in Wikipedia editing and community conventions who is willing to conduct training tutorials on basic editing skills before and during the event.
- Reviewed resources offered by Art+Feminism and connected with a representative of that organization who aided in the planning and execution for the event.
- Circulated a survey (See Appendix Materials) among potential faculty participants in order to gauge topic interests and begin to plan possible editorial tasks. This survey also encouraged potential participants to register a Wikipedia account in anticipation of the event.

- Organized two or three planning and tutorial sessions in which the Wikipedia ambassador trained other facilitators in basic Wikipedia editing and community conventions, processes, and values.
- Visited participating classes in order to introduce issues related to Wikipedia's gender gap as well as the planned activities before the event.
- Publicized the event through multiple departmental and institutional channels.

The actual edit-a-thon event took place during a single day, March 8, 2017, and over a three-hour period. During this session, facilitators and participants took the following steps to complete the service project.

- Participants arrived at the edit-a-thon and facilitators and graduate student volunteers helped with them sign in to the event and sign up for Wikipedia accounts.
- The women's and gender studies program chair kicked off the event while introducing the problematic representation of women in Wikipedia.
- Center for Digital Humanities and Culture co-directors gave introductory remarks on digital humanities, Wikipedia, and participatory culture.
- IUP Libraries faculty shared library resources that may be used as sources for the editing of Wikipedia articles.
- The Wikipedia ambassador reviewed edit-a-thon goals and resources for editing. This part of the session allowed for direct tutorials and training of participants in Wikipedia editing skills. We recommended reviewing resources and strategies for adding sources and content to sub- and start-class articles, sharing previously identified article lists (specifically of targeted articles needing improvement) and other project resources.
- The Wikipedia ambassador provided interactive, hands-on training in Wikipedia policies and editing skills. Wikipedia policies covered included neutral point of view, no original research, reliability of sources, and conflict of interest. The ambassador also provided hands-on training and support for the following skills:
    o   creating new editor accounts
    o   understanding elements of a Wikipedia article
    o   navigating and interacting with the user interface
    o   using the visual editor to add references and content
    o   working with sandboxes
- Participants engaged in an open workshop, collecting sources, identifying articles in need of development and adding references and content to those articles.
- Facilitators troubleshot, assisted in general, and provided ongoing demonstrations and tutorials as needed.
- The women's and gender studies coordinator made closing remarks.

POST PROJECT ASSESSMENT
Methods of Reflection

The graduate student facilitator was asked to reflect upon her experiences before and after the event. The reflective prompts she responded to are included in the Appendix Materials. Undergraduate students in an Introduction to Women's and Gender Studies class participated in an event-related discussion before and after the event facilitated by the women's and gender studies librarian and the course instructor.

Post-Project Feedback

Post-project feedback included a reflection from a graduate student participant and facilitator, who also co-authored this case study, and a project assessment written from the point-of-view of the facilitators.

Graduate Reflection: The graduate student facilitator had a specialization in women's and gender studies and history. With no experience in editing Wikipedia, she didn't know what to expect. Though she was provided with Wikipedia editing training prior to the event, she found the prospect of working with the new technology and helping others with it as daunting but exciting. She considered the event a service to the community because it empowered individuals to do web editing, add to research materials freely available online, and address gaps found there, particularly the gender gap. She believed that the event went well and noted that some of the participants seemed truly excited to edit and that she was glad that she could help them. The event changed the way she viewed using Wikipedia for research. Several of her professors had told her never to cite Wikipedia because of the dynamic nature of its content. The event led her to see the value of information found there as a starting place for research, the importance of consulting sources listed in its articles, and the impact that adding information that was lacking there could have upon future readers. She saw the event as a great way to show people how easy, interesting, empowering, and even fun editing and working with media can be. She saw the event as useful for teachers, staff, and students. She would participate in another edit-a-thon event but recommended changes in event promotion and design that would result in more participants and improved infrastructure to support attendees in the editing process.

Project Assessment and Reporting

The combined promotional efforts of facilitators yielded thirty-six visitors overall. From this group, twenty-four registered participants made a total of seventy-four edits. Together, we improved fifteen articles and created one new article, adding a total of 3,450 words on women and the arts in Wikipedia. These statistics are made possible by the program dashboard, a web application that allows for the management of such events and the tracking of registered editors' contributions. A meeting was held after the event with the main facilitators to review the outcomes of the event. Discussion led us to conclude that the edit-a-thon event was most powerful when it is immediately practical and hands-on. Therefore, we realized that the presentations we scheduled for the beginning of the event could be shortened significantly (or even omitted completely) to allow participants to begin registering and editing as soon as possible. We saw direct experience and direct action as the most attractive and powerful draw for an event like this. Furthermore, such direct editing represents the original impetus and goal of the event.

Second, we all realized how more planning and integration of this project into faculty members' courses could benefit the organization and execution of the event. For instance, if we had given faculty more notice, they could have planned a course assignment and written it into their syllabus to accommodate and integrate the Wikipedia Edit-a-thon. We plan to take advantage of this type of pre-planning in the future.

Finally, we also made some key realizations about space. The library classroom we held the event in, while it did provide computers for all participants, did not allow for much freedom of movement. Additionally, while some of our participants used the computers we made available, many of them brought their own laptops. In the future, we would attempt to secure a more open space to allow for movement among participants and facilitators and to encourage discussion and peer-to-peer interaction.

Given that this event was conceived, planned, and held in a little more than a month, we felt that it was a great success. Planning for the next event included improvements, such as promoting the spring event in the fall semester to faculty, the provision of sample curriculum materials to ease the integration of the event into courses in English, women's and gender studies, and information literacy, working with our Center for Teaching Excellence to promote the event, and developing formal leadership roles for students. With more time to plan and experience from the last event, we expect that this year's event will be even better.

Difficulties Encountered

Student Issues: The main issues students faced stemmed from challenges related to technology, less than ideal presentation content, and time constraints. Technology-based activities can be challenging for students with little to no editing experience and they may become frustrated. Students had difficulty with creating accounts, signing on, and editing entries. Having a number of experienced editors on hand to assist with such difficulties can ease such frustrations and be the difference between a frustrating and empowering experience. Given the drop-in nature of the event, the presentation content and timing were sometimes a problem. Some students dropped in during the background information presentation but were unable to stay long enough to edit, and were disappointed. In the future, the presentation sections of the event will be shorter and designed specifically to build editing skills. Descriptive handouts and experienced editors will be on hand at all times to help those that want to get started editing right away. Facilitators plan to have four "resource stations" staffed with experienced student editors which will help participants with basic tasks related to registration and account creation, topic development and article identification, research, and basic editing tasks, such as source citation. These resource stations will operate throughout the event and thus provide support for participants at any stage in the event process.

Instructor (Facilitator) Issues: Difficulties encountered during the event included some technical problems as we worked to ensure that all participants became registered users both of Wikipedia itself as well as the program dashboard we were using to track contributions. There was some initial issue with this latter element of the workshop which arose from the project timeline. The start and end-times programmed into dashboard had been entered incorrectly, which was preventing participants from registering with the edit-a-thon dashboard. Once we figured out what was causing this problem (the start and end-inputs), we were able to modify the dates and solve the issue. Care should be taken when using the program dashboard to ensure that the start- and end-dates are inputted correctly.

An additional technical issue involved the use of the visual editor in Wikipedia. Wikipedia's visual editor makes editorial work much more accessible to novice users because it allows for what-you-see-is-what-you-get (WYYIWYG) editing. However, we initially had some difficulties activating the visual editor for new Wikipedia users because the toggle was not easily located. Once we were able to identify this issue, all participants could use the visual editor.

Community Partner Issues: One of the central issues involving community partners arose through the differing visions for the event held by Women's and Gender Studies (WGS) and the Center for Digital Humanities and Culture (DHC). The DHC provided introductory remarks on digital humanities, Wikipedia, and participatory culture, but the length of these talks was seen by facilitators and some participants in WGS as too lengthy and/or unrelated to the specific editing event on hand. Recommendations were made for shorter introductory discussion and a more streamlined program to allow for more editing time. This issue also calls for more attention to the alignment of visions for the event between community partners.

Conclusions

The Wikipedia Edit-a-thon held at IUP provided opportunities for building community, teaching critical information literacy and digital writing skills, as well as sponsoring public service to help improve an open-access knowledge project. Community partners, instructors, students, and institutions all benefit from such events in numerous ways, from promoting social awareness and equity goals to sponsoring critical literacy and fostering high-impact research and writing practices. Facilitating an Art+Feminism Wikipedia Edit-a-thon at Indiana University of Pennsylvania also helped facilitators learn more about what is needed for a successful, cross-disciplinary event that engages the university community in Wikipedia editing.

APPENDIX MATERIALS

- Reflective Questions for Graduate Facilitator
- IUP Art+Feminism Edit-a-thon Participant Interest Survey
- Program Overview and Schedule for Art+Feminism Wikipedia Edit-a-thon

Reflective Questions for Graduate Facilitator

- What did you think about working with the edit-a-thon when you first were asked to be involved? Were you apprehensive about working with the new technology? Were you excited? Did you see it as an important event in terms of providing a service to the community?
- What were your thoughts about the event itself and the role you played in helping facilitate the event?
- As you think back on your involvement in the event, has it had an impact on you? Do you think of Wikipedia any differently?
- Would you participate in such an event again?

IUP Art+Feminism Edit-a-thon Participant Interest Survey

The Art+Feminism Wikipedia Edit-a-thon is being hosted March 8, from 10:00 a.m. to 1:00 p.m. It is hosted by Stapleton Library in collaboration with Women's and Gender Studies and the Center for Digital Humanities and Culture at Indiana University of Pennsylvania. Walk-ins are welcome but pre-registration is helpful (bit.ly/IUP-EDIT-A-THON). In addition, we are seeking feedback from faculty who may be interested in bringing students with specific interest areas to the event. If you can please complete the survey below, it will help us anticipate the number of volunteers we can expect. Equally important, it will help the librarians and other organizers to identify relevant entries AND prepare materials in advance for the use of our volunteer editors!

- Including myself, I anticipate bringing approximately how many students and/or guests?
- Primary area(s) of interest.
- Do you have a specific Wikipedia article in mind that you or your students would be prepared to edit? If so, please provide the link below.
- The Art+Feminism organizers will be working to identify "stub" articles which exist but would profit from development. Initiating a new article or revising a mature article can be less successful for inexperienced Wikipedia volunteers.
- Are you interested in receiving pre-training on Wikipedia editing or otherwise helping in the organization of this event? No prior experience is needed. Organizers will be planning to orient volunteers in a brief tutoring session and provide ongoing support throughout the event. However, if faculty or staff would like to be more prepared, we will provide an opportunity for training in advance. Do you have any other comments and/or questions?

Program Overview and Schedule for Art+Feminism Wikipedia Edit-a-thon

Steps to Getting Involved

- Students—please sign up for the event.
- Faculty—please take the survey indicating topics of interest.
- Invite others, share this link: http://bit.ly/IUP-Art-Feminism-Edit-A-Thon.
- Come to the library on March 8th.

OVERVIEW

Stapleton Library, in collaboration with Women's and Gender Studies and the Center for Digital Humanities and Culture at Indiana University of Pennsylvania, will host an Art+Feminism Wikipedia Edit-a-thon March 8, from 10:00 a.m. to 1:00 p.m. in 201 Stabley.

This three-hour event is designed to improve coverage of women and the arts on Wikipedia and encourage female editorship. The edit-a-thon will include an introductory talk, tutorials for the beginner Wikipedian, ongoing editing support, reference materials, and refreshments. People of all gender identities and expressions are invited to participate, particularly transgender and cisgender women. In a 2011 survey, the Wikimedia Foundation found that less than 10 percent of its contributors identify as female. This lack of female participation has led to an alarming dearth of content about women and art in the world's most popular online research tool. Art+Feminism's Edit-a-thons and other initiatives make an impact on the gender gap through crucial improvements to art and feminism related subjects on Wikipedia. Since 2014, more than 280 Art+Feminism Edit-a-thons have taken place across the world, creating and improving an estimated 4,600 articles.

EDIT-A-THON PROGRAM
- 9:50 a.m.—Set-up and sign-ups
- 10:00 a.m.—Lynn Botelho: Introductory remarks and refreshments
- 10:10 a.m.—Ken Sherwood and Dan Weinstein: Remarks on digital humanities, Wikipedia, and participatory culture
- 10:25 a.m.—Theresa McDevitt and other library faculty share library resources
- 10:35 a.m.—Matt Vetter reviews edit-a-thon goals and resources for engaging participants
- 10:40 a.m.—Demonstrations and practice edits; Matt demonstrates a range of particular skill sets, allowing time for practice
- 11:00 a.m.—Open workshop: Participants work on editing tasks. Facilitators help participants one-on-one with questions/issues and additional demos as needed
- 12:00 p.m.—Refreshments
- 12:30 p.m.—Ongoing editing and tutorial demonstrations
- 12:50 p.m.—Closing Remarks: Lynn Botelho

Notes
1.   "Wikipedia: Size of Wikipedia," accessed October 6, 2017, https://en.wikipedia.org/wiki/Wikipedia:Size_of_Wikipedia.
2.   Noam Cohen, "Define Gender Gap? Look Up Wikipedia's Contributor List," *New York Times*, January 30, 2011, 1050–56.
3.   "Our Story: Art + Feminism," *Art and Feminism*, accessed April 7 2017, http://www.artandfeminism.org/our-story/.

CHAPTER NINETEEN

Service-Learning in the Oral History Archives

Juliana M. Nykolaiszyn

Professor/Librarian
Oklahoma State University Library
juliana.nykolaiszyn@okstate.edu

THE ACTIVITY

Description: Within a higher education setting, Bringle and Hatcher look at service-learning as "a course-based service experience that produces the best outcomes when meaningful service activities are related to course material through reflection activities such as direct writings, small group discussions, and class presentations." When thinking deeper about service-learning in academic libraries, special collections and university archives provide a wealth of opportunities for students looking to make connections between coursework, community, and civic engagement. At Oklahoma State University (OSU), elements of service-learning can be found within the library's Oklahoma Oral History Research Program (OOHRP), which actively records and archives interviews on a variety of topics related to Oklahoma history and culture. Involving students in growing their understanding of oral history and gaining insight into practices such as interviewing, transcribing, generating metadata, along with creating products such as podcasts, tends to challenge their basic assumptions and helps them grow beyond what is learned in a traditional classroom setting.

Integrating elements of oral history into service-learning is not a new idea but is a tremendous fit. Engaging in such hands-on work helps students "not only learn about the history of the community but also become actively involved in preserving that history."[2] While the OOHRP employs students to assist with general interview processing, in recent years the department has seen an uptick in history undergraduates enrolling in a practicum course that exposes them to professions in the history field. Select practicum students are placed within the library's oral history department for a sixteen-week experience. While students work through all aspects of oral history, including conducting an interview, the culmination of the internship rests with the creation of a podcast episode. This podcast typically brings multiple elements together in a final digital project that is then shared within the greater campus community and beyond. In addition to their on-site work within the library, which allows for formal and informal learning opportunities, students also take part in traditional class meetings with others enrolled in the course, are required to produce a weekly journal, deliver a final presentation, and complete a final report that details their overall experience, including lessons learned.

Getting Started: Prior to the start of the fall 2016 semester, the OSU Department of History started the process of looking for partners to house potential practicum students for a course titled Jobs in History. Within the OSU Library, two departments were approached to take on students: Archives and the Oklahoma Oral History Research Program. The oral history program ended up with two students during the first semester and continued to work closely with the History Department in subsequent semesters. Looking at preparations within the OOHRP, areas of focus were created for students, readings identified, and departmental faculty/staff members were notified in order to prepare for students involved in the course.

Motivations: There are several motivations for the OOHRP to engage in this partnership with the OSU History Department. First, this experience allows for the creation of deeper connections with undergraduate students. These connections help further a student's knowledge of oral history both as a methodology and as an archival resource. Additionally, students not only engage in hands-on learning but also provide real-world support with the creation of transcripts, the auditing of interviews, and development of metadata, which greatly assists the OOHRP's overall mission in producing accessible resources. Finally, student interactions with oral history faculty and staff tend to be mutually fulfilling, with each party learning from one another based on varied interests and areas of expertise.

THE PEOPLE

Welcoming students into the OSU Library's oral history archives who are looking to learn and grow takes a team to help guide them along the way in order to make the most out of a time-limited opportunity. This effort involves many individuals who take students under their wings in order to provide a general overview of not only oral history practice but also highly skilled and sometimes technical work. In the end, a mix of faculty, staff, and community members all provide an active learning environment, thus enriching a student's educational experience.

Libraries: Oklahoma State University is situated in Stillwater, Oklahoma. The main campus serves 22,967 students as of fall 2017.[3] A land-grant institution, the main campus library supports the university's academic mission through a diverse range of print and electronic resources, technology offerings, and research/data support. The Oklahoma Oral History Research Program was officially founded as part of the OSU Library in 2007 with the "goal of documenting and making accessible the history of Oklahoma and OSU through oral history interviews."[4] The unit employs a team of librarians, oral historians, editors, and student workers to further the mission of the library and university. This also includes cultivating relationships both on- and off-campus with students, faculty, cultural institutions, along with the public.

Instructors: A faculty member from the OSU Department of History serves as the instructor of record for the practicum course and assists in placing students with various sites on- and off-campus. They lead the traditional in-class meetings, review weekly journals, and oversee all work required to fulfill the requirements of the course. This faculty member also keeps in regular contact with site-supervisors in monitoring the overall progress of students.

Additionally, students placed within the Oklahoma State University Library's oral history department are exposed to a wide variety of scholars, including library faculty, who help support their overall learning process. Within the library, students work closely with library faculty and staff throughout the sixteen-week period. They have unique access to a team of professionals with diverse research interests and varied backgrounds, which helps illustrate the interdisciplinary nature of oral history and how it fits together within an academic library setting. The OOHRP's team of faculty and staff includes a mix of academics specializing in broad areas, such as librarianship, oral history, archives, folklore, media production, digital humanities, and metadata.

Courses: Offered through the OSU Department of History, students enroll in the course HIST 4980: Jobs in History-Practicum as part of this experience. Students also have additional opportunities to work with the OOHRP in other capacities in a given academic year through a variety of additional internships and employment opportunities.

Students: Those enrolled in the course are typically undergraduate history majors with upperclassmen status, either juniors or seniors. They tend to be very motivated and understand how to operate both independently and as part of a team environment. Most come to the practicum with little to no knowledge of oral history. Of particular note, most students possess varying levels of familiarity with technology, which provides an additional area for personal and future professional growth.

Community Partners: The focus of this practicum experience has the potential to serve different communities in and around the university. Students engage with different aspects of oral history, which directly benefit the library but also helps in making content accessible to a wider audience, including local communities. Additionally, when a student defines an oral history interview and/or podcast topic as part of required tasks included in this course, this also affects a larger community. For example, one practicum student worked with a series of archival interviews featuring a historic black town in Oklahoma and created a podcast highlighting this rich history on the verge of disappearance.

Finding and Working with Partners: Community involvement is integrated within the interview components of the course. Since students are required to conduct an oral history, they have flexibility in helping to determine the narrator and overall focus of the interview. The student works in collaboration with OOHRP faculty to make a narrator determination, and often the department assists in making introductions to already established contacts within the community. It is then the student's responsibility to follow up and set appointments to complete the interview component. Interviewing once again comes into play when students develop their podcast as they must also conduct a short-form interview with an expert for integration within the program. An expert may take the form of a faculty member but can also include fellow students or even community members in and around Oklahoma.

Benefits

There are many benefits for all parties involved within the scope of this practicum. While an overarching goal is to train the next generation of oral historians, it is also understood that many students aspire for careers in law, politics, education, social justice, public service, and librarianship, to name a few. Understanding a student's career trajectory helps the OOHRP provide a flexible learning environment, often gearing work toward areas of personal and professional interest in a way that is ultimately meaningful for the student.

Instructor Benefits: It is the hope of instructors that students gain an appreciation for the different history-related fields. The practicum experience tends to open students' eyes to the broad nature of the history profession and degree applicability beyond typical assumptions.

Student Benefits: Students develop an understanding regarding the process and practice of oral history, from interview to archive. In addition, most benefit from new skills learned in researching and writing, along with the operation of specialized computer applications, equipment, and technology. They have access to library faculty and staff with varied knowledge, which helps build their communication skills and often leads to additional opportunities to explore areas of interest that can directly impact their field of study.

Partner Benefits: The students' work, especially in conducting oral history interviews and in improving the accessibility of other related content, has greater implications as well. Assisting in keeping history alive within local communities is a direct result of student effort throughout the practicum period. In addition, students develop an understanding of the reciprocal nature of oral history and the importance of giving back to local communities through this work.

Institutional Benefits: Involving students in the work of the library's oral history department has many benefits. In addition to guiding students in further understanding oral history methodology and research, the library may develop a greater understanding of how students interact with existing online content and resources. Additionally, this work is more than an assignment or exercise. It directly makes a difference in the department's efforts to create discoverable collections. Finally, after students complete the practicum, they often are strong candidates for employment opportunities within the library, due to knowledge and skills learned during their time in the program.

THE PROCESS
Expected Learning Outcomes

Students placed within the OOHRP develop practical knowledge about the creation and curation of oral histories. Upon completion of the practicum experience, they will be able to understand how to conduct an oral history interview, develop practical skills in oral history processing and preservation, and create/produce a podcast featuring oral history excerpts. Additionally, students will learn how to interact in a team environment with a variety of professionals and community members, meet desired deadlines, and expand their view of Oklahoma history and culture. Finally, it is the hope of the OOHRP that students will grow an appreciation for the interdisciplinary nature of oral history and understand how it can be integrated across a variety of disciplines.

Curriculum Materials

In order to develop a broader understanding of oral history methodology, students are asked to read select chapters in Donald A. Ritchie's comprehensive how-to text, *Doing Oral History*[5] in addition to Nancy MacKay's *Curating Oral Histories: From Interview to Archive*.[6] For technical learning with respect to audio/video software, students may turn to tutorials housed on Lynda.com, to which the library subscribes. Additionally, students also utilize existing online oral history collections maintained by the Oklahoma Oral History Research Program throughout the semester.

Steps Involved

Once the students are matched with the OSU Library's oral history program, they meet with the head of the department to learn more about expectations and set up a schedule. The following activities typically take place throughout the practicum:

- **Introduction to Oral History:** Students are assigned a variety of readings to familiarize themselves with the practice of oral history. Additionally, they meet individually with members of the department to discuss specific roles and job duties and begin building relationships with oral history faculty/staff. During this introductory period, students also learn more about human subject research and complete training modules required by the Institutional Review Board.

- **Transcription, Auditing, and Editing:** In this phase, students meet with the lead oral history editor to develop an understanding of what happens to an interview once it comes into the library's office. Students are assigned interviews and work through each area of processing, including transcription, audit checking, and editing. They also learn how to create biographies for narrators that are included in final transcriptions. Throughout, they are encouraged to ask questions for further clarification. Feedback is consistently provided on their progress.

- **Metadata:** Next, students learn more about the basics of creating interview accessibility. As a result, a big portion of this area falls within the development of metadata. Students learn about metadata fields and structure. They engage in creating descriptive metadata, including identifying subject, keywords, descriptions, and coverage elements. A discussion of what happens to metadata also takes place, including its use in content management systems.

- **Interview:** As students become more familiar with oral history, they begin leading up to the interview assignment. To get a feel for fieldwork, students shadow an oral historian during an interview session. In this process, they may also engage in other documentary elements while on the road with interviewers, including capturing photographs for the archive. Upon completion of this activity, students then begin researching/discussing potential ideas for an interview they would like to undertake. After making a determination, students follow through in contacting and scheduling interviews, conduct background research, prepare a question guide, become familiar with equipment, learn more about release forms, and are instructed on interview basics before venturing out to record a solo effort.

- **Podcast:** The OOHRP's monthly podcast, Amplified Oklahoma, provides students with the opportunity to learn more about audio production and digital storytelling. Students are asked to identify a subject of interest and create an episode from start to finish. They are responsible for researching the topic, preparing a script, narrating the script, selecting appropriate music, identifying interview excerpts from the oral history archives for inclusion, interviewing a campus or community expert, and editing the production. Students work closely with the OOHRP's podcast producer for guidance and support throughout the creation of the episode.

- **Ongoing Discussions:** Students meet regularly with oral history faculty/ staff to review readings, discuss methodology, address concerns or questions, and receive feedback on progress. Oral history faculty/staff make efforts throughout the sixteen-week period to build deeper relationships with students, foster connections within the greater community, and lead conversations that speak to the interdisciplinary nature of oral history methodology.

POST-PROJECT ASSESSMENT
Methods of Reflection

Throughout the sixteen-week course, students are encouraged to reflect on their experience via weekly journal entries. These entries include lessons learned, questions they may have, and topics of an interesting and/or frustrating nature. Additionally, since students work closely with OOHRP faculty and staff, interaction and questions are encouraged. For future practicum students, it is the department's hope to integrate additional methods of reflection, such as exit interviews with participants as the OOHRP continues to improve and make changes to content covered during the semester.

Post-Project Feedback

While the instructor of record provides feedback to practicum supervisors within the library's oral history department, attending the final student presentations helps shed light on lessons learned throughout their time with the OOHRP. In this format, the students prepare a presentation for a larger group. In many cases, students integrate audio/visual elements into their talk, including excerpts from interviews and/or podcast efforts. Attendance usually includes faculty from the OSU History Department, site supervisors, and all students who participated in the practicum course during the semester. As students describe their experiences in this format, it is interesting to see the resulting growth and/or challenges encountered throughout the process.

Understanding areas where students struggled or faced difficulty assists in how the oral history department has modified involvement in this program. Informal feedback is also solicited. Iris Owens, a practicum student during the spring 2017 semester reflected:

> I came in as a history student that only knew how to use Microsoft Word, and I left being able to use Adobe Audition, various recording equipment, and developed a basic understanding of Microsoft Excel. I learned a new style of writing, which makes it easier for me to transition from "research writing" to a more journalistic style. I now know how to create interview questions, contact people and interview them in a professional manner, and, most importantly, I learned how to make a podcast. I absolutely fell in love with every part of the process, even the monotony of noise reduction.[7]

Students, like Ms. Owens, have grown tremendously throughout the process. Continuing to mix formal and informal reporting methods helps ensure students are getting the most out of the program but also in making greater connections in the world around them.

Project Assessment and Reporting Method

Many factors are considered in assessing the overall success of a student's practicum experience within the OOHRP. These include gauging if opportunities provided a level of reciprocity among the student and stakeholders (community members, library faculty and staff, etc.). Additionally, assessment may revolve around the following questions: Could connections between the hands-on learning components and future opportunities be identified by the student? Were required activities completed within a reasonable timeframe? Were student successes and frustrations equally addressed throughout the semester? Can metrics be identified which illustrate impact (such as podcast listener data, interview downloads, etc.)? With these questions as a guide, the OOHRP can continue developing a meaningful and fulfilling experience for practicum students involved with the library's oral history department.

Difficulties Encountered

Student Issues: Students involved in the practicum experience come to the OOHRP with varying levels of comfort regarding technology and familiarity with oral history. As the semester progresses, students are often asked to complete assignments that may be outside of their comfort zone. Library faculty work with students to help ease difficulties and provide support along the way in the learning process. Additionally, since the practicum schedule can be quite ambitious, timing also plays a major role in making sure students have adequate opportunity to fulfill expectations.

Instructor/Librarian Issues: Issues surrounding library faculty and staff revolve around the number of practicum students placed in the department at any given time. The more students involved, the less likely it is that they will all be on the same schedule. This creates minor scheduling difficulties on the part of library faculty tasked with mentoring students as they move through the process.

Community Partner Issues: Students work with external partners in the completion of the interviewing portion of the practicum. In the case of an oral history interview, many months will elapse before a partner will see a final product from their session with the student. Since the processing of oral histories takes considerable time beyond the practicum period, it is likely partners will contact the library to inquire about the status of the completed work.

Conclusion

While scholars view service-learning as a partnership between student and community, experiences like this also help foster a sense of connection beyond the classroom setting. The OOHRP's practicum students learn how all parts of the oral history process have the potential to influence a community's greater history, including the long-term accessibility of content. Reflection and guidance throughout help the student develop a feel for the gaps in the literature and provide an understanding of strategies to improve such silences in the historical record.

Special collections and university archives, including specialized areas such as oral history, provide the perfect environment to explore service-learning. With a focus on outreach in its many forms, including service to campus and community, welcoming students into the library and providing opportunities for them to grow can make all the difference. As student Iris Owens explains, "…the most important thing I took away from the experience is that academia isn't the only path for liberal arts majors. Although my degree mostly focuses on research and writing, when combined with the skills I learned …I see that the applications of my degree are endless."[8]

APPENDIX MATERIALS

- OOHRP Practicum—Scope of Work Description
- Course Requirements from HIST 4980 Syllabus
- Select Student Produced Podcast Episodes

OOHRP Practicum—Scope of Work Description

The goal of this practicum experience with the Oklahoma Oral History Research Program (OOHRP) is to provide hands-on experience with and exposure to the multifaceted work of an oral history program. The work of an oral historian is not limited to the interview itself. Students will have hands-on interaction with the entire process of oral history work including project management, historical research, conducting interviews, processing, transcribing and prepping interviews for preservation, access, and engagement. Students will be expected to complete assigned tasks in each of these areas, complete contextual reading assignments, and will have access to all members of the OOHRP department for mentorship and honest discussions. At the end of this practicum, students will have a portfolio of sample work created during the semester and a better understanding of how oral history work can apply to a variety of disciplinary work.

Course Requirements from HIST 4980 Syllabus

Participation and Attendance: You must attend and participate fully in discussion during the five class sessions that we will hold, along with all work shifts determined by you and your host supervisor. You must also meet with your host institution supervisor by the end of Week 1 and submit your completed contract to D2L Dropbox.

Weekly Journal: You will be expected to keep a weekly journal during the weeks you spend at your host institution. By the end of each week (Sunday 11:59 p.m. after a given week), you must post your journal reflections to D2L. I prefer that these be typed, but if you write them by hand, please scan or take a photo of your notebook and post that to D2L. These should be one or two pages of text (~300–500 words) that record what you did during the week, what you learned, what questions you have, what was particularly frustrating/interesting/etc. This should be written coherently and in full sentences.

Site Duties: To be determined with host supervisor.

Final Presentation: During the last week of classes, we will gather together to share ten-minute final PowerPoint presentations summarizing what you all learned during your practicum experience. More details to follow.

Final Report: During finals week, you will submit a six- to eight-page (double-spaced) paper detailing what you learned during your practicum experience. You can draw on your weekly journal entries, your final PowerPoint presentation, evaluations from your host supervisor, photographs from your semester of work, outside sources about the connections of your site to the study of history, and other reflections on your experience.

Select Student Produced Podcast Episodes

- Berson, Stephanie. "Boley, Oklahoma." *Amplified Oklahoma*. Podcast audio, February 17, 2017. https://library.okstate.edu/news/podcast/.
- Henagan, Laurel. "Folk Dancing." Amplified Oklahoma. Podcast audio, January 20, 2017. https://library.okstate.edu/news/podcast/.
- Owens, Iris. "A Bull in the Elevator." *Amplified Oklahoma*. Podcast audio, May 19, 2017. https://library.okstate.edu/news/podcast/.
- Schrantz, Christina. "Women in the Legal Profession." *Amplified Oklahoma*. Podcast audio, June 16, 2017. https://library.okstate.edu/news/podcast/.

OSU history student Iris Owens interviewing Ilka Heiskell at her home in Mangum, Oklahoma, regarding her experiences in Germany. (March 2017). Photo courtesy Oklahoma Oral History Research Program, OSU Library).

Notes

1. Robert G. Bringle and Julie. A. Hatcher, "Implementing Service-Learning in Higher Education," *Journal of Higher Education* 67, no. 2 (1996): 223.
2. A. Glenn Crothers, "'Bringing History to Life': Community Research, and Multiple Levels of Learning," *The Journal of American History* 88, no. 4 (2002): 1449.

3.   Institutional Research and Information Management, "OSU Student Profile Fall 2017," *Oklahoma State University*, 2017, https://irim.okstate.edu/StudentProfile.

4.   Oklahoma Oral History Research Program, "About the OOHRP," Oklahoma State University Library, https://library.okstate.edu/oralhistory/about-oohrp.

5.   Donald A. Ritchie, *Doing Oral History* (Oxford: Oxford University Press, 2014).

6.   Nancy MacKay, *Curating Oral Histories: From Interview to Archive* (Walnut Creek, CA, Left Coast Press, 2016).

7.   Iris Owens, e-mail message to author, September 2, 2017.

8.   Ibid.

CHAPTER TWENTY

Privacy, Cybersecurity, and the Constitution:

A Poster Session for Undergraduate American Government Students in the Library

Dr. Aleea L. Perry

Assistant Professor
Indiana University of Pennsylvania
aperry@iup.edu

THE ACTIVITY

Description: Users' increasing dependence on electronic information sources and the proliferation of cybersecurity threats have led libraries to develop educational offerings related to online privacy protection best practices for their users as an expansion of their traditional dedication to protecting patron privacy. Libraries continue to advocate for the development of an informed citizenry and increased civic engagement. Collaborating with outside partners who wish to increase awareness of online privacy best practices and civic engagement is a natural partnership. Within the Indiana University of Pennsylvania's (IUP) Department of Political Science, a course in American Government, PLSC 111: Politics and Democracy in America, introduces and reinforces students' knowledge of the American government system, from its colonial beginnings to current events. Within this course, students learn about the US government, Declaration of Independence, the Articles of Confederation, the Constitution, the Bill of Rights, and how each was developed and evolved with legislative, judicial, and executive actions. Technology and social media are ubiquitous on our campus, and ongoing conversations about uses of social media, such as Snapchat, Twitter, Instagram, and Facebook, and expectations of privacy by students are common. In this class, discussions on the Constitution have invariably included expectations of privacy, cybersecurity, and what role the government actually plays in protecting privacy as contrasting with commonly held student expectations. This exercise arose from such discussions.

In this exercise, students are asked to both consult and consider the Constitution as well as discuss how the Constitution does (or does not) protect them in instances of cybersecurity and/or privacy. In an effort to discuss the issue beyond the boundaries of the classroom setting, a poster session was developed to more effectively share the findings of the students with other outside parties and held in a public academic space, the lobby of the library. For these presentations, students were expected to show and discuss their posters with classmates, other students, faculty, staff, and other interested parties who might be passing by during the class hour. Posters were prepared outside of class time and presented during the normal class hour. This was held in conjunction with National Cyber Security Awareness Month (NASCAM) in October. IUP has hosted a Cyber Security Awareness Month at IUP since 2010, with this year as its seventh year. More informed use of social media and increased awareness of online privacy best practices support student success while in college and their potential for employment after they graduate, so events to share class learning outcomes beyond students in the class to casual visitors to the library can be viewed as an educational service to the broader IUP community. As a result of this activity, students in the class reported an increased awareness of social media privacy policies, terms and conditions of use, and how the Constitution does not cover their privacy in these instances, and the opportunity to share their findings on these topics with those passing through the library lobby during the class period.

Getting Started: The poster session for privacy, cybersecurity, and the Constitution was conceived at a writing workshop held at IUP. The focus of the workshop was to develop writing-to-learn exercises within various courses across campus. At that workshop, the instructor proposed a poster session and learned of public space in the library where a poster session could be held during class hours, ensuring that all students would be available to participate. Another political science professor has used the same public space for a poster session and NATO simulation exercises. As the library has been welcoming of active learning events, such as a poster session or simulation, it was a natural fit for this exercise. A public poster session, beyond the boundaries of the classroom experience, allowed for students' posters to be viewed by more than just the instructor and their classmates. Other IUP students utilizing the library, faculty and staff, as well as outside visitors to the library were potential viewers of student work and provided a larger audience for the themes of cybersecurity, privacy, and the Constitution. In addition, she learned that IUP IT Support Services, the IUP Institute for Cyber Security, and IUP Libraries would be working together to promote National Cyber Security Awareness Month during October and that this activity could both benefit from collaboration with these interested parties and assist them in supporting cybersecurity awareness.

After the workshop, the library was approached about using the space. IUP Libraries had intentionally designed a high-traffic area on the first floor of the main library near the coffee shop as a space that would be available for educational outreach/community engagement events, so it readily agreed. When informed of the activity, members of the IUP information technology security staff offered to come and to view, discuss, and comment on the students' posters. During the poster sessions, IUP Libraries staff also offered to attend and discuss posters with students, tweet the event from the libraries' Twitter account, and otherwise document the event and link it to the larger discussion of IUP's Cyber Security Awareness Month. Conversations with IUP's Institute for Cyber Security, an interdisciplinary committee designed to promote and encourage cybersecurity awareness and practice through teaching, research, and service activities, led to a further display of the posters at the Institute's annual Cyber Security Day conference that was held one month after the poster session.

Motivations: Institutions of higher education have both embraced and struggled with the adoption of technology on campus as a complement to other learning strategies. Organizations such as EDUCAUSE, higher education's largest technology association, listed information security, which is closely linked to online privacy, as one of the top trends of 2017. Recent events on the IUP campus involving the use of social media platforms by students have led to conversations about privacy and social and racial justice issues. As American Government courses include conversations on privacy, the founding documents of government, and how they relate to today's environment, it was a natural progression to include cybersecurity as technology continues to evolve, much like the Constitution.

Although the poster preparation in itself included critical thinking and assessment of the Constitution as well as privacy/cybersecurity, the presentation of the poster was critical to the full understanding of the material presented. By utilizing first-floor library space, near the library entrance and in-library coffee shop, the students were presenting the material not just to each other and to the faculty member but to the greater campus at large. This had a three-fold benefit: (1) the library gained an additional outreach event by showcasing cybersecurity/privacy posters to all visitors during National Cyber Security Awareness Month; (2) access to educational materials on cybersecurity/privacy were not limited to just a classroom setting and students displayed posters in small groups, allowing them the experience of presenting to classmates as well as to the instructor and other library visitors; (3) students had the opportunity to engage with IT Support Services security experts on online privacy topics.

THE PEOPLE

Library: IUP Libraries support teaching and learning efforts of a mid-sized public university which offers degrees from certificates to doctorates in the humanities and social sciences. The libraries have intentionally designed its spaces to draw users in for individual and collaborative work and broader community events. A number of its spaces are frequently used by faculty and students for community building, educational outreach, and actual classroom instruction. Course instructors, including one of the professors in political science, have often used the libraries' inviting spaces for classroom activities, from poster sessions to NATO simulation activities. The Department of Political Science has seven faculty members who teach courses in four major areas, as well as a master of public affairs degree. Within the department, a tenured associate professor works with computer science professors on cybersecurity awareness and training in the Western Pennsylvania region in the Institute for Cyber Security at IUP.

Instructor: The instructor for this course is a second-year, pre-tenure assistant professor in the Department of Political Science. Her teaching pedagogy includes adaptation of current events and actions to introduce and reinforce instruction in American government. The instructor made contact with the IUP government information and outreach librarian who has collaborated with the National Cyber Security Awareness month outreach events by planning events in the library and promoting government sources that offer privacy training materials during a writing workshop, and together they developed the logistics for the poster session in the library.

Course: The privacy/cybersecurity and the Constitution poster session was developed for a 100-level American Government class. This course has three main objectives: (1) to improve students' understanding of the basic institutions and processes of the American political system; (2) to introduce students to several analytical frameworks so that they may critically think, speak, and write about political issues; and (3) to help students develop a greater interest in, and enjoyment of, politics and public affairs. This activity falls under objectives 1, 2, and 3, as it enhances students' understanding of the Constitution while simultaneously engaging critical thinking skills within privacy expectations and their own use of technology.

Students: Undergraduate students from all colleges at the university may take the American Government course as a Liberal Studies Social Science course. As such, many students in PLSC 111 are not political science majors, and/or may not be interested in the course beyond fulfillment of the liberal studies requirement. As such, the PLSC 111 course includes reading discussions, lecture, movie essays, exams, and the privacy/cybersecurity poster session to actively engage students in not just learning about government but observing how it impacts their day-to-day life.

Community Partners: Community partners for this project included the IUP Libraries, the IT Support Center, and the IUP Institute for Cyber Security, and even the National Cyber Security Alliance & the U.S. Department of Homeland Security that leads the month-long awareness campaign. All partners shared interest in supporting the learning objectives of the activity. IUP Libraries offered space for the event and the government information and outreach librarian coordinated the logistics of the session and helped develop the session as a learning-rich project. IUP IT Services staff attended the poster session, offered comments and questions to students, and provided valuable feedback to the instructor and students about the session. The Institute for Cyber Security and the Computer Science Department provided a second poster display during their Cyber Security Day on the IUP campus.

Finding and Working with Partners: Each October, National Cyber Security Awareness Month is celebrated nationally. On the IUP campus, the IT Support Center (ITS) and the IUP Institute for Cyber Security (ICS) has promoted this national effort to increase awareness of cybersecurity threats and best practices through an annual campaign. IUP Libraries outreach staff are always looking for ways to contribute to campus educational efforts and encourage partners to hold events in our spaces, so they have been involved in planning and carrying out related activities for the last several years. In the past, the campus NASCAM campaign has included drop-in, face-to-face educational sessions for students, faculty, and staff, campus-wide informational emails, contests, outreach activities in the library lobby, and an annual Cyber Security Day (formerly Information Assurance Day). The Cyber Security Day features speakers discussing the latest news in cybersecurity and how to promote awareness of cybersecurity. ITS and ICS have been open to collaborations that allow them to efficiently and economically increase their awareness efforts. This assignment was a natural fit with the library's mission of educational outreach, the campus NASCAM campaign to increase cyber awareness and security, and engaging students with cybersecurity, privacy, and the Constitution.

IUP Libraries staff encouraged the instructor when she inquired about using IUP Libraries spaces during National Cyber Security Awareness Month to further ITS and ICS outreach efforts as well as to deepen learning for her students and spread awareness beyond her class as this would allow for maximum exposure of the posters to all patrons entering or exiting the library, as well as a non-threatening environment for students. When they discovered that the sessions would be held at the busiest times of the day and that each of the two seventy-five-minute sessions would have fifty students each on the first floor of the library, a number of challenges presented themselves. By identifying these challenges (space, ensuring clear walkways, and crowding), the library staff and instructor worked together to plan the event. New easels were obtained by the library and the instructor agreed to ask students to alternate showcasing their posters so less space and fewer easels were ultimately needed. In a class of forty-five students, fifteen easels were used, allowing three posters per easel, and three students to present to each other, as well as to the instructor and guests. ITS and the ICS was also pleased to expand its cybersecurity awareness outreach events in this way. Library staff were pleased to visit the sessions and discuss the content with students, and their social media staff were happy to use Twitter to announce the poster session as it was happening and write a blog post about the poster session after the event was over.

Benefits

Instructor: The benefit to the instructor was the active engagement of students in a directed research activity that showcases both fundamental American government documents and current events. She was pleased with both the creativity and thoughtfulness of the posters and was encouraged by her students' feedback on their learning experience. This assignment will be included in future American Government classes.

Students: Students were able to showcase their creativity, critical thinking, presentation, and understanding of the Constitution, cybersecurity, and privacy in a single poster session. By presenting their understanding of the material to each other as well as to library visitors, IT Services staff, other interested students and faculty, students were able to develop confidence in their presentation ability and knowledge.

Partners: The IUP Libraries was able to further their mission to "provide support for teaching, research, and the personal enrichment of members of the IUP community" by hosting this event in their first-floor space. Further, by showcasing a poster session on cybersecurity, the IUP Libraries assisted in the ITS and ICS focus on cybersecurity in a public forum, easily accessible to members of the IUP community at no additional cost. The addition of the poster sessions to the Cyber Security Day program also made the event more visible and may have attracted more attendees. IUP Libraries is also a federal government documents depository and creating an informed citizenry is our mission. Activities that build awareness of cybersecurity and use this timely topic to explore the Constitution is in keeping with that mission.

Institution: IUP recognizes that national and local cybersecurity awareness issues are common and efforts to increase awareness of how to avoid them benefit students. It has celebrated National Cyber Security Awareness Month since 2010, and featuring a publicly available student-based poster session on cybersecurity furthers the active engagement of students in discussions of cybersecurity and privacy in a classroom setting beyond a typical computer science class. By utilizing the Constitution as a basis for privacy rights, the discussion of cybersecurity and privacy moved beyond just the abstract and into the concrete.

THE PROCESS
Expected Learning Outcomes

Students will review, discuss, and consider how Constitutional concepts of privacy may or may not relate to use of technology, including issues relating to cybersecurity. Students will consider how the Constitution, a document which governs our country, is capable and able to address issues never considered by our nation's founders over two hundred years ago. Within the course, students are asked to critically assess current events, the Constitution, the readings, and their own place in the American governmental system; this poster session extended the learning outcomes to consider their own use of technology, cybersecurity, and the Constitution.

Curriculum Materials

Students were directed to view a cybersecurity video developed by the IUP ITS department to better understand cybersecurity and privacy. This video was part of the materials identified by the government services librarian, which also included information on library-based curriculum events. In-class discussions about the Constitution, including the Bill of Rights, discussed possible provisions for privacy within the document. For the assignment, students were asked to address all of the following for full credit on the poster session assignment. Poster and presenter does all of the following:

- identifies the privacy issue;
- includes the Constitutional provision;
- discusses how privacy (or lack thereof) affects students' lives;
- has a creative and eye-catching display; and
- discusses the issue with the professor, classmates, and library patrons during presentation hour in the library.

The Appendix Materials includes the assignment description and rubric.

Steps Involved

The poster idea was borne from class discussions on students' perceptions of privacy and how the government protects (or does not protect) their privacy.

- Prior to the poster session assignment, lectures relating to the Constitution, as well as class discussions on the role of the Constitution, were held to both introduce and reinforce students' understanding of the Constitution. Special emphasis was placed on the First, Fourth, Fifth, Ninth, and Fourteenth Amendments to the Constitution, which include provisions for privacy as the founding fathers had envisioned in 1789. Class discussions focused on current events in cybersecurity, including email phishing, data exposure, and public sector initiatives for cybersecurity.

- In class discussions about the Constitution and the amendments, students were asked to consider their own expectations for privacy and how those expectations include their digital identity.
- For the poster, students were asked to think about what privacy is, what expectations they have for privacy in both the cyber and physical world, and how the Constitution addresses those issues (if it does). Students were asked to quote the Constitution on their poster (where it relates to privacy), discuss privacy itself (as well as their expectations for privacy), and how privacy (or lack thereof) affects their lives. Students were expected to complete the poster outside of class time.
- A full seventy-five-minute class period was allocated for poster display and discussion in the library. Students were asked to bring their completed posters to the poster session, present their posters to their respective easel-mates, discuss their posters with any interested attendees, and present the poster to the instructor. During the session, the instructor circulated around the displays, viewing each poster individually and asking questions of the presenter. As the session was held in the library lobby area, it was open to the campus community as well as the public. Members of the IUP IT Security department, librarians, and fellow campus community members also viewed the posters and asked questions of the presenters. This allowed the presenters to have a casual, yet informative, poster sessions and learn from their fellow classmates as well as those visiting the poster session. Additionally, librarians tweeted about the display, showcasing students and their posters to increase visibility and cybersecurity awareness.
- A post-session discussion was held in the next class session for students to discuss what they learned by doing the poster, what they learned from other posters, and what information they gleaned from visitors to the session itself. Almost universally, students acknowledged that they view their own cybersecurity with a more critical eye after the session.
- At the Information Assurance/Cyber Security Workshop, held at the end of the month, the online privacy and the Constitution posters were put on display a second time. They were featured in the entry of the auditorium where the presentations were held and provided attendees with additional information on how students view their own cybersecurity.

POST-PROJECT FEEDBACK
Reflection Methods

During the poster sessions, students discussed how their views on cybersecurity and privacy practices had changed as a result of the assignment with other students in the groups that shared easels, librarians, and IT Security experts. An in-class discussion of the poster session was also held the class session after the public poster sessions. Students were asked to discuss what they learned, if the knowledge impacted how they use technology, and what information they might share with their peers.

Post-Project Feedback

A number of students reported that they reevaluated their use of social media as well as how they utilize technology. Further, students reported that they were surprised by how the Constitution, while written over 200 years ago, still has relevance in technology and cybersecurity. Students appreciated the opportunity to present in a low-stakes, public environment with campus community members in attendance. Overall, students told the instructor that they enjoyed the assignment and learned from it. Future assignments will include a reflection paper component to allow students to discuss their thoughts on the assignment, what they learned from it, and their suggestions for improvements to the assignment.

The library appreciated the opportunity to host the lively, educational event that promoted both cybersecurity/online privacy best practices and increased civic engagement. In addition to adding an event to the physical library, it also added to the libraries' social media presence when one of the librarians featured the event on the library's Twitter feed. Library outreach was also inspired by the poster sessions to create their own posters to promote online privacy and cybersecurity that were shown on the digital signage across campus. They were so pleased with the outcome of the activity that one of the librarians wrote a newsletter article on the assignment for a local librarian's group (http://www.wpwvcacrl.org/newsletter.html). The IT Security Department welcomed the addition of both a class assignment and an engaging public educational event designed to increased awareness of threats to user privacy.

Project Assessment and Reporting Methods

Overall, the majority of posters met the criteria for the assignment and displayed a thorough understanding of cybersecurity and the Constitution. Posters were creative, informative, and eye-catching—three factors which are important for both learning and sharing knowledge. Students discussed their knowledge with each other, members of the IT department, librarians, and members of the campus community at large, thereby increasing the knowledge base for cybersecurity as well as the Constitution, campus-wide. Holding the session in the library was a perfect way to use a public space to increase knowledge in informal (presentations to classmates) and formal (presentations to the instructor, IT department, and librarians) ways.

Difficulties

Students: The students were initially surprised that the Constitution could be considered with issues of cybersecurity and technology. After a full discussion of the Constitution and how it relates to privacy, students began to better understand the concepts. A video, produced by the IUP IT department, helped to instruct students further in cybersecurity.

Instructor: As this was a first-time assignment, the instructor was very pleased with both the quality of the posters and the seriousness of the students presenting their chosen topic. With the addition of the libraries' location and the audience of fellow students, IT Security staff, and librarians, the assignment reached a much broader audience than expected. She would consider this assignment a success in both learning outcomes and campus outreach.

Partners: The librarians had to work through the logistics of hosting an event with approximately forty-five presenting students. As there was not room for forty-five easels within the lobby, the instructor agreed to have fifteen easels, with three student posters per easel. This allowed for room to view the posters, as well as ease of access to the full library for other library patrons. Combining presenters into easel sharing groups worked well but also had an additional benefit in providing a built-in audience for the presentations. Further, while having such large groups of students so engaged in presentations might have been a bit worrisome at first, in the end, it was a very successful event and a great way to raise awareness about online privacy but also inspire others to come and use the space for their educational outreach events. The IT staff's attendance at the poster session claimed time from their busy days but allowed them a unique opportunity to provide students with feedback on the issues raised in the posters from seasoned cybersecurity professionals. Both groups benefitted from this interaction as it deepened learning for students and brought IT Security professionals in closer touch with their main clientele.

Conclusion

While this poster session was originally conceived as an assignment for an American Government course, the impact was felt well beyond the typical classroom environment. Partnerships with the library and the IT department yielded curriculum materials, two public forums, publicity, and student interactions which led to increased learning outcomes and public impact. As this poster session was developed with and assisted by the government information librarian and the library, students were able to share their knowledge with a larger audience, receive feedback from a greater variety of sources (such as the librarians, IT department, and campus community), and used the library for more than knowledge gain—they used it to share their knowledge of cybersecurity, privacy, and the Constitution with others. The partnership with the IT department offered students an opportunity to critically engage with professionals in cybersecurity and share their knowledge with the campus IT professionals. The on-campus collaboration between three separate departments (Political Science, Library, and IT) showcased student engagement, critical thinking, shared goals, and learning outcomes for the entire IUP community.

This assignment could be utilized by other instructors of American government, public policy, public administration, business, computer science, and marketing to showcase cybersecurity, terms and conditions relative to personal privacy, the Constitution, and public policy. As students increasingly utilize social media and its variants to share information, conduct business, or engage with others, the issues of cybersecurity and privacy could be included in a multitude of disciplines.

APPENDIX MATERIALS
- Privacy Poster and Poster Session Instructions

Privacy Poster and Poster Session Instructions

On October 5, you will present a poster in the 1st floor of the IUP library which discusses our Constitution, privacy, and how this applies to you. See the D2L Content tab for a short video on cybersecurity from the IUP IT Support Center. For this assignment, I encourage creativity—think about what privacy is, what expectations you have for privacy in both the cyber and physical world, and how the Constitution addresses those issues (if it does). Be sure to quote the Constitution on your poster (where it relates to privacy), discuss privacy itself (as well as our expectations for privacy), and how privacy (or lack thereof) affects your life. A standard poster-board-sized poster is required for this assignment, and use of markers, printed signage, and inclusion of eye-catching displays are encouraged. You will be asked to discuss your poster with me, library patrons, and your classmates. Your posters will be displayed during our class hour in the library and may be retained by the library for a month-long discussion on cybersecurity. Class will be held in the library, 1st floor—bring your poster.

Grading rubric will be as such:

Poster and presenter do all of the following: identifies privacy issue; includes Constitutional provision; discusses how privacy (or lack thereof) affects student's life; creative and eye-catching display; discusses issue with me, classmates, and library patrons during presentation hour in Library:

10 points

Poster and presenter do some (but not all) of the following: identifies privacy issue; includes Constitutional provision; discusses how privacy (or lack thereof) affects student's life; creative and eye-catching display; discusses issue with me, classmates and library patrons during presentation hour in Library:

5 points

No poster, no discussion, non-participation:

0 points

TOTAL: 0–10 points

POSTER REQUIREMENTS	POINTS
Used full-size poster board (22 × 28)?	
Student's name is on back of poster board?	
Privacy issue is identified and prominent on the poster?	
Constitutional provision related to privacy issue identified and prominent on poster?	
Discussion of how privacy issue affects student's life prominent on poster?	
Sources of information are cited properly, using APA format?	
Poster is easy to read/understand from distance of 3 feet?	
Poster uses creative display techniques/eye-catching display of data?	
Student is present and attended poster discussion in 1st floor of Library?	
Student discussed poster display with Professor?	
Student discussed poster display with classmate(s)?	
Student discussed poster display with Library patrons?	

Event Image (photo credit: Elin Woods)

CHAPTER TWENTY-ONE

The ABCs of Nutrition and Literacy:

Combining Children's Books with Health Awareness in an Academic Service-Learning Project

Stephanie Taylor-Davis, PhD, RDN, LDN
Professor, Department of Food and Nutrition
Indiana University of Pennsylvania
stdavis@iup.edu

THE ACTIVITY

Description: The ABCs of Nutrition and Literacy Fair is an educational outreach event created and staffed by food and nutrition students and held at Indiana Free Library (IFL), the local public library. It was the result of a collaboration between a professor in food and nutrition at Indiana University of Pennsylvania (IUP) and IFL's children's librarian and held annually since 2014. The four primary goals of the fair are to (1) enhance student learning by providing them with an opportunity to plan, implement, and evaluate a nutrition lesson offered in the community, (2) impact the literacy, nutrition, and health of families with young children, (3) utilize children's literature as a means to promote nutrition and health literacy, and (4) collaborate to extend outreach and diversify programs offered by the students, university, and the library.

This three-hour fair is for families with young children (target ages, two to seven years) and has been held on a Saturday in early fall and staffed by IUP students enrolled in the course, FDNT364 Methods of Teaching Food and Nutrition. Some students in the class volunteer to serve as members of the planning team and work closely with the instructor to provide support, feedback to students, and planning and event logistics. Stations can be found on all three floors of the library. Students set up stations for each letter of the alphabet as well as a few for food, nutrition, and health-related themes. Each interactive station provides nutrition information, displays a children's book, and offers age-appropriate activities. In some cases, food sampling for children and their caregivers is offered.

Upon arrival, attendees are provided with a "map" showing the location of all the stations and a document that specifies what children's book, health topic, activities, and food sampling can be found at each station. Also included is an A-to-Z admission ticket. Each station marks the ticket to record visits, and the ticket can be shown upon departure to receive an age-appropriate gift. Parents/caregivers are asked to complete a short survey to evaluate their child(ren)'s experience upon departure.

The successful event is the result of weeks of preparation. FDNT364 students develop lesson plans for each station. Lesson plans are reviewed by the instructor, planning team members, a food and nutrition graduate student, as well as the IFL children's librarian(s). Included as part of lesson plan development is the selection of a children's book (age appropriate for preschoolers). This requirement prompts students to explore children's literature in order to identify a compatible book either to build the lesson upon or to integrate into the existing plan. As needed, the children's librarian provides guidance or book suggestions.

Getting Started: Over the years, the instructor has facilitated a variety of service-based learning experiences for students in FDNT364, Methods of Teaching Food and Nutrition. This is the only course offered specifically for nutrition and dietetics students with an education-focused component.

Critical for competency and confidence development is the opportunity for students to learn by active engagement. The FDNT364 course includes requirements for a minimum of three real-life teaching experiences: (1) a community-based, instructor-facilitated teaching experience; (2) a student-initiated teaching experience on a topic with an audience chosen by the students with instructor approval; and (3) development of a creative print or electronic media piece. The instructor-initiated experience has taken many forms over the years with locations both on- and off-campus. A primary goal of the instructor-initiated experience is to structure a standardized, relatively non-threatening experience for all students to assure that core competency-building skills are provided under a high level of instructor guidance. Most FDNT364 students have genuine fears about public speaking and have little to no experience sharing nutrition knowledge with others or working with children and/or families.

As a faculty member and dietitian with a background in public health nutrition and lifestyle-related education initiatives, the instructor has an interest in issues concerning poor dietary habits and physical inactivity that pervade this region. With a focus on school-based nutrition education and community health, much of her work has been in the area of health promotion through a demonstration of positive food behaviors and dietary patterns.

For several years, the instructor developed experiential learning opportunities for nutrition students directed toward local elementary school students in connection with some grant-funded projects. To expand student learning by diversifying the audience for various instructional activities, she looked beyond local elementary schools for a venue that would offer low-cost or free space, be welcoming to the community, and attractive to different community audiences. The local public library seemed the ideal location.

During a visit to learn more about how to reserve the local library's conference room, the instructor met the children's librarian. After a conversation with her, and later supervisor approval, an agreement was made whereby FDNT364 students could lead the weekly preschool story time at IFL by combining a short nutrition lesson with a compatible food- or nutrition-related book. Over three years (2011, 2012, 2013), 127 students benefited from this teaching experience at the library while promoting healthy food choices among children and families in the community. Reaching children and families early in an environment comfortable to them offers the greatest potential that nutrition messages will be effectively received by the family. Emphasizing children's books with a food and nutrition focus during the lessons fosters reciprocal messages of nutrition and health.

The nutrition "lessons" incorporated as part of the pre-school story time were well received. There were some limitations relating to occasional poor patron attendance at the story time sessions and student scheduling conflicts. In addition, the librarian had to invest considerable time to schedule multiple student lessons, and she missed her chance to lead programs and to build rapport through story time with patrons. The early venture with preschool story time between the instructor and children's librarian cultivated a relationship and interest to explore other ways to collaborate for a mutual partnership. The librarian suggested an alternative weekend option that would diversify their program offerings and help to extend outreach to bring in new patrons. The instructor and the students brainstormed ideas that could be done as a whole class event and proposed a Food and Nutrition Fair for families.

The first ABCs of Nutrition and Literacy Fair was held in 2014. To date, each year (2014–2017), 133 students have gained valuable teaching experiences through this one-day, all-class, and public library-based event.

Motivations

This academic service-learning project fosters mutually beneficial interactions and relationships for all parties and helps both students and community members involved to develop and enhance knowledge, perspectives, attitudes, skills, and behaviors. The many reasons why the instructor was motivated to initiate and sustain it include:

- By participating in this instructor-facilitated teaching experience, students gain confidence and skill prior to having to plan, implement, and evaluate a self-initiated teaching experience (on a topic using selected strategies with an audience that the student identifies).
- The single event and location accommodates all students at the same time, includes individual accountability and responsibility, and allows the instructor to model how to do large-scale nutrition education as well as community-based programming.
- Across the semester, the development, implementation, and evaluation of this service activity can be matched to topics in the course. The framework of the service activity makes course topics meaningful and relevant to the students (e.g., the ability to go through Gagne's Nine Steps—structured learning and development to address community needs while benefiting students through real-world practice/application of knowledge).
- The format of having students develop a station to offer at the event lends easily to showcasing a variety of teaching approaches (e.g., games, posters, music, decision-making, taste-testing, hands-on activities) across diverse nutrition and healthy eating themes (e.g., food groups, nutrients, specific foods, food and health relationships, food and culture, farm-to-table, and cooking).
- Integrating a food/nutrition-related children's book as part of the lesson plan and featuring the book at the station, encourages students to consider multi-disciplinary approaches and connections as part of nutrition education methods.
- Student reflection assignments are integrated before, during, and after completion of the activity. Students reflect on the experience and connect with course content as well as personal/professional goals set at beginning of the semester and the teaching philosophy statement written at the beginning of the semester.
- Grades earned in the course are based on demonstrated learning, not service or theory alone.
- High-impact practices become seamless between the course and the service activity and produce in students improved motivation and translation of knowledge to new contexts, better learning outcomes, enhanced concern for community, improved interpersonal skills and self-confidence, additional contexts to observe and interact, and enhanced abilities to work with diverse populations.
- Each stage of the service-learning activity takes students out of their comfort zone, motivating them to grow academically and professionally.
- The project allows students to teach topics in the real world. They learn to make decisions, design instruction, solve problems, and think on their feet.

THE PEOPLE

Libraries: The Indiana Free Library is located in downtown Indiana, PA. The library serves community members in White Township, Indiana Borough, Armstrong Township, and Shelocta Borough. It services approximately 32,924 patrons and has approximately 88,000 holdings. The mission of IFL is "to serve and strengthen our community by supporting literacy and lifelong learning." The ground floor of IFL is devoted to an extensive collection of children's materials, and two librarians serve the needs of this population. The library has three floors and many inviting community spaces are in frequent use for a variety of purposes, from educational programming to community meetings contributing to making the IFL a thriving community library.

Students are also supported in developing their projects by Indiana University of Pennsylvania Libraries (IUPL). The Food and Nutrition uses evidence-based practices in the discipline and curriculum at IUP, stressing the development of research skills. By the time students reach upper-level classes, they are likely to have attended multiple library instruction sessions and met with university librarians on the development of research projects. IUPL offers access to a comprehensive collection of information resources, including both the college/professional-level academic materials necessary to support development of the nutritional aspects of student projects and a large children's literature section that supports the development of children's literacy.

Course: FDNT364 Methods of Teaching Food and Nutrition aims to provide students with practice in current teaching techniques and use of resource materials in nutrition education, including classroom instruction and community-based education. Topics include: lesson planning, application of learning theories, learner needs assessment, writing measurable objectives, evidence-based research, selection or development of instructional materials, active learning strategies, goal-setting and behavior change to promote optimal health, communication skills, interpersonal skills, leadership, group dynamics, and assessment and evaluation.

In addition to fulfilling the course description and course-specific objectives, this course is charged with contributing to several knowledge requirements and learning outcomes as part of the IUP Department of Food and Nutrition's accredited Didactic Program in Dietetics. These include:

- Demonstrate how to locate, interpret, evaluate, and use professional literature to make ethical, evidence-based practice decisions.
- Demonstrate effective and professional oral and written communication and documentation.
- Develop a program/educational strategy for a target population.
- Demonstrate counseling and education methods to facilitate behavior change and enhance wellness for diverse individuals and groups.

Students: FDNT364 is typically taken by students with junior status who are nutrition and dietetics majors. Those enrolled have a strong introductory background in nutrition, having taken both FDNT212 Nutrition (for majors, includes chemistry prerequisite) and FDNT213 Lifecycle Nutrition. This course is taught once per year in the fall semester with a class size of typically between thirty to thirty-five students.

Community Partner: IFL is the community partner for this event. Educational outreach is a priority for this library and includes frequent educational programs for age groups from children to senior citizens. Also, as a PA Forward Library, the IFL is committed to providing services and programs that meet all five of the PA Forward Literacies: Basic Literacy, Information Literacy, Civic and Social Literacy, Health Literacy, and Financial Literacy. They address these literacies through a rich collection of resources and a wide variety of programs. This event has particular relevancy for Health Literacy, which is defined as follows: "Libraries can play an important role in helping citizens actively manage their own and their family's well-being, making them effective partners with their health care providers and reducing costs. Some of our Health Literacy programs include Engage for Health and various nutrition programs."[1] This event aligns well with IFL sentiments and is relevant for health literacy.

Finding and Working with Partners: A personal visit to the library by the faculty member to meet with the librarian to discuss course needs and to brainstorm possible service-learning opportunities that could be developed in collaboration with the university faculty and students provided an important foundation. This first visit to meet the children's librarian was followed by a second visit to meet with the director of the library and another staff member in the children's section. The early personal, face-to-face connection between the library staff and the faculty member facilitated the ease for both parties to engage at various stages of the planning, implementation, and evaluation process. Working closely to make the first year's event a success and debriefing after the event paved the way for future events.

As part of the planning process each year, FDNT364 students visit the library as a class for a tour and to hear directly from the librarian(s) about tips to engage effectively with families who typically visit the library. In addition, the librarians review lesson plan drafts, recommend revisions, and provide evaluation comments regarding the stations students develop and their performance on the day of the event. This input is invaluable to the learning for both the student and the faculty member to consider how nutrition education is provided and received from a librarian's perspective. Based on the experiences over the last four years, the following are recommendations to cultivate and sustain a productive and positive partnership between an academic program and community sites for service-learning:

- Start with a smaller project(s) and build to a major event (if a big event is desired) to build trust.

- Enhance communication by connecting early and frequently—faculty to student, student to student, graduate assistant to student.
- Allow the community partner an opportunity to shape the project and to provide feedback at all stages of development and evaluation; always debrief.
- Be organized. It is up to the faculty member to coordinate and lead.
- Discuss expectations frankly with the community partner, including key needs for the success of the project.
- Set expectations, especially for students, and reinforce these often.
- Value the community partner as co-evaluator of student engagement, methods, etc.
- Be respectful. Remember, you are a guest in the community space.
- Champion your host partner. Recognize that this event is a reflection on them and their services as much as it is on the university, you as a faculty member, and your students. Identify ways during the event to promote their service (or product).
- Clean up. Leave the place as good or better at the conclusion of the event.

Benefits

Student Benefits: The activity motivates students to learn and develop because the assignment has an impact on others. It provides them with the opportunity to apply theory to an actual event, bringing course material to life and enhancing practical knowledge and skill development through real-world experience.

Involvement helps students build community and social awareness and increases self-confidence and skills in working across the lifecycle (the lesson includes objectives for child and parent/caregiver as learners). It allows students to set goals and develop greater self-awareness and includes opportunities for reflection and to gain professional experience—while helping others. As a result of their presentations, students have received requests to do additional programming for local organizations or gained employment to work with families in the community.

The graduate assistant and volunteer undergraduate team leaders all gain leadership experience. Learning to work with different personality styles, gaining organizational skills, improving the ability to provide constructive feedback, developing marketing skills, and collaborating with local businesses to advertise are examples of ways team leaders contribute to the event. In addition to being a "résumé builder," students are able to reflect on this experience when interviewing for future employment or applying for internships.

Instructor Benefits: The activity offers the potential to connect teaching, scholarship, and service responsibilities. This is a way to extend classroom instruction by combining meaningful community service and a public demonstration of quality education and training efforts with/for students.

Community Partner Benefits: The Indiana Free Library is able to expand its programming with a high-quality, low-cost educational outreach event connected to health literacy. Our collaboration increases promotion of health literacy as the community has few programs. The interactive design of the stations, drawing in visitors, young and old, to try (new) foods, learn more about food and nutrition, examine children's literature, learn about local initiatives (composting, cooking classes), groups (community garden, student dietetic association), and businesses (e.g., a newly established food co-op), effectively promotes children's literacy, their children's collections, and the health awareness of members of the community in a pleasant and novel way. It allows the library to build connections with university students who are sharing their expertise with library visitors, increasing the likelihood that students will return on their own or collaborate with this or other public libraries when they begin their careers.

Institutional Benefits: Indiana University of Pennsylvania benefits from closer connections with the community, improved learning outcomes for their students, enhanced career potentials, and increased civic engagement. It also is good public relations for the university and for the Food and Nutrition Department, which often see increased requests from community members to do other programming and to serve as a resource after the ABCs of Nutrition and Literacy Fair.

THE PROCESS
Expected Learning Outcomes

The ABCs of Nutrition and Literacy Fair assignment addresses two overall student development goals central to the charge of this course to

- provide experience in the development of theory-based educational programming via assessing needs, developing objectives, creating/selecting accompanying materials and activities, implementing appropriate instructional strategies, assessment and evaluation; and
- plan, teach, and evaluate a lesson(s) that is an appropriate length and level for the target audience using effective instructional materials and methods.

Service-learning as a component of course requirements is an excellent way to promote higher order student competency, such as synthesis, analysis, and evaluation. The Framework for Information Literacy and Higher Education (FILHE; http://www.ala.org/acrl/standards/ilframework) has been applied to this assignment and is noted in parentheses after each expected learning outcome below. Specifically, the expected learning outcomes for this service-learning event (met fully or in part) included:

- Locate, interpret, evaluate, and use professional and other literature to make ethical, evidence-based practice decisions (FILHE: Authority is Constructed and Contextual; Research as Inquiry).

- Apply learning theories (FILHE: Information Has Value; Information Creation as a Process).
- Correctly state, write, and analyze learning/behavioral objectives.
- Locate, research, and/or create educational materials using technology as appropriate (FILHE: Information Has Value; Information Creation as a Process; Searching as Strategic Exploration).
- Select and organize learning experiences appropriate for objectives and target audience (FILHE: Information Creation as a Process; Searching as Strategic Exploration).
- Select and/or prepare, and evaluate instructional materials to promote the learning process (FILHE: Information Has Value; Information Creation as a Process; Searching as Strategic Exploration).
- Write a lesson plan (FILHE: Information Has Value; Scholarship as Conversation).
- Improve verbal and nonverbal communication skills.
- Practice interpersonal skills.
- Reflect to make connections between course content, community/population, site/experience (FILHE: Scholarship as Conversation).
- Employ effective and professional oral and written communication and documentation.
- Demonstrate education methods to facilitate behavior change and enhance wellness for diverse individuals and groups.

Curriculum Materials

Instruction and activities (in- and out-of-class) prepare the students to complete this project. This is the first of three major application projects completed during this course and contributes approximately 12.5 percent toward the student's final grade in the course.

READINGS AND RESOURCES USED TO ASSIST STUDENTS WITH THE ABCS OF NUTRITION AND LITERACY FAIR ARE:

- professional journal articles (position and practice papers) with worksheets to complete to guide reading to answer key questions:
  - o Example Practice Paper: Communicating Accurate Food and Nutrition Information, JAND
- instructor-developed PowerPoint presentation about the event, expectations, and lesson planning process
- websites and documents focusing on literacy, nutrition education, and use of books with children
  - o "Using Children's Storybooks as a Basis for Nutrition Education" (PowerPoint presentation by Connie Evers, MS, RD, LD

o   *Teaching Our Youngest: A Guide for Preschool Teachers and Child Care and Family Providers* (Early Childhood-Head Start Task Force, US Department of Education, US Department of Health and Human Services, 2002)

o   Michigan Team Nutrition Preschool Booklist (for grades K-2; 2006, https://www.education.ne.gov/wp-content/up-loads/2017/07/MichiganTeamNutritionBooklet.pdf)

Reflective assignments, event materials, and grading rubrics are included in Appendix Materials.

Steps Involved

The steps for including this academic service-learning event as part of this fall semester-only course is provided below in timeline format.

Late July:
- Contact the children's librarian to see if there is interest in scheduling the event this year at the library and to identify a Saturday in late September or during the month of October.

Mid-August:
- Finalize the course syllabus and set up support materials and assignments related to the event on the course Learning Management System (LMS).
- Confirm with the department chairperson whether there will be funds available to offset the costs of offering this service-learning event.

Week 1 of the course—late August:
In-class:
- Review the syllabus and emphasize the value of experiential and service-learning opportunities.
- Have students mark their calendars for a visit to the local library as a class (late September) and date of the event (in October).
- Have students initiate applications for required clearances.
- Describe the event to the students.
- Ask for volunteers (the number of volunteers has typically been four or five students, depending on class size, and being sure that twenty-six students are available to cover all letters of the alphabet as "stations" at the fair) to serve as a team leader. These students help to manage the planning and execution of the event by supporting other students to develop stations.
Out of class:
- Establish communication with and between the university Office of Communications and Marketing and the local library to request advertising in the *Indiana Gazette* newspaper.

- Request that the university photographer be available to stop by the event to take pictures.

Week 2 of the course—early September:
In-class:
- Prepare a basket so that all other students can draw their letter of the alphabet as the means to assign station letters. If more than twenty-six students are available, then this number of "theme" stations will also be developed for the event and "theme" should be a choice to draw from the basket.
- Educate students on the lesson planning process; review the lesson plan template and explain its components.
- Explain to students that a portion of some class time will be dedicated to helping them with station development, which includes:
  o letters—each letter will represent a nutrition/food related topic
  o theme tables—selecting an activity that is health/nutrition related
  o develop lesson plan geared for preschool children
  o develop/find handouts for parents/caregivers
  o selecting a book that reflects the station

Homework:
- Assign readings.
- Assign that a draft of the lesson plan should be prepared for the following week.

Week 3—early September:
In-class:
- Review draft lesson plans.
- Share and compare ideas to develop a class "vision" for the event.
- Educate students on topics such as principles and strategies for teaching children and "What is literacy/health literacy?"
- Discuss reputable sources for referencing information.

Homework:
- Assign readings.
- Provide large foam boards for students to create signs for each station (some years these are re-used).

Out-of-class:
- Assign each team leader a group of students (five to seven) to mentor and organize in preparation for the event. Team members also serve as communication liaisons between student groups and the instructor. (This saves time during class and provides students with more personalized attention as they develop their stations and prepare themselves for this teaching experience.)

The instructor meets with the team leaders to review roles and responsibilities, which include the following:

- Share tips on providing feedback when assisting with the review of the lesson plans.
- Support other students and their stations.
- Help with organizing materials/purchases for the stations.
- Serve as a welcoming committee and facilitate traffic on the day of the event.
- Discuss how their evaluation and grade will be different from their peers as they will not have to create a station but will support their group members in a leadership role.
- Be in contact with the instructor and graduate student; explain this is part of graduate assistantship duties.
- Request that they contact local pre-schools, day care centers, and local businesses to distribute flyers to advertise the event.

Week 4—mid-September:

- Send the children's librarian revised draft lesson plans for each station to obtain feedback.
- The class visits the local library (approximately forty-five minutes).
- Meet with the children's librarian and gain insights on working with pre-school children and families.
- Receive a tour.
- Students will consider optimal locations for their stations' given lesson plan and activities.

In-class:

- Educate students on topics such as community-based event planning, implementation and evaluation, and learner assessment and evaluation.
- Team leaders meet with small groups during class to review lesson plans and facilitate peer-to-peer idea sharing and support.

Homework:

- Assign readings.
- Students should consult with team leaders or the instructor as needed to revise lesson plans.

Out of class:

- Work with team leaders on the following:
  - o station map depicting the location of stations throughout the library
  - o parent/guardian guide describing what each station offers
  - o admission ticket
  - o fair evaluation survey
  - o create necessary spreadsheets (e.g., items needed, station themes)

      o   discuss designs for a welcome table

Week 5—late September:
    In-class:
- Team Leaders meet with small groups during class to review lesson plans and consider feedback by the children's librarian.
- Decorated foam letters are turned in and the student contest occurs to determine a favorite decoration (this builds morale).

    Out of class:
- Work with team leaders on the following:
  - o   Identify and make a list of what items are needed by students to carry out the activities of their station and how these materials are going to be secured and by whom.

Weeks 6 and beyond until day before the event in October:
    In-class:
- Confirm that the "items needed" spreadsheet reflects the items needed and how they are to be secured. Address questions and provide support as needed. Lecture topics include communication skills and the importance of teamwork.

    Out of class:
- Students can bring any materials that need to be transported to the library to be stored in the instructor's office (must be clearly labeled with name and station letter/theme).

Day before the event:
    Out of class:
- Team leaders meet at the instructor's office at 1:00 p.m. to help load materials that need to be transported to the library into instructor's van for transport.
- All other students meet in front of the library at 1:45 p.m. to assist in carrying items into the library (up to 2nd-floor conference room for later disbursement).
- At 2:00–4:45 p.m. (although we have done set-up in as little as ninety minutes), using the event station map, the instructor and team leaders direct students in set-up and moving tables in all areas of the library to be used for the event. At the same time, large foam decorative letters representing each letter station are hung from the ceiling and colorful plastic tablecloths are placed to protect surfaces and for decoration. Once this is complete, students take materials to the tables in order to set up their letter/theme stations. Team leaders set up the welcome table and also circulate to be sure students have what they need. No student is permitted to leave until *all* work is complete. The instructor takes attendance at the beginning and end of set-up.

Day of the event:

Out of class:

- 9:30 a.m.—The children's librarian opens the doors thirty minutes prior to the time that the library is open to patrons for last-minute set-up, including the addition of food samples to the station tables.
- 10:00 a.m.–1:00 p.m.—The event takes place.
- 1:00 p.m.–2:00 p.m.—All students bring materials from each station back to the 2nd-floor conference room for clean-up and organization prior to taking materials to the instructor's van to take back to campus. Some students work to receive materials, others put away tables, etc. in the library and clean up to restore the library to its usual operations condition. Students take garbage to the dumpster and pick up anything off the floor.
- 2:00 p.m.–3:00 p.m.—Team leaders return to campus with the instructor to put any materials away or in the instructor's office.

After the event:

- The instructor completes grades and provides feedback to students. The event contributes 12.5 percent of the total grade for the course. Of this, activities and assignments contribute the following, with team leader grading criteria slightly modified as noted:
    - o   10 percent—attendance and participation in- and out-of-class activities, discussions, and assignments related to the event
    - o   20 percent—development and submission of final lesson plan and materials (team leaders are assessed based on performance of roles and responsibilities, including planning documentation)
    - o   20 percent—station set-up, content, aesthetics
    - o   35 percent—student performance on the day of the event: professionalism and positive attitude, engagement with children and caregivers, and teamwork
    - o   15 percent—reflection paper
- The instructor follows up to debrief with the children's librarian.

In-class:

- Class discussion to brief on the event.

Out of class:

- Students complete their reflection papers.

POST-PROJECT ASSESSMENT
Methods of Reflection

Reflection is an ongoing process that occurs during the planning, implementation, and evaluation phases of this event. Continuous assessment and communication are essential for events of this scale. In-class, small-group discussion, co-facilitated by the instructor and planning team leaders, provides opportunities for students to connect course concepts with the event. Additional documentation and tracking of roles and responsibilities are afforded by using the "discussion" section of the course learning management system. The lesson plan assignment and opportunities for revision encourage reflection that occurs independently by students and together as a class. On occasion, students may make short presentations about the development progress for their station or to highlight a success or challenge they experienced on the day of the event. In addition, students may opt to include examples from the event as part of their end-of-semester presentation, where they summarize accomplishments given the personal/professionals goals that they set to meet through their enrollment in the course.

Conversations that occur either face-to-face or via email with the children's librarians provide guidance for students regarding the feasibility and relevance of their station plans for families and in the library setting; they also ensure that the overall logistics for using the site are sound. Also, communication is important to ensure there is not an overlap of similar station themes or food sampling. An evaluation form is distributed to glean feedback from attendees at the event.

An event planning binder is maintained so that from year-to-year the instructor can recall major tasks and document considerations to revise the program for the following year. The instructor is also able to look back on the course learning management system from year-to-year to review assignments, timelines, samples of student work—content for each station over the years and student comments/reflections regarding the event. Reading student reflection papers is very informative as is a post-event check-in with the children's librarian for her input on how the event went, any specific feedback for students, and suggestions for the future. Each of these methods for data and reflection provide important insights to consider.

Post-Project Feedback

Across the four years that the ABCs of Nutrition and Literacy Fair has been offered, positive feedback from various constituencies (e.g., students, children and families, community, librarians, department chairperson) combined with satisfaction regarding the merits of the event by the instructor affirm its value.

A community fair is a good match for student readiness to engage in nutrition education (often for the first time) and develops their abilities and confidence for this service and future programming. When the concept is first presented to them, students are typically uncertain and anxious, but once completed, their reflections indicate overwhelming satisfaction. Students usually report that the goals and objectives they set for their lesson were met but often report that they underestimated the knowledge and abilities of children. Relief is a common emotion reported by students when the event is over and encompasses both this huge responsibility and all of the effort necessary to make it happen is over, but it also relates to the confidence they feel now that their capacity to meet such challenges has been tested. This propels students forward in the course as they embark on planning, implementing, and evaluating a self-initiated teaching experience completed independently or with a partner for an audience that is on a nutrition-related topic of their choice. Typically, students report that if they were to make a change, they would do more hands-on activities with children and have a broader range of ways to tailor an activity so that it has the flexibility to reach participants across a wider range of abilities. Students really enjoy the chance to use their knowledge to answer questions for parents/caregivers and usually are surprised by the great questions children ask. Students who are presenting stations, as well as those functioning as student leaders, are placed in situations that allow them to practice how well they think in the moment, such as when problems must be solved to adjust to unpredictable events. These insights gained through this experiential academic service-learning activity bring nutrition education theory to life for students, helping them to recognize the value of theories and their application. Development in this area improves student ability when completing subsequent lesson planning assignments in the course. At many points, students receive feedback (from the instructor, librarians, parents/caregivers, and children) that enhances their learning, growth, and development as future food and nutrition professionals.

Parents/caregivers who complete the evaluation form overwhelmingly give the fair the highest rating—"excellent"—and all respondents have indicated "strongly agree" or "agree" to the statement, "My child learned something valuable today" and "My child enjoyed the Nutrition & Literacy Fair today." Most families also indicate that, based on the fair, they will consider a change to improve their child's or family food choices. Parent/caregivers freely comment on the good job that students did preparing their stations and interacting with their children. Occasionally, parents/caregivers comment that they liked the opportunity to peruse books showcased at the stations or verbalize intent to look at ways to tie books they select to themes and activities for their children the way the stations did. Some parents/caregivers indicate they are appreciative of the library and the university for hosting the event.

For children, favorite activities generally are those that are most interactive (e.g., walk along the fruit and vegetable rainbow; spin the wheel, paint with potato stamps, make your own mini pizza, fishing game, proper handwashing), feature themes or props that include book/movie character recognition (e.g., Minions, super heroes, Arthur), include an element of competition (bean bag toss, beat the clock, matching game), or emphasize food production (e.g., type of eggs from different animals, where milk comes from, squeezing oranges to make orange juice, foods from the ground versus a tree versus a vine). Stations that feature taste-testing receive mixed reactions both by children and parents/caregivers that include delight (familiar or favorite foods, or those presented in a novel way), fear (unfamiliar or disliked foods), or surprise (taste foods and discover they like them). The least popular stations sometimes are those that may be overstimulating for some children (e.g., jumping and stretching) or where either the student appearance or demeanor is unfamiliar or distracting (e.g., different dress due to culture, student is too enthusiastic, or student is not expressive or inviting enough based on child's temperament). Children really do enjoy using their admission ticket to the fair as a way to collect stickers at each station and track what they have completed and still need to do/see.

For the university, the department, and the library (including librarians), this collaborative effort provides a definitive service to the community that could not come to fruition without such a partnership. The event helps each to meet their respective missions as well as to project positively in the community.

Project Assessment and Reporting Methods

The event, including the number of students participating, number of attendees, and hours of service, are reported to the department chairperson and forwarded to the college dean for inclusion in university productivity reports.

Competencies attained via this academic service-learning activity are reported as part of the reports generated by the department to maintain accreditation of its undergraduate dietetics program.

The library, which receives state funding, participates in an initiative, PA Forward, where library programming is categorized and promoted around five important literacy concepts: Basic Literacy, Computer & Information Technology Literacy, Health Literacy, Financial Literacy, and Civic & Social Literacy. This information is submitted to the state library and the IFL library receives "stars" for certain levels. The IFL is successful in reaching its star goal for Basic Literacy and Civic & Social Literacy. This event can be reported under the Health Literacy category.

Difficulties Encountered

Student Issues: The planning for and putting on this event creates an excellent learning experience for students but can challenge them in ways that other assignments do not pose a challenge. Students were excited but nervous about doing a "real" event. It is often the first time some students have presented in a public forum related to their major, so fear of public speaking, even on the small, individualized scale of manning their station, was sometimes evident. The Saturday event falls outside of the usual class schedule, and students were sometimes unhappy with the scheduling and reported difficulties in juggling work and personal schedules to be involved. There was no alternative to participation unless the student had athletic or military service conflicts or could document medical or other emergency. Student emergencies did, on occasion, occur on the day of the event, so there must be a back-up plan to adjust for absences (e.g., this is where student planning team members can step in to cover stations). They had to choose something to wear that would engage visitors and help promote the educational objective of their stations while still being formal/professional. They had to adapt to circumstances and be flexible enough to modify information or activities to meet learner needs and abilities. Much time and hard work went into preparing and carrying out the event, and for some, working with children and parents was a new experience.

Instructor Issues: The activity adds much to the complexity of the course and requires a lot of faculty time planning, organizing, and adapting the design and timeline to accommodate a service-learning experience. Scheduling visits to the public library had to take into consideration the distance from campus and students' other classes (e.g., the local library is within walking distance, so transportation was not needed, but time must allow fifteen minutes to/from so students can get back on campus for next class meetings).

The event is relatively inexpensive. The Food and Nutrition Department offers some funding but that has decreased in recent years, increasing student responsibility for purchasing. The decision regarding the textbook for the course and its cost was adjusted so that the increased financial burden (which varies based on student decisions about their lesson plan for the station) for expenses related to the service-learning project was offset.

It is a fact of community-based programming that it is often very difficult to anticipate attendance. Efforts are made to minimize competition with other community events by being aware of the community and university calendars when setting an event date, considering the weather, etc. Instructors have to establish a fair way to manage and respond to unforeseen student emergencies. One year, up through the day of set-up (right before the event), faculty were on strike and contractually prohibited from being involved. Student leaders and a graduate assistant cooperated tremendously to set up and volunteered to hold the event on Saturday with or without the instructor. Thankfully, the faculty strike ended late in the afternoon on Friday, so the faculty member was able to go to the event on Saturday. The instructor, who might have high standards for her own work, might have to accept the fact that in spite of everyone's efforts, some stations may not be of high quality, and that might impact the way the entire event will be represented. Feedback and grading requirements, including providing opportunities for student reflection and self-assessment, given the complexity of the event, are substantial. Knowing the rules and procedures for, and making the best use of, established university channels for communication and publicity is also essential.

Community Partner Issues: While cooperation on this project requires effort on the part of the children's librarian, this responsibility is accepted as a requirement of the job of a public librarian. Providing educational opportunities is one of their goals, and having access to community professionals and resources positively projects the library. In addition to state and government aid, the library depends on private donations. Maintaining diverse program offerings may in the long run support fundraising efforts as patrons connect donations with their appreciation for library program offerings. This library-wide event does disrupt the normal library routine but patrons have not expressed discontent about the additional noise or lack of access to areas of the library. In fact, many patrons are drawn to the public library because they enjoy such programming. The event also requires time commitments from the children's librarian, who has had to adapt her schedule to accommodate working with the students and the event. The structure of the library building necessitates being creative when offering community programs. In addition to having activities on three floors, as this event is organized, families are asked to find stations in corners and small spaces tucked between library shelving. Some children enjoy exploring the library and find this an added benefit of attending this program. However, for families with small children, several children of varying ages, and babies in strollers, this can be a disadvantage. Parking is a major problem because of the library's downtown location with limited street parking and a very small parking lot with only a few short-term patron parking spaces. This could keep some families from attending the program but there are many families who would not let this prevent them from offering this opportunity to their children. The library has also experienced some difficulty attracting patrons to attend programming under the Health Literacy category of the PA Forward initiative. The reason why this category of programming is less popular among patrons is unclear.

Although several challenges were listed, none these were insurmountable, nor did they present any significant deterrent to current participation or to participation in the future. Adequate time, clear and responsive communication, and the flexibility to adapt are all hallmarks of success and are important for events such as the one described in this chapter. All parties were committed to the event and made adjustments to work together effectively.

Establishing team leader positions provides volunteer students with leadership experience, and each year their availability and training have served as a buffer to cushion the inevitable, unexpected changes that arise. The team of students provides manpower to distribute and effectively manage such situations. Publicizing the event to attract more attendees, as well as to more effectively reach the intended audience, continues to be a challenge. Considerations for the future are to distribute flyers to schools and to change the title of the event by developing a catchier phrase.

Conclusion

This partnership between the university and the local public library provides direct benefits to students and to community members. The collaborative opportunity is professionally rewarding for both the faculty and the librarians. The academic service-learning project described in this chapter provides a mechanism for experiential educational opportunities for students that may not otherwise be garnered, while offering information and activities to enhance the health literacy and food-based practices of young children and families in the community.

APPENDIX MATERIALS

- Lesson Plan
- Reflection Paper Assignment
- ABC Station Map
- Parent/Guardian Guide to Stations
- Sample Admission Ticket
- Sample Event Evaluation Form for Attendees
- Grading Rubric for Students/Stations
- Grading Rubric for Student Planning Team Leaders
- Grading Rubric for End-of-Semester Presentation
- Pictures

Lesson Plan

Nutrition & Literacy: The ABCs of Nutrition

LETTER: _____ TITLE of Station: _____

LESSON PLAN FOR: Pre-School Children and Families; Indiana Free Library, Nutrition & Literacy Fair

USE DATE: November 14, 2015

DEVELOPMENT DATE:

NAME OF LESSON PLAN DEVELOPER: _____

    NAME OF STUDENT TEAM LEADER: _____

LENGTH/DURATION: 5 minutes

OVERALL GOAL OF THIS STATION:
_____
_____
_____

DESCRIBE THIS STATION:
_____
_____
_____
_____
_____

MATERIALS NEEDED:
Foam Board from which to Cut Letter and Decorate (provided by the department)

LIST OF RESOURCES (provide full citations) USED TO DEVELOP THIS STATION/LESSON:

Lesson Plan

Nutrition & Literacy: The ABCs of Nutrition

Objective #1 for **CHILDREN**:

Content	Learning Experience	Method of Evaluation (as applicable)

Objective #1 for **PARENTS**:

Content	Learning Experience	Method of Evaluation (as applicable)

Reflection Paper Assignment

FDNT 364 Methods of Teaching
Reflection Paper Assignment – ABCs of Nutrition & Literacy Fair

What is a reflection paper?

A reflection paper is an opportunity for you to communicate in writing to your instructor about your feelings, attitudes, emotions and beliefs (affective domain of learning) about your teaching experience. The reflection paper will help you to think about the experience for your own self-assessment and also provide your instructor with this description to go along with your lesson plan and what could be observed in your implementation during the event.

What is the content of a reflection paper?

You should include the following in a reflection paper:

1. Description of the objective(s) you had for your letter or theme station. If you were a team leader, consider the overall goals and objectives you had for the event and your specific contributions.
2. Assess the degree to which you think you accomplished the objective(s) for yourself and for your learners.
3. How you felt *prior to* the event (well prepared? nervous? etc.)
4. How you felt *while* the event was happening, including your performance and how the children responded to your station and the event overall.
5. How you felt *immediately after* the event was over.
6. If you had the opportunity to plan (your station) and participate in this or a similar event for preschool children and their families in the future, what change(s) would you make? Why?
7. What did you learn from this experience?
8. Were you able to work on any of your professional development goals? If so, comment.
9. Are there connections that you can make between your experience and your teaching philosophy?
10. Include any other observations, experiences, or insights that you have related to this project and the event.

Please be honest. Do not write what you think the professor wants to hear, but rather your honest feelings and assessment of the effectiveness of your station and your role as a nutrition educator (or your role as a team leader).

Length?

The length is less important than the quality of the paper. Required length is a **minimum** of **three** *typed* pages and a maximum of five pages (12-point font, Times New Roman, spacing and margins are up to you). Be sure to proof-read your paper – spelling and grammar do count.

ABC Station Map

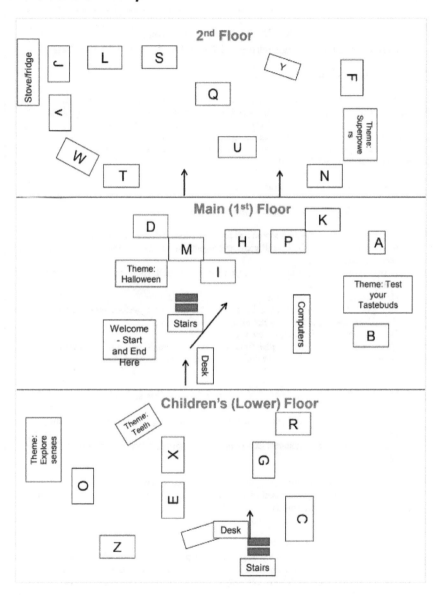

Parent/Guardian Guide to Stations

The ABCs of Nutrition & Literacy Fair

Saturday October 14, 2017

Co-Sponsored by IUP Department of Food and Nutrition & The Indiana Free Library

Foods may contain dairy, nuts, soy, and gluten products

LIST OF STATIONS by LETTER and THEME

Station Letter	Station Title/ Theme	Featured Books	Foods (if available)	Location
Welcome Table	Welcome Guide			1ˢᵗ - Main Floor
A	Apples All Around	Apple Farmer Annie By: Monica Wellington	Apple Chips with & without Cinnamon Sugar	2ⁿᵈ Floor - Upper Conference Room
B	Busy Bananas	Once upon a banana By: Jennifer Armstrong		2ⁿᵈ Floor – Upper Lobby
C	Cute Carrot	The Carrot Seed By: Ruth Krauss	Carrot & Carrot Juice	Children's Floor
D	Dare to Dip	Stanley's Store By: William Bee	Vegetable & Fruit Dip for strawberries, apples, peppers, broccoli, & cauliflower	2ⁿᵈ Floor - Upper Conference Room
E	Excellent Eggplants	Once Upon a Time in the Kitchen By: Carol Odell	Eggplant Pizza Bites	2ⁿᵈ Floor - Upper Conference Room
F	Funky Fruits	Fruits in Suits By: Jared Chapman	Dragon fruit, star fruit, strawberries, & banana	1ˢᵗ - Main Floor
G	Got Guac?	Avocado Baby By: John Burningham	Guacamole & Crackers	1ˢᵗ - Main Floor
H	Healthy Hummus	Vegetable Garden By Douglas Florian	Vegetables, Hummus, & Cracker	2ⁿᵈ Floor – Upper Lobby
I	I Scream for Ice Cream	The Scoop on Ice Cream By: Bonnie Williams	Homemade Ice Cream	2ⁿᵈ Floor - Upper Conference Room
J	Just Juice	Learn Alphabets - Vegetables and Fruits ABC-Z: Alphabet books for toddlers, preschoolers and kids by Joseph Eleyinte	Juice made with green apples, pears, celery, cucumbers	2ⁿᵈ Floor – Upper Floor Back Room
K	Kickin' it With Kiwi	We Love Fruit By: Fay Robinson	Kiwi	1ˢᵗ - Main Floor

Sample Admission Ticket

A B C D E F G H I

Admit One

A,B,C's of Nutrition & Literacy
IUP Department of Food and Nutrition
Indiana Free Library

Sample Event Evaluation Form for Attendees

ABCs of Nutrition & Literacy Fair – Evaluation Form

Thank you for attending the ABCs of Nutrition & Literacy Fair today! Please help us to evaluate today's event and to guide planning for future programs.

Directions: Circle or complete the answers below.

How would you rate the ABCs of Nutrition Fair overall?
Excellent   Good   Fair   Poor

My child learned something valuable today.
Strongly Agree   Agree   Unsure   Disagree   Strongly Disagree

My child enjoyed the Nutrition & Literacy Fair today.
Strongly Agree   Agree   Unsure   Disagree   Strongly Disagree

List your three favorite stations or activities:
1. _____
2. _____
3. _____

Based on what you learned at this Nutrition Fair, will you consider any changes to improve your child's or family food choices? ___Yes ___ No
Explain why:_____

How did you learn about the Nutrition Fair? (Check all that apply)
_____ Librarians or library fliers
_____ Newspaper
_____ Radio
_____ Website
_____ Someone told me
_____ Other:_____

Would you be interested in attending our Nutrition Fair next year? ___ Yes ___ No

What suggestions do you have to improve this event?
_____
_____

Additional comments:
_____
_____

Thank you for your participation!

Grading Rubric for Students/Stations

Presenter _____
Date___
Audience Indiana Free Library Pre-School children's program
Evaluator_____

Yes	No	n/obs	
			Book selection is appropriate for audience and station
			Activity(ies) complement the book theme/topic
			Overall lesson is appropriate for target audience.
			Provides clear explanations of content or instructions for activities.
			Establishes rapport with the children/families
			Exhibits enthusiasm.
			Encourages participation and provides appropriate positive feedback.
			Effectively uses time allotted.
			Overall, the children/families responded positively to the lesson.
			The lesson content was a worthwhile use of library/program time.
			Other:
			Other:

What I Liked Best About the Lesson or What You Did was:

If I Could Change One Thing About the Lesson it would be:

Other Comments:

Grading Rubric for Student Planning Team Leaders

ABC's of Nutrition & Literacy Fair

Team Leader Assignment

Grading Rubric

Prior to the Event ___/30

___/5 Provides support to team members make experience significant

___/5 Ability to identify issues in a real-world situation

___/5 Ability to demonstrate leadership skill within a team

___/5 Implements ethical responsibility within the professional

___/5 Mentoring is consistent throughout assignment

___/5 Engaged attendance during scheduled meetings

During the Event ___/30

___/5 Ability to respond to real-life experience that may occur unexpected during the event

___/5 Connects and integrates classroom material

___/5 Initiates cooperative experiences and promotes skills associated with community involvement and citizenship

___/5 Ability to demonstrate problem-solving skills

___/5 Effectively utilize verbal and nonverbal communication skills with diverse audiences

___/5 Model Professionalism

After the Event ___/15

___/5 Includes structured reflection during and after the service experience

___/5 Engages in reflection throughout the assignment

___/5 Ability to complete instructed tasks in a timely manner

Comments:

Grading Rubric for End-of-Semester Presentations

End-of-Semester Presentation - Evaluation Sheet
FDNT 364 Methods of Teaching Food and Nutrition

Presenter(s): _____
Date: _____
Evaluator: _____

For criteria on the left side, the following scoring system will be used:
✓+ = mastery/thorough (3 pts); ✓ = proficient/adequate (2 pts); ✓- = improvement needed (1 pt)

DESCRIPTION OF ACCOMPLISHMENTS
AND LESSONS LEARNED (3 pts each)

	Connection to objectives
	Connection to professional development goals
	Description of topic
	Description of audience
	Description of context/setting
	Description of strategies
	Description of successes
	Description of challenges
	Description of insights gained
	Ability to translate experience to one that is meaningful/useful for others
	Clarity of explanation
	Evidence of integration of concepts learned during course

General Comments:

MECHANICS OF PRESENTATION (2 pts each)

	Volume; pitch of voice
	Pace of presentation
	Poise; body language
	Professional level of language
	Interest/enthusiasm

ORGANIZATION (1 pt each)

	Appropriate introduction
	Logical organization of presentation
	Appropriate summarization
	Within time limit

MEDIA (as applicable)

	Visual impact
	Connection to presentation
	Appropriate citations/resources

$$\text{Grade} = \frac{\text{Points earned}}{50} \times 100$$

Score = _____ Grade = _____%

Advertising in Local Newspaper for Event (2017)

The Indiana Gazette

PICTURED,
front row, from
left, are
Ashley E.
DeBerry, Emily
Nallin and
Nicole Smith.
Back row: Kate
Geiger,
director of the
Indiana
Library;
Sherita
Jamison,
Justin Brown,
children's
assistant
librarian;
Kelsey Henry;
and Joanne
Mast,
children's
librarian.

JAMIE EMPFIELD/Gazette

Prof, students to teach kids about health

How can we get children excited about eating healthy foods? Indiana University of Pennsylvania professor Stephanie Taylor-Davis, along with students from her course "Methods of Teaching Food and Nutrition," aim to engage children by promoting healthy diets through games and activities.

The Indiana Free Library is hosting this children's nutrition fair on all three floors of the building. From choosing apple chips over potato chips to learning different ways to prepare zucchinis, each student selects a letter of the alphabet and creates activities to excite young children about the featured food item. Families can visit the 26 stations, where they will sample fruits, vegetables, grains and dairy products while playing games and completing activities.

Adults accompanying children will receive information about selecting and preparing healthy foods along with suggestions to continue the fun at home. Each station will also feature a children's book on the theme. Families are invited to come to the library next Saturday between 10 a.m. and 1 p.m.

2014

2015

2016

Notes

1. IFL website, http://www.indianafreelibrary.org/paforward.

CHAPTER TWENTY-TWO

More about Experiential and Service-Learning Experiences for Libraries and Information Literacy Instruction

BACKGROUND READINGS

In 2003, John Riddle wrote that though service-learning had "achieved a widespread currency in higher education pedagogy," he could locate little that "critically" considered how this practice "impacts the mission and services of college and university libraries."[1] A few years later in 2006, Lynn Westney could not report that much has changed.[2] Those who want to learn more about the use of service and experiential learning for libraries and information literacy instruction will be happy to learn that the situation mentioned by Riddle and Westney has changed. This chapter will discuss literature that specifically treats this topic.

The first full-length book to address service-learning and libraries appeared in 2009. *Service Learning: Linking Library Education and Practice* was edited by Loriene Roy, Kelly Jensen, and Alex Hershey Meyers.[3] Roy is a past president of ALA and a librarian educator who has "a personal teaching philosophy of building communities of service." She promoted the use of service-learning experiences in graduate study during her presidency, stressing its reciprocal nature in her description of the practice as "a bridge" between students who were preparing for the profession, faculty who needed to "stay refreshed and connected to today's work environment," and practicing librarians who "need to help prepare new librarians." She defined service-learning as a teaching practice where students "address community needs through the application of course content," "work in cooperation with community members," and "reflect on the activity, gaining a deeper understanding of the course content."[4] The book begins with a historical summary of the use of this pedagogical practice in the professional training of librarians and the controversy which has sometimes surrounded it. It includes chapters on reflection, assessment, and the state of the use of service-learning in graduate programs at the time. Other chapters discuss the connection of service-learning to critical information literacy, the reciprocal nature of the practice, its connection to building communities, and a final chapter with the results of a survey of recent LIS graduates opinions of the value of these experiences to their development as librarians. Much detail on communities served, services offered, how these experiences enrich the LIS students' learning, and benefits for all involved are included. Advocating for the adoption of the practice in programs that offer professional training of librarians, it intertwines theory and practical advice and concludes with an extensive bibliography for those who would like to delve deeper into the topics covered.

By 2014, interest in service-learning and libraries had grown to the point that a Colloquium on Libraries and Service Learning was held. One of the outcomes of this conference was Jennifer E. Nutefall's *Service Learning, Information Literacy, and Libraries*.[5] This volume is designed to "provide a larger context for librarian involvement in service learning," with both theoretical discussions and "practical examples of service learning partnerships."[6] This book is the first to address the use of service-learning in general undergraduate education that involves libraries and information literacy instruction. It begins with a thoughtful chapter which defines and describes the benefits of service-learning, reviews the literature specifically relating to service-learning in libraries, and offers tools such as checklists and rubrics to help librarians expand the practice on their campuses. Later chapters explore the intersection of service-learning and information literacy pedagogies and offer valuable advice on how to design meaningful reflective activities. Tips on finding information for real-world applications and discussion of efforts to build community connections and partnerships are also provided. A final chapter considers the future prospects of service-learning in higher education in general, its impact on librarians and library spaces, and the place of service-learning in LIS education. This much-needed volume fills a gap in the literature and will be very useful to those interested in better understanding or adopting the practice for students in undergraduate general education classes and promoting the quality and expansion of service-learning experiences on their campuses.

Pete McDonnell's *The Experiential Library: Transforming Academic and Research Libraries through the Power of Experiential Learning* appeared in 2016.[7] The volume argues that experiential learning "will increasingly become a key component of what academic and research libraries can offer the learning enterprise" and offers "illustrative examples" of how libraries are embracing these practices to become "more 'experiential' institutions."[8] It defines experiential learning as "learning by doing" or as "a learner-centered educational theory and methodology which places experience at the forefront of learning." It contends that experiential learning "places emphasis on students' active integration of subject knowledge and learning through development and application of skills." He also notes the importance of "reflective observations of the learner's interaction with the material."[9] Most chapters offer both theoretical justification for the use of the practice and practical examples of how meaningful learning experiences were created. Its diverse case studies include those related to the use of experiential learning and inquiry-based projects in information literacy instruction, object-based learning with archival materials, student-designed library exhibits, student-led ethnographic studies, and a first-year experience class with a service-learning element taught by a librarian. It concludes with suggestions designed to encourage others to consider adopting the practice. An engaging and enthusiastic introduction to the topic, it provides much that will help those who want to make information literacy instruction and libraries more experiential to accomplish that end.

Craig Gibson's *Student Engagement and Information Literacy*,[10] published in 2006, argues for closer collaboration among campus personnel in different divisions to better support the holistic development of students and illustrates how information literacy can be a catalyst for transforming the curriculum so that "the classic goals of liberal education are linked with disciplinary learning, community involvement, and lifelong learning."[11] An overview of the concept of student engagement and why it is increasingly important for colleges is followed by case studies, including two that describe service-learning experiences for students in both first-year and more advanced learning communities. An excellent introduction to the concept of student engagement and engaged scholarship, this volume is definitely worth a look.

Distinguishing Between Service and Experiential Learning

Service-learning is generally understood to be a subset of experiential learning. Given that, it is not surprising that there might be some confusion when it comes to use of the terms. It does not help that service-learning itself has been variously defined.[12] Yontz and McCook noted the multiplicity of definitions but also that reciprocity and reflection are central to most.[13] Sook Lim and Catherine Bloomquist have argued that it is essential that service-learning be clearly defined to adequately assess outcomes and maximize learning. They provide a multi-part definition that includes experiential and service elements, some connection to credit-bearing courses, a balance between service and learning, mutual benefit to all involved, the inclusion of reflection, and planning for both "academic and civic learning" outcomes. They specifically exclude practical experiences that are only designed to develop skills to enter a profession.[14]

Getting Started

Frances Yates is a librarian/library administrator who established one of the very few campus centers for service-learning that exist in a library and is operated by librarians. In her 2014 article, she explains how her center got started and how it operates. She explains how libraries are well-suited to play this central role in promoting service-learning on campus, and offers a list of tips for those that might like to add a "service-engagement role to library operations."[15]

Katherine Kott provides practical advice for librarians interested in expanding library support for service-learning on their campuses in a book chapter and online rubric. The book chapter includes things to consider, steps that can be taken, and some tools to assess progress in developing such a program. A matrix included at the end of the chapter is expanded upon in the freely available "Self-Assessment Rubric for Development of Service Learning Programs in Academic Libraries." This tool measures progress on six dimensions of adoption of the practice, from building awareness to the institutionalization of the practice, and provides assistance with measuring current progress and setting goals for improvement.[16]

Maureen Barry developed and taught credit-bearing information literacy courses that included a service-learning element and collaborated with faculty to develop information literacy-related service-learning assignments for classes in other disciplines. In her many writings, she offers practical advice for others who would like to follow her lead. Barry offers advice on what library administrators can do to promote service-learning initiatives,[17] or for librarians who wish to begin working with faculty to develop information literacy elements for classes with a service-learning focus.[18] Reflection is essential to both experiential and service-learning. Instructors may benefit from practical advice on how to develop reflective activities to increase critical-thinking and otherwise improve student learning outcomes. Barry provides such advice in her book chapter on reflection.[19]

In addition to the edited volume mentioned earlier in the book, Jennifer E. Nutefall has also offered useful advice on getting started in articles. Two articles in particular are of note. In an article on the importance of service-learning to libraries, she provides a section called "What can librarians do to connect with service learning initiatives?"[20] In a subsequent article, she offers more recommendations for librarians interested in developing information literacy support for service-learning assignments.[21]

Annotated Bibliographies and Literature Reviews

There are a few bibliographic articles and literature reviews which specifically deal with service and experiential learning and libraries. Ball's article, "Practicums and Service Learning in LIS Education" on the history of their use in librarian professional training, provides a useful bibliography with works dating from 1921 to 2006. It is a bit dated now but is still an excellent resource for historical information.[22] Sanders and Balius's "Experiential Learning and Academic Libraries" is a nicely done and fairly recent annotated bibliography of articles published between 2010 and 2015 related to experiential and service-learning in libraries.[23]

Two shorter and now somewhat dated bibliographies were written by Wallace and Allen. Wallace's "A Librarian's Guide to Service-Learning" provides an annotated list of organizations, journals, books, discussion lists, and articles to provide a starting point for faculty in management and leadership studies who want to learn more about service-learning.[24] Allen's "Service Learning: A Guide to Selected Resources" lists organizations, periodicals, and classic texts that support service-learning course development.[25]

Most current is an article published in *College & Research Libraries News* in the fall of 2017 and written by one of the contributors to this volume. It lists online sources of information relating to community engagement in higher education in general and in libraries, including Maureen Barry's *Service-Learning Librarians Blog*.[26]

Graduate Professional Education and Service and Experiential Learning

Inclusion of applied learning experiences in library and information literacy training is nothing new. Authors have mentioned the educational benefits of using them for the professional training of librarians since at least 1894.[27] Yontz and McCool are just two authors that have argued that service-learning is a "'natural' for library professional education.[28] Roy, Ball Albertson and a host of others continue to argue for its inclusion in the curriculum.[29] Many programs now require internships or practicum as a requirement for graduation.

Mehra and Robins have described how applied experiences have been used to build collection development skills,[30] and Cuban and Hayes have described applied learning opportunities where students develop professional skills while serving in programs that promote community literacy.[31] Obrien, et al. and Roy have discussed how providing reference service in a variety of settings can help prepare students for professional reference work, even as they serve the community.[32] A number of authors have noted that library technology-related courses can be enhanced by service-learning experiences, whether in providing specialized computer training for those with intellectual disabilities, creating web pages to help public libraries do their work, or teaching those searching for a job basic computer skills.[33] Bloomquist, Cooper, and Tilley have discussed the importance of reflection to the learning in graduate education,[34] and Angel and Bossler have promoted the use of service-learning experiences even in classes offered online.[35]

Service and Experiential Learning in Undergraduate Education Courses

Given their power to improve learning experiences for the professional training of librarians, it natural to assume that applied learning activities could be equally valuable for the similar learning experiences of undergraduate students in information literacy courses. Librarians do not typically teach credit-bearing information literacy classes, but Barry and Marrall have and share their experiences in teaching such classes in a number of articles.[36] It is more typical for librarians to collaborate with faculty in other disciplines in designing information literacy assignments for classes with service-based experiences. Blithe, Carrera, and Medaille shared how their libraries provided support for the development of service-based digital storytelling assignments,[37] and Hernandez and Knight intentionally designed information literacy assignments to encourage students to view "the ability to critically evaluate multiple information sources" as "an essential tool of citizenship" when they collaborated with a sex and gender class with a service element.[38] Copeland engaged students and served the community with a History Laboratory project which helped students build twenty-first-century workplace skills while supporting a community history digital humanities resource.[39]

McCleskey and Allison provided information literacy skill development support for an architectural classes where students were asked to do design work for a residential care facility,[40] and Sweet provided detail on librarian involvement in the development and teaching of a class that included an information literacy element as well as a community research service project called "Creating a Sustainable Society."[41]

Herther, Riddle, and Westney offer more theoretical treatments and describe a variety of possible collaborations between librarians and instructors in various disciplines.[42] Gradis and Travis strongly promote the expansion of the use of applied learning experiences in their article which argues that information literacy can be connected to a service-based class in any discipline.[43]

Information Literacy and Service Activities in First-Year Experience Programs

First-year experience classes are also seen as likely to qualify as high-impact practices, and Watts, Blodgett, Nutefall, Wolverton, and Heiselt discuss how librarians have been involved in those with service elements. Watts described a highly successful first-year experience program that included a variety library and information literacy-related service opportunities in classes that spanned a ten-year period.[44] Blodgett described his experience in designing a course called "Beyond Shushing" for first-year students that included service experiences relating to storytime, computer literacy instruction, and studying library usage.[45] Wolverton and Heiselt described a unique first-year program where credit-bearing courses connected to residence hall learning communities, and an academic librarian helped coordinate service experiences in public library settings.[46] Nutefall worked with a writing class for first-year students and helped develop assignments where students researched demographics and social issues relating to the local communities where they provided service.[47]

Library as Community Partner or Host

Libraries, as centrally located institutions that welcome and provide service the university and the wider community and who supply resources and personnel who assist faculty who are developing curriculum, are natural partners to serve as community partners or hosts for service-learning experiences. York, Groves, and Black describe a range of course-related experiential activities that served the public good and were offered through their library from creative scrap paper artistic projects to those in anthropology classes who studied fellow students.[48]

Library Marketing

The use of applied assignments which seek "clients" to help students prepare for work life are common in many disciplines these days. Librarians have discussed how they served as "clients" for classes in English writing to business marketing classes to provide students with a real-world experience in marketing, public relations, and business communication as they assist their peers in learning about how libraries can help them. Chestnut and Meulemans, Nalani and Fiegen, and Duke, MacDonald, and Trimble, and Brock and Tabaei all discussed partnering with students in classes in the development of library marketing plans and advertising campaigns.[49] Mangrum and West asked students in an anthropology class to study their peers and to gather data the role the library played in the student research process through focus groups.[50]

Development of engaging users' guides and training is something that libraries are constantly involved with. Inviting students to collaborate with librarians in this task can help libraries better reach their users, students develop professional writing and presentation skills, and make it more likely students will use the library and benefit from such use. Librarians who described such collaborations include Rhodes and Davis, who worked with English classes to develop new library database guides,[51] and Bisko and Pope-Ruark who discussed how students in a writing and rhetoric class created instructional videos to promote the use of library resources.[52] Meyer and Miller also provide a useful description of how they worked with students in a technical communications class to promote the use of RefWorks.[53]

Library Design

Modern libraries are redesigning both physical and virtual spaces to better serve students. It makes sense to invite students who will be using the spaces and virtual resources to provide input on the redesign, and likely to result in improved spaces that support better learning outcomes as well as help students build their professional skills. Brown-Sica described how her library invited students in graduate and undergraduate architecture and psychology courses to do Participatory Action Research in designing new library spaces,[54] and Watkins and Kuglitsch explain how they worked with students to design subject-based library commons areas.[55] Connolly, Cosgrave, and Krkoska worked similarly on the development of virtual spaces when they collaborated with student programmers to design the library's virtual presence.[56]

Library as a Site for Community Events

Libraries actively seek educational programming and intentionally develop spaces that bring the community together for sharing and development of knowledge. They offer the perfect location for events that raise community awareness of local needs as well as funds to address those needs. Pashia discussed how the library was the site for an empty bowls charitable event which increased awareness of food insufficiency, raised money to address the needs, and included students from art classes who created the objects to be sold.[57]

Next Steps

In 2003, Yontz and McCook wrote that many LIS educators were already using experiential and service-based activities with their students, "without knowing the term or characterizing their activities in this way." They suggested that it was important to make the practice more visible by simply using the term, by "disseminating reports" of what they have done, and "participating in the national dialogue."[58] Many years later, we believe that this is still the case.

This chapter has provided an overview of some of the existing professional literature in this area. The editors agree with Yontz and McCook that it is likely—

without realizing or acknowledging it—that many more libraries and librarians are engaged in promoting experiential and service-learning pedagogical practices on their campuses; it might be simply a problem of nomenclature or lack of communication. But in any case, we urge you to recognize your involvement in a movement that is transforming libraries, information literacy instruction, and higher education, and follow the advice of Yontz and McCook. Share your successes. Everyone will win if you do.

Notes

1. John S. Riddle, "Where's the Library in Service Learning? Models for Engaged Library Instruction," *The Journal of Academic Librarianship* 29, no. 2 (2003): 71.
2. Lynn C. Westney, "Conspicuous by their Absence: Academic Librarians in the Engaged University," *Reference & User Services Quarterly* 45, no. 3 (2006): 200–203.
3. Loriene Roy, Kelly Jensen, and Alex Hershey Meyers, *Service-learning: Linking Library Education and Practice* (Chicago: American Library Association, 2009).
4. Ibid, viii.
5. Jennifer E. Nutefall, *Service Learning, Information Literacy, and Libraries* (Santa Barbara: ABC-CLIO, 2016).
6. Ibid., xi.
7. Pete McDonnell, *The Experiential Library: Transforming Academic and Research Libraries through the Power of Experiential Learning* (Amsterdam: Chandos Publishing, 2016).
8. Ibid., xxvii.
9. Ibid., xviii.
10. Craig Gibson, ed., *Student Engagement and Information Literacy* (Chicago: Association of College & Research Libraries, 2006).
11. Ibid., xiii.
12. Elaine Yontz and Kathleen de la Peña McCook, "Service-Learning and LIS Education," *Journal of Education for Library and Information Science* 44, no.1 (Winter 2003): 58.
13. Ibid.
14. Sook Lim and Catherine Bloomquist, "Distinguishing Service Learning from Other Types of Experiential Learning," *Education for Information* 31, no. 4 (2015): 204.
15. Frances Yates, "Beyond Library Space and Place: Creating a Culture of Community Engagement through Library Partnerships," *Indiana Libraries* 33, no. 2 (2014): 53–57.
16. Katherine Kott, "Service Learning in Academic Libraries in the United States," in *Service Learning, Information Literacy, and Libraries,* ed. Jennifer E. Nutefall (Santa Barbara: ABC-CLIO, 2016), 10–18.; Katherine Kott, "Self-Assessment Rubric for Development of Service Learning Programs in Academic Libraries," Katherine Kott Consulting, last modified January 24, 2017, http://katherinekott.com/wp-content/uploads/2017/01/Service-Learning-Rubric-01.24.pdf.
17. Maureen Barry, "Community Engagement through Service-Learning," *Strategic Library* 4 (2014): 6.
18. Maureen Barry, "Librarians as Partners in Service-Learning Courses (Part II)," *LOEX Quarterly* 38, no. 2 (2011): 4.
19. Maureen Barry, "Avoiding Fluff: Crafting Meaningful Reflection Activities for Service Learning Students," in *Service Learning, Information Literacy, and Libraries,* ed. Jennifer

Nutefall (Santa Barbara: Libraries Unlimited, 2016): 39–50.

20. Jennifer E. Nutefall, "Why Service Learning is Important to Librarians," *OLA Quarterly* 17, no. 3 (2014): 18.

21. Jennifer E. Nutefall, "The Relationship between Service Learning and Research," *Public Services Quarterly* 5, no. 4 (2009): 250–61.

22. Mary Alice Ball, "Practicums and Service Learning in LIS Education," *Journal of Education for Library and Information Science* (2008): 70–82.

23. Elizabeth Ann Sanders and Angela Balius, "Experiential Learning and Academic Libraries: An Annotated Bibliography," *Codex: the Journal of the Louisiana Chapter of the ACRL* 3, no. 3 (2015): 49–74.

24. Lynn M. Wallace, "A Librarian's Guide to Service-Learning," *Academy of Management Learning & Education* 4, no. 3 (2005): 385–90.

25. Barbara Allen, "Service Learning: A Guide to Selected Resources," *Collection Building* 24, no. 4 (2005): 127–32.

26. Anne Gruber, "Community Engagement in Higher Education: Online Information Sources," *College & Research Libraries News*, 78, no. 10 (3 November 2017), 563–66.

27. Melville Dewey, "School of Library Economy at Columbia College," *Library Journal* 9 (1894): 118.

28. Yontz and McCook, "Service-Learning and LIS Education," 66.

29. Roy, Jensen, and Meyers, *Service-learning: Linking Library Education,* viii; Ball, "Practicums and Service Learning in LIS education," 70–82; Dan Albertson and Maryann S. Whitaker, "A Service-Learning Framework to Support an MLIS Core Curriculum," *Journal of Education for Library and Information Science* (2011): 152–63.

30. Bharat Mehra and William C. Robinson, "The Community Engagement Model in Library and Information Science Education: A Case Study of a Collection Development and Management Course," *Journal of Education for Library and Information Science* 50, no. 1 (2009): 15–38.

31. Sondra Cuban and Elisabeth Hayes, "Perspectives of Five Library and Information Studies Students Involved in Service Learning at a Community-based Literacy Program," *Journal of Education for Library and Information Science* 42, no. 2 (Spring 2001): 86–95.

32. Heather O'Brien, Luanne Freund, Leanna Jantzi, and Samantha Sinanan, "Investigating a Peer-to-peer Community Service Learning Model for LIS Education," *Journal of Education for Library and Information Science* 55, no. 4 (2014): 322; Loriene Roy, "The Place of Service Learning in Reference Education," *The Reference Librarian* 55, no. 2 (2014): 168–71.

33. Albertson and Whitaker, "A Service-Learning Framework," 152–63.; Dan Albertson, Maryann S. Whitaker, and R. Alexander Perry, "Developing and Organizing a Community Engagement Project that Provides Technology Literacy Training to Persons with Intellectual Disabilities," *Journal of Education for Library and Information Science* 52, no. 2 (2011): 142–51; Mary Alice Ball and Katherine Schilling, "Service Learning, Technology and LIS Education," *Journal of Education for Library and Information Science* 47, no. 4 (Fall 2006): 277–90; James Elmborg, Heather Leighton, Holly Huffman, Jane Bradbury, Tim Bryant, Denise Britigan, Connie Ghinazzi, Stacy Light, Sarah Andrews, and Chris Miller, "Service Learning in the Library and Information Science Curriculum: The Perspectives and Experiences of One Multimedia/user Education Class," *Research Strategies* 18, no. 4 (2001): 265–81; Raymond Pun, Adan Ortega, and Vanna

Nauk, "Doing Technology: A Teaching Collaboration between Fresno State and Fresno County Public Library," *College & Research Libraries News* 78, no. 6 (2017): 303–15; Loriene Roy, Trina Bolfing, and Bonnie Brzozowski, "Computer Classes for Job Seekers: LIS Students Team with Public Librarians to Extend Public Services," *Public Library Quarterly* 29, no. 3 (2010): 193–209; Maryann Whitaker and Dan Albertson, "Triangulating Findings from an Instruction-based Community Engagement Project," *Reference & User Services Quarterly* 51, no. 1 (2011): 49–59.

34. Catherine Bloomquist, "Reflecting on Reflection as a Critical Component in Service Learning," *Journal of Education for Library and Information Science* 56, no. 2 (2015): 169–72; Linda Cooper, "Student Reflections on an LIS Internship from a Service Learning Perspective Supporting Multiple Learning Theories," *Journal of Education for Library and Information Science* 54, No. 4, (October 2013): 286–98; Christine Tilley, "Reflective Journaling and Fieldwork: A Case Study with Library and Information Studies Students at the Queensland University of Technology, 1994," *Education for Library and Information Services: Australia* 13, no. 2 (1996): 25–34.

35. Christine M. Angel, "Collaboration among Faculty Members and Community Partners: Increasing the Quality of Online Library and Information Science Graduate Programs through Academic Service-Learning," *Journal of Library & Information Services in Distance Learning* 10, no. 1-2 (2016): 4–14; Jenny S. Bossaller, "Service Learning as Innovative Pedagogy in Online Learning," *Education for Information* 32, no. 1 (2016): 35–53.

36. Maureen Barry, "Research for the Greater Good: Incorporating Service Learning in an Information Literacy Course at Wright State University," *College & Research Libraries News* 72, no. 6 (2011): 345–48; Barry, "Community Engagement through Service-Learning," 5–7; Maureen Barry, "Service Learning: Engaging College Students with the Library and Information Literacy Competencies," in *Student Engagement and the Academic Library*, ed. Loanne Snavely (Santa Barbara, California: Libraries Unlimited, 2012), 86–94; Rebecca M. Marrall, "Teaching the Digital Divide: Connecting Students to Community, Knowledge, and Service Learning," Library Philosophy and Practice (2014), 0_1-12.0_1-12.

37. Sarah Jane Blithe, Winter Carrera, and Ann Medaille, "Stories of Service-learning: Guidelines for Increasing Student Engagement with Digital Storytelling," *Journal of Library Innovation* 6, no. 1 (2015): 60.

38. Marcia Hernandez and Lorrie A. Knight, "Reinventing the Box: Faculty-Librarian Collaborative Efforts to Foster Service Learning for Political Engagement," *Journal for Civic Commitment* 16, no. 1 (2010): 2.

39. Sarah Shippy Copeland, "The History Laboratory: Service-Learning at Cleveland State Community College Library," *Tennessee Libraries* 61, no. 4 (2011).

40. Sarah E. McCleskey and David J. Allison, "Collaboration for Service Learning in Architectural Education," *Art Documentation: Journal of the Art Libraries Society of North America* 19, no. 1 (2000): 40–43.

41. Christopher A. Sweet, "Service-Learning and Information Literacy: Creating Powerful Synergies," In *Information Literacy and Social Justice: Radical Professional Praxis*, ed. Shana Higgins and Lua Gregory (Sacramento: Library Juice Press, 2013), 247–75.

42. Nancy K. Herther, "Service Learning and Engagement in the Academic Library: Operating Out of the Box," *College & Research Libraries News* 69, no. 7 (2008): 386–89; Riddle, "Where's the Library in Service Learning?," 71–81; Westney, "Conspicuous by

their Absence," 200–03.

43. Jennifer Gradis and Tiffini Travis, "Information literacy+Service Learning=Social Change," in *IFLA World Library and Information Congress,* last modified February 11, 2014, http://library.ifla.org/1058/1/166-gradis-en.pdf.

44. Margit Watts, "Becoming Educated: Service Learning as Mirror," in *Student Engagement and Information Literacy,* ed. Craig Gibson (Chicago: ACRL, 2006): 33–54.

45. Jayne Blodgett, "Taking the Class Out of the Classroom: Libraries, Literacy, and Service Learning," in *The Experiential Library: Transforming Academic and Research Libraries through the Power of Experiential Learning,* ed. Pete McDonnell (Amsterdam: Chandos, 2016): 43–52.

46. April K. Heiselt and Robert E. Wolverton, "Libraries: Partners in Linking College Students and their Communities through Service Learning," *Reference & User Services Quarterly* (2009): 83–90; Robert E. Wolverton and April K. Heiselt, "US Academic Librarians and Community Service: A Case Study," *New Library World* 111, no. 9/10 (2010): 381–90.

47. Nutefall, "'The Relationship Between Service Learning and Research," 250–61.

48. Amy York, Christy Groves, and William Black, "Enriching the Academic Experience: The Library and Experiential Learning," *Collaborative Librarianship* 2, no. 4 (2010): 4.

49. Mary Todd Chesnut, "Recession-Friendly Library Market Research: Service-Learning with Benefits," *Journal of Library Innovation* 2, no. 1 (2011): 61–71; Yvonne Meulemans and Ann Manning Fiegen, "Using Business Student Consultants to Benchmark and Develop a Library Marketing Plan," *Journal of Business & Finance Librarianship* 11, no. 3 (2006): 19–31; Lynda M. Duke, Jean B. MacDonald, and Carrie S. Trimble, "Collaboration Between Marketing Students and the Library: An Experiential Learning Project to Promote Reference Services," *College & Research Libraries* 70, no. 2 (2009): 109–22; Robert B. McGeachin and Diana Ramirez, "Collaborating with Students to Develop an Advertising Campaign," *College & Undergraduate Libraries* 12, no. 1-2 (2006): 139–52; Sabra Brock and Sara Tabaei, "Library and Marketing Class Collaborate to Create Next Generation Learning Landscape," *Reference Services Review* 39, no. 3 (2011): 362–68.

50. Suzanne Mangrum and Kristen West, "Partnering with Undergraduate Students to Conduct Library Focus Groups," *College & Undergraduate Libraries* 19, no. 1 (2012): 18–32.

51. Naomi J. Rhodes and Judith M. Davis, "Using Service Learning To Get Positive Reactions in the Library," *Computers in Libraries* 21, no. 1 (2001): 32–35.

52. Lynne Bisko and Rebecca Pope-Ruark, "Making the Video: Tips for Successful Library-Class Collaborations," *College & Research Libraries News* 71, no. 9 (2010): 468–83.

53. Nadean J. Meyer and Ielleen R. Miller, "The Library as Service-learning Partner: A Win–win Collaboration with Students and Faculty," *College & Undergraduate Libraries* 15, no. 4 (2008): 399–413.

54. Margaret Brown-Sica, "Using Academic Courses to Generate Data for Use in Evidence Based Library Planning," *The Journal of Academic Librarianship* 39, no. 3 (2013): 275–87.

55. Alexander Watkins and Rebecca Kuglitsch, "Creating Connective Library Spaces," *Enhancing Teaching and Learning in the 21st-Century Academic Library: Successful Innovations That Make a Difference* 2 (2015): 157.

56. Matthew Connolly, Tony Cosgrave, and Baseema B. Krkoska, "Mobilizing the Library's Web Presence and Services: A Student-Library Collaboration to Create the Library's Mobile Site and iPhone Application," *The Reference Librarian* 52, no. 1-2 (2010): 27–35.

57. Angela Pashia, "Empty Bowls in the Library: Makerspaces Meet Service," *College & Research Libraries News* 76, no. 2 (2015): 79–82.
58. Yontz and McCook, "Service-learning and LIS Education," 58.

Authors and Editors

Heather Beirne is a reference and instruction librarian at Eastern Kentucky University Libraries. She holds an MSLS from the University of Kentucky and a bachelors in English from Transylvania University. Before coming to EKU, Heather held positions in both public and academic libraries throughout central Kentucky. She has published several chapters in various anthologies as well as several articles in *Kentucky Libraries* and presented at state, regional, and national conferences related to librarianship and education. Her research interests include library instructional pedagogy, information literacy, news literacy, faculty outreach, library advocacy through library instruction, digital literacy, digital citizenship, and digital storytelling.

Mark Bestoso recently retired from Penn State Behrend (Erie) after teaching business management for twenty-six years. His work and teaching focused on management, international business, and data analysis.

Janet A. Blood, PhD has worked at Indiana University of Pennsylvania since 2004 in the Fashion Merchandising program and is an associate professor. With a background in apparel design and education, Dr. Blood strives to bring out the creative side of her merchandising students with active learning activities and projects. She has won multiple education and design awards and seeks to be a lifelong learner through her own experimentation of new technologies and techniques that can be integrated into the classroom curriculum.

Lola Bradley is a public services librarian at the University of South Carolina Upstate. She teaches LIBR 201: Strategies for Information Discovery face-to-face and online. Her professional interests include instructional design, educational technology, interactive teaching, and information literacy for all ages. In May 2018, she and her colleague, Bree Kirsch, won an award for excellence in online services learning course design.

Leslin H. Charles has a special interest in information literacy, student engagement, and assessment of student learning. Leslin represented Rutgers University Libraries in the second cohort (2014-2015) of ACRL Assessment in Action: Academic Libraries and Student Success. She has also participated in the ACRL Assessment Immersion Program, 2009 and Harvard Leadership Institute for Academic Librarians, 2007. She is the recipient of the *2018 Faculty Award for Outstanding Generosity & Commitment to Students* from the office of Undergraduate Academic Affairs, Rutgers University, New Brunswick. Leslin leads the libraries' efforts to develop pedagogically sound learning experiences and appropriate assessment strategies in collaboration with librarians, teaching faculty, and relevant campus partners.

Caleb Finegan earned his BA (Spanish, 1988) and MA (Latin American Studies, 1993) from Vanderbilt University in Nashville, TN. In 1999, he graduated with a doctoral degree (PhD) from the University of Florida with a concentration in colonial Latin American history. Dr. Finegan currently teaches courses (sometimes in honors) in Latin American history. He has been the Director of IUP's Robert E. Cook Honors College since 2014. From 2007 to 2011, Dr. Finegan also worked as the university's director of civic engagement and student leadership activities.

James Fisk received his MLS from Emporia State University and his MA from the University of Wisconsin-Madison. He just completed his third year at the University of New Mexico-Gallup. His primary duties include bibliographic instruction and research assistance to his faculty colleagues and students. Prior to his tenure in Gallup, Mr. Fisk was a member of the faculty at Morningside College for twelve years, four of which he held the title of college librarian.

Anne Marie Gruber is an instruction and liaison librarian at the University of Northern Iowa's Rod Library. She holds a graduate degree in library and information science from the University of Iowa. Her research interests focus on the library's role in community engagement, particularly information literacy instruction to support student learning and engagement in service-learning experiences.

Russell A. Hall is a reference and instruction librarian at Penn State Behrend (Erie), where he has worked for the past sixteen years. His interests are in information literacy, specifically in how college graduates carry their information literacy skills and mindsets from college into the workplace.

Tanya Heflin is an associate professor of English and dean's associate at Indiana University of Pennsylvania, where she teaches in the Doctoral Program in Literature and Criticism. Her work focuses on recovering the hidden voices of women and multiethnic North American writers from the mid-nineteenth century to the present with a special focus on understudied formats including diaries, scrapbooks, and graphic memoirs. She teaches literature courses that focus on archive use, access to information, and the history of book-banning, and for several years she has coordinated the library-affiliated Banned Books programs by collaborating with students, faculty, and university libraries.

Lara Homsey-Messer is currently associate professor of anthropology at Indiana University of Pennsylvania. A registered professional archaeologist, she teaches undergraduate courses in public archaeology and cultural resource management and serves as the Graduate Coordinator for the MA program in applied archaeology. She is the founder and co-chair of the Center for Teaching Excellence's Service

Learning Teaching Circle. Prior to her time at IUP, she was associate professor at Murray State University and also served as the coordinator for the Office of Service Learning and Civic Engagement from 2012–2014.

Jen Jones, PhD, is an associate professor and department coordinator of communication at Seton Hill University. Her research examines intersections of leadership, communication, and philosophy along with creative pedagogical approaches. She recently provided the workshop "Experiential Learning" for Seton Hill's Teaching & Learning Forum, and presented "Small Teaching in Activity-Based Learning: Expanding Big Ideas" at the Pennsylvania Communication Association Conference. Jones has presented her work at national and international conferences and has served as a reviewer for *Qualitative Research Reports in Communication, Business Ethics Quarterly,* and *Leadership.*

Breanne Kirsch is the university librarian at Briar Cliff University. Previously, she was a public services librarian at the University of South Carolina Upstate. Some of her areas of interest include using educational technology tools in instruction, teaching research skills to students, and games in libraries. She edited *Games in Libraries: Essays on Using Play to Connect and Instruct,* published in 2014. She has presented at a number of library conferences on technology tools and instruction. In May 2018, she and her colleague Lola Bradley won an award for Teacher's Excellence in Online Service Learning Course Design.

Tracy Lassiter is an assistant professor of English at the University of New Mexico-Gallup. Her predominant research areas are pedagogy, information literacy, and petrofiction. She has had articles published in *Imaginations: Journal of Cross-Cultural Image Studies, TESOL Journal,* and *Pennsylvania English.* She had another information-literacy chapter called "Topical Full Monty" published in *Let the Games Begin! Engaging Students with Interactive Information Literacy Games.*

Jeanine Mazak-Kahne is an associate professor of history at Indiana University of Pennsylvania. She teaches courses in public and twentieth-century US history as well as advises students in the department's public history certificate program. She is also the recipient of Faculty Recognition Award for Experiential Education from the University's Center for Teaching Excellence. This award recognized her efforts to foster civic engagement of future public history professionals in an academic setting through collaborative learning initiatives with partners in the university library and local history agencies.

Theresa McDevitt is the government information/outreach librarian at Indiana University of Pennsylvania, where she has served since 1986. She has taught a one-credit information literacy course with a service-learning element for the last five years. She is a co-director of the universities' Reflective Practice faculty development group and has an MLS from the University of Pittsburgh and a PhD in American history from Kent State University.

Juliana M. Nykolaiszyn joined the Oklahoma State University Library in 2007 where she serves as a professor/librarian. Over a ten-year-period, her work focused on the creation and curation of oral histories. In 2017, Nykolaiszyn was named assistant head of Digital Resources and Discovery Services, where she works closely with the library's digitization, metadata, and web services units.

Bethanie O'Dell is the virtual learning librarian and assistant professor at Emporia State University. She received her master of library science and master of science in instructional design and technology from Emporia State in 2016. She provides research support for students on a regular basis and enjoys teaching people about the use of different web tools, emerging technology in libraries, and digital literacy. Her personal research also includes gamification and mobile learning.

Terri Pedersen Summey, PhD, is a professor and research/instruction librarian at Emporia State University Libraries and Archives. Terri earned an MS in library science from North Texas State University and her doctoral degree at ESU's School of Library and Information Management. Her research interests include emotional intelligence, reference services, user experience, embedded librarians, and technology in instruction.

Aleea Perry is an assistant professor in the Department of Political Science at Indiana University of Pennsylvania. She has a PhD in public administration from the University of Illinois–Chicago, with concentrations in public management and financial management. Her teaching pedagogy includes adaptation of current events and actions to introduce and reinforce instruction in American government. Her research interests include work motivation, organizational development, and the politics of public finance.

Amanda Peters is the student engagement librarian at the University of Michigan Library. She has an MLIS from Kent State University and a BA and MA in English literature from the University of Toledo. She has worked at the Shapiro Undergraduate Library for the past seventeen years, and during that time has focused on instruction and outreach to undergraduate students. In her role as liaison to learning communities, she works to promote close relationships between campus learning communities and the library, and continues to coordinate instruction, programs and events for undergraduates, including new student orientation. In the past three years, she has developed and implemented an innovative new program at the UM Library, The Student Engagement Program. She manages forty students as they work as library ambassadors, fellows, and as recipients of library mini-grants.

Janet Pinkley is an associate librarian at the John Spoor Broome Library at California State University Channel Islands where she oversees Access Services. She teaches information literacy across disciplines, coordinates reference services, and finds unique ways for the library to support student learning.

Amy Podoletz is an undergraduate senior communication major at Seton Hill University. She recently interned for the Seton Hill University Archives as a project manager for the Seton Hill University Centennial time capsule. She has extensive experience working at the Hollidaysburg PA Public Library and the Reeves Memorial Library at Seton Hill University. She attended the PA Communication Association Conference and the PA Library Association Conference. She was recently offered an internship at the Altoona PA Public Library. She plans on attending graduate school for information and library science after she receives her bachelor of arts in communication.

Angela Pratesi is the fine and performing arts librarian at the University of Northern Iowa's Rod Library. She holds graduate degrees in library and information studies and music history from the University of Wisconsin-Madison. Her research interests primarily fall at the intersection of information, the arts, and learning.

Stephanie Taylor-Davis is a professor in the Department of Food and Nutrition and Director of the Center for Teaching Excellence at Indiana University of Pennsylvania. Her educational background includes two BS degrees from Lock Haven University (Management Science and Recreation/Fitness Management); a MS in Public Health Nutrition from Case Western Reserve University; and a PhD in Human Nutrition from The Pennsylvania State University. Stephanie is a registered dietitian and licensed dietitian-nutritionist in Pennsylvania. In addition to faculty development, her interests include nutrition education and survey research.

Matthew A. Vetter, MFA, PhD, is an assistant professor of English at Indiana University of Pennsylvania, where he is affiliate faculty in the Composition and Applied Linguistics PhD program. His research asks questions related to technology, writing, and pedagogy, with a specific interest in investigations of the ideological and epistemological functions of digital communities. Vetter has published critical work in Composition Studies, Computers and Composition Online, the Digital Rhetoric Collaborative, Harlot, and publications sponsored by the Wiki Education Foundation. An associate editor at *Kairos: A Journal of Rhetoric, Technology, and Pedagogy,* Vetter also holds an MFA in creative writing from Spalding University.

Angela Waseskuk is the foundations coordinator and instructor of art at the University of Northern Iowa Art Department. She received her BFA in painting from the University of Northern Iowa and her MFA in sculpture and dimensional studies from the New York State College of Ceramics at Alfred University. She also studied at the Yale Summer School of Art in Norfolk, CT. Her research interests include the role of community engagement in the arts and how they contribute to the first-year learning experiences for studio art students.

Cori Woods is a graduate student at Indiana University of Pennsylvania. She is obtaining her master's degree in Public History and aspires to become a museum curator. Along with attaining her degree, Cori works as the graduate assistant for Women and Gender Studies.

Alyssa Wright is the associate librarian for the social sciences at West Virginia University. She has a MA in communication studies and an MLIS from the University of Iowa. Her work centers on improving students' critical thinking and research skills as well as partnering with faculty to craft assignments and lesson plans that address students' information literacy deficits. She teaches courses in information literacy and grant seeking. Her previous teaching experience includes courses in communication, writing, rhetoric, and public speaking at the university and community college level. She serves as the library liaison to psychology, communication studies, sociology, and anthropology.